Feminists in Politics
*A Panel Analysis of
the First National Women's Conference*

Feminists in Politics
A Panel Analysis of
the First National Women's Conference

Alice S. Rossi

Social and Demographic Research Institute
University of Massachusetts
Amherst, Massachusetts

ACADEMIC PRESS

A Subsidiary of Harcourt Brace Jovanovich, Publishers

New York   *London*

Paris *San Diego* *San Francisco* *São Paulo* *Sydney* *Tokyo* *Toronto*

ACADEMIC PRESS, INC.
111 Fifth Avenue, New York, New York 10003

United Kingdom Edition published by
ACADEMIC PRESS, INC. (LONDON) LTD.
24/28 Oval Road, London NW1   7DX

Library of Congress Cataloging in Publication Data

Rossi, Alice S.,   Date
   Feminists in politics.

   Bibliography: p.
   1. National Women's Conference (1st : 1977 : Houston,
Tex.)--Evaluation.   2. Women in politics--United States
--Congresses--Evaluation.   3. Feminism--United States--
Congresses--Evaluation.   I. Title.
HQ1391.U5R67   1982   320'.088'042   82-8807
ISBN 0-12-598280-1   AACR2

PRINTED IN THE UNITED STATES OF AMERICA

82 83 84 85   9 8 7 6 5 4 3 2 1

In tribute to women in the past,
with pride in women of today,
and hope for women in the future

Contents

List of Figures   xiii

List of Tables   xv

Preface   xxi

Acknowledgments   xxv

1

The National Conference in Historical Perspective   *1*

Introduction   1

Long-Term Historical Context   5

The Third Wave of Feminism: 1961–1981   13

The National IWY Commission and
the National Women's Conference   24

Research on the National Women's Conference   34

Dual Roles as Researcher and IWY Commissioner   39

Organization of the Book   43

2

Whom Did We Miss? Response Pattern Analysis   *47*

Introduction   47

The Population: Target and Attainment   48

Data and Coding of Bioforms   52
Response Analysis: Elected Delegates and Alternates   56
Response Analysis: Ford and Carter Commissioners   61
Response Analysis: Secretariat Staff   69
Summary   72

3

Design and Measurement   73

Introduction   73
Major Components of the Research Design   74
Predictor Variables   77
Demographic and Status Variables   78
Overall Design   78
Profile of the Sample   80
Political Experience   84
Feminist Beliefs   91
Measuring the Houston Experience   93
Political Plans   106

4

Conference Organization and Political Behavior   117

Introduction   117
Organizational Categories at the Conference   121
Socioeconomic Characteristics   123
Political Characteristics   125
Organizational Membership   127
Political Activity   130
Role in Houston   134
Expected versus Actual Leadership Role   137
Network Formation   139
Conclusion   141

5

The State Delegation: Formation and Impact   145

Introduction   145
Links between State Coordinating Committees and
State Delegations   150
Organizational Membership and Delegate Role Expectations   161
Structural Characteristics of Delegations   164
Actual Roles Played in Houston   169

Development of Personal Familiarity with Home-State Delegates 171
Network Formation in Houston 180
Conclusion 182

6

The Structures of Affect and Belief 185

Introduction 185
Belief Structure 188
Determinants of Belief Structure 190
Affect Structure 195
Determinants of Affect Structure 201
Belief and Affect Consistency 214
Consensus and Constraint: NOW versus the League of
Women Voters 215
Consensus and Constraint: Pro-Plan versus Anti-Plan Activists 224
Conclusion 232

7

Paths to Political Competence and Action 235

Introduction 235
The Analysis Model 237
Leadership at the Conference 241
Political Competence 249
Holding Office 255
Mainstream versus Movement Political Activity 259
Organizational Membership 263
Family Connections and Political Activity 268
Paths to Political Activism: An Overview 277

8

Looking Ahead: Political Aspirations and Action 289

Introduction 289
Aspiration Measurement 292
Aspiration Typology 297
Determinants of Political Aspirations 301
Impact of the Conference on Political Aspirations 309
Commitment to Implementation of Conference Resolutions 313
Conclusion 317

9

Summary of Findings and Their Political Implications   *321*

    Introduction   321
    Unique Features of the Study   321
    Major Findings   329

APPENDIX A

The Houston National Women's Conference Study   *343*

    October Survey (1977)   345
    February Survey (1978)   367

APPENDIX B

*Alphabetical List of Indices, Operational Definitions,
and Location in Surveys*   *383*

APPENDIX C

*Resolutions Endorsed by National
Women's Conference*   *387*

    1. Arts and Humanities   387
    2. Battered Women   387
    3. Business   388
    4. Child Abuse   389
    5. Child Care   389
    6. Credit   390
    7. Disabled Women   390
    8. Education   391
    9. Elective and Appointive Office   392
    10. Employment   393
    11. Equal Rights Amendment   394
    12. Health   395
    13. Homemakers   396
    14. Insurance   397
    15. International Affairs   397
    16. Media   399
    17. Minority Women   400
    18. Offenders   402
    19. Older Women   402
    20. Rape   403

21. Reproductive Freedom   405
22. Rural Women   405
23. Sexual Preference   406
24. Statistics   406
25. Women, Welfare, and Poverty   407

References   *409*

List of Figures

Figure 1.1   Peaks of Feminist Political Activity in American History   6

Figure 1.2   Timing of Formation and Duration of Organizational
Units Relevant to the National Conference   29

Figure 1.3   Process of Delegate Selection to the National Conference   30

Figure 3.1   Major Background, Predictor and Panel Variables in the
Research Design   79

Figure 3.2   Movement and Mainstream Political Activity Level: Mean
and Range of One Standard Deviation on Scores
Converted to 0–100   114

Figure 4.1   Membership Level in Selected Types of Organizatons by
Conference Status Position: Subsets and Mean
Membership   128

Figure 4.2   Mainstream and Movement Political Activity and Political
Competence by Conference Status Position: Subsets
and Means   131

Figure 4.3   Affect Response to Passage of Selected Resolutions:
Subsets and Means on Enthusiasm Scale by Status
Position   132

Figure 4.4   Commitment to Implementation of Resolutions by
Conference Status Position at Local versus National
Level: Subsets and Means   133

Figure 4.5 Role Differentiation by Status Position: Subsets and
Mean Scores on Houston Activity Measures   135

Figure 4.6 Expected and Actual Leadership Role at Conference by
Status Position: Subset and Mean Scores   138

Figure 4.7 Network Formation by Conference Status Position:
Subsets and Mean Number of New Contacts Made in
Houston by Contact Locale   141

Figure 6.1 Mean Scores on Affect Scales concerning
Selected Groups   196

Figure 6.2 Mean Scores on Affect Scales on Political and
Conference-Relevant Groups by Political Orientation   198

Figure 6.3 Mean Scores on Affect Scales on Ethnic and
Occupational Groups by Political Orientation   199

Figure 6.4 Pearson Correlation Coefficients on Affect Scales:
Anti-Abortion and Pro-Abortion Groups with All
Other Groups   200

Figure 6.5 Belief and Affect Consensus by Organizational
Membership Type: Subsets and Mean Scores   219

Figure 6.6 Feminist Beliefs and Political Characteristics of Pro-Plan
and Anti-Plan Activists at National Conference   227

Figure 6.7 Organizational Membership of Pro-Plan and Anti-Plan
Activists at National Conference   228

Figure 7.1 Major Dependent Variables in the Analytic Sequence   240

Figure 7.2 Ranking of Significant Predictors of Mainstream and
Movement Political Activity Level   263

Figure 7.3 Ranking of Significant Predictors of Membership Level
by Type of Organization   266

Figure 7.4 Political Activity of Mothers versus Fathers by Social
Class of Family of Origin   272

Figure 7.5 Paths to Mainstream Political Activity: Regression
Sequence from Politically Active Spouse through Political
Organization Membership to Mainstream Activity Level   279

Figure 7.6 Paths to Gender- and Sex-Linked Feminist Activity   282

Figure 7.7 Paths to Political Competence   285

Figure 8.1 Mainstream and Movement Political Aspirations by
Level, Pre-Conference versus Post-Conference   293

List of Tables

Table 1.1 Selected Highlights of the Federal Chronology of Actions
Affecting Women: 1961–1978   20

Table 1.2 Racial–Ethnic Distribution of Elected Delegates versus
Total U.S. Female Population, 1976   32

Table 1.3 Timing of Political Events and of Research Process   38

Table 2.1 Sample and Response Rate by Panel Wave and
Sample Category   50

Table 2.2 Panel Response Pattern by Sample Category   51

Table 2.3 Comparison of Panel Analysis Sample, Refusals, and
Total Population on Selected Characteristics of Elected
Delegates and Alternates   58

Table 2.4 Ranking of Demographic Categories by Refusal Rate   60

Table 2.5 Response Pattern by State and Region   62

Table 2.6 State Ratification of ERA and Survey Refusal Rate   64

Table 2.7 Regional Distribution of Elected Delegates and Alternates
for Total Population, Bioform Sample, and Survey
Response Pattern Types   64

Table 2.8 Type of Representation for Total Ford and Carter
Commission   66

Table 2.9 Response Pattern by Type of Representation for Ford
and Carter Commissioners   68

Table 2.10 Response Pattern of Carter Commissioners by
Decision-Making Role on the Commission   69

Table 2.11 Response Pattern by Selected Characteristics of
Secretariat Staff   71

Table 3.1 Social Demographic Profile of IWY Sample   81

Table 3.2 Organizational Membership Profile of IWY Sample   82

Table 3.3 Mean Membership Profile by Organizational Type   83

Table 3.4 Membership in Specified Organizations   84

Table 3.5 Support or Opposition to Selected Causes   85

Table 3.6 Office Holding and Political Activity of Self and Family
Members   86

Table 3.7 Recent Mainstream and Movement Political Activity Level   88

Table 3.8 Political Competence Self Rating   90

Table 3.9 Feminist Beliefs: Items and Indices   91

Table 3.10 Involvement with State Delegations   95

Table 3.11 Special Events Attended at National Conference   97

Table 3.12 Caucus Meetings Attended at National Conference   98

Table 3.13 Groups Worked with at National Conference   99

Table 3.14 Role in National Conference Plenary Sessions   101

Table 3.15 Control of the Conference   103

Table 3.16 Network Formation   105

Table 3.17 Mainstream and Movement Aspirations for Elective
Office: October versus February   107

Table 3.18 Change in Mainstream and Movement Aspirations for
Elective Office from October to February   108

Table 3.19 Political Commitment to Implementation of Resolutions in
Plan of Action   110

Table 3.20 Past and Future Feminist Political Activity   112

Table 3.21 Change and Stability of Political Action on Selected
Issues: Past Political Action versus Future Action on
Resolution Implementation   113

Table 4.1 Socioeconomic Characteristics by Conference Status
Position   124

Table 4.2 Political Characteristics by Conference Status Position   126

Table 4.3 Network Formation by Organizational Structure: Mean
Contacts by Location and Overall Means by
Organizational Position   142

Table 5.1 State Coordinating Committee Membership by
Conference Status   151

Table 5.2 Regression on State Coordinating Committee
Membership of Social Status, Organizational Membership,
and Political Experience   154

Table 5.3   Regression on Elected Delegate Type of Social Status,
Organizational Membership, and Political Experience   158
Table 5.4   Groups Supporting Nomination of Elected Delegate
Types   159
Table 5.5   Expected Role in Houston of Insider and Newcomer
Delegates   161
Table 5.6   Motivation in Delegate Election, Groups Expected to
Work with in Houston, and Expected Role in Houston,
by Membership Level in Feminist and Traditional
Women's Organizations   163
Table 5.7   Expected and Actual Conference Role by Level of
Political Consensus in the State Delegation   165
Table 5.8   Expected Role by Size of State Delegation   168
Table 5.9   Size of City of Residence by Size of State Delegation   168
Table 5.10 Expected Role by City Size and State Delegation Size   169
Table 5.11 Regression on Actual Conference Role Type of Status,
Opportunity, and Contextual Variables   170
Table 5.12 Personal Familiarity with Delegation Members over Time   172
Table 5.13 Frequency of State Delegation Meetings before, during,
and after the National Conference   173
Table 5.14 Effects of State Committee Membership and Frequency
of Delegation Meetings on Personal Familiarity with
Home-State Delegates   174
Table 5.15 Regression on Proportion of Delegates Known Personally
before State Meeting   175
Table 5.16 Regression on Proportion of State Delegation Known
Personally after National Conference   176
Table 5.17 Regression on Network Formation of Contextual and
Activity Variables   181
Table 6.1   Pearson Correlation Coefficients between Belief Indices   190
Table 6.2   Regression on Feminist Belief Indices of Political and
Religious Orientation and Personal Attributes   192
Table 6.3   Regression on Belief Indices of Political and Religious
Orientation and Personal Attributes, Controlling for
Feminist Self-Concept   194
Table 6.4   Regression on Selected Affect Scales of Political and
Social-Demographic Characteristics   202
Table 6.5 R^2 in Regressions on Selected Affect Scales with Same
Set of Political and Demographic Predictor Variables:
October versus February   205
Table 6.6   Regression on Affect toward IWY Commissioners of
Political and Demographic Variables: October versus
February   206

Table 6.7   Affect Scales: Change between October 1977 and
              February 1978   208
Table 6.8   Impact of Conference on Affect toward Selected Groups:
              Regression on February Affect Scales of Conference
              Participation, Controlling for October Affect Score   211
Table 6.9   Membership Level and Overlap in Five Specified
              Organizations   217
Table 6.10 Belief/Affect Consensus: Coefficients of Variation of
              Feminism Measures by Organizational Membership Type   221
Table 6.11 Belief/Affect Constraint: Average within-Individual
              Variability across Thirteen Feminism Measures, by
              Organizational Membership Type   223
Table 6.12 Affect Constraint by Organizational Membership Types:
              October versus February Surveys   223
Table 6.13 Social-Demographic Characteristics of Pro-Plan and
              Anti-Plan Activists at National Conference   226
Table 6.14 Affect Consensus by Caucus Activity Types: Mean
              Scores, October Survey   230
Table 6.15 Affect Constraint by Caucus Activity Types: October
              versus February   231
Table 7.1   Variables in the Analysis Model   238
Table 7.2   Regression on Expected and Actual Conference
              Leadership Role   243
Table 7.3   Regression on Actual Conference Leadership Role,
              Controlling for Expected Leadership Role: Impact of
              Activity in Houston   245
Table 7.4   Regression on Role in Houston   246
Table 7.5   Regression on Pre- and Post-Conference Political
              Competence   250
Table 7.6   Regression on Post-Conference Political Competence
              Rating, Controlling for Pre-Conference Rating   253
Table 7.7   Regressions on Office-Holding Experience: Elective and
              Appointive Public Office and Political Party Office   257
Table 7.8   Regression on Mainstream and Movement Activity Level
              of Ascribed and Status Characteristics, Personal
              Attributes, and Political and Organizational Involvement   260
Table 7.9   Regressions of Organizational Membership on Early and
              Adult Family and Socioeconomic Characteristics and
              Value Orientations   265
Table 7.10 Regression of Husbands' Political Activity on Past and
              Current Status Characteristics   269
Table 7.11 Husbands' Political Activity by Parental Political Activity   271

Table 7.12 Parental Political Activity by Social Class of Family of
             Origin and Race/Ethnicity   273
Table 7.13 Cohort Differences in Parental Political Activity by Social
             Class of Family of Origin   274
Table 7.14 Mainstream and Movement Political Activity Level by Age
             and Parental Political Activity Profile   276
Table 8.1 Mainstream and Movement Political Aspirations:
             Composite Score Distributions, Pre- and Post-Conference   294
Table 8.2 Mainstream and Movement Political Aspiration Change   295
Table 8.3 Stability and Change in Mainstream and Movement
             Political Aspirations between Pre- and Post-Conference
             Surveys   296
Table 8.4 Political Aspiration Typology by Selected Background
             Characteristics, Post-Conference Survey   298
Table 8.5 Most Significant Political and Demographic Characteristics
             of Four Aspiration Types   299
Table 8.6 Regressions on Political Aspirations: Mainstream versus
             Movement, Pre- and Post-Conference   303
Table 8.7 Regressions on Mainstream and Movement Political
             Aspirations by Age   308
Table 8.8 Regression on Post-Conference Mainstream and
             Movement Political Aspirations, Controlling for
             Pre-Conference Aspirations   311
Table 8.9 Regressions on Commitment to Implementation of
             Conference Resolutions   316

Preface

It is several years since the first national women's conference in Houston, Texas, in November 1977. This study was conceived in June 1977, funded in July 1977, fielded in October 1977, and again in February and March 1978. Field administration, data processing, coding, and analysis were all conducted in Amherst, Massachusetts, through the Social and Demographic Research Institute. The analysis and first draft of the manuscript were completed during a sabbatical leave in 1979–1980 and revised during the 1980–1981 academic year.

The study grew out of my personal involvement as a Commissioner on the National Commission on the Observance of International Women's Year and my intellectual concern, going back many years, for the study of social and political movements. Indeed, it had long disturbed me, in attempting to understand the nineteenth-century women's movement, that one could not penetrate far beyond the leaders of that movement in doing social-historical research. One knew a great deal about Elizabeth Cady Stanton and Susan B. Anthony and their collaborators in the suffrage movement, through the memoirs and historical records these leaders and their friends provided for future scholars. But one never knew who the thousands of participants were who attended all the suffrage conventions, how they differed from the general population, what their prior experiences had been, and how participation in the women's movement affected their lives and political hopes.

A conviction grew, in the early months of my involvement as an IWY Commissioner, that future historians should have better data with which to understand today's feminist movement. It did not seem appropriate to leave a historical record on the 1977 conference restricted to media coverage, personal memoirs of key organizers, and archival records that the Secretariat deposited in the national archives. Of greater interest to future historians, contemporary social scientists, and political activists in the 1980s would be an analysis of the whole range of official participants in the national conference, from the IWY Commissioners and Secretariat staff to the hundreds of elected delegates and alternates and appointed delegates-at-large. To gather data from so large a group as this, consisting of approximately 2000 people, required systematic survey research as the method of choice. Such a data set would provide future historians with evidence gathered by the methods and analysis techniques of the social sciences today.

Several substantive and political questions dictated the content of such a survey. High on the list was a concern for the potential recruitment of more women into mainstream politics in the United States, hopefully to some extent from the ranks of those active in the feminist movement. As I became acquainted with the Carter-appointed national Commissioners, it was clear that some had moved from mainstream politics to feminist politics, whereas others seemed on the verge of crossing over from feminist politics to mainstream politics. Was the same thing happening in the country at large? If the feminist movement is not to remain a parallel political structure, working as a lobby group for legislative changes that would improve the status of women, such crossovers from movement to mainstream politics are of critical importance. Since the representation of women at the top of the political hierarchy is still abysmally low, any lack of such crossovers from feminist to mainstream politics implies that the movement itself may come to represent a barrier to the direct political advancement of women. Here the questions became: What have been the political activity patterns in both mainstream and movement politics of the hundreds of delegates who would serve in Houston? What issues have they been active on that led them to a nomination and election to serve as a delegate? Where do they see themselves going politically in the future? Can we anticipate any significant representation of women from this visible population of state-elected delegates to a feminist conference in future state legislatures and the halls of Congress? The substantive focus underlying such questions is the political development of American women and the determinants of aspirations for prominence in both mainstream and feminist politics.

A second substantive question guiding the study concerns the structure of feminist beliefs. While one could anticipate a high consensus among the delegates on such matters as ERA ratification and expanded job opportunities for

women, it was far from clear how much support the delegates would give to
more controversial issues such as abortion, sexual preference, or battered
wives. The abortion issue had been divisive in the first few years of the National Organization for Women (1966–1969), leading to the withdrawal of
some early members who wished to concentrate only on economic and political rights for women. It was not clear in the spring of 1977 whether the issue
of sexual preference and lesbian rights might not be an equivalent source of
divisiveness when support was sought for resolutions on this issue in the Plan
of Action, since the delegate body would be very large, diverse, from all parts
of the country and all walks of life, and whose political activity on women's
issues had been largely on expanded educational and economic opportunities for women and securing the ratification of the ERA.

It was also clear, from state meeting elections in June 1977, that some proportion of the delegate body would be women in opposition to many key issues to be voted on in Houston. Though troubling to me as a Commissioner,
the greater political diversity of the delegate body that was emerging from
these first state meetings was an added attraction to me as a research sociologist, for light can be shed on a political movement through an analysis of
those opposed to the movement as well as those who support it. Hence the
study would tap a full range of belief domains, varying in the extent to which
they would be endorsed or rejected by the elected delegates. This analysis will
be of special interest to social psychologists who study attitude formation and
value systems, and to political sociologists concerned with understanding the
structure of beliefs that are associated with political movements.

A third substantive issue guiding the study concerned the impact the conference itself might have on the participants. Would such participation encourage the delegates to enlarge their political horizons and seek public office
at a higher level than they had ever considered before? Or would the massive
scale of such a conference deflate the political aspirations of the delegates as
they compared themselves with politically skillful leaders with far more experience than they in large-scale political processes? It became clear, for example,
that "outreach" efforts by many state committees had succeeded in electing
women with very little political experience from small towns and cities around
the country. What would be the impact on them of suddenly being thrust into
the limelight of a national conference? If any number of such women lost
ground in personal political confidence, there would be a clear implication
that such unintended long-term consequences of outreach efforts override
the short-term gain of a more diverse delegate body.

A systematic study of the impact of the conference called for a panel design
through surveys administered both before and after the event being studied.
Such a panel study of a political event had never been conducted before,
even for a close analogy to the Houston conference, a national political party

convention. This impact analysis will therefore be of interest to political scientists and sociologists, as well as to political activists concerned with the efficacy of alternative action strategies.

The book is organized around these three central substantive issues. The IWY Commission and the study of the conference is placed in the context of feminist history in Chapter 1—both the long-term history that reaches back to Seneca Falls in 1848 and the short-term history of more recent post-1965 political developments. Design, variable measurement, and response pattern analysis occupy Chapters 2 and 3. Those interested in political organization and group formation will find Chapters 4 and 5 of special interest. Affect and belief structure and an analysis of the differences between Pro-Plan and Anti-Plan activists at the conference are covered in Chapter 6. The past political development of the delegates and their political aspirations, including how those aspirations were affected by the Houston experience, is the focus of Chapters 7 and 8. Readers who wish a brief overview of the study and its findings will find Chapter 9 of help, for it lays out the major respects in which the study is unique, provides a summary of the major findings, and discusses their implications for the future position of women in American politics.

A subject index is not included in the volume; instead, the reader will find a detailed table of contents and lists of all figures and tables. In addition, there are three appendices that include (a) the survey instruments; (b) an alphabetical list of indices and operation definitions and location in the surveys; and (c) the full text of the 25 resolutions in the Plan of Action that were endorsed by the Houston conference.

Acknowledgments

There are a number of people whose help was critical to the study. It is a great pleasure to acknowledge my indebtedness to them here. Above all, my gratitude to the hundreds of delegates who responded not once, but twice, to my request for their help in filling out a long questionnaire. Between the two instruments, the delegates responded to over 500 discrete questions. These are enormously busy women, most of them employed, running households of their own, yet devoting hours every week to voluntary organizations and political efforts on behalf of women. It was clear from reading their responses, and even more from the statistical analysis, that they gave careful consideration to the questions in the survey. Many wrote notes, telephoned, and sent news clippings and further encouragement and help to the research. No researcher could hope for a better sample of cooperating respondents.

My second, and equally important, source of support and hence of gratitude is to the Ford Foundation and in particular to Mariam K. Chamberlain, program officer of the Education and Public Policy division, who responded so quickly to my proposal seeking funds to conduct the study. With a firm conference date ahead in November, it was imperative in June to secure quick funding, which the foundation granted within a few weeks of receiving my proposal. When costs exceeded the budget, the foundation granted supplementary funds and twice extended the time period for their use when the preliminary data analysis indicated sufficient robustness to warrant more extensive statistical treatment than first envisaged. The same patience was shown when the gestation period of the manuscript turned out to be longer than expected.

Third, the study could not have been conducted without the help provided by IWY Commission Secretariat staff. Kathryn Clarenbach, its executive director, was an enthusiastic supporter from start to finish. She provided address labels, information from IWY Commission files, and mailing envelopes, to say nothing of social support. Her keen eyes also picked up errors of fact in a first draft of early chapters. Very special thanks are due to Shelah Leader for her help in one aspect of the response pattern analysis reported in Chapter 2.

Many of the national IWY Commissioners themselves were of great help either directly or indirectly, typically without realizing how much I was learning from them. Simply having the opportunity of close observation during many tense and troubling IWY Commission meetings was a political education for me. Tucked between heavy agenda meetings there were also personal occasions to connect anew with people known from the early days of the founding of the National Organization for Women, such as Kathryn Clarenbach and Dorothy Haener; to learn about the work of the IWY Commission under appointments by President Ford from Gerridee Wheeler and Elizabeth Athananakos; to deepen my understanding of the special problems confronting Latinas from Carmen Delgado Votaw and Cecilia Preciado-Burciago, of Asian-American women from Rita Elway, of women abroad from Mildred Persinger, and of the special problems in the union movement from both Addie Wyatt and Dorothy Haener. And of course, there were many dozens of lessons in pragmatic politics from working with such women as Mildred Jeffrey, Mary Anne Krupsak, Connie Plunkett, and Liz Carpenter.

A dozen or more undergraduate sociology majors must go unnamed but acknowledged for their loyal and enthusiastic help in the mundane tasks of mailing, keeping ledgers, and coding questionnaires, under the quiet competence of Ann McMurray's supervision. Cindy Deitch served as my chief research assistant in the field, in coding, in data processing, and in early data analysis. Lucy Fischer helped with computer work, and Aida Rodriquez with a review of the literature on women in politics. Janet Gans and Ruth Backes, together with Cindy Deitch, served as my assistants in Houston, supplementing my own observations of conference happenings and floor management with their own interviews and observations. That fieldwork was critical to the design of the second questionnaire, for it fed into decisions about which exposure variables were needed as measures of who did what during the Houston event itself.

A very special note of thanks and ongoing appreciation is due to Eleanor Weber-Burdin for her patient instruction and prompt response to requests for help with computer problems. She is the quiet steady presence at the Social and Demographic Research Institute, without whom many of us would make countless errors in the computer work that flows out into the world from SADRI offices. Much the same can be said for the help of Jeannie Reinle, whose magic fingers on the keyboard have turned the manuscript into final shape. Their cheerful, competent help is gratefully acknowledged.

I have left for last two very special categories of people for whose help I have a very special appreciation. The first is my "women's group," a group of women who are advanced sociology graduate students, and a colleague, Naomi Gerstel. The composition of the group has changed over the years of the study, as students completed their dissertations and moved on to first academic appointments, but they have been a vital part of my life, providing intellectual stimulation and personal support during the long months of the data analysis and writing of the manuscript: Cindy Deitch, Lucy Fischer, Aida Rodriquez, Beth Schneider, Kathy Daly, Mary Ford, and Naomi Gerstel have provided personal support and loyalty for which I am very grateful.

Last, and of most personal and professional significance, my love and boundless thanks to the two Peters in my life. My son, Peter Eric, first steered me through the intricacies of regression analysis, time series, and auto correlations while still a student of econometrics himself. It was an incredible first experience in the joy of supplementing a mother–son relationship with an intellectual collaboration. It is most difficult of all to acknowledge properly the role of my husband, Peter H., whose help and magical expertise as a data analyst and patient teacher have left their mark on all my work, as his tender partnership and loving support have left on the 30 years of life we have shared.

Needless to say, whatever errors of analysis or interpretation have slipped through the sharp review of my friends and kin are the responsibility of the author alone.

1

The National Conference in Historical Context

Introduction

At 9 A.M. on Saturday, November 19, 1977, Commissioner Gloria Scott brought the first plenary session of the National Women's Conference to order. She did so with the gavel presented to Susan B. Anthony by the National American Women Suffrage Association in 1896. The gavel, on loan from the Smithsonian Institution, had been used 60 years earlier at suffrage conventions. Its use in 1977 symbolized the continuity of American women's efforts to secure equality and justice, while underlining the uniqueness of the occasion as the first publicly funded national women's conference in American history.

The conference itself lasted a mere 4 days, but back of those 4 days were many months of intense preparation by thousands of people. Back of those months of direct efforts was a year of political activity in the Congress to secure the funding for the conference. That such a conference was held at all was in turn due to the political efforts by the contemporary feminist movement from the mid-1960s on.

The impact of the conference in the years since 1977 is more difficult to assess. Such impact is less visible than the event itself or the political efforts that preceded it. An analysis of conference impact would have to be charted by the political action of participants in recent years and the agenda of dozens of organizations that were involved in one way or another with the conference. It would also have to embrace the impact of the conference on the lives of thousands of people who did not participate directly as delegates in Houston, those lesser known observers across the country who viewed the proceedings on television, read press accounts of the deliberations, or listened to delegates describe their political and personal experiences in Houston to hundreds of groups in their home communities. An unknown number of such listeners have joined the thousands of contacts the delegates made in Houston and at their state meetings, enlarging the networks of women across city and state boundaries who share the commitment to the expansion of the rights and options of their sex in American society.

Historical evidence on the conference is widely scattered and varied, from the official report of the national Commission—*The Spirit of Houston* (1978)—to dozens of cartons of Commission records stored in the national archives and hundreds of oral history tapes gathered in Houston by scholars who interviewed the delegates on their response to the political events in which they were involved. There is also no question but that correspondence files, personal diaries, and journals contain historical evidence of the delegates' observations and experiences of the Houston meeting. Still other difficult-to-trace but important evidence of conference impact will be preserved in stories added to the oral tradition within the families and friendship circles of the delegates, much as stories about the suffrage movement in the first two decades of the century are preserved by the daughters, nieces, and granddaughters of those earlier feminists.

The study reported in this volume will contribute a new set of data about the conference and its impact on the participants, for it reports the involvement in, reactions to, and impact of the conference upon all those officially associated with it as Commissioners, elected delegates or alternates, appointed delegates-at-large, or members of the Secretariat staff. Two questionnaires were mailed to each person in these five official categories: the first was sent a month before the conference began, the second, 3 months after it had ended. This book traces the past political activities of the conference participants, what they actually did during the conference, the impact of the conference on their commitment to political action in the future, and their aspirations for holding elected office in American politics or in organizations associated with the feminist movement.

The study is unique on several counts. For one, it is unusual for any aspect of a social movement to be studied in essentially quantitative terms: Most of what we know about social movements is of a descriptive, qualitative variety. This is true of studies of the temperance and suffrage movements in the nineteenth century, and has been true in twentieth-century research on religious sects, cults, and political movements. There are, of course, good reasons for this emphasis on qualitative and descriptive studies. Membership in a social or political movement tends to be diffuse and changeable: People move in and out of such movements; there is typically no self-conscious record keeping on the part of movement leaders; all too often, a movement never reaches a stage of organization that entails routine record keeping. As a result, what we know about past social movements tends to be based on spotty historical records: diaries, minutes of meetings, local press accounts, biographies or autobiographies of the founders or of prominent individuals who played leadership roles during the course of the movement's history. Thus, our knowledge of the suffrage movement in the nineteenth and early twentieth centuries comes from newspaper accounts, pamphlets, and speeches at meetings of organizations committed to the goals of the movement; correspondence, memoirs, and biographies of such national leaders as Elizabeth Cady Stanton and Susan B. Anthony, and similar personal records from lesser figures that are tucked away in local libraries and historical societies.

But we have no evidence on which to give an aggregate sketch of the thousands of people who flocked to the suffrage conventions during those earlier decades or of those who did the organizing and preparatory work between conventions. Consequently, we cannot tell how the individuals who comprised the bulk of the membership in a past social movement compare with those who never attended a single meeting. Without such information, we cannot tell how much consensus existed among movement participants on the issues that brought them together and activated their political efforts, or the extent to which members differed from the larger public on such issues.

The spottiness of the historical record is also related to the fact that the research methodology appropriate to a quantitative analysis of a social movement did not exist in the late nineteenth or early twentieth centuries. Systematic sampling, focused interviews, and structured questionnaires are quite modern procedures. Future historians will have an unprecedented variety of evidence about social and political life in American society beginning in the 1930s, when the modern methodology of the social sciences became established. Each decade since then has seen increasing reliance on surveys and opinion polls to study a wide array of issues of lively contemporary concern. Numerous organizations poll their members to assess their attitudes on issues relevant to the agenda of the organization, just as newspapers and magazines poll subscribers to determine the market they represent for advertisers.

Despite the ubiquity of public opinion polls and surveys of special populations, little use has been made of the new research techniques in studies of the political process, special political events, or political movements. A notable exception are the endless surveys conducted in connection with electoral campaigns; these assess voter inclinations or predict election results in close contests. If one wanted to obtain a sample with a high probability of including men and women who would become prominent in national politics 10 or 20 years from now, a good net to cast would be a sample of delegates to a national political party convention. In precisely the same way, a sample of delegates to the national women's conference is highly likely to contain women who will become prominent in national politics in the future, either in mainstream politics in the Congress or in movement politics in the leading women's rights organizations.

Yet there has been little research on political party conventions. Prominent among them are the studies by McCluskey of the 1956 presidential conventions and by Kirkpatrick of the 1972 conventions (Kirkpatrick, 1976; McCluskey, 1958, 1960, 1964). Both studies were limited to only one contact with each delegate, either by personal interview or by written questionnaire. These studies provide useful profiles of the delegates' differences in political experience, demographic characteristics, and party positions. Thus, Kirkpatrick shows how delegates to the 1972 Democratic convention differed from delegates to the Republican convention that year on such factors as age, sex, educational attainment, or occupation, and how male delegates differed from female delegates in social and economic characteristics, political experience, and aspirations for future office holding.

What has *not* been studied is the *impact* of serving as a delegate to the party conventions: Does such participation dampen or stimulate political aspirations? Since it is probable that both effects can be found, an analysis of the differences between those who are "turned on" and those who are "turned off" by their service as national delegates would be of particular interest. This is exactly what the present study attempted to do, by obtaining data on political aspirations from the delegates both before and after the national women's conference.

Women have been conspicuous by their absence from American political life for most of the nation's history. Even in the late 1970s, although they represented 51% of the population, women were only 1% of U.S. Senators, 4% of U.S. Representatives, 5% of county officials and, even on very local levels, only 9% of mayors and city councilors. This underrepresentation of women in politics at all levels of elective office is a critical issue to political activist and social scientist alike. The women in this study are of very special interest in this connection, since they have had a great deal of political experience of a variety of sorts. It is likely that many of the feminists who will attain national prominence in politics in the next few decades were respondents in our study. What they have told us of their backgrounds, political experience, and political aspirations may help to unravel the reasons for the scarcity of women in politics and indicate what it would take to increase their numbers in elective office.

A last unique feature of the present study concerns the researcher's role vis-à-vis the population and the event under study. Both McClusky and

Kirkpatrick were political scientists who worked exclusively as researchers when they studied the delegates to the political party conventions. They were not themselves delegates to the party conventions they studied. By contrast, I served simultaneously as a National Commissioner and a research investigator during 1977 and 1978. This dual role presented special advantages and distinct disadvantages, which will be described later in this chapter.

But first, I wish to place the national conference in its historical context, both the long-term context of the past century of feminist political action and the short-term context of the current feminist renaissance of the last two decades.

Long-Term Historical Context

There were many women in colonial America who were concerned for the position of women in their communities but, like Abigail Adams, who admonished her husband "not to forget the ladies," they represented isolated individual voices rather than collectively organized efforts to change the status of women. The Seneca Falls, New York, public meeting in 1848 was a significant event in the history of American women precisely because it was one of the first attempts to organize collective action for change in the position and rights of women. Hence it is the 130-year span from 1848 to 1980 that provides the broadest historical canvas against which to place the current feminist movement. No detailed chronicle of this larger history will be attempted here; that has been done by other scholars. Rather, I wish to develop a particular theme concerning the cyclical nature of feminist political action over the past 130 years. It is an important theme because it speaks to the question of whether and when any feminist social movement "ends."[1]

An examination of organized political action by women on issues bearing on their own rights suggests a cyclical pattern, illustrated in Figure 1.1. Three peaks of organized efforts are shown in this graph: The first occurs between 1848 and the Civil War; the second between 1900 and the passage of the suffrage amendment in the early 1920s, and the third from the mid-1960s to the present. The graph also suggests that each peak, or wave, is separated from the next by roughly 50 years, or two generations.[2] Many young women

[1]This thesis is more fully developed in "Feminism and Intellectual Complexity" (in Rossi, 1973: 615–621).

[2]Quite disparate social scientists have noted this pattern of alternation between generations. Hansen (1952) noted that ethnic societies tend to emerge two generations after a peak in a particular group's immigration to the United States, just as Southern history and literature flourished two generations after the Civil War. Hansen suggests that sons forget what grandsons wish to remember, meaning that the second generation is so occupied with problems of assimilation and social mobility that they tend to repress ethnic identification, whereas the third genera-

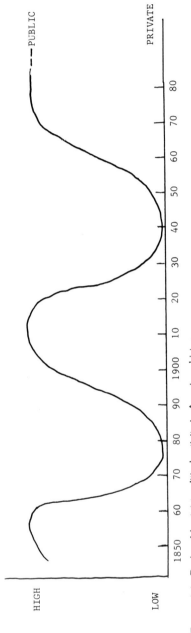

Figure 1.1. Peaks of feminist political activity in American history.

now in their twenties have grandmothers who participated in the suffrage campaigns that followed the first World War. Some of the middle-aged women involved in the contemporary feminist movement are themselves the daughters of suffragists. Many such individuals were in fact among the delegates to the national women's conference and hence respondents in our study. The emotional salience of this link between the generations was caught in the delegates' responses to an open-ended question that asked them to describe the most memorable aspect or experience of their attendance at the Houston conference. A number of women pointed to these personal links between themselves and women who had been active on women's issues earlier in the century. In a few cases, the links crossed three generations, as in the following instance of a middle-aged delegate:

> I had a very strong sense of being part of history. I remember my mother telling me of her experience as a young law student marching for suffrage. She visited my daughter in Houston during the conference and they both enjoyed the gavel to gavel coverage on public broadcasting. I felt a great responsibility for the example my mother had been for me all my life, as I hope I have been for my daughter.

Another woman illustrates the same point of cross-generational linkage involving a delegate 50 years older than herself:

> Talking to an 80-year-old delegate from my home state was a real high for me. I told her about my family and especially about my mother who was a 1920s political activist. When I gave her my maiden name, she almost shouted "then YOU are Mabel's DAUGHTER." That gave us a tremendous feeling of the links between us, of the continuity across the fifty years' difference in our ages.

Some of the links the delegates commented on were not backward to an older generation, but forward into the future, through the women's own daughters. Reading their comments, one senses the presence of family history in the making. The women's participation in Houston will become an important part of family history for themselves and for their daughters and granddaughters in much the same way that the political activities of the suffragists in the first two decades of the twentieth century have been kept alive

---

tion (the grandsons of the immigrants) are more secure socially and economically than their parents and can indulge the backward search to their ethnic roots. This thesis, although attractive, may need the same qualification developed in the text; that is, the middle generation may not reject the ethnic and religious heritage of the immigrant generation so much as limit their observance of ritual to the privacy of their families and homes. The third generation feels freer to act-out the values of their fathers and grandfathers in public associational life. Hence it is the dialectic from public to private and back to public arenas that may lead the historian to assume more radical breaks between proximate generations than in fact exists, because historians' "evidence" tends to be limited to public records.

in their memories from stories their mothers told them. Thus, one woman wrote:

> There were two highlights for me. One was the passage of the ERA and Minority Women's planks. The other was having with me and watching their reactions, my 11- and 13-year-old daughters, forming a special tradition and bond between us. I wondered how many women there in Houston had mothers who attended suffrage meetings years ago.

This woman's daughters were young adolescents who will probably remember their experiences in Houston without hearing stories about the event. But one was also aware, in Houston, of younger children and even babies who came to Houston with their mothers. These younger children will need the repetition of family stories about the event to make such memories vivid when they in turn reach adulthood. An example of this link to the future is the peak experience reported by a young delegate in her twenties:

> The absolute highpoint for me was walking into the Coliseum for the first time with my two-month-old daughter in my arms, and seeing that enormous word across the whole back of the stage—W O M A N.

Many of these quotations from individual delegates suggest a continuity between proximate generations, yet the cyclical pattern shown in Figure 1.1 suggests discontinuity, for the valley between peaks is two generations (50 years). The pattern in historians' treatment of the history of feminism is one of discontinuity. The subtitle of O'Neill's (1969) study of the suffrage movement early in this century is *The Rise and Fall of American Feminism,* clearly projecting a radical discontinuity to the movement over time. Are the women who report that their mothers were activists merely exceptional cases, whereas the general rule was for feminism to skip generations? Or was there a shift, over time, in the arena in which feminist ideas were manifested? Historians have access largely to a special kind of evidence; that is, written *public* records, press accounts of demonstrations or marches, organized efforts at legislative reform, minutes from the records of organizations involved in the social movement they study, etc. The interesting question is, What happens between the peaks of public organized action? Do women revert to the traditionalism of an earlier generation, or are they working through and into the stuff of their private lives, the values espoused by their more activist mothers and aunts?

It may be a misreading of the past to interpret the cyclical pattern shown over the past 130 years as the rise and fall of feminism, for this assumes that during the valleys between the three peaks, women lost the gains made by the preceding generation and returned to traditional conceptions of a woman's life. Perhaps we should view this cyclical pattern as a dialectic between public and private arenas of life. This conception acknowledges the peaks, those times when organized feminist efforts were conspicuous on the public political arena. But during the periods of seeming quiescence, a dialectical interpretation argues against the loss or denial of the values of the preceding generation of activists and stresses instead that, during the quiet periods, women may have been applying or acting on the same values that took their mothers into suffrage marches on the streets of New York City or Washington, D.C., but in less conspicuous, nonpolitical ways. The difference between proximate generations is therefore the arena in which feminist ideas are detectable in the lives of women.

Indeed, the aftermath of the first wave of feminism following the Civil War was decades of great expansion in women's higher education and in white-collar clerical and professional jobs for women. These were years during which the most prestigious eastern women's colleges were established. The typewriter came into use in the 1870s, opening up a whole new occupation to women. The daughters of the 1850s activists may have been deflected from direct political activity and public visibility into private education and em-ployment. Daughters may have done the same thing in the aftermath of the second wave, retreating in the 1930s and 1940s into private consolidation of the gains made by their mothers. During the 1930s, when feminism was supposedly dead, women earned a greater proportion of advanced degrees than at any other time before 1970.

So, too, the proportion of women in the labor force continued to climb during the 1940s and had increased dramatically by the late 1950s; this has significant implications, since labor-force participation tends to lower the polit-ical participation of women for the simple reason that politics in America is an extracurricular activity over and above responsibilities in work and family. Political roles, like work roles, have been premised on male incumbency: Just as most jobs in the economy were structured on the assumption that women carried men's family and household responsibilities, so too, most roles in the polity assume wives are at home to care for children and tend the house. Between 1920 and 1960, the descendants of the suffragists poured much of their energy into education and employment (Chafe, 1972). If they were married, they did double duty at work and at home. Such a profile leaves women little time or energy for political involvement during the years when men their age are getting established in politics—their 30s and 40s. This is why female politicians have been older, on average, than men in politics, and why they are more often widows or unmarried women than married women with children.

On the other hand, as increasing numbers of women move into the labor force, their perspectives begin to shift from an orientation turned inward to

domestic and neighborhood matters to an outward orientation with concern
for the larger society and their place in it. Although *The Feminine Mystique*
(Friedan, 1963) focused on middle-class homemakers in affluent suburbia,
the women who responded most keenly to the book were those already
oriented to the world beyond their homes through paid employment, volunteer work, or attendance at colleges and universities. It was the employed
woman whose children were well along in school who joined with single,
divorced, and widowed women in the early phase of the "women's rights"
movement in the middle-to-late 1960s; similarly, much younger women (the
majority still unattached and attending school) were drawn to and active in
the formation of the "women's liberation" movement in the late 1960s and
early 1970s. But this is a story I shall return to later in this chapter.

The general point of this discussion is that there has been much more
continuity between the generations than the public record of organized political action would suggest. This continuity is particularly characteristic of members of proximate generations at their most intimate points of contact—within
the family, between parents and children.[3] We do not generally find very
radical discontinuities in basic values from one generation to the next, once
children are beyond the limit-testing and rebellious stage of adolescence.
Children may differ from their parents in superficial ways—in consumer
habits, hair and clothing styles, or food preferences—but they are more apt to
be like their parents in underlying values and predispositions such as their
degree of sociability, their manner of relating to people younger and older
than themselves, and to members of their own and the opposite sex. Were
this not the case, were the family not serving as a major factor in assuring
some stability of norms and customs through time, there would be no persistence of cultural differences that distinguish one nation from another or,
within American society, one ethnic or religious group from another.

[3]There is evidence of intergenerational stability of basic political values in studies of radical
American youth in the 1960s. It had been assumed by many social scientists that these dissenting
young people were "oedipal rebels" rebelling against their fathers. According to this view, college
administrators, government and military officials were targets for anger psychologically displaced
from the dissidents' fathers. On the basis of this thesis, it was thought that the sons held a set of
political and personal beliefs radically different from that of their parents. Research has shown the
case to be quite otherwise: There is, in fact, a good deal of value continuity between parents and
their activist children. The parents of radical youth were political liberals (although apathetic), not
conservatives. What their children did was to bring the liberal views of their parents from the
private side of life to the public arena, on city streets and in social movements for justice and a
peaceful world (Brewster-Smith, Block, & Hahn, 1968; Flacks, 1967; Haan, 1968; Keniston,
1967, 1968). Such evidence further supports our thesis that proximate generations may differ in
public activity but less often in basic values and beliefs. Whether the same pattern would hold for
parents of feminist daughters is not known, but would be an important topic for scholarly
investigation.

At the same time, it is important to recognize that social changes or extraordinary historical events have an influence not only on the young, but on people of all ages. The concept of adult stability has had to yield in recent years as developmental psychologists have come to realize that we are not fixed entities when we enter adulthood, but continue to grow and change as we move through the life cycle (Brim & Kagan, 1980). Some of this change takes place through the intimate exchanges between parents and grown children. A parent is no more a fixed and finished product than a child is a *tabula rasa*. Parents learn to cope with constitutional and temperamental differences among their children and, within the parameters set by these differences, they transmit their values, prejudices, and tastes to their children. But the young in turn exert an influence on their parents, as many middle-aged mothers know who have argued out, thought about, and changed ideas due to the influence of their daughters. This reciprocal influence can then contribute to both value continuity and gradual change over longer stretches of time.

This reciprocal influence is also a process of quiet, subtle change that earlier historians had not noted; yet it is this process of working ideals into private life that may take place between the peaks of highly visible public activity in the long-term historical context. One can see this in longitudinal studies of the past 15 years in which sex-role attitudes are found to have changed not only among younger women but, significantly, among older women as well (Thornton & Freedman, 1979). So too, the passage of the suffrage amendment would have been a hollow victory had women not gone on in subsequent decades to use the suffrage won by the preceding generation. To use the suffrage required changes in knowledge and habits for millions of women. To meet the need for such new knowledge was the driving force behind the emergence of the League of Women Voters, yet this organization is rarely seen as having played any vital role in feminist history until it endorsed the Equal Rights Amendment (ERA) in recent years. League activities took place at the less conspicuous pole of the dialectic and never made newspaper headlines as the suffrage activities had done.

Our general thesis concerning the dialectic between public and private manifestations of feminist ideas and action in the long-term historical context can be applied to individual lives as well. Many names prominent in the early phase of the recent feminist renaissance are no longer in the public eye. An author or a political leader may be visible for a few years, then fade from public view. Indeed, it was with some surprise that I noted, in a study of feminists prominent in women's history in the nineteenth century (Rossi, 1973), that their feminist activism often took place during a very short span of 5–10 years in their early adulthood, after which they withdrew into private obscurity. We tend to think of women like Susan B. Anthony and Elizabeth Cady Stanton, early leaders who remained active well into old age, but they were not typical cases. Public roles exact a high price in time and energy, particularly in social movements that pioneer new ideas that trigger emotional heat and political opposition. It is understandable in simple human terms that most individuals tend to remain in the public limelight for only a short portion of their adulthood rather than the whole of their lives.

Social movements that persist over time may be those that accept this toll and encourage a circulation of leaders with fresh energy to replace those who become "burned out," drained by their efforts on the public stage. Many of the older women at the national conference in Houston reported their awareness of this necessity, and found pleasure precisely in the realization that there were so many competent and vigorous younger women to take their place. One such woman wrote:

> I am 69 years old, and while the conference was able to stir up all my old fire for a while, the best thing of all was to see so many politically capable young women to carry on the work.

Another woman wrote:

> The greatest experience of all for me was to see all the new emerging leaders to continue our struggle. I have given ten years to the movement, and really want now to work at a less feverish pace and in quieter circles. Anne Saunier is only the most visible of the new faces; there were dozens and dozens of such young women in Houston.

Even in our noisy times, these "quieter circles" contribute to significant social change. A striking 76% of the delegates in our survey reported that they "work for women's rights" on their current jobs. They are not employees in feminist organizations. These women work as government officials, clerks, social workers, teachers, health-care workers, lawyers, physicians, and nurses, to name a few. Their contributions to the feminist movement are not easily seen, but they are having important effects by promoting changes in customary practices in the workplace such as promotion guidelines and job definitions. Such individual efforts gradually add up to a significant change in the nature of the economy and of women's place in it.

In addition, there is an important commonality in the occupations women are concentrated in: Women prefer and are, in fact, most often found in people-serving occupations; they are far less often found in occupations dealing with inanimate material objects and machines. This means that women's work roles involve a high level of contact and interaction with people every day, providing a good vantage point in the social system from which, by verbal persuasion and personal modeling, women can be effective agents of social change in values and practices without ever stepping up onto a political soapbox.

The pleasure that shows in the remarks of older delegates to Houston concerning their replacement by younger leaders may also reflect a potential advantage women could have over men in politics. Since women have rarely had helpmates to cover home and child care when they were extremely active in politics, they have acquired a flexibility, stamina, and range of interests and skills that do not leave them in a personal vacuum when they contemplate withdrawing from politics, or when they have to adjust to a political defeat. They move on to other things. In addition, women's ability to put other people before themselves may make it easier for them to accept, indeed, to encourage the circulation of leadership that most benefits the movement. Men who have wielded power in industry or politics may "hang in there" beyond their usefulness to the organization or to the party because their lives would be empty if they stepped down. Since their lives never had much in them but their struggle for and exercise of economic or political power, they are apt to have neither alternative spheres for gratification nor the ability to acquire new passions to give meaning to their lives.

There is one added implication of the dialectic interpretation I have given to the cyclical pattern of feminist activity over the past 100 years and more. There is comfort in the view that periods of political quiescence are not necessarily periods of reversal or demise. At numerous points during the 1970s, the media have announced that feminism was "dead" or "dying" as a movement. Some of these announcements were undoubtedly motivated by the fantasy that the announcements themselves would contribute to the demise of the feminist movement. Unfortunately, one heard this assessment in some feminist circles as well. But if social change is best achieved when there are periods of rest during which new ideas are woven into the fabric of private lives, then those who gave so much time and energy during a peak period of political activism can take heart: Those efforts were not in vain; activists need not despair, but should look for the evidence of the effects of their efforts in women's homes, jobs, and private relationships, rather than the arena of politics. This is a cheering thought in the early 1980s, when backlash and stiffening opposition consume the energies of so many feminists and their organizations, for the moral of the dialectical interpretation of the history of the feminist movement is that we may lose a few battles, yet win the war.

The Third Wave of Feminism: 1961–1981

The national women's conference did not emerge from a political vacuum: It was preceded by a particular set of events and organizational developments within the feminist movement. In the previous section, I labeled this the third wave or peak in the long-term context of American feminist history. In this section, I shall locate the national conference in the short-term historical context of this third wave.[4]

There is an imperfect understanding in the social sciences of what combination of forces stimulates the emergence of a new social movement or the resurgence of an older one into public visibility. Hence scholars disagree on the specific date or event that can serve as a marker to the first phase of a movement's history. Such markers have several general characteristics: They are apt to be public, perhaps unique, typically affect large numbers of people, and are often identified as significant only years later, when the movement can no longer be ignored. Seneca Falls (1848) was without doubt a peak event in the personal lives of participants, but it was only defined as a significant marker decades later, when the suffrage movement was highly organized and publicly visible.

We may be too close to the origins of the third wave of feminism to identify its most significant beginning point or best symbolic marker. Some might say the publication of Friedan's *The Feminine Mystique* in 1963 is such a marker because of the enormous response to it among American women in the years following its publication. Others might argue that the formation of the Kennedy Commission on the Status of Women (1961), or the publication of its final report (*American Women,* 1963), both of which preceded Friedan's book, are more appropriate markers. Still others might claim that the founding of the National Organization for Women (NOW) in 1966 is a better marker event. A sociologist might prefer less specific political events or publications as starting points, preferring instead to point to the 1950s, which showed a sharp rise in the employment of married women, coupled with the beginning of what has become a long-term decline in the fertility rate (both trends apparent by 1960). But whatever marker we select, it in turn begs for an explanation in terms of preceding events that stimulated it. In that sense, there is an arbitrary quality to placing chronological dates on any ongoing, particularly recent, history of a social process or political movement.

The task is made somewhat easier if it is guided by some conceptual scheme that provides the criteria for classifying events. Almond and Powell's (1966) concepts of the three stages in a political process can assist us in charting the emergence and direction of the third wave of feminism. They differentiate among the following three stages in a political process: (a) *interest articulation,* when the emphasis is largely on a critique of existing social and political circumstances; (b) *interest aggregation,* when interests are gathered together in some organizational form that facilitates political action and assures public visibility; and (c) *rule-making,* when there are organized

---

[4]Several good descriptive histories of these early years of the contemporary feminist renaissance are Freeman, 1975; Carden, 1974; Hole and Levine, 1971.

efforts to influence policy and laws made by government, through elections, legislation, lobbies, etc.

The "fit" of this schema is undoubtedly better when dealing with a discrete, single-issue political movement than with one that has shown a broadening of issues and goals over time. Thus, the schema fits the earlier two waves of feminist history better than the third wave because the earlier waves tended to focus on the single issue of the suffrage. The Seneca Falls meeting in 1848 was followed by numerous town and city meetings at which women expressed their grievances and clarified the demands they made upon the larger society for change—the *interest articulation* stage of Almond and Powell's schema.

With the emergence of formal suffrage organizations and the numerous conventions that occurred during the last few decades of the nineteenth century, the movement shifted to the second, or *interest aggregation,* stage. The last intensive push of the movement in the first few decades of the twentieth century, under the leadership of Carrie Chapman Catt, represents the transition to the third, more mature stage of *rule-making* and tightly organized political tactics in canvassing, lobbying, etc. until the suffrage amendment was ratified by the required number of states.

The "fit" of this schema is much looser in the case of the third wave of feminism because the goals of the movement have broadened over the past decade, from their initial focus on the economic rights of women in their public roles to the rights of women in the private sector, covering such matters as marital division of labor, reproductive rights, protection from sexual harassment and abuse, etc. One issue may be at the stage of interest articulation, whereas another has moved on to the stage of rule-making. Hence to divide the third wave of feminism into stages is only a crude device at best, a way of locating the national women's conference in relation to broader developments in the short history of the third wave of feminism. I suggest 1961 as a beginning marker, 1966 as the transition to the second stage, and 1972 as the transition to the third stage.

Interest Articulation: 1961–1966

The first stage begins with the establishment of the Kennedy Commission on the Status of Women in 1961 and ends with the founding of the first feminist organization, NOW, in 1966. The key motivation of the Kennedy Commission and the state commissions which followed was rooted in the Soviet challenge to the American government through the successful launching of Sputnik in 1957. The government was not motivated so much by the *rights* of women as it was by a concern for *womanpower,* then viewed as the last untapped reserve from which the labor force could be expanded to meet the Soviet technical challenge in the race for technological and political supremacy in space and on earth. Hence the recommendations of the Kennedy Commission, and of the state commissions that followed, centered on the expansion of educational and economic opportunities for women. The objective was to ease female movement into technical and scientific fields or to release men for work in such fields by enlarging women's representation in the less technical occupations that had absorbed a large proportion of male labor. It is significant that, during the third wave of feminism, the first legislative action by the U.S. Congress to have a direct impact on women was the passage of the Equal Pay Act in 1963.

The state commissions followed the lead of the national Commission and inquired into the special circumstances facing women in the economies of the individual states. Periodically, representatives from the state commissions convened in Washington, D.C., to report on the progress of their work at the state level. In the process, countless thousands of women experienced rising expectations for governmental action. They expected the government to implement, rather than simply receive and file away, the recommendations they brought from their state commissions to the Washington, D.C., meetings. When these expectations were frustrated, as they were, by inaction on the part of the federal government, the spark was ignited that led to the formation of a political organization independent of the federal government—NOW (1966). The shift from the public to the private sector, and the effort to recruit members to the new organization, represents the transition from the stage of interest articulation to interest aggregation. Hence 1966 is a useful turning point in recent feminist history.

The primary goals of NOW in its founding year were closely modeled after those of civil rights organizations and of the Kennedy Commission itself; that is, to expand women's economic rights and opportunities. NOW was to be a kind of NAACP for women, seeking expanded economic opportunities, equal pay for equal work, and institutional change such as child care centers to facilitate the double duties of women at home and on the job. At that point, child care centers were not seen as desirable for the development of young children so much as necessary aids to permit women to carry traditional family responsibilities while filling jobs away from home. NOW quickly became known as the *women's rights* organization, and the stereotypical NOW member was an older, middle-class, white, married, and employed woman.

Interest Aggregation: 1966–1972

The founders of NOW were in fact more diverse than was thought for, within a year, there was strong internal pressure to advocate social and legal changes for women outside the school and the workplace. The right of a woman to control her own body through access to contraception and to safe abortions for unwanted pregnancies and the ERA were endorsed at NOW's second annual convention, causing some members and officers to withdraw. Independent organizations were created by those who wished to adhere to the narrower task of fighting economic discrimination. The Women's Equity Action League (WEAL) had its origins among the early NOW members who resisted the enlargement of the issues on NOW's agenda in 1967.

During these same 2 years, there was a counterpart spinoff of women in the anti-war and civil rights movements who were frustrated by male leadership and strongly influenced by a varied set of radical beliefs concerning the roots of women's oppression. This was a diffuse movement of small local groups, largely unnamed, that focused on consciousness-raising and were highly resistant to formal organizational structures. Neo-Marxist in political perspective, the keynote of such groups was no longer "make room for women," but more fundamental calls for basic structural changes in the economy, the government, and the family. Key words of the time were *oppression, male chauvinism,* and *patriarchal power.* Kate Millett's *Sexual Politics* (1970) and Shulamith Firestone's *The Dialectic of Sex* (1970) spoke for the *women's liberation* perspective as Betty Friedan's *The Feminine Mystique* had spoken for the *women's rights* perspective several years earlier.

With age, class, and politics sharply dividing many of the women who held these two perspectives, the early 1970s were understandably marked by a great deal of dissension and turmoil when the two forces met head on within an organization like NOW or in coalitions formed at the local level. The media gleefully described these clashes as evidence of fragmentation and predicted the demise of the feminist movement. While NOW was struggling to increase its membership and firm up its organizational structure, liberation group members were decrying elitist control and struggling to work in a participatory democratic mode yet finding the lack of structure an impediment to effective political action. Jo Freeman, an early observer of this strain, called it "the tyranny of structurelessness" (Freeman, 1972–1973). It was a complex mix that considerably strengthened both wings of the feminist movement. The infusion of younger women with background experience in consciousness-raising groups helped to radicalize the liberal goals and tactics of the local chapters and national board of NOW, and growing political experience helped the radicals to modify their earlier rigid emphasis on participatory democracy yet retain their healthy stress on minimal bureaucratic hierarchization in the women's liberation sector of the movement. The latter emphasis is apparent in the loose organizational structure of the women's health centers and the women's studies movement in subsequent years.

During 1969–1972, women's caucuses emerged in professional associations and on campuses across the country. They were characterized by strong infusions of young graduate students and faculty women and a minimum of organizational trappings. By 1972, many of the academic women's caucuses had moved to more formal organizational structures such as the Association of Women Psychologists (AWP) and the Sociologists for Women in Society (SWS).[5]

Rule-Making: 1972−1981

The year 1972 was a critical turning point in the feminist third wave, showing several early indicators of the political developments to follow over the next 8 years. Congress approved the ERA in 1972, opening the door to the need for focused political efforts to secure its ratification in at least 38 states within the 7-year period designated. By the time the national women's conference was held in 1977, only 3 states more were needed for ratification. Congress passed the 3-year extension bill in 1978, under the impetus of the strong support provided by the national conference and the concerted political lobbying for extension by NOW.

The year 1972 was also important for the National Women's Political Caucus (NWPC), a nonpartisan organization founded in 1971 and aimed specifically at applying pressure for greater representation of women and of women's issues in the mainstream of both political parties. NWPC has been dedicated to supporting women candidates for public office and to lending financial and other help to male candidates who are strong advocates of women's rights. The 1972 political party conventions were the first to feel the full weight of feminist political pressure, not merely for platform endorsement of women's rights but for a sharp increase in the number of women in the ranks of delegates to the conventions themselves. The Democrats increased the percentage of women delegates to their conventions from 13% in 1968 to 39% in 1972, whereas the Republicans increased female representation from 17 to 30% between the two conventions (Kirkpatrick, 1976). Also of considerable importance was the widening support for the ERA from an increasing number of major women's organizations in the country, from traditional ones like the League of Women Voters, the Girl Scouts, the American Association of University Women (AAUW), the Federation of Business and Professional Women's Clubs, to such newer organizations, closer to the feminist movement from their founding, such as the National Black Feminist Organization (founded in 1973), and the Coalition of Labor Union Women (CLUW) (founded in 1974).

[5]Rossi and Calderwood (1973) provide an overview of these developments and an assessment of the status of academic women as of 1973. See especially Klotzburger (1973: 359−392) for a sketch of the development of women's caucuses in the major disciplinary professional associations.

The label used to refer to a social movement is a good indicator of the degree of perceived consensus on the part of the public. It is also a good political barometer to the amount of fragmentation or cohesion within the movement itself. From 1966 to 1972, one could only speak of *wings* or *sectors* to a diffuse, uncoordinated social movement. On the liberal side, there was the *women's rights,* or *women's movement,* and on the radical, *women's liberation,* or *women's lib* as the press insisted on calling it. Since 1972, the label increasingly used both within the movement and by the larger public is the *feminist movement.*[6]

This is not to suggest that every individual or every organization supporting the ERA, child care, or equal pay for women would take kindly to the *feminist* label. There may not be anyone within NOW who would reject the label, but many members of the League of Women Voters or the Federation of Business and Professional Women's Clubs would undoubtedly do so, despite the fact that both organizations endorsed the ERA. We shall see in the course of the analysis reported in later chapters that organizations like NOW and the League differ significantly in their individual and collective consensus on an array of issues concerning women. It is precisely because the feminist movement has added new issues and objectives to the feminist agenda over the years, that it could hardly be otherwise. Consensus may have been high on the kinds of economic issues with which the movement was occupied in the mid-1960s, but this was not so on issues that emerged in the mid-1970s, such as sexual preference, women's health, rape, and displaced homemakers. On still other issues, like easy access to abortion, there are longstanding counter-values some feminists hold that preclude their endorsement of abortion, although they share a high degree of consensus on economic and political rights for women.

Table 1.1 brings together some of the major developments in the historic sketch given thus far, together with other selected highlights in the more recent chronology of federal actions affecting the status of women. What such an overview does not communicate is the overlap of key individuals across these varied actions and decisions. Federally employed women who were prominent on the Kennedy Commission or on state commissions helped to found NOW and Federally Employed Women (FEW). For example, Catherine East, a NOW founder active in Kennedy Commission work, went on to serve as Executive Secretary of the Citizens Advisory Council on the

---

[6]*Feminist* and *feminism* are terms with a much shorter history than many people realize. They appeared for the first time in a book review in an 1895 issue of the British journal, *Athenaeum.* They appeared there in quotation marks, which they lost by the turn of the century. We now speak of the nineteenth-century political movement as a *feminist* movement but, at the time, it was simply called the *woman's movement.* It is a significant transition point when organizations or coalitions use the new label to describe themselves as collectivities.

Table 1.1
Selected Highlights of the Federal Chronology of Actions Affecting Women: 1961–1978

Year	EXECUTIVE ACTION	LEGISLATIVE ACTION	JUDICIAL DECISIONS
1961	Kennedy Commission on the Status of Women (Executive Order 10980)		
1963	Kennedy Commission Report, AMERICAN WOMEN Interdepartmental Committee on Status of Women & Citizens Advisory Council on Status of Women set up in Dept. of Labor	Equal Pay Act passed	
1964	First National Conference of State Commissions on Status of Women (also held in 1965 and 1966).	Civil Rights Act of 1964 (Title VII prohibits discrimination in employment because of race, sex, religion, color, national origin.	
1965			Griswold v. State of Conn. (State law banning contraceptives struck down as unconstitutional)
1966			White v. Crook (exclusion of women from juries a violation of equal protection under 14th Amendment.)

1967	Task forces established to update recommendations of 1963 Kennedy Commission Report. FAMILY LAW AND POLICY (First government document recommending far-reaching change in law affecting marriage and divorce, abortion, domicile, custody). Executive Order 11246 (Prohibits discrimination by federal contractors, amended to include sex discrimination -- basis for affirmative action plans.)	Repeal of law restricting military rank held by women.	Weeks v. Southern Bell Telephone (First successful appeals court decision interpreting sex provision of Title VII - Civil Rights Act of 1964.)
1969	President's Task Force on Women's Rights and Responsibilities (Nixon)		
1970	Task Force Report, A MATTER OF SIMPLE JUSTICE		Bowe v. Colgate Palmolive (First court test of real effects of labor laws that apply only to women.)
1972	Civil Rights Commission given jurisdiction over sex discrimination	ERA approved by Congress Equal Employment Opportunities Act of 1972 (gives EEOC enforcement authority)	

(continued)

Table 1.1 (*continued*)

Year	EXECUTIVE ACTION	LEGISLATIVE ACTION	JUDICIAL DECISIONS
1972		Title IX of Education Amendments Act (prohibits sex discrimination in most federally assisted educational programs.)	
1973	First time President's Economic Report includes a chapter on "The Economic Role of Women"	Foreign Assistance Act (provision for integrating women into development efforts.)	Doe v. Bolton; Roe v. Wade (Decisions to abort a matter between woman & physician.)
1974		Public Law 93-392 (establishes August 26 as Women's Equality Day.) Public Law 93-495, Equal Credit Opportunities Act (Prohibits discrimination in credit on basis of sex or marital status.)	

22

1975	National Commission on Observance of International Women's Year appointed	Public Law 94-197 establishes National Commission, amended to cover national conference	Stanton v. Stanton (Court struck down state law on child support that defined males as minors until 21 and females under 18)
1976	IWY Commission Report, TOWARD A MORE PERFECT UNION.		
1977	National Women's Conference, Houston		
1978	IWY Commission Report, THE SPIRIT OF HOUSTON President's Advisory Committee on Women established.	ERA extension to June 30, 1982 passed.	

Status of Women within the Department of Labor, and later joined the Secretariat staff of the International Women's Year (IWY) Commission under President Carter. Similarly, Kathryn Clarenbach was active as the Chairperson of the Wisconsin state commission, key organizer and first Chairperson of the Board of NOW, and Executive Director of the IWY Commission. Marguerite Rawalt had a long and distinguished career as a lawyer defending women's rights and played important roles in the formation of the NOW Legal Defense Fund and as a consultant to the 1967 Task Force on Family Law and Policy in the Department of Labor. Dorothy Haener's involvement in the feminist movement began as a union activist and official in the United Auto Workers in Detroit; she later served on the Board of NOW, has been active in ERAmerica and the Coalition of Labor Union Women, and served as a Commissioner on the IWY Commission. These are only a few illustrations from the hundreds of women from government, academe, unions, publishing, and business who have provided continuity to feminist political efforts and whose sociometric links to each other have been critical to the communication across organizations that contributes to the expansion and effectiveness of a social movement.

With this general historical background, we can move now to the more immediate history of the development and organization of the IWY Commission and the national women's conference for which it was responsible.

The National IWY Commission and
the National Women's Conference

National commissions come into being through presidential (executive) order, by mandate of a Congressional law, or by a combination of both. It has been politically customary and expedient to diversify such commissions in terms of ethnicity, region, and occupation of the men and women invited to serve on them, but it is not uncommon for the majority of the commissioners appointed at any particular time to share the political party affiliation of the president appointing them. Since it is one of the prerogatives of an incoming president to review all existing national commissions and to change their composition through new appointments, the work of a commission can be seriously affected by the timing of presidential elections, and in particular by any shift in the political party occupying the White House. Commission reports released shortly after the installation of a new administration may be rejected or studiously ignored by an incoming president; President Nixon, for example, publicly rejected central recommendations of the Johnson-appointed commissions on pornography and on population.

The history of the National Commission on the Observance of International Women's Year illustrates the effects these factors can have. The 38 months of its existence, from January 9, 1975, to March 31, 1978, spanned the shift from a Republican administration under President Ford to a Democratic administration under President Carter. The Commission also involved both executive orders and public law. On the other hand, the final report of the IWY Commission was submitted to the same president (Carter) who had changed the personnel serving as Commissioners during the 7 critical planning months immediately preceding the national conference. Thus, the history of the IWY Commission is important to an understanding of the organizational structure of the national women's conference and will be reviewed here for that reason.

The United Nations had declared 1975 to be International Women's Year and, in observance of that fact, President Ford appointed a National IWY Commission by Executive Order 11832 on January 2, 1975. This 35-member IWY Commission, under Presiding Officer Jill Ruckelshaus, was charged with coordinating efforts across the country in observance of International Women's Year, examining data on recent trends in the status of American women, and making recommendations to the President in a final report by the end of 1975. Because it took place so soon after the U.N. declaration, there was an international aura to the establishment of the U.S. Commission that made the State Department an appropriate setting to house the IWY Commission and its Secretariat staff. In November 1975, the life of the IWY Commission was extended for 6 months, by an amendment to the executive order, to give the Commission additional time to prepare its report, . . . *To Form a More Perfect Union,* which was released in June 1976. Thus, President Ford, who appointed the IWY Commission in the first place, was also the recipient of this first report from the IWY Commission.

There was no provision in the executive order for a national women's conference. Like the model provided by the earlier national commission on the status of women under President Kennedy, the IWY Commission's charge centered on data gathering, testimony before the Commission, reports on specialized topics, an assessment of the impact of existing or pending legislation on the position of women, and the publication of a report on its findings and recommendations for action. But it was only 5 days (January 14, 1975) after President Ford signed the executive order establishing the IWY Commission that Bella Abzug and Patsy Mink introduced bills in Congress specifically for the purpose of holding a national women's conference. As in most legislative history, it took several months to gather support from men and women in Congress behind the bill and to monitor its passage through the legislative process. The bill's authors had in mind the bicentennial year ahead (1976) and the hope that a national women's conference that same year would strike a new and memorable historic note for that very reason.

Public Law 94-167 was not passed and signed by President Ford until December 24, 1975, making it unlikely that anything of the magnitude of a national women's conference could be organized in time to be held during the following, bicentennial year. The law did not establish a new national commission: It charged the existing IWY Commission to appoint coordinating committees in each of the 50 states and 6 specified territories. These committees would be responsible for organizing state meetings during 1976 for the purpose of electing delegates to a national conference to be held at some unspecified date and for submitting a report on its work and recommendations to the President and the Congress within 120 days of the national conference.

Appropriations to the IWY Commission under Public Law 94-167 were not made until 6 months after the signing of the bill and hence were not available until June 1976, about the same time the IWY Commission released its first report. (The amount of money appropriated—$5 million—was one-half the amount requested in the original bill.) The IWY Commission appointed several regional coordinators from the Secretariat staff to draw up lists of people to serve on the 56 state or territory coordinating committees. After staff review, the full IWY Commission voted on the state committee membership lists. Thus, the important first step of putting the organizational machinery for the national women's conference in place was completed shortly after the national elections in November 1976.

During the winter of 1976 and the early spring of 1977, the Secretariat staff developed administrative procedures for coordinating the work of the 56 committees, prepared working documents to assist the states in running workshops and panel discussions on a range of issues affecting women, and developed guidelines for handling the allocation and expenditure of funds the state committees received from the national Commission. Secretariat staff and IWY Commission members were also involved in drawing up a set of specific resolutions from the Ford Commission report to assure that all state meetings took action on at least a core agenda, regardless of the many new resolutions presented by local groups that wished to tailor recommendations to a state plan of action or to urge the addition of new resolutions to the agenda for the national conference.

During these late winter months, the Carter administration reviewed the composition of the IWY Commission and its charge under the public law mandating the national women's conference. In March 1977, President Carter announced his appointments to the IWY Commission, released an Executive Order expanding the Commission to include at most 43 members, and specifically charged the Commission to proceed in its efforts to organize and convene the conference in keeping with the public law. Bella Abzug was appointed Presiding Officer, replacing Elizabeth Athanasakos, who had served in the post in 1976 and early 1977.

Athanasakos was one of the Ford appointees who were reappointed by President Carter, thus providing important links of continuity between the Commissions of the two administrations. This continuity was much greater for the Secretariat staff than for the IWY Commissioners themselves: 25% of the Carter Commissioners had served on Ford appointments as well, whereas 70% of the Secretariat staff (as of October 1977) had been hired during the Ford administration.

There was a decided shift from Republican to Democratic majorities on the IWY Commission as a result of this transition between administrations; issue priorities and more subtle matters like the style of administrative management changed as well. An example of this contrast can be seen among the IWY Commissioners drawn from the ranks of publishers and editors: They ranged from a conservative publisher like Helen Copley (Copley Newspaper, California), who served only on the Ford Commission, to moderates like Lenore Hershey (editor, *Ladies Home Journal*) and John Mack Carter (editor, *Good Housekeeping*), who served on both Commissions; to very liberal Gloria Steinem (editor, *Ms. Magazine*), who was first appointed to the Carter Commission. Only the Carter Commission had officers from explicitly feminist organizations like NOW (Eleanor Smeal, president) and the National Gay Task Force (Jean O'Leary, co-president).

There was also a decided contrast in leadership style between the two Commissions: The first Commission was led in the consensus-building style of Jill Ruckelshaus; the second in the more erratic, tough-minded approach of Bella Abzug. A Ford appointee who remained on the Carter Commission often drew the comparison in the informal conversations we shared during the monthly meetings of the Carter Commission. It had been a pattern, for example, for Jill Ruckelshaus to hold a hospitality meeting the evening before the Commission met, during which it was possible for the Commissioners to talk informally, share news, discuss the agenda, and become better acquainted with each other in a relaxed atmosphere. By contrast, Bella Abzug's pattern more often involved early morning shuttle flights from New York City to Washington, D.C., and a rather frenzied style of chairing the Commission meetings. It was a contrast between charm, intelligence, and low-key administrative savvy on the one side, and the unusual combination of an abrasive style and political charisma on the other. Both Commissions became cohesive working groups over time, but for quite different reasons. The cohesive spirit that developed under Ruckelshaus and Athanasakos grew out of an internal group process, whereas the Abzug Commissioners developed group solidarity as a response to external criticism and to Conservatives' efforts to disrupt their work. A Commissioner who served on both Commissions summed up the difference by saying that the Ford Commission was a good one *because of* the presiding officers, the Carter Commission *despite* its presiding officer. My impression from conversations with staff members is that the same assessment would be given by many members of the Secretariat staff as well.

This contrast in leadership can be easily overdrawn, however, since it is also the case that far more diversity of political and feminist views existed among the Carter Commissioners than among the Ford Commissioners. In keeping with the general demographic correlates of Democratic party affiliation, the Carter-appointees added a spicy blend of union, racial, ethnic, and lesbian voices to the IWY Commission's deliberations and decisions through the summer and fall of 1977. Then, too, the sheer pressure of responsibility that mounted as the conference date drew near added its own note of crisis to try the nerves and spirit of the most tough-minded leader. The combination of enthusiasm and concern for possible political disruption in Houston was shared by the delegates themselves: In the survey fielded in October, before the conference, 87% of the delegates reported high levels of enthusiasm about the coming conference and 57% reported high levels of concern that political opponents of the conference would disrupt it. At its last meeting in Washington, D.C., before the conference, the IWY Commission greatly increased its budgeting for security guards in Houston, so seriously did they view the prospect of trouble.

The important issue to note in this brief history is the points of organizational continuity and of change as a consequence of the restructuring of the national Commission following the change in administrations from Republican Ford to Democratic Carter. Clearly, there was a conspicuous change at the national level as Bella Abzug replaced Elizabeth Athanasakos as Presiding Officer. But the professional core of the Secretariat staff was in place in 1976 and continued through the Carter years of 1977 and early 1978. With this staff's assistance, the Ford Commission set in place the state coordinating committees, and it was these committees that were responsible for organizing the state meetings at which delegates were nominated and elected. The core agenda of resolutions considered at the state meetings were strongly influenced by the set of recommendations made by the Ford Commission in its 1976 report. Since the state committees typically brought a slate of nominees to the state meetings, and a large proportion of the committee-endorsed nominees were elected, the influence of the state committees established during the Ford administration extended to the conference itself. (See Figure 1.2 for a schematic overview of events from 1975 to early spring 1978.)

The Carter Commission inherited this basic structure in early spring 1977. It is interesting to note, with the help of the organizational flow chart in Figure 1.3 at which points the newly composed Commission could exert direct impact on the national conference. These included the details of managing the national conference, including the selection of a site, the mode of seating delegates, the activities that would take place in addition to the plenary ses-

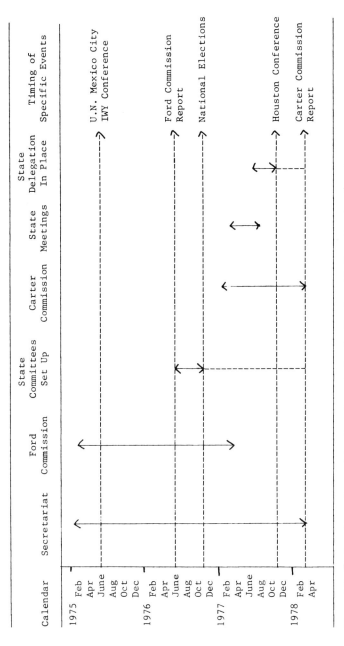

Figure 1.2. Timing of formation and duration of organizational units relevant to the national conference.

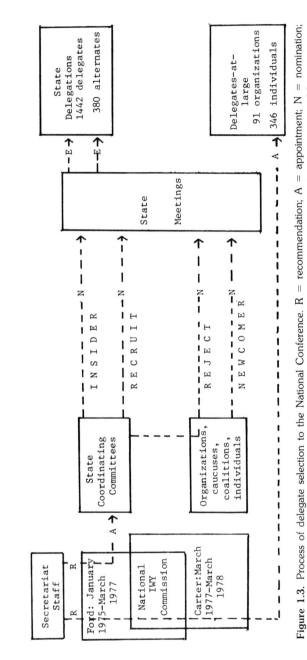

Figure 1.3. Process of delegate selection to the National Conference. R = recommendation; A = appointment; N = nomination; E = election. Insider = Committee member nominated by committee; Reject = Committee member not nominated by committee; Recruit = Nonmember nominated by committee; Newcomer = Nonmember not nominated by committee.

sions, and the hiring of local site personnel. But the key powers of the Carter Commission to affect the outcome of the national conference were through the final set of substantive resolutions in the National Plan of Action, the power of appointment of the delegates-at-large, and the management of the floor during the plenary sessions of the conference.

The official justification for the provision of appointed delegates-at-large under Public Law 94-167 was to provide a means for correcting any lack of representation of significant categories of individuals or of organizations in the elected delegate body. It was expected that the elected delegates would underrepresent racial and ethnic minorities, the less well-educated, the poor, and younger women. To find out to what extent there was, in fact, such underrepresentation, the Secretariat required that all state committees forward to Washington, D.C., biographical forms filled out by the elected delegates and alternates (*bioforms*) so that the IWY Commission could compare the demographic profile of elected delegates with recent census information on the female population and correct any underrepresentation by appointing appropriate delegates-at-large.

It was my impression, as a member of the IWY Commission committee that drew up the lists of potential delegates-at-large, that many Carter Commissioners expected to find a marked underrepresentation of racial and ethnic minorities in the elected delegate body. Although this was never explicitly discussed among us during committee meetings, it was my sense that this expectation was rooted in the knowledge that the state coordinating committees had been set in place by the Ford Commission and that a large proportion of the elected delegates were either members of or nominated by the state committees. As it turned out, the expectations were wrong; if anything, the elected delegates showed an overrepresentation of racial, ethnic, and religious minorities (see Table 1.2). As a result, the pressures on the delegate-at-large selection committee of the national IWY Commission were the more usual ones of a patronage variety, with Commissioners submitting names for committee consideration that represented their own political constituencies and organizational affiliations. This was not inconsistent with racial, ethnic, class, and age diversity of the delegates-at-large, of course, since the Carter Commissioners and the selection committee members in particular, were themselves from very diverse backgrounds.

A good way to show the continuity of influence of the state coordinating committees from their establishment in 1976 through the national conference in November 1977 is by the extent to which the state delegations included people who had been members of the coordinating committees before their nomination and election or who had the endorsement of these committees although they were not members. The four types of delegates shown in Figure 1.2 (Insiders, Recruits, Rejects, and Newcomers) identify the four

Table 1.2

Racial–Ethnic Distribution of Elected Delegates versus Total U.S. Female Population, 1976

RACIAL/ETHNIC GROUP	National Distribution[a]	Elected Delegates[b]	Surplus/ Deficit[c]
Caucasian	84.4	64.5	–
Black	10.4	17.4	+
Hispanic	4.3	8.3	+
Asian–American	.6	2.7	+
American Indian	.4	3.4	+
Hawaiian	–	.5	
Alaskan Native	–	.4	
All Other	.6	2.8	+

[a] Data from Bureau of Labor Statistics (June 1977) based on estimates of all females 16 and over in U.S. as of 1976.

[b] These figures are based on information from delegate biographic forms submitted by elected delegates from 48 states to the Commission Secretariat. Excluded from the base N were 8.7% of the forms that did not state racial/ethnic group membership. These were the figures the Commission committee charged with appointment of delegates at large used in drawing up suggested candidates for the appointed delegate category.

[c] A "+" indicates a significant surplus in delegate body compared to total female population.

major routes to eventual election as a delegate. The *Insiders* are elected delegates who were members of their state committees and enjoyed the endorsement of the committee as nominees. The *Recruits* are elected delegates who were not members of the state committees but had their endorsement. *Rejects* are committee members who did not receive committee endorsement, but managed to be nominated and elected nonetheless. Finally, the *Newcomers* are people who had been neither committee members nor nominees on the slates of the committees: They either sought nomination and election on their own or had the support of local groups and organizations in the state. The distribution of these four types among the elected delegates and alternates in our survey was as follows:

Insiders	35%
Recruits	30%
Rejects	6%
Newcomers	29%

The combination of Insiders plus Rejects (41%) represents the actual extent of overlap in personnel between state delegations and the state committees. State committee endorsement is represented by the combination of Insiders and Recruits—a high 65% of the total elected delegate body. Totally "new blood" (the Newcomers), people with no official ties to nor support from the state committees, were 29% of the final elected delegate body. That two-thirds of the elected delegates were either members of the state committees or had their endorsement is an index of the long and influential reach of the committees set up during the Ford administration.

That long reach of the Ford appointees needs some qualification, since an important part of the story is not visible in the account given thus far. I have not investigated the extent to which the state coordinating committees were in turn drawn from among those prominent in the states for their service on the state commissions on the status of women. For those states with which I am familiar, there was clearly a good deal of overlap. In light of the huge job confronting the small Secretariat staff that carried the responsibility for setting up the state coordinating committees and the presence on that staff of people who had been active in their own state commissions and the national association of state commissions, one surmises that this was a prominent source for possible appointees to the state coordinating committees. State commissions, like national commissions, are creatures of the executive branch (often subject to legislative approval) and hence tend to follow the customary practice of appointing people who represent the ethnic, racial, and religious diversity of the state, or at least such diversity as is represented in the party that occupies the governor's office. Hence some of the diversity that showed up in the profile of elected delegates and alternates was rooted not simply in successful outreach efforts on the part of the coordinating committees but in the diversity of the committees themselves and of the state commissions from which many committee members were drawn.

Following the national conference, many of the same people who were delegates and served on the state committees returned to their responsibilities on the state commissions. They have not been having an easy time of it. Many are newly stimulated and focused in their efforts as observers of and lobbyists for specific bills in the state legislatures. To an extent that we cannot measure, there is a new clarity of political effort as a consequence of the national Plan of Action adopted in Houston and of the enriched and enlarged network of contacts with like-minded people serving on commissions in other states.

Similarly, the far-right activists in many states have since shifted attention to the state commissions. Governors elected to office by conservative, right-to-life supporters have dismissed some state commissions by "sunsetting" them, as occurred in Colorado. This means they were abolished under laws that require the commissions to be reviewed every few years to determine whether there was still a need for them or whether or not they had been working efficiently. Other state commissions have been changed by the appointment of far-right commissioners by newly elected conservative governors. In Massachusetts and Wisconsin, where conservative governors (King and Dreyfus) defeated liberal candidates (Dukakis and Schreiber), the state commissions were dismissed yet, in both states, the ex-commissioners have continued to function and possibly are even more alert and critical now than they had been as members of the state commissions. In Massachusetts, the commissioners were held together as a Women's Commission in Exile and expanded their number to include women from community organizations and more radical feminist groups. In Wisconsin, the ex-commissioners continued their work by initiating a Wisconsin Women's Network and expanding the membership to include representatives of some 55 organizations and hundreds of individuals. But there are a growing number of state commissions that now include antifeminist members, appointed under the guise of wanting to represent "all" women in the state, a move that Kathryn Clarenbach describes as similar to appointing Ku Klux Klan members to civil rights commissions (Lindsey, 1980).

But now let me turn to the study itself, first placing it in the historical context of the Commission's work and then describing the advantages and disadvantages of my having served dual roles as both Commissioner and researcher.

Research on the National Women's Conference

It is doubtful that this study would have been conducted if it were not for my serving as a Carter-appointee on the national IWY Commission. The idea for the study only emerged in early June of 1977, roughly 5 months before the conference, and was largely the result of political developments at state meetings during the spring months. It became clear between March and June that many state meetings were producing delegations with a very different kind of heterogeneity than anyone on the IWY Commission or the state committees had expected. There were early warnings of this in the legal suits filed by far-right groups who wished to halt the IWY Commission's activities and prevent the national conference from taking place. But the events at the state meetings were of even greater concern to the IWY Commission: There were organized campaigns to flood the meetings with anti-IWY individuals who registered and voted for an agreed-upon anti-IWY slate of nominees. In some states, anti-IWY registrants so outnumbered all other participants as to assure the election of sizable numbers of anti-IWY delegates.

In retrospect, the IWY Commission probably showed an exaggerated concern over these developments, since there was never any question that the anti-IWY delegates would represent more than a small proportion of the total elected delegate body. It also became clear by early June that the political heterogeneity of the delegate body that troubled me as a national IWY Commissioner, interested me as a researcher. It was then my belief that both the IWY Commission itself and its opponents in the conservative, anti-ERA, and right-to-life groups, held mystical views of each other that assumed far more divergence of opinion than might in fact be the case on many issues affecting the lives of women. Whether true or not, the presence of anti-ERA and anti-abortion delegates in Houston made research on the delegate body of *more,* rather than *less,* interest to a research sociologist.

Were this newly anticipated diversity of political views in the delegate body the only rationale, it is doubtful that the study would have been undertaken, since it would mean carrying responsibility for work as an IWY Commissioner and a researcher simultaneously, on top of a full-time job as a professor of sociology. In addition, there would be very short notice to prepare for any systematic research, even assuming success in securing funds for the study. It was clear by June that there were numerous small-scale research projects being developed to investigate one or another aspect of the conference. The IWY Commission was self-conscious about providing an adequate descriptive account of its work, so writers were already under contract to write the story of the conference. This gave assurance of excellent qualitative and descriptive accounts of the work of the IWY Commission and the experience of the national conference. The press would undoubtedly cover the dramatic highlights of the conference, and reporters would surely write up their impressions from countless interviews with participants at the conference.

But all this reporting would not provide the kind of evidence only a systematic study could provide. The delegates whose views would be sought out and reported in the press were likely to be those who played conspicuous roles in caucuses, state delegations, or on the floor of the Coliseum during the debates. But who would report on the delegates who sat quietly, never sought to speak from a microphone, yet who may have been the hard-working members of delegation committees? The odds seemed high that future histo-

rians dealing with this conference would be as frustrated by the absence of
data on the participants who did not fill leadership roles as past historians
have been in analyzing the feminist movement in the nineteenth century.
Descriptive studies or press accounts can not represent the full-bodied aggregate voice of the delegates involved in the conference proceedings. Only
systematic surveys can hope to capture that.

An important dimension of the research idea that had begun to germinate
was to study the impact of various kinds of participation in the conference on
the delegates' plans for future political activity or their aspirations for political
careers. Would the conference contribute to the delegates' subjective sense of
political competence? Would the delegates come away from Houston with
higher levels of political aspirations? If delegates had only been politically
active on the local level and then had the experience in Houston of being
active on the national level, would they shift their own political aspirations
from the local to the state or national level? On the other hand, would some
delegates lower their political aspirations once they had had the opportunity
in Houston to observe others they took to be more competent in politics than
themselves?

These were the kinds of questions that emerged as the idea for the study
began to take shape. But for such a study to succeed, it would have to be
independent of the IWY Commission itself, particularly if I were to seek
cooperation from delegates opposed to the conference all told or opposed to
several resolutions on highly controversial issues. This argued for the desirabil-
ity of seeking funds from outside sources, of conducting the research from a
base away from Washington, D.C., and of publishing the results as an independent venture rather than as sponsored work under the auspices of the
IWY Commission itself.

At the same time, it would be useful to have the informal support of the
IWY Commission and the cooperation of the Secretariat staff in order to gain
access to mailing lists, information about the history of the IWY Commission
and plans for the conference, as well as for the myriad small services difficult
to anticipate in advance for a study on this scale. The tentative plan for the
study was therefore presented to the IWY Commission at its June 16 meeting
and was enthusiastically approved by the Commissioners. To move quickly
enough to field the study before the conference, it was imperative that a very
tight budget be drawn up, since this would increase the probability of funding
without a lengthy proposal review process. To keep the budget down, the
IWY Commission agreed to provide mailing envelopes and approved my use
of the government franking privilege as a national IWY Commissioner. I had
requested this because postage for two mailings with return envelopes to a
sample as large as mine could easily run to several thousands of dollars.

With IWY Commission approval in hand, I approached several possible funding sources during the following week; a proposal was drafted and sub-mitted to the most likely sponsor, the Ford Foundation, on June 21. By early July, word came that the project would indeed be funded by the Ford Foun-dation. The summer months were devoted to the design of the first question-naire, which I wanted to have in the mail by early October, thus allowing a 6-week period before the national conference for the fielding of the first wave of the study. Details of the actual design and the variables included in the questionnaires are presented in Chapter 3. Here I wish merely to sketch the overall scope of the project and to discuss the ways in which the simultaneous roles of political participant and researcher turned out to be both advantage-ous and frustrating.

Even under the best of circumstances, the design and fielding of a large-scale study in 4 months is difficult; this represents about one-third the time ordinarily devoted to this phase of a research project of this kind. The strengthening of opposition to the conference in conservative circles also necessarily affected the research, for it became clear as the field stage ap-proached that it might be difficult to obtain a good response rate from dele-gates who opposed the work of the IWY Commission. I used every possible device to assure confidentiality and independence of the research from the IWY Commission: The cover of the questionnaire prominently displayed the information that it was being privately funded by the Ford Foundation and that the University of Massachusetts was the research locale. On the other hand, the use of government franking privileges meant that the mailing ar-rived in State Department envelopes, since this was the federal agency within which the Secretariat was housed.

Despite the explanatory cover letter and my availability by telephone to any delegates that might have doubts about the purposes and sponsorship of the study, the many conflicting signals came through to the potential respondents who received the mail packets—State Department, Ford Foundation, Univer-sity of Massachusetts, Social and Demographic Research Institute, and the dual affiliation of the principal investigator as both professor of sociology and national IWY Commissioner—were bound to blur and complicate the picture in the minds of many respondents. My optimistic expectation in July of an 80% response rate was even then unrealistic in light of the very short time for the preconference field stage: The complex associations of the researcher with the IWY Commission, the heightened political atmosphere by October, and the fact that most mail questionnaires rarely exceed a 50% response rate all contributed to a more sober expectation by the time the survey got under way.

The design and fielding of the *second* wave proceeded at a more leisurely pace in the 2 months following the conference. The second questionnaire was mailed by early February. I allowed a longer period of field time for the

Table 1.3

Timing of Political Events and of Research Process

Date	P o l i t i c a l	R e s e a r c h
1977		
Jan		
Feb		
Mar	Carter Commission Appointed	
Apr		
May	State Meetings: Delegate	
June	Elections	Proposal submitted to Ford Foundation
July		Proposal funded
Aug		FIRST WAVE Design, Pretest
Sept		Printing
Oct	Delegates-at-large Appointed	Fielding (Cut off: Nov. 21)
Nov	National Conference-Houston	
Dec		Coding SECOND WAVE Design
1978		
Jan		Printing
Feb		Fielding
Mar	Commission report submitted to President	(Cut off: Apr. 1)
Apr		
May		Coding
June		
July		Data Merged, begin Data Analysis

second survey both because it was feasible to do so and because the rate of return in the first few weeks suggested a lower response rate to the second survey than to the first. Undoubtedly, the first wave benefitted by the crest of enthusiasm and anticipation that characterized most of the delegates in the weeks just prior to the conference. By the dark, wintry days of February, that glow was considerably dimmed. (Table 1.3 shows the timing of the research process in relation to the timing of the political process of the IWY Commission's work and the conference itself.)

Dual Roles as Researcher and IWY Commissioner

A common method in social research is that of participant observation: A researcher moves into organizations, families, neighborhoods, or political conventions for the exclusive purpose of observing at first hand the flow of events, the interactions among people, the affect behind the spoken word. It is known to all that the researcher is present as an observer. Field participation of this kind is grafted to the basic role of social researcher. In this research project on the national women's conference, the balance was reversed: The research role was grafted to the already existing role as political participant and IWY Commissioner. In short, I was an observing participant rather than a participant observer.

Either type of dual role is complicated, since special restraints are imposed on both roles when they are combined. Against my expectation, I gained no major advantage as an IWY Commissioner because I was conducting research, but suffered several clear disadvantages. On the other hand, there were both advantages and disadvantages from a research point of view in combining the two roles.

Advantages of the Dual Roles

Being a member of the IWY Commission had several advantages for the research. In addition to the franking privilege and the mailing envelopes provided by the Secretariat, I had easy access to the sample because the Secretariat provided mailing labels for all six categories in the sample design; that is, members of the Ford and Carter Commissions, the Secretariat staff, the elected delegates and alternates and, when they became available in October, at least a portion of the appointed delegates-at-large.

My status as an IWY Commissioner helped me to design the instrument: I had foreknowledge of the things planned for Houston, both for the plenary sessions and for the cultural, social, and political events supplementing those sessions, and I knew the resolutions that would comprise the core agenda or Plan of Action as it was called at the conference. It was also of considerable help to know what responsibilities would be carried by which IWY Commissioners during the conference itself and to have had the experience of serving on the delegate-at-large selection committee, where I had observed the flow of nominations that passed under committee scrutiny and decision.

Most advantageous of all, however, was my exposure to the very diverse kinds of people who served as IWY Commissioners, since this helped me to assure that the survey covered the wide array of past political activity, organizational involvement, and future political commitments that needed to be tapped in the questionnaire. It was also helpful to have observed the areas of cleavage among the IWY Commissioners, since this was undoubtedly matched by similar cleavages in the delegate body. Such cleavages became apparent at monthly meetings of the IWY Commission, as Commissioners took positions, argued points and voted on the substantive issues before us. In our midst there was diversity in race, occupation, age, religious belief, sexual preference, and style and extent of family responsibility. Differences were also apparent in their patterns of earlier political involvement on issues affecting women: Some members had long been active and nationally visible on issues affecting women's roles in politics or the economy; others had been involved exclusively with farm women, health, international affairs, or gay rights issues. The diversity, as it manifested itself in IWY Commission deliberations, contributed directly to assuring that the instrument I designed during the summer months, and again in the winter months following the conference, surmounted my own limited and special perspective on feminist activity and political commitments.

Another advantage for the research of my political involvement with the IWY Commission concerned the lower-than-hoped-for response rate. When the probable range of the final response rate became clear in March, it was possible to do something few studies are ever able to do: All elected delegates and alternates to the conference were required to send in autobiographical forms, called *bioforms,* that contained information on their organizational and political affiliations, age, race, ethnicity, religion, and income level. When the probable response rate was estimated and found to be lower than we could easily accept, we approached the Secretariat and secured permission to photocopy all the bioforms turned in by the delegates and alternates immediately after the state elections. This permitted me to compare those delegates who responded to one or both waves of the study with the delegates who refused to respond to one or both waves of the study, at least on those factors covered in the biographic form. This meant I could pinpoint the respects in which the sample differed from the total population on the variables of political orientation, age, race, ethnicity, religion, and income level. The results of this analysis of respondents versus refusals are reported in Chapter 2.

My dual roles as researcher and IWY Commissioner also stimulated an interesting correspondence with many potential and actual respondents, some of whom had crossed my path in earlier political activity but with whom I had had limited contact in the intervening years. It also helped me to identify other researchers who were considering or actually conducting research of a similar or supplementary variety at the local or state level. We enjoyed a fruitful exchange of ideas when our respective research projects became known to each other. A few IWY Commissioners also went out of their way to inform me of things that they thought would be of interest to the research. This advantage, however, was more than offset by my difficulty in relating to other IWY Commissioners, some of whom seemed to hold back from discussing their role at the conference with me. My strong impression was that it was precisely those who played the most important roles in floor management at the conference who were the least inclined to talk frankly in our contacts in Washington, D.C., and in Houston.

Disadvantages of the Dual Roles

The disadvantages of my dual roles as researcher and IWY Commissioner to the success of the research project were few in number but important. For one, the timing of the research was necessarily geared to the timing of the IWY Commission's work and of the conference. The time-consuming and anxious period when a study is in the field was the same time during which, as an IWY Commissioner, my work load was heavy and my anxiety about how things would go in Houston was at its peak. Since the research was not planned long in advance, there was no opportunity to lighten teaching and university obligations during the months when the combination of research and political responsibilities was heaviest.

A second disadvantage has already been cited; this is the confusion that undoubtedly existed among some unknown proportion of the sample as a result of my double identity and the array of symbols on the mailing they received. The study required that I maintain a field ledger with names and addresses of the sample in order to check in returns and mail reminder letters midway in the fielding phase of both surveys. That I used a panel design for the survey also meant that the ledger had to be maintained for several months. I cannot gauge to what extent this compromised the promise of confidentiality in the eyes of potential respondents, although the cover letter assured the delegate that the ledger would be destroyed in due course. A last disadvantage was the pressure I received from some IWY Commissioners who wished to learn of the survey results before they were sufficiently well analyzed to merit any serious feedback to the IWY Commission. I did present an overview profile of some results from the first wave at a January meeting of the IWY Commission, but there was no point at which it was possible to report results from the panel analysis since the second survey was still in the field when the Commission submitted its final report to the president at the end of March 1978.

The major disadvantage of the research role for the political role was the restraint the research imposed on any visible partisanship on the issues before the IWY Commission and the conference. There were many issues before the IWY Commission that I had strong views on, but as a researcher, my job was to be as objective as possible, to be able to view things from many points of view. The result was a good deal of tension between inner conviction and outward behavior. At times this meant interviewing a colleague on the IWY Commission or a delegate at the conference to understand the reasons behind their strong convictions, while not expressing my own opposed views. It meant not taking a place on the lines at the microphones when politically I wished to do so. In short, there was pressure to adhere to a low-key political style when my desire was for strong advocacy.

A second, less burdensome disadvantage, was the decision to seek out those whose views were most dissimilar from mine, to assure that the questionnaires would avoid the blinders that might otherwise affect their design. Even this disadvantage had its positive sides. There were at least a dozen women with whom I talked by telephone or corresponded who showed great patience in explaining why they were opposed to the IWY Commission and the conference resolutions. These encounters across the gulf of opposing values were not unique to me for, as seen in the chapters to follow, many delegates reported such contacts with people they disagreed with as among the high points of their experience in Houston. No doubt these contacts stood out precisely because of the human tendency to polarize our political opponents into people very different from ourselves. Such polarization was clearly apparent at the national conference: The program itself labelled the 26 resolutions to be voted upon as the Plan of Action, and Pro-Plan and Anti-Plan caucuses were quick to form. At the same time, the delegates talked together, shared meals, rode the hotel elevators, and traveled on chartered flights, with numerous opportunities for the ardent Pro-Plan and Anti-Plan delegates to moderate the images they held of each other. An example of this softening of image is the following account of a delegate's experience flying back to her home state after the conference:

> On the return charter flight, I found myself seated with two "majority" delegates and there was an uneasy silence between us at first. Then I expressed respect for the courage and conviction they showed at the conference. In a long and amiable conversation we agreed that proximity had bred tolerance and respect for opposing values, increased commitment to work actively for the views we supported, and recognition that in spite of the differences between us, there were issues on which we could and should work together.

There were several dozen similar comments in the postconference questionnaire.

I shall draw upon these comments at numerous points in the chapters to follow, but one general observation is relevant here. Over 500 respondents filled in the open-ended question on their most memorable experience in Houston, but the majority did not do so: They left the question blank. It is tempting but misleading to infer from the comments of a minority that what they report was representative of all the delegates. From the qualitative comments made by both Pro-Plan and Anti-Plan delegates, one gains the strong impression that both groups softened their image of their political opponents during the conference. In fact, many Pro-Plan delegates gave examples of conversations they had had that, they were convinced, had changed the minds and votes of Anti-Plan delegates. But statistical analysis of the impact of the conference on the Pro- and Anti-Plan delegates suggests otherwise: The Anti-Plan delegates came away with a greater consensus (less variance) in their feelings toward groups opposed to them on significant political issues, whereas the views of Pro-Plan delegates became less extreme and more varied from each other. Far from having been influenced by talks with Pro-Plan delegates, several Anti-Plan delegates carefully explained that they had examined the resolutions before they came to Houston and had decided their vote in advance. This is not to say that interpersonal influence was not at work, but only to underline that, on an aggregate basis, the net effect does not support the idea of great Pro-Plan influence over Anti-Plan delegates.

This example illustrates a major advantage of a systematic study over qualitative interviews or media reports: Since the latter are based on a limited and selective subsample of the participants in an event, the impressions one gathers may be totally misleading if they are generalized to the larger population. Statistical analysis provides less colorful prose but a closer approximation to what people think and feel than human-interest stories obtained from a small number of personal interviews.

Organization of the Book

The response rate to the preconference survey in October 1977 was 63% (1320 respondents); to the postconference survey in February 1978, 51% (1207 respondents). The major focus of the study was on the *impact* of the conference, which can only be analyzed with data provided by those who responded to *both* surveys. This represented only 42% (983 respondents) of the total number of questionnaires mailed to the sample (2087 cases). Although a sample of 983 cases is more than adequate for most statistical analyses, the low panel-response rate was a cause for concern. Hence the first analysis covered in the book is a response pattern analysis (Chapter 2). This comparison of respondents with nonrespondents was made possible by the unique possession of autobiographical data on almost every elected delegate and alternate, whether she responded to the surveys or not.

Chapter 3 introduces the respondents and the measures used in our analysis. It begins with a specification of the major substantive questions underlying the design of the study; moves on to a profile of the sample as provided by the marginal responses to key questions in both the pre- and postconference surveys; and describes the construction of the major indices used in the book.

Chapter 4 focuses on the organizational structures of the IWY Commission and the Houston conference. It explores the past political experiences, positions on feminist issues, roles in the Houston conference, and political aspirations that differentiate the five major organizational categories in the sample: Commissioners (Ford versus Carter appointees), elected delegates, elected alternates, delegates-at-large, and Secretariat staff members.

Elected delegates and alternates comprise, of course, the vast majority of the respondents (83%). Although IWY Commissioners and Secretariat staff members, by contrast, were only 5% of the sample, they were of obvious special importance as planners and managers of the conference and the final report from the IWY Commission; hence they represent important categories for comparison with the elected delegates.

Chapter 5 focuses on an organizational variable that cuts across the five major categories in the sample: the state delegation. Anyone who saw the television coverage of the Houston conference will remember how the Coliseum floor where the plenary sessions were held resembled the floor of a political party convention, with delegates seated together under their state banners. Delegates often had additional symbols (armbands, hats, flowers) of the state delegations they belonged to, symbols that maintained their state identification when they were away from the Coliseum floor or moving around on the floor. The state was a unit of organization for the conference due to the requirement of proportional representation and pragmatic concern for floor management and communication; the intent was not to provide political units with any direct meaning in terms of the formal agenda of the conference.

The state delegation was an interesting, informal social unit of great relevance to our understanding of the conference experience and of the delegates' future plans for political activity and office-seeking. Most delegations traveled together, were housed together, and held numerous meetings before, during, and after the conference. The new, personal ties they formed among themselves may have continuing salience to the formation of formal political coalitions and informal networks in their home states. Since each delegation only came into being as a formal organizational unit as a result of the state meeting elections in the summer of 1977, a panel study could reveal something of the process of group formation and of changes in individuals' identification with the state delegation over the course of time.

Chapter 6 explores the general belief and affect structures of the delegates: where they stood on specific issues and how they felt toward a variety of groups in American society (political, racial, ethnic, feminist, and antifeminist). Belief consensus is explored by comparing members of two specific organizations well represented in the sample: NOW, an explicitly feminist organization, and the League of Women Voters, a traditional women's organization officially linked to the feminist movement only in its endorsement of the ERA. A second comparison concerns the differences and similarities between respondents identifiable as Pro-Plan or Anti-Plan activists. Chapter 6 includes an analysis of the differential impact of the conference on these two political groups.

Chapter 7 presents the most complex statistical analysis in the book, in an effort to explore and to model the paths to political activity and competence. A major concern of the chapter is with the development of the political woman in American society. I explore expected and actual leadership roles in Houston; what political involvements in the past are most highly associated with high ratings on political competence; how the conference affected these subjective ratings; and the correlates of past office-holding in mainstream and feminist politics.

Chapter 8 deals with the political aspirations of the sample and the impact of the conference on those aspirations. It builds on the conceptual model outlined in Chapter 7 and attempts to determine what overall profile characterizes women with very high political aspirations for elected office. Since the level of past political experience is extraordinarily high in a sample of this kind, as compared to a general population survey, the few in the sample with very high aspirations represent a rare category indeed among American women. In light of the low proportion of women in elected office at any level of government, this analysis has special importance for current and future efforts significantly to increase the presence of women in the political process.

The final chapter, Chapter 9, summarizes the major findings of the study and discusses their implications for the role of women in American politics.

2

Whom Did We Miss?
Response Pattern Analysis

Introduction

The field phase of a research project almost always involves some anxiety. This is particularly the case for mail surveys, for there are many factors involved over which the researcher has little or no control. Are the mailing addresses correct? Will the questionnaires be forwarded if the person has moved? Will the cover letter make the survey sound interesting? Will the respondent fill out the questionnaire before it gets misplaced or forgotten? If it is filled out, will it actually reach a mailbox? At every step of the way, there is a risk to the final response rate of a study.

This chapter describes the fielding of the study and the results in terms of response rate. There was no problem of sampling in the study since the goal was to reach a known total population.[1] There were, however, problems in

[1] It is more precise to say I attempted a *census* of a total known population rather than a random sample drawn from that population. Hence in a formal statistical sense, the respondents in the data-set do not represent a *sample* of the population but a proportion of a total population census. There is no formal concept to refer to the respondents in a statistically accurate yet euphonious manner, so I will use the term *sample* despite its departure from strict definitional accuracy. Furthermore, tests of statistical inference are appropriate only to true samples from a population. While it is not clear that response errors in the data-set work in the same way that sampling errors work in true samples of a population, I shall nonetheless rely on tests of significance throughout the analysis in the book, as the best approximation to some confidence in what should be considered a firm or meaningful result.

the study involving one category, appointed delegates-at-large. There is also an interesting analysis that is seldom possible in social research: I had an alternative source of information on at least some character-istics for almost all individuals in the population, so it was possible to compare those who responded to the survey with those who did not. In most studies, the "refusals" are unknown and one must make esti-mates of the way in which their absence might bias the results, typically by comparing those who did respond against some known distribution of charac-teristics in a city or regional population (e.g., comparing sample from County X with census data on the county). By contrast, in this study I was able to compare the refusals among the elected delegates and alternates with the respondents on age, race, ethnicity, religious affiliation, income, and political orientation. Special analysis was also done on the response pattern of IWY Commissioners and Secretariat staff members.

The Population: Target and Attainment

The study design called for a survey of the total population of individuals in six categories relevant to the national conference: (a) elected delegates, (b) elected alternates, (c) appointed delegates-at-large, (d) Ford-appointed IWY Commissioners, (e) Carter-appointed IWY Commissioners, and (f) members of the Secretariat staff.

Public Law 94-167 and commission deliberations in keeping with that law established the number of elected delegates and alternates as proportional to state population but with a minimum of 12 delegates per state or territory; there would be 1442 delegates elected at state meetings. There were to be five alternates for each state or territory, for a total of 280 elected alternates. The alternates for each state were those five individuals in a ranked votes-cast list following the cut-off for the number of elected delegates allotted to a state. Since the elections took place at state meetings (the last of which occurred in late summer of 1977), the Secretariat had names and addresses for all elected delegates and most alternates by the time the study was ready to field in early October. Commissioners and Secretariat staff members were also known in advance, and hence posed no special problem in fielding.

This was not the case for appointed delegates-at-large. The law specified only that this category should exist, to be appointed by the IWY Commission, in order to rectify any underrepresentation in the elected delegate body of important categories in the adult female population. The IWY Commission set the number at 400 and decided to invite both specified individuals and or-ganizations, the latter to decide themselves who would represent them. The IWY Commission secured the cooperation of the Bureau of Labor Statistics to provide recent statistics on the female adult population 16 years of age or older (as of June 1977). Tallies on the elected delegates were late, for it required cooperation on the part of the state committees to forward the bioforms of the elected delegates and alternates to the Secretariat office in Washington, D.C. By late September, the delegate-at-large selection committee had to work with incomplete tallies if the appointed delegates were to be in place before the conference dates.

It was soon clear that the outreach efforts of the states had more than succeeded in assuring an ethnically diverse delegate body. Bureau of Labor Statistics put the proportion of non-Caucasian women in the population at 16%, whereas the proportion of such delegates from the tabulations available to us in late September stood at 36%. The committee's efforts were then concentrated on trying to increase the proportions of younger and lower-income people and to widen the range of organizational representatives.

Lists of individuals and organizations to invite became ready only in early October, at the time the first survey was mailed. It took several weeks for the organizations the IWY Commission approached to decide whether to accept the invitation and to determine who would represent them. I held off on mailing to people in this category as long as possible, but by late October there was no choice but to use the only available list of names and addresses, which was for the 280 individuals who had been invited to serve as delegates-at-large. Not all of them accepted, of course, which lowered their interest in responding to the survey. I could not include any organizational representatives in the first survey, since they only became known to me after the Houston conference. This is why the first mailing was sent to 280 individuals invited to serve as appointed delegates, whereas the second mailing went to 545 people, those on the earlier list plus the additional individuals and organizational representatives who accepted the IWY Commission's invitation. The final roster of delegates-at-large included 346 individuals and 92 organizational representatives. The major impact of this awkward timing was to lower drastically the proportion of the delegates-at-large who would appear in the panel subsample: Less than one-half the final appointed delegates even *received* both surveys.

The classification of individuals in the remaining five categories of the population involved minor problems compared to this difficulty with the delegates-at-large. The IWY Commissioners were known, of course, but nine had served on both Commissions, having been reappointed by President Carter. The final classification kept them as *current Carter Commissioners,* thus reducing the category of Ford-only Commissioners, or *ex-Commissioners* as I shall refer to them on occasion. In addition, some of the ex-Commissioners were elected as state delegates. Such cases were kept in the Commissioner category, to keep that small category as large as possible. A few cases involved members of the Secretariat staff who were elected as delegates; here, too, they were retained in the Secretariat staff category to

Table 2.1

Sample and Response Rate by Panel Wave and Sample Category

CATEGORY	October Survey			February Survey		
	Number Sent	Number Responded	Response Rate	Number Sent	Number Responded	Response Rate
Elected Delegates	1417	944	67%	1422	764	54%
Elected Alternates	269	154	57%	278	141	51%
Appointed Delegates at large	280	154	55%	545	249	46%
Carter Commissioners	46	21	46%	46	24	52%
Ford Commissioners	38	18	47%	38	11	29%
Secretariat Staff	37	23	62%	39	18	46%
TOTAL	2087	1320	63%	2368	1207	51%

Table 2.2
Panel Response Pattern by Sample Category

Category	Subtotal Number	Response Pattern							
		Both Waves		October Only		February Only		Neither Wave	
		N	%	N	%	N	%	N	%
Elected Delegates	1417	699	49	245	17	65	5	408	29
Elected Alternates	269	114	42	40	15	27	10	88	33
Appointed Delegates at Large	543	120	22	34	6	129	24	260	48
Commissioners	84	32	38	7	8	3	4	42	50
Secretariat Staff	37	18	49	5	14	–	–	14	37
Total	(2350)	983	42%	331	14	224	10	812	35

keep it as large as possible. Last, there was a delay in the mailing of names and addresses to the Commission from a few territory committees (e.g., the names of the alternates from Puerto Rico and the Trust territories were not known in time for the October mailing). As a consequence of difficulties of this sort, the sample frame for elected delegates was 1417 rather than 1442; for elected alternates, 269 rather than 280.

Table 2.1 shows these adjusted figures and the number and rates of response obtained to each of the two waves for the six categories. The overall response rate for the October survey was 63%, for the February survey, 51%. The month before the conference was undoubtedly a peak of anticipatory enthusiasm, with the research project riding the crest of this anticipation and doing fairly well in the response rate as a result, especially for a mail questionnaire with only one reminder letter. By February 1978 that psychological facilitation no longer applied and the response rate fell accordingly.

The category with the highest response rate in both waves was the elected delegates; the sharpest fall-off between waves was shown by the Ford-appointed Commissioners and members of the Secretariat staff. Although they were not officially involved in IWY Commission work immediately prior to the conference, the Ford Commissioners may have felt greater commitment at that time and hence responded quite well to the first wave of the study. That commitment may no longer have held them as respondents by the time the February survey arrived in their mail. For many members of the Secretariat staff, February 1978 was a frenzied month, rushing to complete the report, sorting through and packing IWY Commission papers for filing in the national archives, and personally searching for alternate employment once the IWY Commission's work was completed—all to be done by the end of March when the IWY Commission closed its office and funding ended. This combination of factors may have lowered the staff's response rate to the second survey.

Although response rates of 63 and 51% are respectable for a mail questionnaire (many of which never exceed 40%), a panel analysis is dependent on response not to one but to both surveys. Here there was a total of 983 cases, 42% of the population that received both questionnaires. As the details of Table 2.2 show, 331 previous respondents were lost in the second mailing and 224 new ones were gained. The final total refusal rate stood at 35%, the percentage that did not respond to either wave of the study.

Data and Coding of Bioforms

For an analysis that would rely heavily on the panel subsample, a response rate of 42% was worrisome indeed. But since the bioforms filled out by elected delegates and alternates were on file with the Secretariat in

Washington, D.C., I sought and obtained permission from the Executive Director of the Secretariat in early March 1978 to photocopy all the bioforms before they were boxed and shipped to the national archives the following month. With data from these forms, it was possible to compare the ways in which individuals who refused to respond to either survey differed from those who responded to one or both surveys.

There were several problems to using the information from the bioforms. For one, not all states used the exact form recommended by the Secretariat: Some made changes in accordance with the state coordinating committee's preferences or sense of appropriateness to their local circumstances. Most forms were filled out hastily by the nominees during the hectic first day of the state meetings. Many forms had illegible entries on them, or entries that had become illegible on the photocopies. Still other delegates left some of the questions blank, especially those dealing with age, income, and religion. But from a research perspective, they were useful in this sense: All such problems of omission, alternate forms, and near-illegible entries may be assumed to have little to do with response pattern differences. However poor the data, the same problems held for people who did not respond to either survey as for those who cooperated by responding to both.

Furthermore, the set was remarkably complete, given the circumstances under which the delegates filled out the forms and the cooperation required of the state committees to forward an intact set to the Secretariat in Washington, D.C. The total population of elected delegates and alternates comprised 1722 people. There were only 90 cases for which there was no bioform, which means forms were available for 95% of the population. The sample ledger contained 1686 names of elected delegates and alternates: There was no bioform for only 54 cases, hence a 96.8% coverage. Last, there was no relationship between missing bioforms and the response pattern to the survey: Missing forms characterized 3% of both the two-wave respondents and the two-wave refusals.

Consequently, for at least the information contained on the bioforms, the total population as represented by the bioform sample could be compared with both the refusals and the panel subsample, thus permitting an identification of the respects in which the panel subsample differed from the total population of elected delegates and alternates.

Almost all the states used the 1-page, letter-sized form prepared by the Secretariat staff. Most of the space was devoted to listing the major political and other organizations the nominees had been active in and what officerships they had held in those organizations. At the bottom of the form were simple categories to check-off age, religion, race, ethnicity, and income. The addresses on the form permitted a classification of people by state and hence by region. The most important information, however, had to do with political affiliations, because I expected much lower response rates from delegates at the two extremes of a general political continuum: Those of a more radical persuasion might have viewed the conference and the research project as part and parcel of a reformist politics they abhorred, whereas those of a very conservative political persuasion, might have been part of an organized opposition to the IWY Commission generally, and the Houston conference, in particular.

The data on the bioforms most relevant to these political considerations were the organizational listings. They were remarkably detailed, perhaps understandably so from the perspective of a candidate seeking to win an election as a delegate to Houston, for the forms were available for inspection by voters at most state meetings—in folders, tacked to bulletin boards, or otherwise displayed in public settings. A general political orientation code was constructed, based on the profile of organizations the individual belonged to. In more than one-half the cases, this was a relatively clear-cut coding decision. A nominee who indicated membership in the John Birch Society, the Eagle Forum, and a local anti-abortion coalition was readily classified as *very Conservative*. A nominee who indicated membership in a Radical Feminist Coalition and the Progressive Workers Party was similarly an easy case to code as *Radical* in general political orientation.

More difficult decisions were involved in differentiating between *Liberal* and *very Liberal*. Here various combinations of organizational memberships were inspected: A profile of Democratic Party, Women's Democratic Forum, and League of Women Voters was classified as *Liberal*, whereas a profile of Democratic Party, Black Women Organized for Action, and the Coalition of Labor Union Women was classified as *very Liberal*. A major rule in coding decisions was that membership in a women's rights organization merited coding at least as far left as *Liberal*, with the remaining organizations an individual belonged to determining whether to code as *Liberal*, *very Liberal* or *Radical*. The *Mixed or Nonpolitical* category was reserved for cases mentioning only professional or social organizations, or groups working on such issues as aging, health, alcohol abuse in which there was no additional clue to political views. Republican Party members were coded as *Conservative* unless an additional organization was cited that merited a different decision. Thus, for example, Republican Party and NOW membership was coded as *mixed* rather than *Conservative*.

The final political orientation code and examples of the kinds of organizations or combinations of organizations that were used in the coding process follow:

Radical   Any membership in radical feminist groups, Progressive Workers Party or organization, Democratic Socialist Organizing Committee or other Socialist organizations, or in a gay rights organization.

Very Liberal	NOW, WEAL, CLUW or other union affiliation; American Civil Liberties Union; NAACP; Black Women's Political Caucus; National Women's Political Caucus; ERAmerica; pro-choice abortion groups (e.g., NARAL); Democratic Party if linked to any of above.
Liberal	Democratic Party with or without such organizations as League of Women Voters, Women's Democratic Forum, Democratic Club, but no civil rights or welfare organizations.
Mixed/Nonpolitical	No mention of organizations illustrated in other codes, but mention of organizations like BPW, AAUW, IWY state committee, health issue groups on such issues as alcohol abuse, rape, drugs, aging, health planning, youth or school groups. Or combinations of both conservative and liberal organizations (e.g., Republican Party and NOW).
Conservative	No women's rights group; women's service organizations and Republican Party; church or sorority groups in combination with mildly conservative political groups.
Very Conservative	Any mention of organizations like IWY Citizens Review Committee, Eagle Forum, Relief Society, John Birch Society, Pro-Life, Right to Life, Mormons, Heritage Foundation, STOP ERA.

A second qualitative code was developed using the information on the highest organizational officership held. If organizations were listed but no mention was made of any officership, it was assumed the person was simply a member. All mentions of officerships were coded in terms of the top or highest level of such posts, taking into account the office itself (president versus secretary) and the level of the organization (local versus national). More specifically, the code was as follows:

Local Only	Highest office held was any officership in a local organization or local chapter of regional or national organization (president/board member/convener/chair).
State–Low	Any office except top officer in a statewide organization or state chapter of a national organization (vice-president/vice-chair/co-chair/board member).
State–High	Top office in a statewide organization or state chapter of a national organization (president/chair/convener/regional executive).
National	Any office in a national organization (president/vice-president/secretary/treasurer/board member).

Response Analysis: Elected Delegates and Alternates

Table 2.3 gives a detailed summary of the distribution of six coded variables for the bioform sample, the two-wave panel of elected delegates and alternates for whom there were bioform data, and the two-wave refusals, that is, those delegates and alternates who did not respond to either survey. The last column of Table 2.3 shows the refusal rate for each of the categories on the six variables shown. Table 2.4 permits an easy overview of the results by ranking the specific categories from very high to very low refusal rates.

On political orientation, a key variable concerning which I had serious questions of sample bias, the highest refusal rate of all was from women with *very Conservative* political affiliations (67%), whereas the lowest refusal rate was among those with *very Liberal* political affiliations (15%). On religious affiliation, Catholic women had high refusal rates (35%), whereas Jewish and agnostic women had very low refusal rates (11% and 20%, respectively). Typical of most mail surveys, those with low income were more apt to refuse (38% here) and those with high income and presumably higher educational attainment were least apt to refuse to participate in the survey (13%). Note, however, from the base Ns, that the income item was most apt of all variables to be left blank on the bioforms.

Clearly, there is a strong demographic patterning to the profile of refusals as there is on political affiliation. On the other hand, most of the subgroups with very high refusal rates are relatively small as a proportion of the total population, as indexed by the bioform sample. Thus, although women under 25 show a high refusal rate (38%), relatively few delegates and alternates in the population are in this age group (6%). Similarly, the delegates coded as *very Conservative* have a high refusal rate (67%) to be sure, but they represent only 7% of the population. As a consequence, when the distribution of the panel subsample is compared to the distribution of the total bioform sample on any of the coded variables, there are only slight differences between the two. If a criterion is set at a 5% or more difference, then the panel sample compared to the total population tends to show the following slight tip toward over- or underrepresentation: *The sample slightly underrepresented Catholics, blacks, and conservative women and overrepresented white, very liberal women who had held positions as top officers of state or national organizations.*

There is some evidence that the decision to respond or not to respond was not purely an individual decision for many potential respondents. During the weeks before the national conference when the study was in the field, there were legal cases on file in the courts attempting to ban the holding of the national conference altogether or charging the IWY Commission with lobbying efforts specifically prohibited by Public Law 94-167.

Rumors were widespread, and there was evidence in my contact with potential respondents that some conservative organizations were applying pressure on those of their members who had been elected as delegates to Houston not to cooperate with the study. Several phone calls from such women gave evidence of this pressure. For example, a woman from Indiana phoned to ask pointed questions about the survey, why I, as an IWY Commissioner was doing the research; what I expected to "get out of it," and whether the results would be fed back into IWY Commission reports. When my answers seemed to calm her concerns, she sighed and said she wished she "could" answer the questionnaire, but "I've been told not to." Pressure of this sort from the conservative right relaxed after the November conference, with the result that, in February, there was an increase in the response rate of conservative women who had refused to respond to the October survey. Two women attached notes to their February questionnaires indicating they were glad to be able to fill it out, now that "we have not been told not to this time."

Indirect evidence on an aggregate level of political factors affecting the response rate was also apparent. On a regional level, the refusal rate was highest among delegates from the Midwest (40%) and Southwest (39%), lowest among those from New England (17%) and the Border states (19%). But the greatest variation in refusal rate was not by region but by states within a region. In the Mid-Atlantic region, the range was not very great—only 16%—from Pennsylvania (11%) to New York (27%). In the Midwest, the range was 50%, from a low 6% refusal rate in South Dakota to a high 69% in Indiana. In the Mountain region, state variation ranged from a low of 5% in Idaho to a high of 61% in Utah. Table 2.5 shows response pattern by state and by region.

From the reports submitted by IWY Commissioners who served as federal officers at the state meetings and from the state committee chairpersons, it became clear by September that 11 states had elected delegations that were predominantly opposed to the IWY Commission and its recommendations: Alabama, Hawaii, Indiana, Kansas, Mississippi, Missouri, Montana, Nebraska, Ohio, Oklahoma, and Utah. Of these, only Alabama showed a refusal rate of less than 50%.

Even stronger evidence of the impact of political climate at the state level is found in Table 2.6. Here the states are classified according to whether they have ratified the ERA or not; within each category, the distribution of the states is shown on their refusal rate. Slightly more than one-half the 15 nonratified states had refusal rates over 35%, as compared to only 17% of the states that had ratified the ERA. An inspection of bordering states dramatically underlines this point: The refusal rate in nonratified Mississippi was 71%, but its neighbors, ratified Tennessee, had a low 13% refusal rate and ratified Arkansas only 9%. In the Southwest, nonratified Utah had a refusal rate of

Table 2.3

Comparison of Panel Analysis Sample, Refusals and Total Population on Selected Characteristics of Elected Delegates and Alternates (Source: Bioforms filled out at state meetings by nominees.)

Characteristic	Bioform Sample	Panel Analysis Sample	Two-Wave Refusals	Refusal Rate	
AGE					
25 or less	6.2	4.9	7.8	38%	(91)
26 – 55	79.3	79.1	78.2	29%	(1167)
56 or older	14.5	15.9	14.0	28%	(214)
100% =	(1472)[a]	(709)	(444)		
RELIGION					
Protestant	41.7	41.2	41.9	29%	(559)
Catholic	25.8	21.1	32.1	35%	(345)
Jewish	8.2	11.9	3.2	11%	(110)
Other	13.9	11.8	15.8	34%	(186)
None	10.3	14.0	7.0	20%	(138)
100% =	(1339)	(645)	(396)		
RACE/ETHNICITY					
Caucasian	62.0	71.5	57.4	27%	(881)
Black	17.0	11.2	19.1	34%	(241)
Latina	7.7	6.2	9.8	35%	(110)
Asian	2.0	1.8	1.6	24%	(29)
Indian	1.1	.9	1.2	33%	(15)
Other	10.2	8.5	10.6	28%	(145)
100% =	(1421)	(680)	(425)		

Low	18.4	14.1	21.0	38%	(168)
Medium	73.9	74.5	74.9	32%	(675)
High	7.8	11.3	4.1	13%	(71)
100% =	(914)	(432)	(295)		
POLITICAL ORIENTATION					
Radical	2.5	2.3	2.8	32%	(41)
Very Liberal	32.3	43.8	16.5	15%	(524)
Liberal	14.1	17.3	10.0	20%	(229)
Mixed/nonpolitical	29.7	25.3	32.1	31%	(482)
Conservative	7.8	4.2	12.2	45%	(127)
Very Conservative	7.1	2.6	16.5	67%	(115)
No Information	6.5	4.6	10.0		
100% =	(1624)	(784)	(479)		
HIGHEST ORGANIZATIONAL POSITION HELD					
No Officership	25.6	23.1	29.1	33%	(416)
Local Only	31.8	29.1	33.9	32%	(517)
State – low	10.8	11.7	8.4	22%	(176)
State – high	17.0	21.2	12.6	22%	(276)
National	8.1	10.1	6.0	22%	(132)
No Information	6.6	4.8	10.0		
100% =	(1625)	(784)	(480)		

[a]N's vary greatly by variable since not all forms included certain categories, and nominees frequently did not fill out all categories.

Table 2.4
Ranking of Demographic Categories by Refusal Rate[a]

Refusal Rate	Demographic Categories
67%	Very Conservative political orientation
45%	Conservative political orientation
38%	25 years old or younger
38%	Low income
35%	Latina-American
35%	Catholic
34%	'Other' religion
34%	Black-American
33%	Indian-American
33%	No officership held in organizations belonged to
32%	Medium Income; Radical political orientation
32%	Highest organizational officership at local level
31%	Mixed on non-political orientation
29%	26-55 years old
29%	Protestant
28%	56 years or older
28%	'Other' ethnicity
27%	Caucasian
24%	Asian-American
22%	Highest organizational officership at state/national level
20%	Liberal political orientation
20%	No religious affiliation
15%	Very liberal political orientation
13%	High income
11%	Jewish

[a]Variables included on bioforms: age, race/ethnicity, income, religion, political orientation, organizational membership and officership.

61%, whereas its ratified neighbors showed a low of 5% in Idaho, 6% in Wyoming, 16% in Colorado.

Although the state variation in response pattern is thus seen to be very great, this is of relatively little concern in the analysis reported in this book. At most, it is region of the country that is utilized as a variable in the analysis, rather than state. From the point of view of regional distribution of the panel sample and refusals, compared to the bioform sample or the full population distribution, there are only minor differences. Table 2.7 indicates not more than 4% difference between the panel subsample and the total population of all delegates and alternates from any particular region. Thus, 20.3% of the panel respondents are from the Midwest, whereas 24.5% of the total population of delegates reside in the Midwest. The reverse pattern, again slight, holds for New England, where 11% of the panel reside, although that region represents 8.1% of the total population.

Although it was disappointing to obtain a much lower response rate than one had optimistically expected, it was encouraging to find from the analysis of the bioforms that the sample of elected delegates and alternates showed only minor departures from the total population. There were even enough cases of delegates who worked against the Plan of Action to compare with Pro-Plan delegates.[2]

Purely on the basis of category size, there were sufficient cases of elected delegates and alternates in every category of age, race, and politics for the kind of analysis I envisaged. In the case of Commissioners and Secretariat staff members, however, the prospect was less rosy. Since there were only a few dozen people involved in either category, special effort was expended to determine whether there were any detectable biases among those who responded to the survey. First, let us examine the IWY Commissioners.

Response Analysis: Ford and Carter Commissioners

Since both the Ford- and Carter-appointed Commissioners were nationally known individuals, their response pattern analysis involved a quite different task from that of the elected delegates. Table 2.1 shows that just under one-half of the IWY Commissioners responded to the first survey; however, whereas the Carter Commissioners showed a slight improvement in response rate to the February survey (52% response versus 46% in October), the Ford Commissioners showed a decline in response rate to the second survey (29% versus 47% in October). Excluded from the total Commissioner category in

[2]This optimism must be qualified, of course, by the realization that I cannot tell how great the departure of the sample from the population of elected delegates and alternates might be on variables *not* measured by data from the bioforms.

Table 2.5

Response Pattern by State and Region (elected delegates and alternates only)

STATE AND REGION	Population N	Bioform Sample N	Survey Response Pattern		
			Both Waves	One Wave	Neither Wave
NEW ENGLAND					
Maine	27	27	78.9	21.1	--
Vermont	17	14	57.1	42.9	--
New Hampshire	19	19	94.7	--	5.3
Connecticut	27	27	63.0	22.2	14.8
Rhode Island	19	18	55.5	16.7	27.8
Massachusetts	39	39	48.8	17.9	33.3
Regional Total	140	136	64.0	19.1	16.9
MID-ATLANTIC					
Pennsylvania	65	64	56.3	32.8	10.9
Delaware	17	9	44.4	44.4	11.2
New Jersey	45	45	55.6	24.4	20.0
New York	93	88	45.5	27.3	27.3
Regional Total	220	206	51.0	29.1	19.9
MIDWEST					
South Dakota	19	18	88.8	5.6	5.6
North Dakota	17	17	70.6	17.6	11.8
Wisconsin	33	29	62.1	24.1	13.8
Iowa	27	27	59.3	25.9	14.8
Minnesota	31	28	71.4	10.7	17.9
Michigan	53	48	58.3	14.6	27.1
Illinois	63	60	31.7	25.0	43.3
Kansas	25	23	21.7	30.4	47.8
Missouri	35	35	20.0	22.9	57.1
Nebraska	21	21	4.8	33.3	61.9
Ohio	61	54	24.0	13.0	63.0
Indiana	37	35	14.3	17.1	68.6
Regional Total	422	395	40.5	19.7	39.7
SOUTH					
Arkansas	23	23	78.3	13.0	8.7
North Carolina	37	33	60.6	21.2	18.2
South Carolina	27	27	64.2	15.9	19.8
Virginia	35	35	57.1	22.9	20.0
Georgia	35	32	50.0	28.1	21.9
Louisiana	31	31	51.6	16.1	32.3
Florida	45	45	46.6	15.6	37.8
Alabama	29	29	24.1	31.0	44.8
Mississippi	25	24	16.7	12.5	70.8
Regional Total	287	279	49.8	19.7	30.1

(continued)

Table **2.5** (*continued*)

STATE AND REGION	Population N	Bioform Sample N	Survey Response Pattern		
			Both Waves	One Wave	Neither Wave
BORDER					
Tennessee	31	31	48.4	38.7	12.9
Kentucky	29	29	69.0	17.2	13.8
Maryland	31	29	72.4	6.9	20.7
District of Columbia	17	17	41.2	35.3	23.5
West Virginia	23	23	47.8	21.7	30.4
Regional Total	131	129	57.4	23.3	19.4
SOUTHWEST					
New Mexico	19	18	50.0	27.8	22.2
Texas	63	60	45.0	25.0	30.0
Arizona	23	11	36.3	27.3	36.3
Oklahoma	27	24	16.7	8.3	75.0
Regional Total	132	113	38.9	22.1	38.9
MOUNTAIN					
Idaho	19	19	89.5	5.3	5.3
Wyoming	17	16	87.5	6.3	6.3
Colorado	25	25	68.0	16.0	16.0
Nevada	17	16	56.3	18.8	25.0
Montana	19	18	22.2	27.8	50.0
Utah	19	18	16.7	22.2	61.1
Regional Total	116	112	55.8	23.3	20.9
PACIFIC					
Oregon	23	23	60.9	34.8	4.3
Alaska	17	15	60.0	20.0	20.0
California	101	96	55.2	22.9	21.9
Washington	29	28	50.0	17.9	32.1
Regional Total	170	162	55.8	23.3	20.9
EXTERNAL					
Guam	17	16	43.8	43.8	12.5
Puerto Rico	17	17	23.5	41.2	35.3
Virgin Islands	17	17	23.5	29.4	47.1
Samoa	17	17	17.6	29.4	52.9
Hawaii	19	20	30.0	15.0	55.0
Trust Territories	17	13	--	38.5	61.5
Regional Total	104	100	24.0	32.0	44.0
TOTAL N	1722	1632			

Table 2.6
State Ratification of ERA and Survey Refusal Rate (in percent)

State Refusal Rate	Ratified	Not-Ratified
35% or more	17	54
20% - 34%	34	33
Less than 20%	49	13
100% =	(35)	(15)

Table 2.7
Regional Distribution of Elected Delegates and Alternates for Total Population, Bioform Sample, and Survey Response Pattern Types

REGION	Total Population	Bioform Sample	Survey Response Pattern		
			Both Waves	One Wave	Neither Wave
New England	8.1	8.2	11.0	7.1	4.8
Mid Atlantic	12.8	12.6	13.3	16.6	8.5
Midwest	24.5	24.2	20.3	21.5	32.6
South	16.7	17.1	17.6	15.2	17.4
Border	7.6	7.9	9.4	8.3	5.2
Southwest	7.7	6.9	5.6	6.9	9.1
Mountain	6.7	6.9	8.1	4.9	6.2
Pacific	9.9	10.0	11.5	10.5	7.1
External	6.0	6.1	3.0	8.8	9.1
100% =	(1722)	(1632)	(788)	(362)	(482)

the analysis to follow are the members of Congress appointed to the IWY Commissions, all of whom were sent questionnaires, but all of whose offices returned them with cover letters indicating a general policy opposed to responding to surveys. In addition, those IWY Commissioners who served on both the Ford- and Carter-appointed Commissions are counted in both commissions, since the object here is to compare respondents and refusals with the two, full IWY Commissions (minus members of Congress). Hence the base number varies in Tables 2.8, 2.9 and 2.10 from those reported in Tables 2.1 and 2.2.

The major focus of this response pattern analysis was to determine if the profile of respondent commissioners differed in any major respect from the total commissions on the characteristics most likely to have determined their initial appointment by the two presidents. The data used were the brief biographies of the Commissioners written by the Secretariat staff for publicity purposes. Each biographic sketch was examined and coded on the dominant overall reputation of each individual in terms of the groups or interests she represented and for which reason she was highly likely to have been invited to serve on the IWY Commission.[3] Three major categories were used in this code, tapping *political, occupational,* and *organizational* representation.

Each of these three categories was made more specific by adding three or four subcategories to provide the most efficient classification of the cases. Thus, for example, the *political* category was divided into *wives of politicians* (e.g., the honorary appointments of Rosalyn Carter and Betty Blanton); women holding *elective or appointive office* (e.g., a judge or lieutenant governor); and those prominent at the *national level of their political party* (e.g., member of the national committee of the Republican Party).

The *occupational* category does not follow any particular logic of job classification, but is simply the distribution of occupations represented among the IWY Commissioners who seem to have come into national visibility through their job prominence rather than their political or organizational affiliations: They include presidents of business enterprises, publishers or editors, actresses, union officials.

The *organizational* category covers affiliations of three types: *traditional women's organizations* like the Y.W.C.A., the League of Women Voters, and the American Association of University Women; *feminist organizations* like NOW or the Women's Action Alliance; and organizations primarily focused on *ethnic, racial, or religious* membership, like the National Council of Catholic Women or the National Urban League.

[3] I shall refer to the respondents as *women* or *delegates* throughout the book, since only eight respondents were male and 95% of the respondents were delegates rather than IWY Commissioners or Secretariat staff members. In fact, three of the Carter-appointed and seven of the Ford-appointed Commissioners were male.

Table 2.8 shows the distribution of IWY Commissioners on the two Commissions using the total and the detailed representation code. As seen from the three-category code, the Ford Commission showed greater occupational and political representation, whereas the Carter Commission showed more representation of an organizational variety. Contrasts between the two Commissions in subcategories are particularly striking in the following respects: There was greater representation on the Ford Commission of people holding office, running a business, and holding a professional job; and on the Carter Commission, there was greater representation of ethnic, religious, and traditional women's organizations.

Table 2.8
Type of Representation for Total Ford and Carter Commission (in percent)

Major Category	Subcategory	Total Commission	
		Ford-appointed	Carter-appointed
POLITICAL		37	26
	Wives of politicians	–	7
	Elective/appointive office . .	26	12
	National political party . . .	11	7
OCCUPATIONAL		48	30
	Business executive	13	2
	Arts/media	17	19
	Academic/professional	13	2
	Union/farm	5	7
ORGANIZATIONAL		15	44
	Ethnic/racial/religious	5	25
	Traditional women's	5	12
	Feminist	5	7
	N	(38)[a]	(43)[a]

[a] Those Commissioners who served on both the Ford and Carter Commissions are counted in both columns.

More important to our present purposes is the fact that the profiles of respondents show largely the same pattern as the total Commissions: that is, greater occupational and political representation among Ford Commission respondents, greater organizational representation among Carter respondents (see Table 2.9). For both Commissions, the refusal rate was highest from those with political affiliations and lowest from those with organizational affiliations. Both the total and the respondent group reflect the tendency for a Republican administration to favor political and business affiliations in appointment to commissions and for a Democratic administration to give stronger representation to the media and to ethnic, racial, and religious organizations.

One further step was taken in the response pattern analysis, but it was limited to the Carter-appointed Commission, since it drew on my own observations as a member of that Commission. A code was developed that classified all the members of the Carter Commission on their role in the decision making that took place on the IWY Commission. By further dividing each category in this code into IWY Commissioners who responded to at least one survey or refused both, I can make at least a small effort to determine whether the sample of IWY Commissioners was biased toward or away from the core decision makers on the IWY Commission.

To protect the confidentiality of survey responses from the IWY Commissioners, only general characteristics are given in the descriptions of each of the four categories in the code on decision-making roles:

1. *Core leaders* are IWY Commissioners whose views were critical in discussions of major issues during monthly IWY Commission meetings; who played prominent roles on committees and in the actual management of the national conference through close coordination of their efforts on the floor, in caucuses, and in IWY Commission deliberations in Houston.

2. *Adjutants* to Core Leaders are IWY Commissioners who regularly attended IWY Commission meetings, played important roles on committees, and had close work and political ties to the core leaders.

3. *Representatives* are IWY Commissioners who regularly attended IWY Commission meetings, who typically spoke from an organizational perspective, but who had less influence on decision making and fewer ongoing political ties to the core leaders than did adjutants.

4. *Symbols* are IWY Commissioners who rarely (or never) attended IWY Commission meetings, seldom participated except to make a report on an individual assignment, or did not attend in person but sent a representative as an observer to IWY Commission meetings.

Table 2.9
Response Pattern by Type of Representation for Ford and Carter Commissioners (in percent)

Administration	Response Pattern	Type of Representation			
		Political	Occupational	Organizational	100%=
FORD	Total Commission	37	48	15	(38)
	Respondents	30	45	25	(20)
	Refusals	45	49	6	(18)
CARTER	Total Commission	26	30	44	(43)
	Respondents	15	31	53	(32)
	Refusals	54	30	18	(11)

Table 2.10

Response Pattern of Carter Commissioners by Decision-Making Role on the Commission[a]

Decision-Making Role [b]	Case Distribution			
	Total Commission	Respondents	Refusals	Percent Refusal
CORE LEADERS	10	7	3	30%
ADJUTANTS	9	8	1	11%
REPRESENTATIVES	14	14	0	0%
SYMBOLS	10	3	7	70%
N =	(43)	(32)	(11)	

[a] Subjective Rating of Commissioners on decision making role on commission.

[b] Cf. text for description of code.

Table 2.10 shows the distribution of respondents and refusals into these four types of commissioners. The majority of refusals were among those least involved in the work of the IWY Commission, the *symbols,* who had a 70% refusal rate. Like their lack of attendance, their refusal seems to reflect low interest in the work of the IWY Commission. The more "solid citizen" members of the IWY Commission, the *adjutants* and *representatives,* who were always present and frequently carried out the decisions made at the meetings, were well represented in the respondent sample as well: Only 1 of the 23 IWY Commissioners in the combined *adjutant* plus *representative* categories refused to respond to both surveys.

Core leaders showed a 30% refusal rate. Whereas this was not as high as for those who graced the IWY Commission by name only, from the point of view of critical decision making, the three individuals represented by this refusal rate of 30% were, in my view, among the five core leaders whose judgments counted the most in the decisions made by the IWY Commission and thus were carried into the national conference itself.

Response Analysis: Secretariat Staff

A quite special approach had to be taken to explore the response pattern of those who served on the Secretariat staff. It must also be reported that it was not until I attempted this analysis of response pattern that I learned the original list of staff members had been short by some 10 individuals. It is a difficult category compared to any other in the study since staffs tend to change with normal bureaucratic turnover and with the waxing and waning of the volume of work handled by the Secretariat office. The sample was based on a mailing list provided by the administrative head of the staff in early October 1977, in response to my request for a full listing of all members of the administrative, professional, support, and secretarial staff. Since some staff turnover occurred before the national conference, additional questionnaires were sent to staff replacements as they were hired. After the conference, the staff also went into a period of contraction, which lowered the response rate of the Secretariat category to the February survey. A few members of the professional staff resigned before the conference and were appointed as delegates-at-large.

To investigate what differentiated staff respondents from staff refusals, I enlisted the aid of a former staff member, herself a professionally trained social scientist, with a request that she code each of the staff members on a list of those who had been sent the two surveys, without knowing who had been a respondent or a refusal. After some discussion, we settled on a list of 35 men and women for this check. The codes consisted of four variables as follows:

1. Level of position on staff: top administrator, professional, support staff
2. Political party affiliation
3. Whether the person joined the staff under the Ford or Carter administration
4. Feminist orientation (strongly feminist, moderately feminist, slightly feminist, or nonfeminist)

For each of the four codes, a *don't know* or *not sure* category was provided as well. Since the feminist-orientation variable was a very subjective rating (as opposed to the sheer factual nature of the other three codes), I rated those staff members with whom I had had contact during the year, as a reliability check on the former staff member's ratings. In only 3 of the 22 cases did my rating differ at all from hers, and since she had better knowledge of her colleagues from daily contact than I could have from monthly IWY Commission meetings, her ratings were used in Table 2.11.

Not shown in Table 2.11 is the political party affiliation of the staff members that I had requested of my associate. She commented that she was surprised to realize she could rate only 4 of the 35 staff members on this variable: She simply did not know with any assurance what the political party affiliations were of most of her daily associates, an interesting indicator of both the work overload of the staff and the independence of feminist goals from party politics in this work group, despite their presence in offices of the Department

Table 2.11

Response Pattern by Selected Characteristics of Secretariat Staff (in percent)

Characteristic	Total Staff	Respondents[a]	Refusals	Refusal Rate	
POINT OF HIRING					
Ford Administration	68.6	63.6	76.9	42%	(24)
Carter Administration	31.4	36.4	23.1	27%	(11)
	(35)	(22)	(13)		
STAFF LEVEL					
Top Administrative	11.4	13.6	7.6	25%	(4)
Professional	60.0	68.2	46.2	29%	(21)
Support/Secretarial	28.6	18.2	46.2	60%	(10)
	(35)	(22)	(13)		
FEMINIST ORIENTATION					
Strongly Feminist	40.0	59.1	7.7	7%	(14)
Moderately Feminist	5.7	4.5	7.7	50%	(2)
Slight/Non-Feminist	42.9	31.8	61.5	53%	(15)
Don't Know/Not Sure	11.4	4.5	23.1	75%	(4)
	(35)	(22)	(13)		
STAFF LEVEL AND FEMINISM					
Top Admin./Professional					
Strongly Feminist	52.0	66.7	16.7	7%	(13)
All Others	48.0	33.3	83.3	50%	(12)
	(25)	(18)	(7)		
Support/Secretarial					
Strongly Feminist	10.0	25.0	0.0	0%	(1)
All Others	90.0	75.0	100.0	67%	(9)
	(10)	(4)	(6)		

[a] Responded to one or both surveys.

of State in the highly politicized atmosphere of Washington, D.C., during the years that involved a national election and change of the political party in power!

As seen in the last column in Table 2.11, the refusal rate was much higher among the support staff than among the administrative and professional staff; it was lower among those who joined the staff under the Carter administration than among those who joined under the Ford administration; and it was decidedly lower among those with a strong feminist orientation than among those with a minimal or unknown position on feminism. When feminist orientation and staff level were examined simultaneously, the highest refusal rate was found among nonfeminist support staff (67%), the lowest rate among strongly feminist professional and administrative staff (7%). (There was only one strongly feminist support staff person; she responded to both surveys.) Thus, the modal profile of the Secretariat staff refusals was a woman hired to a support or secretarial position during the Ford administration for whom the position was merely a job rather than an opportunity to combine a feminist political persuasion with paid employment.

Of more direct relevance is how the Secretariat respondents as a group compare to the total Secretariat staff (the first two columns in Table 2.11). The contrasts are less extreme here, reflecting the fact that 63% of the staff responded to at least one survey. Respondents were not significantly different from the total staff regarding when they were hired, but are somewhat more likely to be feminist and professional rather than support staff. It is of interest to note the distribution of feminist orientation by staff level, for it projects a Secretariat headed by strongly committed administrators, backed up by a polarized professional staff, and supported by a largely neutral, if not antifeminist, support staff. All 4 top administrators were strongly feminist; the professional staff was divided into 9 strongly feminist and 12 with minimal or unknown views; the support staff consisted of 1 strong feminist, 2 of moderate persuasions, and 7 with minimal or unknown positions on feminism.

Summary

Standing back from the specialized methods used to analyze the response pattern of elected delegates, alternates, IWY Commissioners, and Secretariat staff members, one notes some commonality in the profile of refusals. We tended to "miss" more of those with conservative or radical political affiliations; very young, low-income, or minority group members; and those with lukewarm or antagonistic views toward the IWY Commission. The panel sample is therefore somewhat biased toward those with supportive views toward the IWY Commission, feminism generally, and with a profile tipped to very liberal politics and a high level of experience in organizations and organizational leadership at the state and national levels.

3

Design and Measurement

Introduction

Most members of the United States Congress have probably served as delegates to national political party conventions sometime in their political careers. Analogous to this is the probability that any woman with feminist beliefs who holds office at the national level in the years ahead will have been in Houston in 1977 serving in some capacity with the national conference. The delegates to Houston had to be nominated and elected in their states or to have been sufficiently visible on women's issues to have been invited to serve as an appointed delegate-at-large or a member of the IWY Commission itself. It follows that if ever there was a pool of likely future women candidates for high state and national office who are dedicated to women's rights, it is the sample of Houston participants. Consequently, the primary focus in the design of the study was past political experience and personal aspirations for political action and elective office-holding.

In this chapter, I describe the major clusters of variables that were central to the study design, in particular the panel items that appeared in both surveys. Chief among such panel items are measures of political action and aspirations. It is change on these panel items between the first and second surveys as a function of participation in Houston that represents the key analysis problem in the study. Hence the second major category of variable to be described is the Houston *exposure variables,* measures designed to tap what it was that the delegates actually did in the political process that took place at the Houston conference. Following the description of these key variables, I will introduce the sample itself, showing the marginal distribution of responses to the major questions in the surveys and describing the indices constructed to facilitate their analysis. A chronology guides the presentation from background characteristics and past political experience through the Houston conference and on to the delegates' plans and aspirations for political activity.

Major Components of the Research Design

Mainstream and Movement Aspirations

Political aspirations linked to feminist commitments need not translate into careers in elective public office. Alternate routes exist in either appointed public office or in the voluntary organizations specifically dedicated to a feminist agenda. I therefore distinguish between *mainstream* (i.e., elected public office) and *movement* (i.e., elected office in a women's rights organization) political aspirations. Much of the political energy of feminists in the 1970s was channeled into activist organizations, and the question arises whether this is a route to prominence in mainstream politics or not. One approach to answering this question is an analysis of the characteristics that predict movement leadership aspirations as opposed to mainstream political leadership. To the extent that the two political paths draw upon similar characteristics, there is at least a potential for crossover from movement to mainstream politics.[1] To the extent that these characteristics differ, movement politics may not put women politicians into the Congress or the Cabinet. Hence political aspirations of these two major types were a central focus of the study. Within each type, I distinguish the *level* of aspirations (i.e., local, state or national).

Action on the Issues: Past versus Future

A second substantive focus of the study was the issues on which women have been politically active over the 1970s and how they relate to commitments to political action in the future. We know little about what attracts one group of women to work on job discrimination, another on health issues, and

[1]It should be noted, of course, that shifts from movement to mainstream politics or vice-versa flow not just from personal characteristics, but are affected by the political climate that characterizes a particular period in history. In a conservative era, women with a radical orientation may restrict activity to movement politics, while in a very liberal era, the same women might shift to activity in mainstream politics. Hence, radical orientation might be a negative predictor of mainstream activity in one era but a positive predictor in another era.

yet a third on child abuse; nor do we know how such commitments relate to the kinds of issues people expect to be involved in as they look to the future. It may be that older women have concentrated their political efforts on issues affecting women at work and in politics, whereas younger women have been more attracted to issues dealing with marriage, child care, sex preference, health care, etc. One general expectation built into the design of the surveys was a distinction between issues that are *sex-linked* (issues dealing with the unique physiological aspects of being female, such as abortion, contraception, sexual preference) and issues that are *gender-linked* (issues dealing with the social, economic, or political aspects of gender identity, such as educational and economic opportunities, access to politics, child care to assist the working woman, etc.). I predicted that these two clusters would differentiate along age and political lines among the women in the sample. Past and future political action on a detailed range of substantive issues therefore represents the second major cluster of variables in the study design.

Political Activity in Houston

A third focus in the research design concerns the political process that took place in Houston itself: Who did what, when, and with whom. This interest serves two purposes: One is simply a description of what took place in Houston. Second, and more important, I needed information on what people did in Houston to serve as *exposure variables* to explain change in or stability of issue commitment and political aspirations between October and February.

At the heart of the research design, then, are two kinds of variables: panel questions asked both in October 1977 and in February 1978, and intervening exposure variables asked in February about the role played by the women at the November conference. Several additional panel variables will be important in the analysis. One is a measure of *political competence*, based on six questions (to be described later) that were asked on both surveys. The idea here was that the delegation and conference experience provided an unprecedented and intense opportunity to learn or to hone political skills, and hence we may be able to tap the extent to which it is an increase in the subjective sense of political competence that explains whether political aspirations increased between the October and February surveys. I have in mind, for example, a woman from a small midwestern town who has served on a local school board, done well at it, and thought of herself as a potential nominee for city council, whose experience in Houston encouraged her to raise her aspiration from a city council member to a state senator. On the other hand, a pressure-cooker experience like the Houston conference may deflate aspirations as readily as it may raise them. In any event, political competence may serve as a necessary subjective precondition to high political aspirations.

Affect Scales

Another focus of the study concerns the diverse groups that were involved in the conference. The United States is a polyglot society in terms of race and ethnicity, but this diversity is not evenly distributed throughout the population. In some areas of the country, one seldom encounters a Black, or Latina, or American-Indian face. Opportunity, age, and politics are implicated in the complex of subjective feelings that people have toward groups they do not belong to themselves. In the surveys, I devised a set of *feeling scales,* or barometers, as a panel variable, to explore both the determinants of affect toward a variety of groups and the impact of the Houston experience on these subjective feelings of distance or affinity.

The groups ran the gamut from political groups (liberal, radical, conservative) to racial and ethnic ones (Black, Latina);[2] from issue-oriented groups (pro- or anti-ERA, pro- or anti-abortion, lesbian groups) to specific organizations (NOW, the National Women's Political Caucus, the IWY Commissioners) and to occupation-related groups (labor unions, business and professional groups, farm and rural groups).

Expected versus Actual Leadership Role in Houston

The surveys also included a quasi-panel question that asked about the leadership role the women expected to play or did play in Houston. This direct self-assessment question asked, "Which of the following best describes your probable role?" (or, in February, "your actual role"), with five response categories ranging from a "key person, someone whose views will be sought out and taken into account" to "not much of a participant." That some of the women experienced a deflation of their leadership expectations is suggested by the finding that 43% expected to be either "key" or "important" people in Houston but only 35% reported later on that they had in fact been either key or important people at the conference. This obviously hides a good deal of turnover: Some people found they were unexpectedly more important and others less important than they thought they would be when questioned before the conference. Three analysis questions will be posed concerning the leadership variable: What predicts who had expected to be important leaders in Houston; how their activity in Houston affected the leadership role they

[2]The actual word used in the questionnaire was *Hispanic-American,* but in discussions with members of this ethnic group since the study was designed, a strong preference was shown for *Latina* rather than *Hispanic,* on the grounds that Americans of this ethnic heritage do not by and large identity with Spanish culture, but with the Latin American cultures from which they and their families have come. Hence I shall use *Latina* rather than *Hispanic* throughout this volume.

had expected to perform before Houston; and how the level of leadership they had experienced in Houston influenced their political plans and aspirations.

Predictor Variables

Thus far the central variables in the study have been sketched, along with the role I expected them to play in the analysis of the data. There is, in addition, an important category of *predictor variables,* those variables that will help to explain variation in political aspirations or issue commitments, or whether political aspiration levels differ when directed toward mainstream, as opposed to movement, politics. These predictor variables are of three types: organizational membership, past political experience, and ongoing beliefs and attitudes.

Organizational Membership

The most important of the predictor variables are an array of questions concerning organizational membership. They are of key importance because it is largely through organizational membership and activity that political careers are made. Hence a variety of questions was asked not only to get the overall number of organizations the delegates belonged to, but to get separate estimates for a number of specific *types* of organizations: civic, civil rights, educational, feminist, job-related, political, religious, service, and social or cultural organizations. Delegates were also asked if they were members of eight specific organizations: NOW, AAUW, League of Women Voters, Business and Professional Women's Club, National Abortion Rights Action League (NARAL), Eagle Forum, National Gay Task Force, and Coalition of Labor Union Women (CLUW). The range and average number of organizations the women belonged to is a good index of the highly experienced network-builders in this unusual sample: The range was from zero (only 7 women) to 79 organizations, with a membership mean of 12.8 organizations!

Political Experience

The second type of predictor variable deals with past political experience. This includes the extent of mainstream political activity at the precinct, city, state, and national levels; a parallel set of questions were asked regarding the extent of movement political activity on the 16 issues discussed and voted on at most state meetings. In addition, the women were asked if they had been active in such liberal causes as civil rights, anti-war, zero population growth, environmental protection, etc. and whether they had held elective or appointive office in the past. Last, several general questions were asked concerning political orientation (from radical to very conservative), political party preference, experience of and aspirations toward service as a delegate to political party conventions, and voting record.

Beliefs and Affect

The third category of predictor variables are measures of beliefs and affect: These include the delegates' perceptions of the extent to which particular groups in the population supported feminist goals (e.g., the general public, Congress, employers, the courts); self-ratings on a feminist to antifeminist continuum coupled with similar ratings concerning their spouse (if married), best friend, son, and daughter (if they had a child above the age of 12).

An attitude scale on abortion was included that has been in use in national surveys since 1963. It lists five conditions and asks, for each of them, whether legal abortions should be available. Last, attitude questions of the agree–disagree variety were asked and scores were developed to tap four belief domains: marital equity, child care, economic rights, and the relation between the feminist movement and the abortion and sexual preference issues.

Demographic and Status Variables

The last category of variables in the design are demographic variables familiar from national surveys: age, education of self and spouse (if married), marital status, number of children, age of youngest child, religious affiliation, religious observance, current occupation, employment status, social class, own and family total income during the preceding year, race, ethnicity, residence in terms of city size and state, and household composition.

In addition, the delegates were asked if any member of their families had been active in politics (mother, father, spouse, or siblings) in case early exposure to political ideas and activity might have been an important link in the chain of experiences that led these women to a seat on the floor of the national conference.

Overall Design

Figure 3.1 summarizes the major variables in the design of the study and places them on a time frame with respect to both the life of the respondents

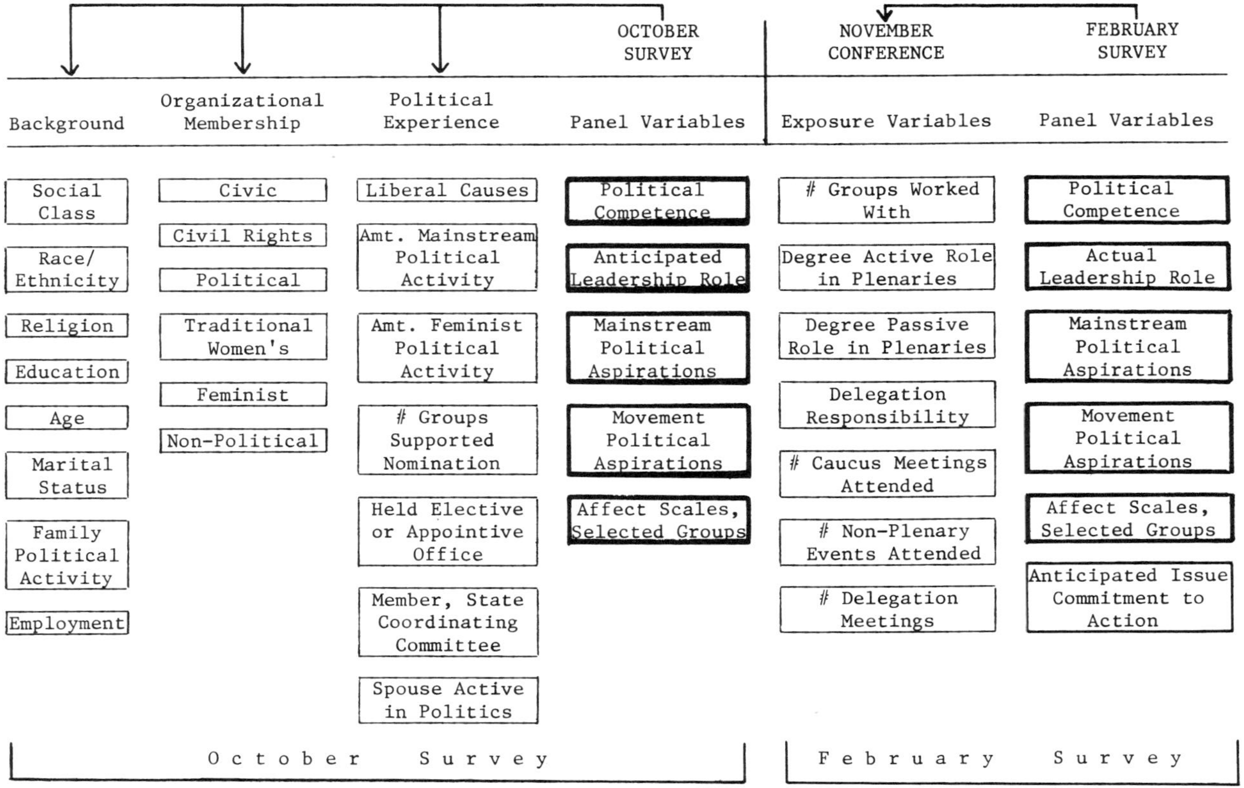

Background
- Social Class
- Race/Ethnicity
- Religion
- Education
- Age
- Marital Status
- Family Political Activity
- Employment

Organizational Membership
- Civic
- Civil Rights
- Political
- Traditional Women's
- Feminist
- Non-Political

Political Experience
- Liberal Causes
- Amt. Mainstream Political Activity
- Amt. Feminist Political Activity
- # Groups Supported Nomination
- Held Elective or Appointive Office
- Member, State Coordinating Committee
- Spouse Active in Politics

OCTOBER SURVEY — Panel Variables
- Political Competence
- Anticipated Leadership Role
- Mainstream Political Aspirations
- Movement Political Aspirations
- Affect Scales, Selected Groups

NOVEMBER CONFERENCE — Exposure Variables
- # Groups Worked With
- Degree Active Role in Plenaries
- Degree Passive Role in Plenaries
- Delegation Responsibility
- # Caucus Meetings Attended
- # Non-Plenary Events Attended
- # Delegation Meetings

FEBRUARY SURVEY — Panel Variables
- Political Competence
- Actual Leadership Role
- Mainstream Political Aspirations
- Movement Political Aspirations
- Affect Scales, Selected Groups
- Anticipated Issue Commitment to Action

October Survey

November

February Survey

Figure 3.1. Major background, predictor and panel variables in the research design. (Heavy boxed variables are the major panel items in the study.)

and the survey from which the data were obtained. (The full questionnaires are in Appendix A.) A number of specific items have not been mentioned, either because they are of a peripheral, supplementary nature or because they do not figure in the analysis reported in this volume.

Appendix B provides a handy reference for identifying the specific questions used to form scores and indices in the analysis. The indices of greatest importance to the core analysis will be presented in the last section of this chapter, but others encountered in the substantive chapters that are not dealt with here are defined in the alphabetical Index List in Appendix B.

Profile of the Sample

Table 3.1 provides a social introduction to the delegates since it brings together familiar social demographic characteristics in a profile of the women in terms of family status; racial, ethnic, and religious backgrounds; and socioeconomic characteristics. The first impression the demographic profile gives is one of diversity: There are women under 20 as well as over 70 years of age; widows and divorcees as well as young married women; those with large families and those with no children; some living alone, others only with children, still others with spouse, children, and a relative; women at home and women who hold down not only a full-time job but an extra part-time job as well. There are 77 women who hold a degree in law and over 100 who did not graduate from high school; women who never attend religious services and others who attend several times a week. (In fact, one woman objected to the code for religious observance with a marginal comment that she goes to church "at least once a day," and the code did not permit her to report this.)

In some respects, the modal profile of the women in the sample is not very different from one we would encounter in a national probability sample: She is a woman in her early forties, married, the mother of an adolescent son or daughter, white, Protestant, middle-class, employed full-time. The delegates differ from such a national profile in tending to work for the government, having higher educational attainment, a smaller family, and a higher probability of being non-Caucasian. The older women in the sample are less representative of their birth cohort than the younger women: Many of the women now in their forties and fifties went against the trend of their age cohort in remaining single, having smaller families, obtaining more education, and being employed full-time.

But it is when we turn to the women's organizational life that we encounter their most striking characteristic: These are joiners par excellence. As noted previously, they hold membership in a high, mean 12.8 organizations. Table 3.2 shows the variety of types of organizations the delegates belong to as well

Table 3.1
Social Demographic Profile of IWY Sample (in percent)

FAMILY STATUS CHARACTERISTICS	SOCIO-ECONOMIC CHARACTERISTICS

CURRENT MARITAL STATUS

Married	58.0
Single	19.0
Separated or Divorced . .	17.4
Widowed	5.6

100% =	(1307)

AGE

16 - 30	16.2
31 - 40	28.7
41 - 50	28.3
51 - 60	19.2
61 - 81	7.5

100% =	(1306)

NUMBER OF CHILDREN

None	32.3
One or Two	35.1
Three or Four	23.6
Five or More	9.0

100% =	(1311)

AGE YOUNGEST CHILD

Under 5	11.9
6 - 10	19.6
11 - 20	39.8
21 or Older	28.8

100% =	(864)

HOUSEHOLD INCLUDES

Spouse	58.7%
Child(ren)	48.5%
Non-Kin	11.8%
Kin	8.8%
Alone	17.2%

	(1278)

RELIGIOUS PREFERENCE

Protestant	46.9
Catholic	20.2
Agnostic, Atheist . . .	14.3
Jewish	9.4
Other	9.1

100%=	(1285)

EDUCATIONAL ATTAINMENT

	Self	Spouse
High School of Less .	9.5	18.1
Some College	19.7	14.4
College Graduate . .	14.8	15.1
Some Graduate Work .	16.7	9.7
Master's Degree . . .	25.3	16.6
Advanced Degree . . .	14.0	26.0

100% =	(1282)	(999)

EMPLOYMENT STATUS

Full Time Plus Part Time .	10.1
Full Time	52.8
Part Time	15.7
Unemployed	4.5
Not Employed	17.0

100% =	(1292)

EMPLOYER

Federal Government	9.5
State or Local Government .	34.7
Non-Profit, Service Organ. .	25.7
Private Business	18.6
Self-Employed	11.6

100% =	(1234)

SOCIAL CLASS		Family of
	Now	Origin
Upper Class . . .	5.3	4.4
Upper Middle . .	38.3	22.1
Middle	41.3	35.0
Working	13.7	33.1
Lower	1.3	5.4

100% =	(1273)	(1294)

RACE/ETHNICITY

White	71.8
Black	13.7
Latina	6.4
Asian	2.3
American Indian/ Alaskan Native . .	2.7
Pacific Islander . .	1.2
Other	1.9

100% =	(1301)

Table 3.2
Organizational Membership Profile of IWY Sample

TYPE OF ORGANIZATION (N = 1283)	Mean	Range	Percent Distribution				
			None	One	Two	3-5	6 or More
Political	2.15	0-15	15.7	25.6	24.6	29.5	4.7
Civic	1.61	0-30	35.1	27.0	17.3	16.9	3.8
Educational . . .	1.56	0-36	30.0	29.2	19.5	18.3	3.1
Feminist	1.55	0-15	30.5	27.3	19.9	20.4	2.0
Job-Related . . .	1.46	0-33	37.6	23.9	17.1	19.1	2.2
Civil Rights . .	1.19	0-10	42.0	26.1	18.2	12.2	1.5
Social/Cultural .	1.11	0-41	47.7	24.4	13.9	12.6	1.5
Religious	.92	0-20	42.6	38.7	10.1	8.0	.7
Service	.78	0-10	54.5	26.8	12.1	5.7	.8

as the variation in mean membership by each organization type. The highly political nature of the sample is underlined by the types of organizations in which the respondents show the highest mean membership: political, civic, educational, and feminist organizations; the lowest overall membership is in religious, service, and cultural organizations. Only 16% of the women belong to no *political* organizations at all, whereas 43% belong to no *religious* organization, the reverse of what a national sample would show.[3] Table 3.3 underlines this general point further: When the types of organizations are clustered into political versus nonpolitical organizations, there is higher mean membership for the *four* types of political organizations ($M = 6.6$) than for the *five* types of nonpolitical organizations ($M = 4.9$) in these summary codes.

Membership in specifically feminist organizations as well as in traditional women's organizations is typical of the sample, as suggested by the similar mean membership in the two sets of organizations shown in Table 3.3. Table

[3]It is also quite possible that the sample departs in several important respects from the total population of delegates, since the response pattern analysis reported in Chapter 2 indicated that the panel sample has an overrepresentation of women with very liberal political views, no religious affiliation, and high levels of organizational involvement.

Table 3.3

Mean Membership Profile by Organizational Type

TYPE OF ORGANIZATION	Mean	Standard Deviation	Range
Total Organization Membership, all types	12.8	8.25	0-79
Total Political Organizations[a] . . .	6.6	4.55	0-37
Total Non-Political Organizations[b]	4.9	4.27	0-54
Specified Organizations:			
Feminist[c]	.69	.80	0-3
Traditional Women's[d]	.70	.87	0-3
# Groups Supported Nomination at State Meeting	2.4	1.50	0-5

[a]Sum of Civic, Civil Rights, Feminist and Political Organizations.

[b]Sum of Educational, Job-Related, Religious, Service, Social and Cultural Organizations.

[c]Membership in National Organization for Women (NOW), National Abortion Rights Action League (NARAL), and National Gay Task Force (NGTF).

[d]Membership in American Association of University Women (AAUW), League of Women Voters (LWV), and a Business and Professional Women's Club.

3.4 gives greater detail on actual membership levels in 10 specific organizations. At the top of the list are a feminist organization, NOW (43% of the sample are NOW members), and a traditional women's organization, the League of Women Voters (31% of the sample); the next two organizations are similarly a feminist organization (NARAL) and a traditional women's organization (AAUW), both with membership levels of about 20%. By contrast, membership in an organization specifically opposed to the national conference and the agenda it endorsed, the Eagle Forum, is very low at 2%. The National Gay Task Force is only slightly better represented, with 3.5% members in the sample.[4]

[4]Once again, it should be noted that this is a conservative estimate of the incidence of members of either group, since the sample contains a lower proportion of both radical and conservative delegates than the total population.

Table 3.4

Membership in Specified Organizations

ORGANIZATION	Percent Members of . .
National Organization for Women (NOW)	42.6%
League of Women Voters (LWV)	31.1%
American Association of University Women (AAUW)	21.3%
National Abortion Rights Action League (NARAL)	20.9%
Business and Professional Women's Club (BPW)	17.8%
Coalition of Labor Union Women (CLUW)	6.4%
Federally Employed Women (FEW)	3.6%
National Gay Task Force (NGTF)	3.5%
Eagle Forum	2.0%
National Congress of Neighborhood Women (NCNW)	1.5%

Political Experience

Experience in Liberal Causes

As might be inferred from the diversity of organizations the delegates belong to, political action and experience in the lives of these women have not
been limited to the issue of women's rights. Civil rights, as we know from the
recent history of the feminist movement, was often the precursor to political
concern for the rights of women. In this sample, three-fourths report having
given time or money to civil rights efforts; from one-third to one-half of the
sample have also been involved in anti-war, Third World, or environmental
protection issues; one-fourth have contributed to the zero population growth
movement. As shown in Table 3.5, ERA ratification has been the top concern
of the Houston delegates, whereas pro-abortion issues have been supported
to only a slightly greater extent than have environmental protection issues.

Own and Family Members' Political Experience

For at least one in four of the delegates, their own political activity over the
years represents a continuity across the generations in their families. Table 3.6

Table 3.5

Support or Opposition to Selected Causes

CAUSE:[a] Percent Gave Time a/o Money to . . .	Actively Supported	Not Active	Actively Opposed
LIBERAL CAUSES			
Civil Rights	75.6	19.6	1.2
Pro-Environmental Protection . .	49.1	45.7	1.3
Cooperation with 3rd World . . .	36.5	57.5	1.5
Anti-War	33.8	53.5	7.2
Zero Population Growth	25.3	67.4	3.3
Anti-Nuclear Energy	14.6	73.6	5.9
Index: Score Range 0-6, Mean = 2.5			
FEMINIST ISSUE CAUSES			
Pro-ERA	80.0	13.0	3.8
Pro-Abortion	57.2	32.8	6.1
Anti-Abortion	7.0	44.4	43.3
Anti-ERA	5.7	34.8	54.5

[a]Questions 41a-j, October survey. Index is for active support, from none to all six causes.

shows that a third of the women themselves have held elective and/or appointive office in mainstream politics and in political party organizations; but a high proportion, 25%, also report that their fathers have been active politically, another 16% that their mothers have been politically active. Their siblings, by contrast, are not like themselves, for lower levels of political activity are reported for their brothers (14%) and sisters (11%) than themselves and their parents. Slightly more than one in four delegates also report their husbands have been active in politics (among those who are or have been married).

It is interesting to note that there is a positive correlation between *parental* political activity and *spouse* political activity ($r = +.22$), suggesting that some of the women grew up in and continue, as adults, to move in a highly politicized family world. Indeed, some of the delegates may have met the man they married in the political networks they shared with their parents.

Table 3.6

Office Holding and Political Activity of Self and Family Members

OWN OFFICE HOLDING[a]	Public Office	Political Party
Both Elected and Appointed . . .	11.0	13.8
Elected Only	6.5	11.1
Appointed Only	18.0	6.6
Neither	64.6	68.6
100% =	(1251)	(1228)

FAMILY MEMBERS' OFFICE HOLDING[b]	Percent Held Office	
Local Office	17.8%	(1274)
State Office	8.7%	(1259)
National Office	1.9%	(1243)

FAMILY MEMBERS' POLITICAL ACTIVITY[c]	Percent Active	
Mother	16.3%	(1229)
Father	24.7%	(1245)
Brother	13.8%	(998)
Sister	11.0%	(988)
Husband	26.7%	(1008)

[a]Question 30A, B, October survey.

[b]Question 32a-c, October survey.

[c]Question 33a-e, October survey. A Family Political Activity Index was constructed based on Q. 32a-c and Q. 33a-d (excluding husband). Two points were given for office holding at the local level, four points at the state level, six points for the national level; specific political activity reported for mother and siblings was given two points each, for father, one point. Total Score Range was 0-19, with a mean of 1.59.

Past Mainstream and Movement Political Activity

Table 3.7 shows the distribution of political activity level in mainstream politics and in two clusters of feminist movement politics. Half the women report having been *very* or *extremely* active in city and state politics, 29% in national politics. Only one in five report no activity in mainstream city and state politics. The index used in later chapters combines the four levels of past political activity, with special added weights for state and national activity, as noted in Table 3.7, Footnote *b*.

The measures of feminist movement activity are based on reported levels of political activity on the 16 issues listed in Table 3.7. These were issues that were considered core items on the agenda of most state meetings. In Table 3.7 they are ranked from highest to lowest activity level, as reported by the delegates in the sample. All the issues with high activity levels are issues that have been on the feminist agenda since the 1960s (ERA, education, employment, abortion), whereas the issues that have emerged in more recent years show moderate to low levels of reported activity (retirement benefits, sexuality, sexual preference, rural women, international relations). Looking down the column of issues in this table is to take a historical journey over 15 years of movement history. The women have become involved in the feminist movement at different points in their own lives, with the result that many older women have poured their political energies for a long time into issues affecting women's opportunities in higher education and the workplace, whereas many younger women first became politically active on issues affecting the private side of life such as rape, sexuality, and sexual preference.

Intercorrelations among the 16 activity issues show a differentiation between sex-linked and gender-linked issues with, on average, much higher correlations *within* each cluster than *between* the two clusters. Thus, the mean correlation coefficient among the five items in the sex-linked cluster was $r = +.432$; among the six items in the gender-linked cluster the mean correlation was $r = +.397$. By contrast, the mean correlation of the 30 coefficients that pair items *between* these two clusters was only $r = +.222$.

Having been active or not on farm issues and on international relations showed no particular clustering and many insignificant correlations, whereas activity on media issues, homemaker rights, and the ERA cut across the two main clusters. Consequently, three indices were constructed from the 16 activity level measures: An overall index that uses all 16 items will be referred to as *movement activity level;* a 5-item *sex-linked activity level* index uses abortion, family planning, sex preference, sexuality, and rape; and a 6-item *gender-linked activity level* index uses health care, education, employment, child care, retirement benefits, and housing. Score range and means are shown at the bottom of Table 3.7. (See also Appendix B.)

Table 3.7

Recent Mainstream and Movement Political Activity Level (in percent)

TYPE OF POLITICAL ACTIVITY	Activity	Level		
MAINSTREAM POLITICAL **ACTIVITY LEVEL**[a]	Not At All	Somewhat	Very	Extremely
Precinct/Neighborhood	25.7	35.9	18.7	19.7
Town or City	18.7	30.5	26.1	24.7
State	20.6	30.6	23.7	25.1
National	29.6	40.6	16.9	12.9

Index: Score Range 0-11,[b] Mean = 5.98 (1201)

MOVEMENT POLITICAL ACTIVITY LEVEL[a]	Not Active	Somewhat Active	Very Active
ERA Ratification	15.6	27.7	56.7
Education	18.4	37.4	44.2
Employment	19.9	35.8	44.3
Child Care	32.1	44.2	23.7
Abortion	32.6	40.9	26.5
Health Care	37.8	37.6	24.6
Homemaker Legal Rights . . .	37.8	38.3	23.9
Rape	40.5	36.6	22.9
Family Planning	49.0	35.8	15.3
Mass Media	49.9	34.0	16.0
Housing	54.2	28.7	17.1
Retirement Benefits	56.1	28.9	15.0
Sexuality	56.9	26.1	16.9
Sexual Preference	61.8	24.7	13.5
International Relations . . .	63.3	24.3	12.4
Farming/Rural Life	77.5	15.6	6.9

Indices:

Total: Score Range 16-48, Mean = 28.62 (1208)

Sex-Linked Activity:[c] Score Range 5-15, Mean = 8.63 (1236)

Gender-Linked Activity:[c] Score Range 6-18, Mean = 11.30 (1257)

[a]Mainstream political activity from Q. 25a-d, October survey; Movement activity from Q. 49a-p, October survey.

[b]Different weights were used to give more points to activity on the state and national levels. For precinct and city: Not At All = 0,

Several interesting patterns are visible even at this stage of introducing the sample. It was noted earlier that parental and spouse political activity were positively correlated. There is also an association between the women's own political activity and that of their husbands, but only with mainstream politics ($r = +.220$), not with their feminist involvement in movement politics ($r = +.003$ to sex-linked activism, $r = +.095$ to gender-linked activism). On the other hand, involvement in mainstream and movement politics by the delegates is significantly correlated ($r = +.388$), though more so on gender-linked issues ($r = +.362$) than on sex-linked issues ($r = +.262$). Even at this level of analysis with correlational patterns, there is a suggestion of the different routes taken into mainstream than into movement politics. One imagines, for example, the woman who grew up in a family active on the local political scene, who met her husband through these early political networks and shared with him a general interest, and modest level of activity, in mainstream political parties and local political issues. For such a woman, feminist involvement may have been an offshoot of general political involvement. One thinks of a League of Women Voters member whose parents and husband have been active locally, whose first feminist political participation has been in efforts to secure ERA ratification following the League's endorsement of the amendment.

Still other women, far less educated than the typical League member, may have become involved in feminist politics through their own prior experiences with issues affecting them as women workers and as activists in local politics. This is suggested by the finding that mainstream political activity is not correlated with educational attainment: Equally high levels of political activity were found among women with a high school diploma as among college graduate women. For still other delegates, feminist political participation was preceded only by political action on civil rights issues or anti-war protests.

Political Competence

In light of the varied political experience the women already had had before they became nominees for election as delegates to the national conference, it is scarcely surprising to find that their overall judgment of themselves as

---

Some or Very = 1, Extremely = 2; for state: Not At All = 0, Some or Very = 2, Extremely = 3; for national: Not At All = 0, Somewhat = 1, Very = 2, Extremely 4.

[c]Sex-Linked Movement Activity is based on Abortion, Family Planning, Rape, Sexual Preference and Sexuality items. Gender-Linked Movement Activity is based on Child Care, Education, Employment, Health Care, Housing and Retirement Benefits.

Table 3.8
Political Competence Self Rating

ITEM[a]	Rating Level			
	Very Low or Low	Moderate	High	Very High
Remaining alert for long hours at at time	3.2	19.8	44.8	32.2
Getting acquainted with a large number of people	4.8	22.8	39.0	33.4
Debating an issue well	6.7	33.5	36.8	22.9
Speaking well before a large audience	4.6	26.4	36.8	32.2
Accepting compromises well	7.1	38.2	39.6	15.1
Knowledge of parliamentary procedures	17.3	43.1	30.1	9.7

Index: Score Range 6-30, Mean = 22.5 (1271)

Correlations: Coefficient Range .17 to .53, October survey.

[a]Question 39a-f, October; Question 39a-f, February survey. Distribution shown is for October.

political beings is very positive indeed. The majority of the women see themselves as very competent on such political skills as speaking well before large audiences, debating an issue well, feeling comfortable while getting acquainted with lots of people, accepting compromises gracefully, and remaining alert for long hours at a time. As seen in Table 3.8, the only item that showed even a modest level of *low* competence ratings is knowledge of parliamentary procedures. This was also the component of political competence that showed most shift on the February survey compared to the October self-rating: Table 3.8 shows that only 10% of the women gave themselves top ratings on parliamentary savvy in October; we shall see in a later chapter that this jumped to 15% by February, with a corresponding decline in low ratings. Ann Saunier, by example, was an effective teacher of parliamentary procedure to many women in Houston!

Feminist Beliefs

Five measures were constructed to study a range of belief domains that have been central to the feminist agenda in recent years: Economic rights, marital equity, child care, and abortion have been areas of major concern to feminists since the 1960s. The fifth index studies more current issues: It is a new measure, called *bottom-line feminism,* which measures the excluding or including tendencies of the delegates in their use of the feminist label. It includes items like whether someone can be called a feminist if he or she does not work for lesbian rights or opposes abortion or the ERA.

Table 3.9 shows the response distribution on the items in these indices, the score range and mean on the indices, and the correlation range between pairs of items in each index. There is not much variance in this sample on the individual items, and often rather little on the indices for three belief areas. Over 90% of the respondents subscribe to the feminist stance on the *economic rights* index, and almost as skewed a distribution is shown for *marital equity.* The same pattern is shown for the *abortion* index, with a mean score of 4.24 pressing the upper limit of the score (5.0), although the endorsements of specific items in the index show the same general pattern of high approval of legal abortions for health reasons and lowered approval for social reasons that has been found consistently in national probability sample surveys.

Child care is a more sensitive issue, with not nearly as strong a level of approval across the items. On an item that has been used in national surveys since the early 1960s, 90% of the delegates endorsed the view that working mothers can have just as close a relationship to a child as do women who stay at home. A similarly high percentage indicated that they would place a child of their own in a child-care center (although for most women in the sample, this is no longer a personal issue since their children are mostly beyond that stage of development). Views on whether the child benefits from child-care centers were not nearly so skewed: Twenty percent of the women were "not sure" and another 6% felt that children do not benefit from child-care centers. On whether they prefer a center to a relative for child care, 20% would prefer a relative and another 27% were "not sure."

That there are no firm criteria on the grounds of which women would be included or excluded from the feminist ranks is apparent from the distribution of responses to the items in the *bottom line feminism* index. One-third of the delegates would not automatically exclude a woman who opposed the ERA from the feminist label. Two-thirds leave the issue of abortion outside the definition of *feminist,* and a very strong majority (73%) take the view that one can be a feminist without working for lesbian rights. The sensitivity of the latter issue is further shown by the sharp split in views on whether or not the lesbian

Table 3.9

Feminist Beliefs: Items and Indices (in percent)

INDEX	ITEM	AGREE[a]	NOT SURE	DISAGREE

ABORTION[b]

It should be possible for a pregnant woman to obtain a legal abortion if . . . . .

		AGREE	NOT SURE	DISAGREE
	Mother's health endangered	93.8	3.7	2.5
	Chance of fetal defect	89.0	4.1	6.9
	Family income too low	75.9	8.5	15.7
	No desire to marry man	75.1	8.6	16.2
	Married, wants no more children	74.0	8.2	17.8

Index: Score Range 0-5, Mean = 4.24 (1273)

CHILDCARE[c]

		AGREE	NOT SURE	DISAGREE
	Would not personally use child-care center	5.2	4.5	90.2
	Working mother just as close to child as mother at home	89.9	4.3	5.8
	Preschool child suffers emotion-ally if mother works	14.3	10.6	75.2
	Preschool child benefits from childcare center	73.4	21.1	5.5
	Personally prefer a relative to care for child	18.9	27.0	54.1

Index: Score Range 5-25, Mean = 20.6 (1240)

Correlations: Coefficient Range = .26 to .51

ECONOMIC RIGHTS[d]

		AGREE	NOT SURE	DISAGREE
	Consider women as seriously as men for executives, politicians, President	96.5	.9	2.6
	Woman should have same job opportunities as a man	95.2	1.4	3.5
	Woman's job must be kept when she has a baby	90.1	6.2	3.7

Index: Score Range 3-15, Mean = 14.21 (1284)

Correlations: Coefficient Range = .53 to .65

MARITAL EQUITY[e]

		AGREE	NOT SURE	DISAGREE
	Helping husband more important than wife having career	6.9	4.9	88.1
	Better if husband the achiever, wife the homemaker	7.2	5.6	87.2
	Men should share housework . . .	94.2	2.5	3.2

Index: Score Range 3-15, Mean 13.5 (1274)

Correlations: Coefficient Range = .36 to .69

(continued)

Table 3.9 (continued)

INDEX	ITEM	AGREE[a]	NOT SURE	DISAGREE
BOTTOM LINE FEMINISM[f]				
	No Feminist if oppose ERA	67.1	11.0	21.7
	Lesbian issue more harm than good to women's movement . . .	38.9	27.4	33.7
	No Feminist if oppose abortion .	31.3	15.6	53.1
	No Feminist if not work for lesbian rights	15.5	12.1	72.5
Index:	Score Range 4-20, Mean = 11.95 (1275)			
Correlations:	Coefficient Range .23 to .41			

[a]Response categories for abortion items were Yes, Don't Know and No. On all other items, five category code differentiating Agree Strongly from Agree, Disagree Strongly from Disagree. Condensed in table above.

[b]Question 43a-e in October survey. Items abbreviated throughout table.

[c]Questions 47b, e and 51c, g, i in October survey.

[d]Question 47f, h, i in October survey.

[e]Question 47a, d, g in October survey.

[f]Question 51b, e, h, j in October survey.

issue has done "more harm than good" to the women's movement: Thirty-nine percent of the delegates agreed with this statement, one-third disagreed.

Measuring the Houston Experience

The 4 days most delegates spent in Houston provided a good test of their ability to "remain mentally alert" for long hours at a stretch. For many people, the "day" began before 6 A.M. and did not end until the early hours of the following day. Caucus and delegation meetings took place at all hours of the day and night. The IWY Commissioners themselves held two meetings that began at 11 P.M. A few delegates referred to meetings between 2 A.M. and 4 A.M. in describing their most memorable experiences at the conference (memorable not because of the hour but because of the substance of the meetings).

Attendance at such meetings was part of what it took to be significantly involved in the political process of the conference and thus provided the criteria for the design of the exposure variables. These variables will be important in explaining stability and change in political commitments and aspirations.

Two kinds of measures were developed to study actual participation in Houston. One concerns the frequency of meeting with the formal organizational units relevant to that political process—the state delegation, the caucuses, the organizations the delegates belonged to, and/or represented at the conference—and the respondent's formal status category (delegate, alternate, IWY Commissioner, Secretariat staff member), which was, predictably, related to differential involvement in the Houston political process. The second type of measure deals with the extent and style of participation in the plenary sessions themselves, such as standing on microphone lines, trying to change someone's vote, passing along messages.

State Delegation

A variety of questions was asked about the delegates' relationship to the state delegation: how much responsibility the women carried within the state delegations; the frequency of delegation meetings before, during, and after the Houston conference; and the extent of personal acquaintance within the delegation at the same three time points. Table 3.10 provides a profile of these aspects of state delegation membership. In the October survey, two-thirds of the delegates reported that their delegation had met at least twice; one-fourth reported that four or more meetings had been held before they left for Houston. During the conference, there was also great variation among the delegations: The modal pattern for individuals was two or three meetings, but one-fifth of the women reported only one meeting; another one-fifth, four or more meetings. The profile changes in the aftermath of the conference: Almost one-half the delegates reported no delegation meetings at all in their state since the Houston conference, whereas close to 30% reported two or more.

The data in Table 3.10 also capture something of the process of group formation that the delegations underwent. Many women were already acquainted with a great many of their sister delegates even before the newly elected body held a formal meeting: One-third of the women had known at least *one-half* of the people elected at their state meeting before the delega-

Table 3.10

Involvement with State Delegations (elected delegates and alternates only)

FORMAL MEETINGS OF DELEGATION	Before Conference[a]	During Conference[a]	Since Conference[a]
Not At All or DK	9.2	5.9	46.4
Once	24.9	20.5	26.5
Two or Three Times	40.4	51.5	19.6
Four or More Times	25.5	22.0	7.5
100% =	(889)	(868)	(856)

PERSONAL ACQUAINTANCE WITH OWN STATE DELEGATES	Before State Meeting[b]	After State Meeting But Before Conference[c]	After Conference[c]
80% or More	15.1	44.5	55.5
50% - 79%	20.0	19.4	15.6
25% - 49%	21.9	19.5	15.3
Less than 25%	36.1	15.4	12.6
None	6.9	1.2	.8
100% =	(1082)	(1041)	(883)

RESPONSIBILITY WITHIN STATE
DELEGATION[d]

Chair, co-chair or vice-chair	7.3
Committee chair or task force leader . . .	12.5
Committee or task force member	8.2
Other responsibility	21.2
No special responsibility	50.7
100% =	(883)

[a]Questions 14a-c, February survey.

[b]Questions 14A-B, October survey.

[c]Question 17A, February survey.

[d]Question 16, February survey.

tion met as a body. This reflects the fact that so many elected delegates had served on their state coordinating committees, as well as the fact that in many states, coalitions that were already in place at the local and state level brought nominations to the state meetings. The fact that the delegates reported a mean of 2.4 groups that supported their nomination for election (Table 3.3) is an index of this overlap of constituencies across action groups and organizations to which the elected delegates had enduring ties.

But there were also people elected who were totally new to the majority of the delegation, a pattern that was clear when state meetings were flooded with Anti-Plan people who won a number of seats in the delegation but who had no prior involvement in the work of the state coordinating committees: Somewhat more than one-third reported that they knew less than 25% of their delegation before the state meeting. By the time they arrived in Houston, this profile had already shifted: from *one-third* before the state meeting, there is now *two-thirds* who felt personally acquainted with at least *one-half* of their delegation. This extensive familiarity is only increased slightly by the time the conference ended. Finally, special official responsibility was a facilitator of increased knowledge of delegation members: Serving as an officer, committee or task force chair, or simply a committee member was reported by one-half the delegates in the sample.

Houston Events

From Saturday morning, November 19, to Monday noon, November 21, the conference was in plenary session for approximately 23 hours. A full 64% of the sample reported they had been present at the plenary sessions for not less than 22 of those hours; another 24% reported attendance for 20–21 hours. This high attendance profile pushed meetings of delegations, organizations, and caucuses to the early morning and late night hours (except for impromptu caucus meetings during the plenary sessions when a resolution was undergoing amendment). The long hours devoted to the plenary sessions cut into the time available for participation in other activities in Houston. In a day centered on a 10-hour plenary session, it is remarkable that so many delegates had the energy to attend other events in Houston. Many people simply skipped meal hours or postponed them to the very late hours on Saturday and Sunday.

Table 3.11 must be viewed with these time restraints in mind. Certain of the events listed here were ongoing, for example, the exhibits in the convention center were open throughout the conference so that many delegates managed to fit in an hour here and there to tour the exhibits, touch base with friends running them, or purchase momentoes of the conference. The activi-

Table 3.11

Special Events Attended at National Conference

EVENT[a]	Percent Attended
Exhibits in Albert Thomas Convention Center	88.4%
ERA Reception	53.3%
Torch Rally	33.5%
ERA Ratification Assembly	31.0%
Seneca Falls South Activities	23.6%
NOW Reception	20.3%
Workshops/Lectures	20.0%
Music Hall Gala	18.3%
Peace and Disarmament Hearing	9.9%
International Visitors Reception	5.8%

Index: Score Range 0-10, Mean = 2.97

[a]Question 8a-j, February survey.

ties in Seneca Falls South were also scheduled for long hours on each of the 3 days, though they attracted far fewer delegates than the convention center exhibits (24% versus 88%). Workshops and lectures were held throughout the conference, but they were more for observers and visitors than for the delegates themselves, which explains the low 20% attendance shown on this dimension of the Houston experience.

The remainder of the events shown were held at specific hours on a particular day. The ERA ratification assembly and reception, as well as the Torch Rally, took place on Friday, the day before the plenary sessions began. Many delegates were still in the throes of settling in at the congested hotels during that day, or were in caucus and delegation meetings rather than at these more public events. Nonetheless, one-half the sample reported having been present at the ERA reception Friday night—scarcely surprising to anyone who tried to move across that crowded ballroom floor to connect with a friend or to get a better view of the First Ladies on the low podium.

Caucus Meetings

The frequency of attendance at caucus meetings is necessarily a much lower profile than that shown on the general events listed in the preceding table. Except for the Pro-Plan Caucus (two-thirds of the delegates report having attended at least one Pro-Plan Caucus meeting), the remaining caucuses were focused on quite specific issues and resolutions of primary interest to the group involved. Hence the figures in Table 3.12 must be viewed against the proportion of the total sample most likely to have a personal interest in a given caucus. For example, although only 14.3% attended at least one meeting of the Black Caucus, Black women were only 13.7% of the total sample to begin with, so a very high proportion of Black delegates were involved in this caucus. Many delegates attended caucus meetings out of interest or a desire to help, even if they themselves were not members of the

Table 3.12

Caucus Meetings Attended at National Conference (in percent)

CAUCUS[a]	Frequency		
	None	One	More Than One
Pro-Plan	34.6	35.9	29.6
Black	85.7	8.1	6.2
Latina	89.7	4.7	5.5
Labor	90.8	6.0	3.2
Lesbian	91.1	5.0	3.9
Welfare	91.7	7.0	1.2
Native-American	93.0	4.5	2.6
Asian	94.0	3.8	2.3
Disabled	95.2	3.8	1.1
"Majority" Anti-Plan	95.6	2.6	1.9
Youth	96.6	2.6	.8

Index: Score Range 11-33, Mean = 12.9 (1136)

[a]Question 7a-k, February survey.

Table 3.13

Groups Worked with at National Conference (in percent)

| GROUP[a] | Frequency | | | |
	Not At All	Not Much	Some	A Great Deal
Own state delegation	14.8	7.2	23.3	54.7
Delegates who belong to same organization(s) you do	23.2	11.5	39.9	25.4
Pro-Plan caucus	25.5	14.3	37.7	22.5
An issue-oriented caucus	31.6	10.5	32.4	25.5
Non-delegate observers	42.5	17.5	30.1	10.0
Individual IWY Commissioners	57.7	16.2	19.9	6.1
Delegates who belong to same political party you do	63.2	12.6	18.3	5.9
IWY Secretariat staff	78.7	10.4	8.0	3.0
"Majority" (Anti-Plan) Caucus	94.5	1.7	1.7	2.1

Index: Score Range 9-36, Mean = 18.8 (1139)

[a]Question 9a-i, February survey.

category affected. Thus, for example, 10% reported having attended at least one Latina Caucus meeting, which is higher than the 6.4% who identified themselves as Latinas. A similar profile holds for the remaining ethnic groups on the list of caucuses shown in Table 3.12. This is largely due to the fact that members of the racial and ethnic caucuses cooperated in submitting a substitute, composite Resolution on Minorities.

Other people attended caucus meetings out of curiosity or a desire to become informed about an opposing group. There were Anti-Plan observers at Pro-Plan Caucus meetings, and probably the reverse as well. Hence sheer caucus attendance is a weak measure of political participation in Houston. A more useful measure is derived from a series of questions about the extent to which the respondents "worked with" a variety of groups at the conference. The marginal profile of responses is shown in Table 3.13. A high score on this index is a good indicator of high involvement in the political process in Houston, for it means having worked with a variety of people and groups—state delegations, caucuses, IWY Commissioners, Secretariat staff—and sister members of particular organizations active at the conference.

The response distribution shown in Table 3.13 also suggests that the most active groups in the political process in Houston were the state delegations, the Pro-Plan Caucus, and organizations of more enduring membership. This is also consistent with the responses given when the delegates were specifically asked if they had worked to amend or substitute any resolution in the Plan of Action: Fifty-four percent said they had been involved in such efforts; of them, 11% reported having begun these efforts before they came to Houston, 56% during the conference itself. When asked with whom they worked in these efforts, 66% reported working with their state delegation and a caucus relevant to the issue involved, another 43% with an organization they belonged to.

Plenary Session Participation

The major exposure measures are those dealing with the plenary sessions themselves, since this was at the heart of the political process in Houston. What role the women played on the Coliseum floor is therefore of central importance to the analysis. We know already that most were in attendance for almost all the long hours the conference was in session. How active they were on that floor is measured by the items in the *active plenary role* index: Making an effort to persuade someone else how to vote, explaining procedures to someone else, passing messages, taking time out for a caucus meeting, and attempting to speak from a floor microphone are the five activities that comprise the index. Those who scored high on this index were clearly highly involved in the political process of resolution amendment, floor management, and consensus building. They include the leaders of the action taking place on the floor.

Leaders do not exist in a vacuum; there must be people to inform and persuade. Hence items were included that would reveal more passive roles in the conference proceedings: people who sought explanations from others, asked others how to vote or took their suggestions, or engaged in some personal withdrawal like dozing off, leaving the floor, or vacillating in attention. I expected the item on leaving the floor to "get away from it all" to cluster with the other passive items, but it did not do so. Apparently, both active and passive participants sometimes felt this way, for this item correlated no more significantly with the passive items than with the active items.

There was no significant patterning to the correlations between either of the last two items shown in Table 3.14 and the active and passive clusters: Neither "voting for something you personally opposed" nor "against something you really supported" related in any consistent way to the items in the active and

Table 3.14

Role in National Conference Plenary Sessions

INDEX	ITEM	F r e q u e n c y			
		Not At All	Once	A Few Times	Many Times
ACTIVE PLENARY ROLE[a]	Explained a procedure to someone else	9.6	12.2	53.4	24.8
	Passed along messages as part of floor operations	23.3	6.0	41.6	29.1
	Attended a caucus meeting . . .	32.2	18.8	33.0	16.1
	Tried to persuade someone how to vote	32.4	11.6	43.0	13.0
	Stood on microphone lines . . .	47.5	17.5	25.7	9.3
	Index: Score Range 5-20, Mean = 12.4 (1094)				
	Correlations: Coefficient Range .20 to .46				
PASSIVE PLENARY ROLE[b]	Asked someone to explain a procedure	45.7	15.2	33.7	5.4
	Looked to others for how you should vote	61.6	13.8	22.4	2.3
	Dozed off or lost track of what was going on	70.6	9.4	19.1	.9
	Index: Score Range 3-12, Mean = 5.11 (1107)				
	Correlations: Coefficient Range .25 to .28				
MISC.[c]	Left the floor just to "get away from it all"	58.3	14.2	24.7	2.8
	Voted for something you personally opposed	77.4	15.5	6.7	.4
	Voted against something you personally supported	93.6	4.4	1.6	.4

[a]Question 19a, b, h, j, k; February survey.

[b]Question 19c, f, i; February survey.

[c]Question 19d, e, g; February survey. These items did not show any consistent pattern of significant correlations with other items in either the Active or the Passive Plenary Role indices.

passive role clusters. The response distribution on these two items is of intrinsic interest, however, for they suggest what many have reported about participation in the Houston conference: The time constraint and the force of Pro-Plan caucusing meant for many participants that they gave their "ayes" to resolutions they might have preferred to revise, amend, or simply reject. The collective will of the body politic in Houston was in the direction of swallowing personal reservations and supporting the plan by voting favorably on all its resolutions. One in four women reported having done this at least once. The counter-pressure, voting against something one personally supported, was a pressure that applied most of all to the Anti-Plan delegates: Since they were a small portion of the delegate body, the frequency of this occurrence is necessarily small, affecting only 6% of the sample.

There is some evidence that many delegates felt the Pro-Plan majority voted against their personal beliefs more often than Anti-Plan delegates did. The delegates were asked about their overall perception of this collective pressure with a direct question: "How would you compare the Pro-Plan and Anti-Plan delegates in the extent to which they voted against their individual beliefs?" [Question 25, February survey]. Half of the delegates saw no difference between the two groups (46% on the grounds that neither group did much voting against their beliefs, a small 5% that both groups did a lot of such voting); another 20% opted out of the question with a "don't know" response. But among those who perceived a contrast between the Pro-Plan and Anti-Plan groups, twice as many cited the Pro-Plan as the Anti-Plan group (19.5% versus 10.3%, respectively) for voting against personal belief. This is consistent with many qualitative comments the delegates made about the Anti-Plan delegates: That they admired and respected these delegates for the strength of their convictions under the difficult circumstances of being a very small minority at an overwhelmingly Pro-Plan convention.[5]

The general sense of haste and pressure to reach consensus is apparent in the responses to two other questions asked in February. The delegates were

[5]I should also report a research failure in one effort to investigate the collective pressure for support of the Plan of Action. I listed all 26 resolutions in the second survey and asked respondents how they had actually voted and how they would have voted "if time, technology or the rules had permitted a secret ballot rather than a standing vote." A comparison of the reported *actual* vote with the *preferred* vote showed no significant differences in response distribution except on the sexual preference resolution, but even here there was only a minor contrast: Twelve percent reported that they had voted against this resolution, 17% that they would have preferred to cast a negative vote. But it was also the case that on every resolution, including the sexual preference item, a much larger number of respondents did not answer the *preferred* vote question than did not answer the *actual* vote question. (Three percent gave no answer to actual vote, 15 percent to preferred vote.) I have no way of knowing to what extent the fivefold increase in "no answers" on the preferred questions were from people who were opposed to the resolutions rather than from those who objected to the question being asked. My inference is that it was largely objection to the question rather than attempts to hide real feeling, because there was little variation in the number of "no answers" across the 26 resolutions.

asked "If time permitted, would you have preferred to further amend any of the resolutions adopted in Houston?" [Question 20, February survey]. Only 17% said *no* to this question. One-half of the delegates said they would have preferred to amend "one or two" resolutions; 18% said in their view this applied to "three or four" resolutions, 11% to "five or more" resolutions. They were also asked: "Many people at the Houston conference felt great time pressure because of the length of the agenda and the shortness of the conference. If you had to decide to reduce the number of resolutions OR add a day to the duration of the conference, which would you do?" [Question 21, February survey]. The delegates favored, by close to 3 to 1, adding a day to the conference (52.1%) over reducing the number of resolutions (18.0%). Only 14.7% held out for both more time and fewer resolutions, and 12.2% said "neither: it was fine as it was." The general view projected by these responses is that none of the resolutions were superfluous; all were important, and hence it was additional time, not agenda reduction, that would have helped.

Conference Control

Judging from comments made on the floor of the Coliseum and reported in the press at the time of the convention, there was a vocal minority among the

Table 3.15
Control of the Conference (in percent)

ITEM[a]	Frequency				
	Strongly Agree	Agree	Neutral	Disagree	Strongly Disagree
The resolutions in Houston were railroaded through	8.6	12.7	8.0	36.2	33.9
The floor management was inconsistent with a democratic process	7.4	9.3	12.2	40.1	31.0
No one could get to a mike without the approval of a Pro-Plan floor manager	5.8	6.9	15.2	37.0	35.1
The conference was controlled by big city Eastern Democrats .	4.1	8.5	20.6	39.0	27.8

Index: Conference Control: Score Range (4-20), Mean 8.6 (1160)

Correlations: Coefficient Range .53 to .73.

[a]Questions 28c, d, h, i, February survey.

delegates who took strong exception to the control wielded by the chair in keeping the flow of convention deliberations fast paced. One heard charges from some delegates that they couldn't get to a microphone in time or without the permission of a floor manager; that message passing and signals were widely used to instruct groups and delegations how to vote on a substantive or procedural issue.

These comments were the idea-source for the four items used to construct an index on *control of the conference.* Table 3.15 shows the response distribution of the four items in this index. There was, indeed, a fairly large proportion (21%) who took the view that resolutions were "railroaded through" or that floor management was not consistent with a democratic process (17%). But the vast majority of the delegates rejected the issue, either out of pragmatic experience and expectations concerning how a long agenda in a short time can be completed in a body as large as that in Houston, or whose own support for the Plan of Action encouraged their acceptance of floor management devices they may not have totally approved on general preference or ethical grounds.

Network Formation

We began the overview profile of the IWY sample by noting the extensive organizational networks within which the delegates have acted politically. One last set of questions from the February survey shows the process of network-building itself. To attend a conference as large as this one, and to mingle with other women from across the country whom you can realistically expect to be like yourself in their dedication to improving the position of women in American society, is to be highly predisposed toward doing what has been natural in American politics throughout our history: to talk, exchange names and addresses, and promise to "keep in touch." This is what network-building and constituency formation in politics is all about. Despite advance awareness of this tendency from observing interactions during the conference, in particular during the last day, I was astonished by the sheer number of new contacts the delegates report having made in Houston. The question clearly emphasized a "new" contact and a "definite plan to keep in touch," yet the 1120 women who responded to this question reported they had made 25,581 such contacts, for a mean of 22.4 new contacts per person! (See Table 3.16.)

Some portion of these new contacts, clearly, was from the ranks of the respondents' own state delegations, particularly in the large delegations in which delegates would find it difficult to become acquainted with very many people prior to their prolonged proximity to each other in Houston. These are vital new ties, however, for they provide a network for future political action

Table 3.16

Network Formation (in percent)[a]

NEW CONTACTS MADE IN HOUSTON	Mean	Distribution			
		None	1-5	6-15	16+
Own Community or City	5.2	49.3	25.2	15.6	9.9
Own State But Not Own City . . .	8.9	30.7	27.6	23.9	17.9
Other State	8.3	35.4	30.3	18.9	15.5

   Total # Contacts Made: 25,581 (1120)

   Mean Total No. Contacts: 22.4

[a]Question read: "What is your best estimate of the number of people
   you met for the first time in Houston with whom you plan to keep in
   touch?" Estimates given separately for "people from your own local
   community or city," "people from outside your city but within your
   state," and "people from another state." N shown is mean across the
   three items. Question 32a-c, February survey.

on a statewide rather than a local level. It is also clear that a large proportion
of the new contacts were made across state lines: One-third of the delegates
reported having made six or more new contacts in Houston with women from
other states, for a high mean of 8.3 cross-state contacts.

Houston Aftermath

Most delegates carried their responsibilities back home with them. When
asked whether they had engaged in any efforts to publicize the Houston
conference in their home communities, they reported a high level of such
activity: Eighty-six percent gave a talk about the conference to at least one
local group; 60% gave an interview to a local paper; and 52% appeared on a
local radio or television show. So too, a positive afterglow was evident in the
ratings of their overall level of satisfaction with the conference at three time
points: When they were leaving Houston, 1 week after Houston ended, and
the time they filled out the second survey (which varied from mid-February to
late March). The proportion giving top ratings of "very satisfied" declined
only slightly over this period, from 61% as they left Houston to 54% at the
time they filled in their questionnaires 3 or 4 months later.

Political Plans

There now remain only the measures of political aspirations and commitment to implementation of the resolutions to complete this introduction to the major variables in the study design. The most important measures concern personal interest in holding elective office in mainstream and movement politics.

Up to this point, response distributions shown in the tables were based on the total survey at either time. Now it is appropriate to restrict the cases to those who responded to *both* surveys, for it is this subsample on which a change analysis can be conducted. It should be noted, however, that no significant differences were found in aspirations or commitments between the full-survey samples and the panel subsample.[6]

Political Aspirations

The panel question on political aspirations was a direct, single-item measure of level of interest in seeking elective office. It was asked separately for public office (mainstream politics) and for women's rights organizations (movement politics) at each of three levels: local, state, and national. Table 3.17 shows the marginal distribution of responses to each of these six items for both October and February. Several essential points emerge from these responses. For one, there is a remarkably high level of interest in seeking elective office in both mainstream and movement politics. When we combine "moderate" and "high" interest levels, the range in October was from 26% for national public office to 58% for state office in a feminist organization. Second, interest levels are higher for local and state office than for national office, and this holds for both mainstream and movement political aspirations. Third, at every level, aspirations are higher for movement office than for mainstream office. Last, there is no evidence, at this rudimentary level of data presentation, of any dramatic surge of political aspirations as a consequence of the intervening experience of participation in the national conference. Indeed, in five of the six comparisons between October and February, there

[6]In no case did the difference exceed 1 or 2%. For example, there were 1288 people who answered the question concerning aspirations for elective office at the national level in the October survey, 963 of whom also answered the same survey question in February, a loss of 322 respondents. But the proportion who reported a high level of interest in a national public office differs by less than 1% between the two groups, 13.4% among the 1288 people who responded to the October survey, 12.6% among the 962 who responded to both surveys. The same pattern held in comparing the panel subsample with the total number who responded to the February survey.

Table 3.17

Mainstream and Movement Aspirations for Elective Office: October versus February (in percent)

OFFICE	LEVEL	SURVEY	LEVEL OF INTEREST				
			NONE	A LITTLE	MODERATE	HIGH	N
ELECTIVE PUBLIC OFFICE[a]	LOCAL	October	42.5	17.3	20.7	19.6	(968)
		February	39.6	18.9	21.0	20.5	(957)
	STATE	October	39.3	15.6	21.2	23.9	(970)
		February	39.1	18.5	20.2	22.2	(962)
	NATIONAL	October	58.2	15.6	13.6	12.6	(962)
		February	60.5	16.0	12.6	11.0	(948)
ELECTIVE OFFICE, WOMEN"S RIGHTS ORGAN.[b]	LOCAL	October	31.7	12.9	22.2	33.2	(955)
		February	34.5	13.2	19.7	32.6	(954)
	STATE	October	31.1	11.4	24.7	32.8	(953)
		February	35.6	12.4	20.4	31.5	(957)
	NATIONAL	October	35.9	14.4	21.8	27.9	(953)
		February	42.0	15.5	19.0	23.5	(953)

[a]Question 26a-c, October survey; Question 41a-c, February survey.

[b]Question 28a-c, October survey; Question 42a-c, February survey.

were fewer women with high aspirations after the conference than before (the exception being local public office).

If there was a tendency for roughly the same number of people to raise as to lower their political aspirations over the 5-month period between surveys, the response distribution shown in Table 3.17 may mask a good deal of individual change. It is only in a turnover table that we can gauge the extent to which aspirations were stable or changed during the 5-month period. Table 3.18 shows this change profile for the six types of political aspirations investigated. Assuming that it was the intervening experience of participation in the national conference that affected the changes in aspirations shown in Table 3.18, then it is clear that there were both positive and negative impacts upon the delegates' aspirations. A good deal of change took place on all six measures of political aspirations. A "much lower" rating means, for example, a shift from October to February from a "high" to a "low" level of interest or from a "moderate" to "no" interest in the office in question.

It is only local public office that shows a net increase in aspirations over time. The predominant impact, if this can be attributed to the conference

Table 3.18

Change in Mainstream and Movement Aspirations for Elective Office from October to February (in percent)

CHANGE PATTERN	Mainstream			Movement		
	Local	State	National	Local	State	National
Much Lower[a]	11.6	10.4	12.7	15.0	14.6	16.4
Lower	9.6	10.9	10.6	11.9	13.1	14.4
No Change	55.3	60.3	61.0	52.0	52.0	52.2
Higher	10.6	9.5	7.3	10.2	11.2	8.4
Much Higher	12.9	8.9	8.4	10.9	9.1	8.6
100% =	(944)	(951)	(933)	(930)	(932)	(927)
Net Change in Percent[b]	+2.3	-2.9	-7.6	-5.8	-7.4	-13.8

[a] Lower level of aspiration in February than in October.

[b] Sum of raised aspirations minus sum of lowered aspirations; hence a "-" indicates extent to which there was more lowering than raising of aspirations over the five month period.

experience, was in the direction of lowered, not raised, aspirations. This is particularly the case for women's rights organizations. As seen from the summary net change figures in the last row of Table 3.18, at each level, the balance is more strongly tipped to lower aspirations for movement office than for mainstream office. It will be a major task of the analysis in Chapter 8 to explore why it was that some women showed a lowering of political aspirations while others reported higher levels of aspirations in February than in October. Another task will be to explore why the overall change was more negative concerning feminist organization prominence than concerning mainstream political prominence.

Implementation of Resolutions

The delegates were asked to rate whether they would "probably" or "definitely" work for the implementation of each of the 26 resolutions voted on in Houston. Since it seemed likely in December, when this instrument was designed, that there would also be a minority of delegates who would work against some of the resolutions, it seemed important to assess the extent of such opposition for each of the 26 resolutions. In the interest of saving space in the instrument, a composite response category was used that included degrees of active support, no activity, or active opposition to each resolution. There were very few cases of active opposition, however; on average fewer than 2% of the delegates were actively opposed. Only four issues showed active opposition reaching 3% or more: 3.5% on child care, 5% on ERA ratification, 7.5% on reproductive freedom, and 9.1% on sexual preference. This ranking probably reflects the intensity of feeling among those who voted against these resolutions. In light of the small number of cases in the active opposition category, they were combined with "no activity" in Table 3.19 and appear simply as "no plan to be active."

The resolutions are ranked in Table 3.19 from highest to lowest commitment to personal political efforts to implement the resolutions. A predictable top priority is efforts to ratify the ERA. It is somewhat surprising to note a few "new" issues very high on the rank order along with longstanding major concerns of the feminist movement: Battered wives, child abuse, and rape are among the top 10 priorities for intended future political action, along with employment, education, politics, abortion, child care, and problems of minority women. Somewhat more specialized interests are clustered at the bottom of the ranking: issues of personal concern to relatively few women (rural women, artists and humanists, women in business); issues very recent in their emergence (statistics on women, insurance); or issues like sexual preference, which has top priority to relatively few women in a personal sense and poses complex political problems for many otherwise dedicated feminist activists.

Since the specific resolutions that would be in the national Plan of Action were not known in detail at the time the first survey was fielded in October, I did not ask about past political efforts on all the issues that were finally embedded in the 26 resolutions voted on in Houston. Hence there was no way to design an exact repetition of items to serve as panel measures of past and future political activity on feminist issues. Three of the 16 issues included in the October survey were not among the final resolutions in the Plan of Action (sexuality, family planning, housing). Not on our October list, but appearing as Houston resolutions were: child abuse, credit, battered wives, disabled women, arts–humanities, elective–appointive office, insurance, minority women, criminal offenders, statistics, and welfare and poverty. Under these circumstances, I opted to let the data on implementation speak for themselves, by constructing indices for those issue items that clustered most strongly in the post-Houston survey without regard to whether they matched an issue included in the October survey. In addition, a total score

Table 3.19

Political Commitment to Implementation of Resolutions in Plan of Action (in percent)[a]

RESOLUTION TOPIC	Commitment		
	No Plan to be Active [b]	Probably Active	Definitely Active
Equal Rights Amendment	12.6	13.9	73.5
Battered Women	22.8	34.4	42.8
Employment	26.9	25.9	47.1
Minority Women	29.9	26.6	43.6
Education	30.2	28.8	41.1
Elective/Appointive Office . . .	30.5	26.2	43.3
Child Abuse	31.7	30.3	37.7
Reproductive Freedom	36.3	18.9	44.9
Child Care	36.9	30.1	33.0
Rape	32.9	28.8	38.3
Homemakers	37.7	27.6	34.7
Women, Welfare and Poverty . . .	40.3	27.5	32.2
Older Women	40.4	26.9	32.7
Health	40.9	28.1	31.1
Credit	46.8	25.8	27.4
Disabled Women	50.7	24.9	24.5
Committee of the Conference . .	52.2	19.9	27.9
Media	52.3	25.5	22.3
Offenders	52.9	24.4	22.6
Business	53.3	24.4	22.3
Rural Women	54.8	23.3	22.0
Insurance	58.8	20.0	20.2
International Affairs	59.7	19.3	21.0
Sexual Preference	60.9	18.4	20.7
Arts and Humanities	61.4	20.5	18.1
Statistics	69.8	14.4	15.8

[a] Cf. Appendix C for full wording of these resolutions.

[b] Question 40a-z, February survey, "No plan to be active" includes a very small proportion who report they will work against the resolution. Cf. text.

was constructed, based on anticipated activity level over all 26 resolutions, the closest parallel to the total score on past activity across the 16 issues tapped in the first survey.

Intentions have softer edges than past behavior, with the result that the correlations among the 26 issues in planned future activity tend to be quite high. It was necessary to raise the criterion to a correlation coefficient of r = .50 for acceptance of items in a subscore. One cluster with correlations from r = .62 to r = .71 consists of resolutions on rape, battered wives, and child abuse, suggesting a focus on *victims of violence.* A second cluster, with coefficients ranging from r = .52 to r = .67, suggest a focus on *victims of society:* Minority women, welfare and poverty, criminal offenders, disabled women, older women, health, and rural or farming women are included in this cluster. The third, unexpected cluster, concerns *money management,* with coefficients ranging from r = .57 to r = .69. It includes the four resolutions dealing with business, credit, insurance, and statistics. These three subscores, together with the composite index on all 26 issues, will be used in the analysis reported in subsequent chapters.

There is, of course, a strong and positive relation between past feminist activity and plans to be active in the future. The correlation between the two composite scores of past and planned political activity is r = +.461. There are, however, important differences in the level of association when past and planned activity is specified in terms of issue sphere. Table 3.20 shows the extent to which past concentration on sex-linked and gender-linked issues relate to political action plans. Those who have been active on public gender roles in such areas as education, employment, and politics tend to anticipate political action at a higher level on all issues than those whose efforts have been focused on private sex-linked questions such as sexual preference, sexuality, or abortion (i.e., all the correlations between past *gender*-related activity and future activity are higher than the correlations between past *sex*-linked activity and future political action).

Since the 1960s, the feminist movement has broadened its agenda to embrace an increasingly diverse range of issues. It may be that individuals who were active in 1970 have added new issues to their private spectrum of concerns that motivate their political action. Women who first became active feminists only in recent years may tend to work on a narrower range of issues. This may be why women who have been active on gender-linked issues like economic discrimination are more likely to express commitment to future work on the sex-linked issues in the *Victims of Violence* index (r = .405) than women whose past activities centered on sex-linked issues tend to show for future gender-linked activity in the *Victims of Society* index (r = .224).

Since there was no exact issue replication in the two surveys, I can only sketch the turnover profile for the 12 issues for which activity ratings were

Table 3.20

Past and Future Feminist Political Activity (Pearson correlation coefficients)

| | P a s t   F e m i n i s t   A c t i v i t y | | |
FUTURE FEMINIST ACTIVITY LEVEL	Sex-Linked Activity	Gender-Linked Activity	Total Activity Level
Victims of Violence	+.313[a]	+.405	+.417
Victims of Society	+.224	+.469	+.415
Money Management	+.146	+.410	+.356
Total Future Activity Level	+.271	+.481	+.461

[a]All coefficients are significant at .001 level.   Base Ns range from
819 to 926 cases.

obtained in both surveys. Section A in Table 3.21 brings forward some of the
results shown in Table 3.7 on the level of past political activity on the 12
issues. The profile of change shown in Section B of Table 3.21 is assessed
against them, and the ratios of expectations for more activity versus less
activity are shown in Section C of Table 3.21.

Despite the high level of political activity on ERA ratification that characterized the delegates in the past, the balance is tipped to even greater effort in
the future, with a ratio of 2.95 between increased and decreased effort. The
plight of rural women was the issue on which the least amount of political
effort was reported in October (only 22% of the delegates), and shows the
greatest change when future plans are compared to past efforts: Six times as
many delegates expect to be more active as plan to be less active
than they have been on this issue. It was our impression, from informal conversations, that many women from large urban centers first came
to appreciate the special problems confronting women in rural and farm areas
through contacts with rural members of their own and other state delegations,
much as American women have learned to see women's issues in a different
light when they have had contact with women from underdeveloped countries. The shift shown so dramatically in Table 3.21 in the increased plans for
future attention to problems of rural women may reflect these urban–rural
encounters among the delegates. Only two issues show a balance tipped to
less, rather than more, activity in the future. On education and employment,
there are more delegates who report lower activity plans for the future than

Table 3.21

Change and Stability of Political Action on Selected Issues:
Past Political Action versus Future Action on Resolution Implementation

ISSUE	A. % ACTIVE ON ISSUE IN PAST	B. FUTURE ACTIVITY RELATIVE TO PAST ACTIVITY			C. CHANGE RATIO: More:Less[a]
		Will be MORE Active	No Change	Will be LESS Active	
ERA	84.4%	23.0	69.1	7.8	2.95
Education	81.6%	19.4	52.9	27.7	.57
Employment . . .	80.1%	21.0	56.3	22.7	.92
Child Care . . .	67.9%	28.8	50.3	20.8	1.38
Abortion	67.4%	31.3	51.6	17.1	1.83
Health	62.2%	30.1	48.6	21.2	1.42
Homemakers . . .	62.2%	30.3	50.6	19.2	1.58
Rape	59.5%	34.7	49.9	15.5	2.24
Media	50.0%	24.9	53.2	21.9	1.14
Sex Preference .	38.2%	19.7	67.4	12.8	1.53
International Relations	36.7%	23.7	62.7	13.6	1.74
Farm/Rural . . .	22.5%	36.8	57.3	6.0	6.22
Base N:	(1544) October Survey	(983) Panel Subsample			

[a]Ratios below 1.00 indicate less activity in future than in past; ratios above 1.00 indicate more activity planned in future than shown in past.

had reported past political activity in the October survey. Concern for schools and colleges may be specific to life span phase: Once having left school or campus, feminists may take their concerns into a larger community context, shifting, for example, from student health care to women's health centers, or sexism in textbooks to issues of credit, political opportunity, or displaced homemakers. It may also be the case that the anticipated hard push for ERA

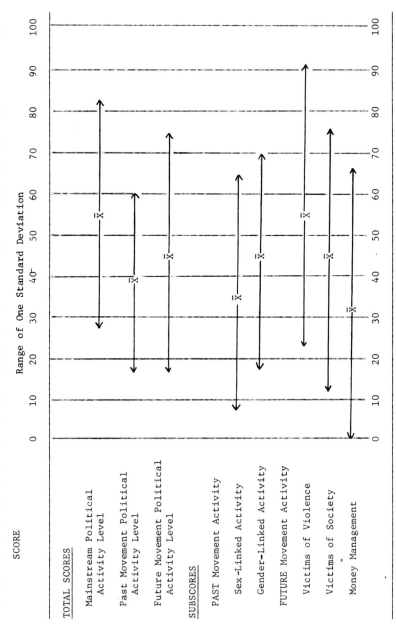

Figure 3.2. Movement and mainstream political activity level: Mean and range of one standard deviation on scores converted to 0–100.

ratification is seen by many delegates as the best route to expand women's opportunities in education and employment. Should the amendment fail to become ratified, there may be a new resurgence of political effort on specific issues affecting women in education and the economy.

Variance in Political Activity Level

Although the delegates showed a higher level of consensus on affect and belief measures, there was a great deal of variance among them on both past and future political activity levels. This is apparent in the percentage distributions on the items and on the score range shown for the indices in previous tables. To bring these political activity measures together in one place and in a way that permits comparison, the indices have been converted to a $0-100$ score range in Figure 3.2, where we can gain a comparative sense of both the sample average (as measured by the mean) and the amount of variance (as measured by 1 S.D.) on the indicators of political activity introduced in this chapter. An inspection of Figure 3.2 shows in a graphic way, the considerable variance that exists on the indices of political activity, both past and present. Past mainstream political activity has been higher than past feminist political activity. A comparison of future with past activity level as measured by the subscores suggests a heightened commitment to action dealing with sex-linked, victim-of-violence issues in the future.

More important, all the political activity measures show a good deal of variance, which suggests there is a lot of room within which to explore and explain the pattern of political commitment and aspiration among the delegates to the national conference. It is to this exploration that the remaining chapters are devoted.

4

Conference Organization and Political Behavior

Introduction

The formal organization of the Houston conference was an unusual hybrid of two familiar forms in American political and government life: a political party convention and a national commission. The analogy to a political party convention was apparent to anyone viewing the sweep of the Coliseum floor through the eye of a television camera or from an observer's post in the gallery: There were delegates seated by state, sections marked off for the press, television cameras, invited guests, and observers, and a gallery for the public. On the other hand, the conference was organized and administered not by an ongoing political party, but by a temporary, executive-appointed national commission. Like other national commissions, as described in Chapter 1, the IWY Commission reflected the administration in executive power at the time of its appointment and reappointment. The use of a Secretariat staff to provide information, prepare reports, and otherwise facilitate the work of the IWY Commissioners was similar to the organization of other national commissions, a similarity that extended to the requirement of a final report from the IWY Commission to the president and the Congress.

On the other hand, the chief responsibility of the IWY Commission was the organization of a national conference of elected delegates. Here the IWY Commission leaned on the familiar device of state elections and the situational device of seating state delegations together and taking formal votes on a set of resolutions. No other format for the seating of delegates was even considered by the IWY Commission; an inquiry about the rationale for following the format of a political party convention at an IWY Commission meeting was greeted by the presiding officer and many IWY Commissioners with a blank and uncomprehending silence. How else could a body as large as this one be managed in a way that would permit us to get through a complex and controversial agenda?

The purpose of this chapter is to examine the characteristics of those who occupied the six formal status positions involved in the conference: The elected delegates, elected alternates, appointed delegates-at-large, the Secretariat staff, the Ford Commissioners and the Carter Commissioners. Several of these status categories were further differentiated by office and function. At the top of the organizational structure, the Presiding Officer, Bella Abzug, was aided by three dozen or so national IWY Commissioners. The Secretariat staff was headed by an Executive Director, Kathryn Clarenbach. The elected delegates were divided among 55 states and territories, each headed by a chairperson. Only the elected alternates and the delegates-at-large lacked any formal leader, chairperson, or officer.

But even with this degree of functional differentiation of duties, the formal leadership structure was unwieldy for any smooth operation of potentially controversial and disruptive plenary sessions. Hence there was also an informal smaller organizational structure limited to those with a good deal of political experience and dedication to the successful endorsement of the Plan of Action. This informal structure was a four-tier organization of which many who attended or observed the conference were probably unaware. It can only be sketched in broad strokes here, with no identification of specific individuals involved, since my knowledge of its composition and operation involved privileged access as an IWY Commissioner as much as observation as a researcher.[1]

The major outline of this informal structure can be described by drawing on an analogy to the military. The four tiers consisted of the following categories:

1. *The generals,* or *key managers,* of the conference were the Presiding Officer and 3 national IWY Commissioners who had a considerable

---

[1] It was the major responsibility of the three research assistants who attended the Houston conference with me to position themselves at various posts on the floor of the Coliseum in order to observe and report on the structure and function of this informal control system. They took brief notes while on the floor and later amplified them on tape recorders in our hotel suite. Once back in Amherst, Massachusetts, the tapes were transcribed and staff meetings held to discuss and compare field observations. These reports and discussions were invaluable sources for the design of the second wave questionnaire, and for the informal organizational sketch in the text. Grateful acknowledgement is here made to Cindy Deitch, Ruth Backes, and Janet Gans for their help in this endeavor.

amount of experience in party politics or in organizations that have engaged in lobbying efforts in connection with Congress or the national parties.

2. *The captains* consisted of 11 state delegation chairpersons who convened the Pro-Plan Caucus in New York City to coordinate political efforts in Houston to assure the adoption of the national Plan. Several IWY Commissioners also served as captains.

3. *The lieutenants* were key delegates scattered through a number of delegations or from the amorphous delegate-at-large body, thus widening the network outward from the 11 delegations in which captains served as pivots for quick decision making as the business of the plenary sessions was conducted. The captains and lieutenants carried the responsibility for signaling delegations (or the Pro-Plan portion of a delegation) on how to respond as resolutions before the body underwent the amendment or substitution process.

4. *The corporals* consisted of about 10 young women with access to the floor who had been hand-picked by the Presiding Officer. They served as message-bearing "runners" between the generals close to or on the podium and the lieutenants and captains at various spots on the floor of the Coliseum. These *runners* ran down the aisles with messages and provided the connective tissue tying together the four tiers of the informal organizational structure of the conference during the plenary sessions.

An informal structure of this sort is commonly found at political party conventions, the only difference between the two types being that the political activity of the former is as advocates of a particular set of resolutions rather than of particular candidates for nomination to the presidency and vice-presidency. But the existence of the informal structure of the national women's conference was not public knowledge even to all of the IWY Commissioners, much less to the larger delegate body or to those in Houston as observers and media reporters.[2]

Nor was it clear, in advance of the conference itself, exactly how this informal structure would function. Many state delegations held meetings before they arrived in Houston at which they gave careful consideration to the tentative Plan of Action, formulated amendments to resolutions in the Plan, or drew up additional resolutions they hoped to submit for discussion and a vote

[2]It was a source of amusement to my staff when a leading newspaper printed a picture described as a "typical group of delegates exchanging news and opinions" that we recognized as a huddle of generals and captains making procedural decisions to get over a parliamentary snag in the deliberations. The most detailed and accurate depiction of the structure and workings of this informal organization was published by the *Village Voice* in New York City the week following the conference.

in Houston. Many such hopes were frustrated as the Pro-Plan Caucus applied pressure to minimize amendments or substitution moves, if only to assure that the whole agenda was covered in the time available in the four major plenary sessions. At the IWY Commissioners' meeting late Friday, the night before the first plenary session, there was still open discussion about how to proceed. Several people connected with the New York delegation and the national IWY Commission argued for a quick adoption of the Plan as it then stood, leaving amendments to "new business" on the agenda for the last plenary session on Monday morning. Legal counsel and several IWY Commissioners argued against this on the grounds that a resolution, once passed, could not later be amended; others warned that many delegations and caucuses were prepared to submit amendments and would be angry if deprived of an opportunity to do so. The outcome of the discussion was on the side of an open amendment process, subject only to the powers of persuasion by the lieutenants and captains in the informal structure to curb and channel this process, using the promise that resolutions not considered in Houston would be reviewed under new business at the last Houston session or, following the conference, by the IWY Commission.

I do not know whether the Anti-Plan Caucus had a comparable informal structure to rally votes for or against particular resolutions, since I was not privy to its deliberations and had limited vantage points to observe any such structure in operation during the plenary sessions. My research assistants, who had access to the floor, were not sure whether or how this might have operated, although it was clear, on some resolutions, that response had been well organized in advance (e.g., the demonstration on the floor after the delegates voted favorably on the Reproductive Freedom resolution).

Cutting across the formal organizational structure and working either with or against the informal structure were a variety of organizations and caucuses whose activities centered on specific issues. Their presence was highly visible in the form of ribbons, buttons, and armbands that adorned the delegates, supplementing the symbols most states adopted (flowers, hats, scarves, buttons, and armbands) to identify the delegations away from their seats on the floor of the Coliseum. Many delegates carried six or more such identifying symbols on their persons, making for as colorful imagery on the television screen as in the situation itself. Several organizations had conference headquarters, press staffs, their own caucuses, and special scheduled events. Thus, for example, NOW had permanent headquarters on the eighth floor of the Hyatt Regency Hotel for registration, press releases, messages, and coordination of caucus efforts. Despite the fullness of the formal agenda of the conference, NOW held NOW Delegate Caucus meetings, NOW Observer meetings, a reception, and press conferences. The National Abortion Rights Action

League (NARAL), similarly, held a reception for Pro-Choice delegates and contributed to caucuses and workshops on abortion and related issues.

There were two characteristics of the conference that departed markedly from political party conventions. The successful outreach of the state committees assured a more heterogeneous delegate body than is typical of party conventions (at least until the precedent-breaking conventions in 1972) with regard to race and ethnicity. Any camera sweep of the plenary sessions caught the conspicuous presence of significant numbers of Black, Latina, Native-American, Asian-American, and Pacific-American women. Related to this diversity was the spread in the level of occupational and political experience in the delegate body: There were women on welfare as well as state-court judges; experienced politicians as well as women away from their home communities for the first time for any purpose other than family visits. The second marked contrast to party conventions was the conspicuous absence of men, who appeared in any number at all only as observers or visitors in the gallery or camera crewmen on the floor. No man wielded a gavel. One delegate's observation sums it up:

> If it weren't for the state banners and the nature of the resolutions on the agenda, the closest thing in my experience to Houston was a national convention of nurses, where women filled both the floor and the podium.

The diverse social characteristics of the participants in Houston will be encountered as quantitative variables in the chapters to follow. The caucuses and ongoing ties to organizations will also appear as part of the analysis of what happened in Houston and what impact political activity there had on the delegates' perceptions of their roles and on their plans for the future. In this chapter, we concentrate on the official positions they held *as* delegates and contrast them with alternates, Secretariat staff members, and IWY Commissioners. Hence this chapter provides an aggregate portrait, a sketch of the similarities and differences among the six status positions in the formal organization of the conference. It sketches their personal background, political and organizational experience, what they did during the conference, and what they have carried away from it.

Organizational Categories at the Conference

Since the profile covers both the expectations of the respondents (as provided in the October survey) and their actual experience and roles in Houston (reported in the February survey), the analysis is restricted to the panel subsample that responded to both waves of the study.[3] The categories to be described, together with their numerical and proportional representation in the panel sample, are as follows:

Category	Number	Percentage
Elected delegates	701	71.3
Elected alternates	110	11.2
Appointed delegates-at-large	120	12.2
Carter Commissioners	21	2.1
Ford Commissioners	14	1.4
Secretariat staff	17	1.7
	983	

In Chapter 2 we explored the response rate from five of these six categories (all but the delegates-at-large). It is a useful reminder, particularly in light of the small numbers in the Secretariat staff and IWY Commissioner categories, to briefly sketch the major respects in which the panel respondents differ from the total population in each of the status positions of interest in this chapter.

Elected Delegates and Elected Alternates

Compared to the total elected delegate and alternate population, the respondents in these positions include fewer low-income and more high-income women; fewer radicals or conservatives, more very liberal women; more white, fewer racial and ethnic minorities; more Jewish and agnostic women, and fewer Catholics (Tables 2.3 and 2.4).

Secretariat Staff

Respondents were more apt to be top administrative and professional staff members than secretarial and clerical members, and the professional staff are

[3]The reader should be alerted to the fact that the substantive chapters of the book are based on this panel subsample of 983 respondents, even when all the variables in a particular analysis stem from one rather than from both surveys. While the case N at numerous points could have been much larger had I opted to work with all three samples (the full October survey, the full February survey, and the panel subsample), such a decision would also have produced confusingly large differences in case Ns across the tables in the book. The response pattern analysis supported the choice of simplying the analysis by restriction to the panel subsample, since there were only minor differences between those who responded to only one survey rather than both. The differences found are greater between refusals and respondents than between one versus two-wave respondents. Since 983 cases are sufficient for any statistical analysis reported in the book, this lent further justification to the decision. One last reason will become evident in later chapters dealing with change analysis, where the same set of predictor variables are regressed on panel variables measured in October compared to February.

more feminist in their personal identification than are the total staff (Table 2.11).

IWY Commissioners

Both Carter and Ford Commissioner respondents were less apt to be political representatives and more apt to represent a variety of organizations than were either of the total IWY Commissions (Table 2.9). On a subjective rating of the decision-making role of the Carter Commissioners, respondents were more apt to be at the middle level of decision making as adjutants of the core leaders and less apt to be either the generals in the informal structure or symbolic appointees who rarely attended IWY Commission meetings (Table 2.10).[4]

Delegates-at-Large

No response pattern analysis was possible here, but it should be remembered that there were two categories of at-large delegates, those appointed as representatives of specific organizations and those appointed as individuals to round out the representation profile of the total delegate body. Since only the individuals invited to serve as at-large delegates were known at the time of the first survey, the panel subsample includes no organizational representatives in the at-large delegate category.

Socioeconomic Characteristics

An inspection of Table 4.1 quickly shows that there was more diversity in socioeconomic characteristics *within* the status category positions than *between* them: IWY Commissioners and Secretariat staff members, like the delegate body itself, show considerable variation in educational attainment and income level. On the other hand, more than one-half of every status position shows educational attainment beyond a college degree. The majority, in all six groups, were employed full-time, although homemakers are slightly more prevalent among the elected alternates. Secretariat staff members are, by definition, in the work force. There is also great variance in the

---

[4]Note that, in the response pattern analysis, those people who served on both Commissions were counted twice so that the comparison of respondents was with the total, larger Commissions appointed by the two presidents. In the classification used in the analysis in this chapter, the Ford Commissioners reappointed by President Carter are included only as Carter Commissioners since it is their responsibilities as Commissioners in relation to the national conference that is relevant to the analysis.

Table 4.1

Socioeconomic Characteristics by Conference Status Position (in percent)

| CHARACTERISTIC | Elected | | Delegates | Commissioners | | Staff |
	Delegates	Alternates	At Large	Carter	Ford	
EDUCATIONAL ATTAINMENT						
Some High School or Less	7.9	10.1	7.7	9.5	--	--
Some College/College Graduate	32.1	39.5	32.5	28.6	45.5	29.4
Some Graduate Work/ Master's Degree . .	45.0	40.4	41.8	47.6	36.4	52.9
Advanced Degree . . .	15.0	10.1	18.0	14.3	18.2	17.7
EMPLOYMENT STATUS						
Full Time	60.0	61.7	62.0	71.4	63.6	88.3
Part Time	18.0	7.5	14.0	19.0	18.2	11.7
Not Employed	21.0	30.8	24.0	9.6	18.2	--
OWN ANNUAL EARNINGS						
(1976) Under $10,000 .	22.6	40.2	25.0	15.8	25.0	5.9
$10,000-$20,000 . . .	39.5	48.3	26.9	21.1	12.5	58.8
$20,000-$30,000 . . .	16.6	6.9	27.0	15.8	37.2	29.4
$30,000 or More . . .	4.7	4.6	21.2	47.4	25.0	5.9
TOTAL FAMILY INCOME						
(1976) Percent $30,000 or More . . .	36.3%	37.0%	45.8%	71.4%	80.0%	35.3%
N[a] =	(699)	(108)	(119)	(21)	(14)	(17)

[a]There is slight variation in base N from one variable to another.

earning levels shown by women in all six groups, although here the IWY Commissioners and the appointed delegates stand out in having a much higher proportion with high earnings than the elected delegates and alternates: Whereas only one in ten of the elected alternates had earned more than $20,000 the preceding year, this held for more than *one-half* of both the Ford and Carter Commissioners. The same profile holds for total family income, with *one-third* of the delegates and Secretariat staff members reporting incomes over $30,000, whereas roughly *three-quarters* of the IWY Commissioners did so. A comparison of the respondents' earnings with their total family income at this high level suggests that a larger proportion of the Carter Commissioners provided a significant proportion of the total income of their households than was true for the Ford Commissioners. On the other hand, low earnings (under $10,000) is a characteristic of at least *one-fifth* of the women in all status categories except the Secretariat staff.

Not reported (because there were no striking differences) are the ethnic and religious affiliations of the women in the varied status positions. The Ford and Carter Commissioners show profiles very little different from the elected delegates in this respect. The only significant contrast was the profile of the Secretariat staff, over 90% of whom were white, and which included twice as many women with no religious affiliation (35.3%) as any other group (other groups averaged about 15%).

Political Characteristics

The sharpest difference among status positions in political characteristics is the predictable contrast between Ford and Carter Commissioners. Ford Commissioners were either Republicans or Independents, whereas Carter Commissioners were either Democrats or leaning that way, with no Independents among them. There is clearly greater similarity of political orientation and party affiliation between the Carter Commissioners and the delegates than between the Carter and the Ford Commissioners. Despite their greater tendency to party Independents, the Ford appointees were twice as likely to have campaigned for Ford in the 1976 election as were Carter Commissioners to have campaigned for Carter.

The Secretariat staff profile shows a much greater tip to the very liberal or radical end of the political continuum and consistently much less tendency to be affiliated with the Republican party than any other status position. The Secretariat staff's profile is of relatively firm beliefs but little political affiliation or activity: Few had campaigned for either candidate, none had held elective office at any point in the past, although one-fifth had held appointive office (often on state commissions on the status of women). Both Commissioner categories have had more actual political experience (both elective and appointive) in public office than any other category. Last, there was a slightly larger representation of conservative views and party affiliation among the elected alternates than among the other delegate types. This accounted for the considerable pressure felt by many delegates to remain on the floor during the plenary sessions so that their places would not be taken by the more conservative alternates.

Table 4.2

Political Characteristics by Conference Status Position (in percent)

CHARACTERISTIC	Elected Delegates	Elected Alternates	Delegates At Large	Commissioners Carter	Commissioners Ford	Staff
POLITICAL ORIENTATION						
Radical	8.6	7.3	4.9	5.0	--	11.8
Very Liberal	41.2	28.4	32.0	35.0	18.2	47.1
Liberal-Moderate . . .	45.2	51.4	59.8	60.0	45.5	29.4
Conservative	5.0	12.8	3.3	--	36.4	11.8
POLITICAL PARTY						
Republican	8.5	18.7	8.3	10.6	45.5	--
Independent, lean to Republican	2.8	2.8	3.3	5.3	9.1	5.9
Independent	8.1	9.4	5.0	--	36.4	17.6
Independent, lean to Democratic	20.9	23.4	20.7	36.9	--	29.4
Democratic	59.9	45.8	62.8	47.3	9.1	47.0
1976 CAMPAIGN PARTICIPATION						
% campaigned for Carter	31.3%	20.4%	30.6%	30.0%	--	6.3%
% campaigned for Ford	6.6%	13.9%	5.0%	10.0%	72.7%	--
OFFICE HOLDING[a]						
Held Elective Office .	,16.6	15.7	10.2	25.0	27.3	--
Held Appointive Office	31.9	23.1	23.0	56.3	63.7	23.5
Neither	62.9	73.1	71.8	43.8	36.4	76.5
N =	(698)	(110)	(119)	(21)	(14)	(17)

[a]Percentages exceed 100% since many held both elective and appointive office.

Organizational Membership

The remarkably high level of organizational membership in this sample has already been noted (Table 3.3). Since voluntary associations are a major conduit for political action and the development of political careers, the study gathered rich detail on organizational membership. A good deal of variance can be expected on the organizational membership profile of the six conference status positions.

With six status positions to be compared across a half-dozen or so types of organizations, it is useful to follow an analysis procedure that simplifies the patterns to be described. There were several key questions to be put to the data: Are there significant differences across the six status positions in organizational and political characteristics? Do the status positions cluster differently from one characteristic to another? Which status positions are most alike, which are most dissimilar? To answer such questions, two major procedures were followed. For one, an analysis of variance determined whether there were any statistically significant differences across the six status positions. Second, the Duncan Multiple Range Test was used to determine which groups were most alike, and which were most dissimilar. (The Duncan Test gives a systematic procedure for comparing all possible pairs of group means and clusters those groups into homogeneous subsets whose means are not significantly different from an alpha level set at .05.)

The results of the first application of these two procedures can be seen in Figure 4.1, but they require a few words of explanation to facilitate reading the figure. (This same mode of analysis will be followed on other topics in the remainder of this chapter as well as in Chapter 6 on the structures of affect and belief.) The results of significance tests in the analysis of variance are shown in brackets below the variable label in the left-hand column. They indicate whether or not the mean scores shown on each type of organizational membership differ significantly among the six status categories. Thus, for example, the six status positions differ significantly on political organization membership but not on feminist organization membership or involvement in liberal causes.

The specific level of organizational membership associated with each status position is measured by the mean number of organizations shown in brackets either directly below or to the right of each status position in the figure. Thus, for example, Figure 4.1 shows that Carter Commissioners belong to a mean of 17.3 organizations, whereas the Secretariat staff members show a mean organizational membership of only 7.4.

The oval shapes in Figure 4.1 cluster the six status categories into the subsets shown by the Duncan procedure: Categories within a particular subset show no significant differences in mean organizational membership level.

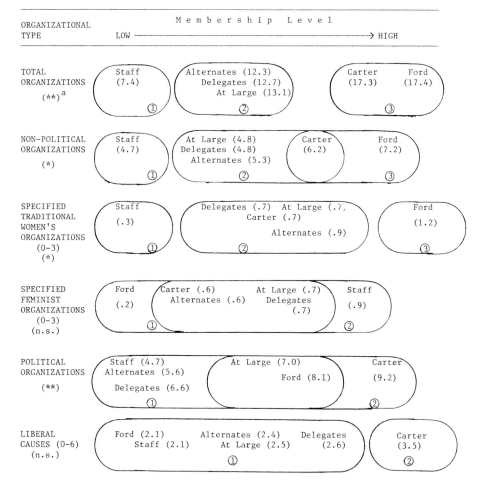

a Significance level on oneway analysis of variance. Cf. text for description of Duncan Subset classification procedure and convention for substantive data presentation in this analysis.

"Delegates" are the elected delegates; "at large" the appointed delegates.
  * p ≤ .05
  ** p ≤ .01

Figure 4.1. Membership level in selected types of organizations by conference status position: Subsets and mean membership.

Overlapping ovals indicate that particular status categories are not significantly different from the means of two subsets. In some cases, of course, the differences between means are so minor one can almost be certain by inspection that they are not significantly different. Carter Commissioners who show a mean of 17.3 organizations are certainly not different from Ford Commissioners with a mean of 17.4. Hence they both appear in the same subset in the top row of Figure 4.1. All three types of delegates (elected delegates, alternates and appointed delegates) are similarly alike in showing moderate levels of total organizational membership (Subset 2 in the top row of Figure 4.1). By contrast, the Secretariat staff shows a significantly lower membership level than any other status type, as indicated by its position in a separate subset.

The number of subsets can be seen both by inspection and by the circled numbers within the ovals shown in the figure. Subsets typically range from 1 to at most 5 in Tables 4.1 and 4.2, but, in all cases, the subsets are ordered in relation to the dependent variables. Thus, on total organizational membership, Secretariat staff members are demarcated as a separate subset (1) with the lowest organizational membership mean ($M = 7.4$) to the left of the row, the Ford Commissioners in subset (3) to the right of the row, with the highest organizational membership mean ($M = 17.4$).

Following a given status position down Figure 4.1 provides an overview of that group's organizational profile in relation to the other status positions. Thus, for example, the Ford Commissioners show a very high total organizational membership and are similarly high in membership in nonpolitical and traditional women's organizations. The Carter Commissioners differ from the Ford Commissioners in showing the highest political organizational membership and involvement in liberal causes. Secretariat staff members are consistently in a separate, low membership subset or share a low membership level subset with other status groups. Secretariat staff members are joiners only in feminist organizations. Indeed, when membership was examined in two specific organizations in the feminist code (NOW and NARAL), we found that 66% of the Secretariat staff members were NOW members, compared to about 38% of the Carter Commissioners and only 18% of the Ford Commissioners. None of the Ford appointees belong to NARAL, but an average of one in four in all other status categories are members (data not shown).

The three categories of delegates and alternates differ from each other on only one of the organizational membership indices: Appointed delegates show high membership in political organizations, more like the IWY Commissioners than the alternates and Secretariat staff members. This is at odds with our expectation: Since the appointment of delegates-at-large was heavily influenced by the desire to diversify the delegate body, we expected them to be less involved in political, and more involved in nonpolitical, organizations compared to other delegates. That the reverse holds may indicate that those appointed delegates who responded to the survey tended to be more politicized women.

Political Activity

Figure 4.2 brings together the major indices of mainstream and movement political activity in recent years, as well as the index of political competence. The strongest group differences are shown on the latter index, with Ford Commissioners showing the highest mean score on political competence and Secretariat staff members the lowest, a pattern consistent with the level of experience these two groups show in mainstream politics. It is the Ford Commissioners who were most active in the 1976 presidential campaign, just as they show (in the second row of Figure 4.2), the highest level of past activity in mainstream politics. Carter Commissioners show mainstream political activity levels closer to the delegates than to the Ford Commissioners. (It should be remembered, however, that those Carter Commissioners who have been most prominent in national party politics did not respond to the surveys and hence are not represented here.)

On past political activity in the feminist movement, the delegates themselves take the lead with the highest mean on movement activity level. They are followed by the Commissioners. Only a few Commissioners were appointed because of their involvement in such issues as sexuality, family planning, abortion reform, or sexual preference, whereas many delegates had the support of local groups with whom they had worked on precisely these issues. It is of interest that Secretariat staff members do not show any elevation of activity on these issues despite their very liberal political orientation and high membership in feminist organizations.

Part of the reason for this low political activity level among the Secretariat staff may be the demanding nature of their jobs. If ever there was a group whose jobs were themselves the channels for contributing to feminist political efforts, it is the Secretariat staff. Indeed, all of them responded a "great deal" when asked to what extent they contribute to women's rights efforts on their jobs. Women in other status positions also show lower employment profiles or are working in occupations with few legitimate outlets for feminist efforts, so they have been obliged to seek out specifically political contexts for feminist activity.

But this is not the whole story. Another aspect emerges when the status categories are examined for their subjective response to the passage of four specific resolutions (ERA, Minorities, Reproductive Freedom, and Sexual Preference). As anyone might expect who witnessed the scene when the ERA

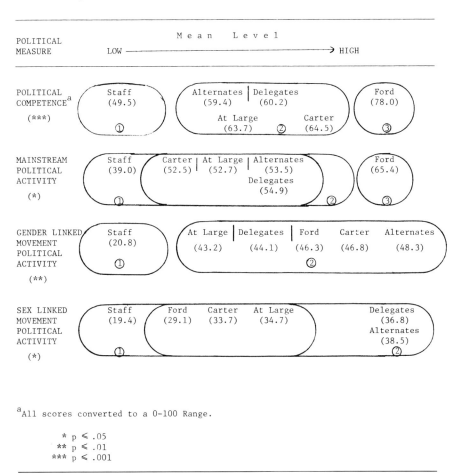

Figure 4.2. Mainstream and movement political activity and political competence by conference status position: Subsets and means.

and Minorities resolutions were passed, there is little differentiation among the six categories in their response to the passage of the ERA and Minorities resolutions. On the converted scores, which theoretically could range from zero to 100, no group showed a mean below $M = 85$. Ford Commissioners, most apt of all to have been single-minded in their concentration on the ERA ratification campaign, showed no variance at all, whereas alternates, who included a conservative minority in opposition to the ERA, were least enthusiastic. The Duncan procedure showed no subset patterning in the response to the Minorities resolution, as one might expect.

Response to the Reproductive Freedom and Sexual Preference resolutions

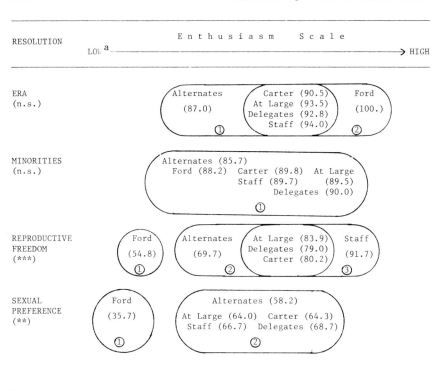

RESOLUTION   E n t h u s i a s m   S c a l e
                    LOW a ───→ HIGH

ERA   Alternates   Carter (90.5)   Ford
(n.s.)   (87.0)   At Large (93.5)   (100.)
                            Delegates (92.8)
                               Staff (94.0)
                     ①   ②

MINORITIES   Alternates (85.7)
(n.s.)   Ford (88.2) Carter (89.8) At Large
                              Staff (89.7)   (89.5)
                                     Delegates (90.0)
                          ①

REPRODUCTIVE   Ford   Alternates   At Large (83.9)   Staff
FREEDOM   (54.8)   (69.7)   Delegates (79.0)   (91.7)
(***)   Carter (80.2)
                  ①   ②   ③

SEXUAL   Ford   Alternates (58.2)
PREFERENCE   (35.7)   At Large (64.0) Carter (64.3)
(**)   Staff (66.7) Delegates (68.7)
                  ①   ②

a Score converted to 0-100 range, where 0 = highly depressed, 100 = highly enthusiastic when resolution(s) passed.

** p ≤ .01
*** p ≤ .001

Figure 4.3. Affect response to passage of selected resolutions: Subsets and means on enthusiasm scale by status position.

was quite another matter. Note that these measures tap not how people voted,
but how they felt when the resolutions passed. There is much more variance in
these private feelings than in the actual vote itself. In this case Ford Commissioners constitute a separate subset with the lowest levels of positive response
to the passage of both resolutions. On the abortion issue, as on the ERA, the
minority among the elected alternates who held conservative views in opposition to abortion tipped the category toward the Ford Commissioners,[5]

[5] It should be kept in mind that the underrepresentation of conservative respondents in the
sample compared to the population may contribute to some unknown extent to the pattern
shown in the text, particularly on issues of great salience to conservative delegates, like abortion.
Nor do we know how the response bias in the delegate and alternate categories differs from that
in the Secretariat staff and Commissioner categories.

whereas Secretariat staff members, with more secular and feminist views, generally, constitute a separate subset with highly enthusiastic responses to the passage of the Reproductive Freedom resolution. The Carter Commissioners are closer to the delegate groups than to the Ford Commissioners, with moderate levels of enthusiasm toward the two controversial issues.

An interesting pattern differentiates the status categories when respondents were asked how committed they were personally to working toward the implementation of at least some of the resolutions passed in Houston. The question first asked about plans for such political activity at the city or state level, then at the national level. Figure 4.4 shows the subset clustering that differentiates these two levels. The IWY Commissioners take the lead on both measures. They have already reached a high level of state and national visibility on the core agenda items of ERA ratification, economic opportunity, and political access for increasing numbers of women, and could hardly be expected to do other than show high levels of commitment in the future. What is interesting is that the delegate groups show higher average scores of commitment to action on the city and state levels than on the national level,

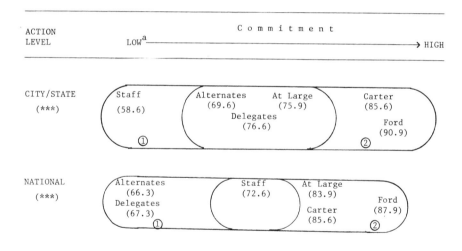

^aHere, as in other tables using the Duncan subsets for graphic presentation, "low" is a relative term comparing one group with the others. On a scale of 0 to 100, even the "low" average score of 58.6 shown for the Staff on the city and state level, is a moderate level of commitment.

*** p ⩽ .001

Figure 4.4. Commitment to implementation of resolutions by conference status position at local versus national level: Subsets and means.

whereas Secretariat staff members show the reverse: more commitment to national efforts than to city or state levels.

To some extent, this pattern reflects the fact that most of the Secretariat staff lives and works in the Washington, D.C., area. Many of the Secretariat staff women have moved on from the IWY Commission to other federal agencies, congressional staffs, and extragovernmental organizations and firms in Washington, D.C. Many of them are now in positions where their feminist concerns are as legitimate a focus of their daily tasks as they were while they worked for the IWY Commission, and these jobs have been and continue to be, at the national level. Though few in number, these women are a steady source of pressure from critical posts within the government and thus are contributing to the extension of the rights of women. By contrast, most delegates have been active in feminist politics at the local and state levels, and it is here that they expect to continue to work in the future.

Role in Houston

The indices of activity levels during the conference in Houston were designed with the delegates in mind. The extent to which people were engaged in such activities as working with a caucus, delegation, the IWY Commission, the Secretariat staff, nondelegate observers, or organizations they belonged to together comprise the measure labeled *number of groups worked with*. To score high on this measure is far easier for the delegates themselves than for the Carter Commissioners or the Secretariat staff, for the simple reason that the latter two groups were charged with explicit responsibilities that absorbed much of their time and energy during the Houston conference.

This is important to bear in mind when comparing the six organizational categories on the activity level shown in Houston (Figure 4.5). Many members of the Secretariat staff were using their professional expertise throughout the conference: Thus, a staff lawyer concentrated on legal and security issues; a journalist on preparation of press releases and negotiations with the hundreds of other journalists present to cover the conference. So, too, the Carter Commissioners carried special responsibilities during the conference: Several worked closely with the caucuses that pressed for revision of specific resolutions. One Carter Commissioner was in charge of floor communication between the chairperson on the podium and the array of security people on the floor of the Coliseum. A special committee of Carter Commissioners was established to negotiate with the hotel in coping with a housing crisis that began 2 days before the conference officially convened. Other Carter Commissioners worked closely with the local arrangements committee, whereas still others oversaw the workshops and lectures that supplemented the ple-

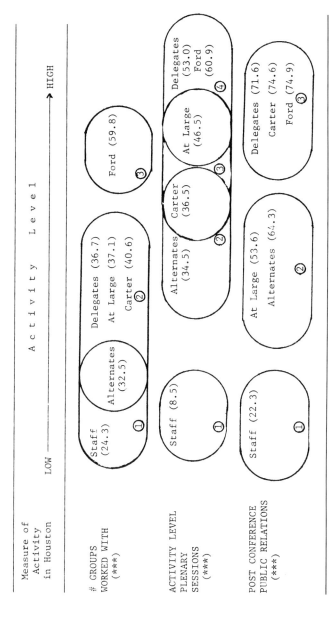

Figure 4.5. Role differentiation by status position: Subsets and mean scores on Houston activity measures; all three scores converted to 0–100 range; $p \leq .001$.

135

nary sessions. This role specialization restricted the time available to engage in the particular range of activities that would produce a high score on the measures used in the study.

By contrast, the Ford Commissioners had a degree of freedom to use their time and energy to suit their own preferences and commitments. As nationally visible and politically experienced people with many ties to members of the delegations, they were clearly sought out and drawn into a great variety of activities. This is most clearly shown in the top row of Figure 4.5, where the Ford Commissioners represent a distinct subset with the highest average score on the number of groups they worked with in Houston. So, too, on the index on activity level during the plenary sessions, the Ford Commissioners share the highest activity cluster with the delegates, whereas the Carter Commissioners were more like the alternates in level of activity during the plenaries. With no vote and highly differentiated assignments, Secretariat staff members were minimally involved in plenary session activities.

The same point of role differentiation accounts for the profile shown in the last row of Figure 4.5, which shows the level of activity engaged in during the immediate aftermath of the conference, when people returned to their home communities. As national figures, both Carter and Ford Commissioners were in high demand (or sought out such opportunities themselves) for radio and television appearances and talks to local groups and organizations about the Houston conference and the national Plan of Action. Secretariat staff members, concentrated in the Washington, D.C., area and with their own public relations specialist, were least likely to play a significant public role following the conference.

This aftermath role was frequently an important high point for the delegates, often against any expectation that they would become newsworthy upon their return to their home communities. Typically, delegates from small towns were most surprised by their sudden prominence in the local press. One woman wrote:

> It's been really hard for me, coming from a very small rural community, population 1000. I so often feel my ideas make me different from everybody around me. In Houston, at last, I felt a "part" of the world. And that gave me courage to enjoy the "notoriety" of the local press when I got home.

Apparently, the tone of the local press was not, in this instance, very supportive of the national Plan. Another woman had a more positive, but equally surprising, experience:

> I am amazed that after so many years feeling an oddball and pariah, my church ran a special article on me as a delegate to Houston, even reporting without criticism that I had supported the sexual preference and reproductive freedom resolutions. That could not have happened even a few years ago.

Local friends clearly paved the way for the return of another woman who wrote:

> I was astonished when I got home to find my friends had already arranged for a radio interview and made several dates for me to speak to local groups. There was a local reporter at the airport seeking me out, something that could never have happened before, and probably would not have happened without the advance work by my friends.

Expected versus Actual Leadership Role

A more general question that has fewer limitations due to role specialization in Houston was one that asked people what best described the role they expected to play in Houston: Did she expect to be a *key person* whose views are sought out and taken into account; an *important person* whose views are paid attention to; an *interested participant* who tries to make her views known; an *interested bystander,* concerned with the issues, but who will not influence decisions; or *not much of a participant.* This question was repeated, with appropriate language changes, in the February survey, to find out what role the participants actually played at the conference. As a panel variable, I shall analyze, in a later chapter, what determined whether or not the participants' expectations of leadership meshed with their actual leadership role.

Figure 4.6 shows the pattern for both expected and actual leadership role by status position, with several interesting results. Overall, there was a clear falling-off from expectation, as indicated by the predominance of minuses in the last row, labeled *Shortfall from leadership expectation.* It is one thing to feel important after winning a state election, quite another to retain that feeling after encountering the mammoth size and scale of the conference. It is the phenomenon of the big fish from a small pool feeling small indeed in a large sea. Even the most experienced delegate must have felt a bit intimidated by the size of the Coliseum and the thousands of participants and observers.

There were fewer surprises for the most experienced participants: The Ford and Carter Commissioners seemed to know in advance that their roles were distinctly different. Though equally prominent nationally, the Ford Commissioners expected and experienced less important roles for themselves than the Carter Commissioners did. Hence there is both sharp subset differentiation and an insignificant drop in leadership actuality compared to expectation among the IWY Commissioners. Some realism also seems to have dictated the responses of the alternates: They would not even be regular voting participants in the deliberations, although many undoubtedly had hoped to do more than they in fact did. They appear here as the category with the lowest expected and reported leadership role.

LEADERSHIP ROLE   L e a d e r s h i p   I m p o r t a n c e
AT CONFERENCE   LOW ──→ HIGH

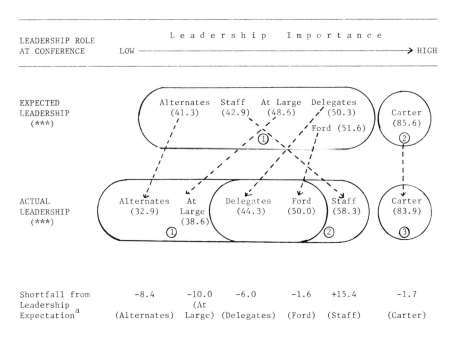

EXPECTED
LEADERSHIP
(***)

ACTUAL
LEADERSHIP
(***)

Shortfall from   -8.4   -10.0   -6.0   -1.6   +15.4   -1.7
Leadership   (At
Expectation[a]   (Alternates) Large) (Delegates) (Ford) (Staff)   (Carter)

[a]Extent to which actual leadership was more or less important than expected.   "+"
indicates actual role was <u>more</u> important than expected, "-" that actual role was
<u>less</u> important than expected.

*** p ≤ .001

Figure 4.6. Expected and actual leadership role at conference by status position: Subset and
mean scores.

   The delegates-at-large show the sharpest shortfall from expectations, which
is also understandable. Individually, these were experienced, politically competent women, many with a history of heading up national voluntary associations. As delegates-at-large, however, they were seated together to the rear of
the Coliseum floor, 400-strong but with no organizational means to forge a
meaningful political entity. Some at-large delegates were observed to work
closely with their home-state delegations. A few were tied into the informal
leadership structure, serving as lieutenants. But, as a group, they were not
conspicuous in the way many of them must have expected to be: There is a
shortfall of 10 points in the mean of their actual leadership compared to their
expected leadership role in Houston.
   The elected delegates also showed a shortfall from leadership expectation
when they reported to us in the February survey. Of course, this shortfall

measure hides the fact that many *individuals* found themselves more important than they expected to be. Here we note only the aggregate level of change. (In a later chapter, individual turnover and change between expected and actual leadership role will be explored).

The group that showed the greatest overall change was the Secretariat staff, whose low expectation of leadership in the October survey (close to that expressed by the alternates) rose to a markedly more important actual role that is exceeded only by the Carter Commissioners. To one close enough to have observed the Secretariat staff for months in Washington, D.C., and then again in Houston, the real question is not why the Secretariat staff had so important a role in Houston, but why they expressed such low expectations for leadership in the October survey. I suspect the answer lies in the great contrast in their roles in Houston compared to those in Washington, D.C. Most of the Secretariat staff's contact with the state delegates during the planning months was by phone or by mail; their interaction was greatest with the IWY Commissioners whose tasks they facilitated or whose decisions they implemented. In Washington, D.C., the Secretariat staff was clearly of lower general status than the IWY Commissioners. In Houston, however, they were among the most knowledgeable people present: They knew the layout of the conference, what the rules were, and where things were located. It was to them that delegates turned with requests for extra space to hold caucus meetings or for solutions to other logistical problems. The Secretariat staff was therefore constantly turned to for advice, information, and a varied array of assistance. There are countless crises during even the best planned event, so the knowledge and administrative savvy of the Secretariat staff members were put to the test throughout the conference. The result may well have been the realization that they were far more important to the actual running of the conference than they had expected to be while they were the overworked and often underappreciated facilitators of the IWY Commissioners' work during the earlier months in Washington, D.C.

Network Formation

The Houston scene was a beehive of social interaction, some of it casual brushes while using elevators, waiting on lines for food, registration, entry or exit from the Coliseum floor, sharing taxis, and other such activities of a service or obligatory nature. Other social contacts were more purposefully related to the business of the conference or to the sharing of political experience and plans for action on issues affecting women. In the course of these interactions, many old friendships were reaffirmed and new ones begun, although it is probably the case that the nature of the situation defined the new contacts as of potential political utility; we cannot assume personal friendship was involved.

I noted in Chapter 3 that an enormous number of new contacts were made in Houston: Each respondent made an average of 22 new contacts with whom they plan to keep in touch. This average is summed across three types of new contacts: People who lived in their own town or city; outside their local city but within the same state; or from another state entirely.

Far more than chance was involved in the likelihood of making few or many such new connections; there were structured determinants as well. If you were a delegate from a small town, there would be little likelihood of meeting someone in Houston from your own town, whereas a woman from New York City or Los Angeles might establish several such contacts. The sheer number of times a large delegation met before going to Houston could affect whether or not the new contacts were from one's own state. Many delegates met each other for the first time on the flight to Houston and these connections are counted in the overall total of new contacts reported by the women. By the same process, a large delegation, seated together and holding many caucus meetings in Houston, restricted the opportunity to connect with people from other states. The delegates-at-large were in an optimal situation to connect with women from states other than their own since they did not meet as at-large delegates and were seated among women from a wide range of states and regions of the country.

The relevance of at least some of these considerations is apparent in the results shown in Figure 4.7. There is very little differentiation by status position on the average number of new contacts made with people from their own home cities, though it is interesting to note that it was the Secretariat staff members who showed the highest number of contacts. This probably reflects their residence in Washington, D.C. and the prominence of women from federal agencies who participated as observers, ran workshops and exhibits, or served as at-large delegates in Houston.

New contacts with people from their home states show quite a different pattern: Here it is the IWY Commissioners who take the lead with the highest number of new contacts. One Carter Commissioner was so impressed by her experience on this score that she described it as one of the most memorable things about the conference. She said, "I left with a list of almost a hundred women from my state I'd never met before, and that's going to be very helpful on at least a half-dozen pet projects of mine." The elected delegates follow the IWY Commissioners with a mean of 9.7 new contacts with people from their own states. This reflects the opportunities traveling together, often sharing hotel rooms, and working together as a delegation, provided.

Contacts made with people from other states show yet a third profile. Here the Carter Commissioners clearly took the lead, with a mean almost twice as large as that of the Ford Commissioners ($M = 22$ versus $M = 13$). It is highly

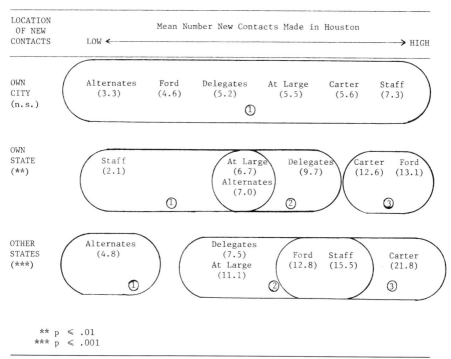

LOCATION OF NEW CONTACTS	Mean Number New Contacts Made in Houston
	LOW ←————————————————————→ HIGH

OWN CITY (n.s.)

Alternates (3.3)   Ford (4.6)   Delegates (5.2)   At Large (5.5)   Carter (5.6)   Staff (7.3)
①

OWN STATE (**)

Staff (2.1)   At Large (6.7) Alternates (7.0)   Delegates (9.7)   Carter (12.6)   Ford (13.1)
①   ②   ③

OTHER STATES (***)

Alternates (4.8)   Delegates (7.5) At Large (11.1)   Ford (12.8)   Staff (15.5)   Carter (21.8)
①   ②   ③

** p ≤ .01
*** p ≤ .001

Figure 4.7. Network formation by conference status position: Subsets and mean number of new contacts made in Houston by contact locale.

likely that this difference reflects the official roles played by the Carter Commissioners, which involved other people seeking them out for a variety of reasons. Ford Commissioners, by contrast, if they wished to "work the floor" would seek out others they already knew to support positions they espoused. The same tendency for others to seek them out that held for the Carter Commissioners probably also affected the Secretariat staff's experience as well, and hence they made more contacts with people from other states than even the Ford Commissioners.

Table 4.3 makes the actual network data more accessible, by showing the net effect of the three quite different patterns on the grand means in the last row: The Carter Commissioners lead with a mean of 40 new contacts, and the alternates trail with the lowest overall mean, less than one-half that number, 15 new contacts.

Conclusion

To summarize the data presented in this chapter, I shall sketch an overall aggregate profile for each of the six status positions. The profiles for a particu-

Table 4.3
Network Formation by Organizational Structure:
Mean Contacts by Location and Overall Means by Organizational Position

| Location of New Contacts | Staff | Organizational Position | | | Commissioners | |
		Elected Delegates	Elected Alternates	Appointed Delegates	Ford	Carter
Own Community/ City	7.31	5.17	3.32	5.52	4.63	5.59
Own State . .	2.07	9.73	7.01	6.68	13.13	12.61
Other States .	15.50	7.54	4.79	11.11	12.75	21.84
Overall Mean	24.88	22.44	15.12	23.31	30.51	40.04

lar category will include only those characteristics that were especially noteworthy, for example, characteristics on which elected delegates were the highest or lowest, on average, of all six status positions.

IWY Commissioners

The Ford and Carter Commissioners were alike in several respects that marked them off from the other four status categories: Both their own earnings and that of their total household were higher than in any other status position. They are highly experienced politically, showing the highest levels of political activity in mainstream politics (especially in having previously held public office), and rating themselves high on political competence. They are "joiners" par excellence, with a mean of 17 organizational memberships.

The major differentiation between Ford and Carter Commissioners lies in their political affiliations: Ford Commissioners are split between Republicans and Independents, whereas Carter Commissioners show strong Democratic party affiliation with no Independents among them. Also, Ford Commissioners were highly involved in Ford's presidential campaign, whereas Carter appointees were not as highly involved in his campaign, perhaps reflecting the strong northeastern, urban, and "regular-party" nature of their ties to the Democratic party.

There are also differences between the two sets of Commissioners in the kinds of organizations they have been most active in: Carter Commissioners show the highest mean membership in political organizations and participation in liberal causes during the past decade, whereas the Ford Commissioners show the highest involvement in traditional women's organizations and the lowest involvement in feminist organizations or liberal causes.

As one would expect from their political expertise and prominence on the national scene, both sets of Commissioners played active and important roles in Houston. Because they were not bound into specific assignments, the Ford Commissioners showed the highest level of political activity during the conference in terms of activity level during the plenary sessions and the large number of groups they worked with, on both of which they exceeded the Carter Commissioners. Though slightly lower on average than the Carter Commissioners, compared to other status positions, the Ford Commissioners showed high leadership expectation and actuality.

Differences emerged between the Ford and Carter Commissioners on their aggregate response to the passage of the more controversial resolutions at the conference: Ford Commissioners showed the least enthusiasm of all the status categories when the resolutions on abortion and sexual preference were passed, a pattern consistent with their past emphasis on gender- rather than sex-linked feminist issues and their organizational affiliation with traditional women's organizations rather than liberal causes.

Looking toward the future, both sets of Commissioners anticipate a high level of commitment to the implementation of the major resolutions passed at the conference, both in their home towns or states and at the national level. So, too, as highly visible and recognized figures, they came away from Houston with the highest level of new contacts they expect to keep in touch with, although the more conspicuous role played by the Carter appointees gave them the higher average.

Alternates

The *elected alternates* were in the unenviable position of having serious restrictions on their participation in the work of the conference. On the other hand, this clearly was no surprise to them, as reflected in the fact that they reported the lowest expected, as well as actual, leadership role in Houston. This group included more conservative women than did any other status position, and the smallest proportion of full-time employed women as well. Role restraints also show in the fact that the elected alternates report relatively low averages on plenary session activity or on the number of groups worked with during the conference. Their lack of access to voting roles on the floor was probably a factor restricting the number of new contacts they could make during the conference as well, for this group shows the lowest mean of all status positions.

Appointed delegates-at-large were like the Carter Commissioners in generally showing a high level of political organization membership and a high level of commitment to future activity at the national level to assure implementation of the resolutions in the Plan. But they probably also included the largest proportion of women whose expectations were frustrated at the conference: As a group, they showed the largest shortfall in actual leadership roles reported in February compared to their expectations in October.

  Elected delegates, compared to all other status positions, have a moderate level on most of the characteristics reviewed in this analysis: moderate levels of organizational membership, self-rated political competence, new contacts made in Houston, and participation in mainstream politics. As a group, however, they were close to the Ford Commissioners in playing active roles during the plenary sessions and working within their state delegations and the variety of groups that organized in behalf of voting for or amending the resolutions of particular interest to them.

Secretariat Staff

As a group, the Secretariat staff profile is unique among the six status positions. Composed largely of administrative and professional women of very liberal or radical political beliefs and strong involvement in feminist organizations and issues, the Secretariat staff nonetheless showed very low levels of actual political action outside their jobs: They had low averages on participation in liberal causes, mainstream politics, or gender- and sex-linked feminist politics; low organizational membership, except for feminist organizations; and low self-ratings on political competence. Although they were specialists in terms of their job-dictated roles during the conference, they scored low on the measures used to study direct involvement in political activity in Houston.

On the other hand, they experienced far more important leadership roles than they had anticipated in Washington, D.C., and they showed high profiles on network formation as a consequence of the conference, particularly with people from their own city and from other states. Unlike almost all of the delegates and IWY Commissioners, the Secretariat staff's employment in connection with the IWY Commission has taken a major investment of time but has provided an important channel for active contribution to the expansion of women's rights. For almost everybody else, political activity has been an extracurricular time investment on top of job and family roles. For the Secretariat staff members, their jobs were, by definition, a significant contribution to the feminist movement.

5

The State Delegation: Formation and Impact

Introduction

Both mainstream politics and traditional women's organizations differ from feminist politics in an important organizational respect: Both have organizational and administrative units at the state level as well as at local and national levels. Thus, a voluntary organization like the League of Women Voters has a wide local base in the form of some 1275 local chapters that are affiliated at the state level through 50 associations and topped by a national organization whose elected officers and board members plan and coordinate the work of the 150,000-member organization.

By contrast, since the mid-1960s, the feminist movement has been organized at the local and national levels but has had relatively weak organization at the state level. This is curious in a sense, because the National Commission on the Status of Women, appointed by former President Kennedy, had spawned smaller versions of itself with the appointment of state commissions on the status of women in most of the states by the mid-1960s. But these state units were appointed bodies with no constituencies: They were executive creatures of the governor, and hence of the political party in power at the time they were established. Like the national IWY Commission itself, a turnover in political party in control of a governor's office typically led to a reconstitution of the state commissions.

It was against this background that the initial emphasis in NOW was the

145

recruitment of a national membership and the development of local, city-based chapters. As the organization grew, regional rather than statewide coalitions of local chapters developed. Only the growing concentration of NOW's finances and political efforts to secure ERA ratification encouraged political organization at the state level. It is in the states in which ratification has been most difficult to secure that coalitions have formed between NOW chapters and the more traditional women's organizations like the League of Women Voters and AAUW to coordinate efforts to secure ratification.

Many of the delegates to Houston from unratified states seized the opportunity represented by the national conference to develop cross-state coalitions with delegates from other nonratified states, explicitly in order to learn and discuss strategy with them. A few examples from our qualitative file illustrate this. One woman wrote:

> Coming from Virginia, where anti-ERA house leader, Jim Thompson, was defeated on November 8th for which NOW was largely responsible, I was impressed and thrilled that so many people sought us out from the Virginia delegation to ask details about our election strategy. Everybody was so buoyed up by it and I felt great to provide not only a "high" for so many people, but real practical political advice as well.

Another delegate, also from an unratified state, spoke to the same theme:

> The most important thing to me was the ease of knowing where people were who have been dealing with the same problems I am, from nonratified states. This is the clearest need of all just now: to identify state leaders and build connections between them when they are facing similar political problems in their states. I want to work now for a coalition of state leaders from the unratified states. My Houston contacts are a boon in that regard.

Even more explicitly, another delegate reports development of this sort that began in Houston:

> By far my most significant experience in Houston was a coalition meeting of the top three Pro-ERA leaders in unratified states, for a special caucus. We decided we needed an "ERA connection." Too often we relate only vertically (up to the national organization headquarters, down to our local city level). So we've begun a good lateral set up. Two states lost in 1977 by the good ole back-slider vote switches, so we feel strategy development is the key, and want to have a by-invitation-only ERA strategy convention crossing organizational and state lines to make some grass roots decisions in common.

ERA ratification was unique among the resolutions in the Plan in its need for sharply focused political effort at the state level. Most other resolutions call for action at the level of national legislation or local political effort, or simply have no particular political geographic unit within which political action is especially relevant. Child-care centers are most likely to develop through either federal legislation and appropriations or locally based voluntary or employer-coordinated efforts. The issues that have been the special concern of women's liberation groups stimulated local development of programs, in some cases facilitated through federal appropriations. This would hold for such issues as battered women, child abuse, health, and rape. Since the mid-1970s, local groups have applied for and secured federal monies to establish crisis centers for battered wives and rape victims. Like the organizational structure of women's liberation groups themselves, the political action is highly concentrated at the local level, with diffuse connections through national networks (e.g., the National Women's Health Network) rather than at the state level. Apart from the ERA, the only issue on which geography was particularly relevant did not even appear in the Plan: The desire on the part of the delegation from the District of Columbia to make statehood for the District a special resolution. When this issue came up at an IWY Commission meeting, the chairperson ruled it out of order as not relevant to the national Plan.[1]

The weakness of the feminist movement at the state level was apparent at many state meetings at which delegates to the national conference were nominated and elected. In a number of states in which Pro-Plan nominees lost (Ohio is a prime example), slates of nominees came from *several* city-based coalitions of feminists, against which a statewide *single* slate of nonfeminist nominees could easily win. With one city's feminist slate competing against another city's slate as well as the Anti-Plan slate, it was not surprising that several delegations contained a heavy representation of Anti-Plan delegates.

That state delegations were chosen as units in the political organization of the national conference had little to do with remedying the weakness of state-level organization in the feminist movement. It was chosen on purely pragmatic grounds, as a useful means by which to choose delegates in proportion to population and to manage the conference in a way familiar from party conventions. So, too, it was pragmatic concern for floor management and communications that dictated the proximate seating of the delegates

[1]This should not be taken to mean there is nothing to do at the state level by those concerned for the lives of women. Clearly there is a great deal to be done, tailoring problem definitions and solutions to the special characteristics of a given state (ethnic and income distribution of a state population; specific occupational concentration of a county or state; age distribution, for example). Many state coordinating committees developed specific state plans of action for precisely the reason that there were unique issues particular to their states. The major point is that few of the resolutions in the national Plan called for primarily state-level political action.

under state banners on the floor of the Coliseum. The state delegation was merely an additional tool through which caucusing on specific issues or overall endorsement of the Plan could be marshalled.

The low salience of the state as a political unit is also demonstrated in the responses of the delegates when they were asked to rate how important a number of factors were in why they sought their nominations: Ninety-four percent stressed their desire to influence a particular issue; 84% to participate in an historic event; 59% to represent a particular organization. By contrast, when we asked for more directly personal, political motivations, only 26% claimed that they sought the nomination as conference delegate to strengthen their position in local or state party politics, 20% to help their own political careers. Although some portion of this latter group had their sights on seeking office in the state legislature, this was much less a focus than was local public office, so considerably less than 20% of the delegates viewed their election as delegates from the point of view of their own ascent to political visibility at the state level.

Pragmatic administrative decisions can have powerful unintended consequences, however, and it is the burden of this chapter to trace what happened to the delegates as a consequence of their participation in the state delegations. Since significant political careers rarely bypass state-level participation and visibility, an analysis of the delegations is important to our concern for women's political aspirations. The delegation was the most stable social ecology for participating in the national conference, off as well as on the floor of the Coliseum, before and after as well as during the Houston conference. State delegations typically met several times before leaving for Houston; many delegations flew to and from Houston on chartered flights; typically they were housed together in the same hotel if not the same floor; many state delegates shared rooms, taxis, meals away from the conference; they sat close to each other through the 23 hours of the plenary sessions; and, in many cases, the point of greatest political presssure they experienced was from delegation leaders tied into the informal political structure that worked to secure the passage of all the resolutions in the Plan. And many delegates who wished to amend resolutions in the Plan organized support for their amendments through their delegations.

Whether the state delegation was a meaningful social entity or not varied greatly among the delegates, depending on their own individual characteristics and the characteristics of the delegation as a structural entity. Hence an analysis of the formation and impact of the state delegations is of interest on both sociological and political grounds. Sociologically, it is of interest since the delegation was a social group of short, but intense, duration, a major ecological entity through which the participants experienced the national conference, and a group of potential continuing political relevance as the source of new contacts to build networks at the state level in the years since. This latter point is of special importance from the point of view of how the national conference may have contributed to filling the weak link of state networking in feminist politics. Whatever the long-term effect of the national conference on the attainment of feminist goals in the country at large, a significant by-product may lie precisely in the development of contacts outside the delegates' home communities, in an enlarged political network across the state.

The analysis of the state delegation was facilitated by a question asked in both waves of the study. In October, the delegates were asked how they viewed their role in Houston—whether as individuals, as members of a delegation, or as representatives of an issue caucus or organization. I shall refer to these as *Solo, Team member,* and *Representative* roles. In February, the delegates were asked which of these three roles best described what they had actually done while in Houston. A comparison of these anticipated and actual roles, and of what determined these role choices, provides an opportunity to explore the process of group formation as a function of individual and structural characteristics.

A number of predictions are plausible in such an analysis. In light of the intensely packed days and nights the delegations spent together, one would predict a general increase in *Team member* and a decrease in *Solo* roles between the pre- and postconference surveys. One would expect a marginal loner in an otherwise politically cohesive delegation to depart from the general trend toward Team member role definitions, holding to a Solo or Representative role by the February survey. Even in October, before the conference, one would expect those who had served on their state coordinating committees to show a head-start in cohesive affiliation and hence to show a Team member role expectation more frequently than those who had *not* served on the state committees. One might even entertain the hypothesis, rooted in general sociological ideas, that delegates from small towns would tend to a Team member role expectation, whereas those from politically diverse and activist urban centers would tend to Representative roles. Along similar lines, I predicted that the sheer size of a delegation would affect role choice: Small delegations may cohere more readily than large delegations since it is easier to get acquainted with everybody on a 12-member delegation than on a 50-member delegation. Long experience in traditional women's organizations may be conducive to a ready absorption as a delegation Team member, whereas membership in feminist organizations, typically of shorter duration and often with strong commitments to very specific issues affecting women, may be conducive to Representative, rather than Team member, roles.

I turn first to an analysis of the ties the delegates had to their state coordinating committees, what background factors were associated with different types

of connections the women had to the state committees, and how those patterns affected the roles they expected and then actually played at the national
conference.

Links between State Coordinating Committees
and State Delegations

It is hardly surprising that 39% of the sample reported that they were
members of their state coordinating committees, since these committees were
in charge of organizing and running the state meetings, and election as a
delegate was the major route to an active political role in Houston. This
linkage between the state committees and participation in Houston held not
only for the elected delegates and alternates, but for the IWY Commissioners
and appointed delegates-at-large as well, as seen in Table 5.1.

Almost three-quarters of the Ford Commissioners were state committee
members (73%), and hence they continued to be vitally involved in the
conference despite stepping down from the national IWY Commission in the
spring of 1977. So, too, the majority of the Carter Commissioners held membership on their state committees: Slightly more than one-half were serving in
this capacity when President Carter appointed them to the national IWY
Commission in March 1977. Hence, for the majority of both Ford- and
Carter-appointees, there was overlap and continuity of involvement in conference plans from 1976 through early 1978, in part through their ties to state
coordinating committees and the state delegations.

A significant percentage of the appointed delegates-at-large (36%) had also
served on their state committees. Indeed, following the state meeting elections, many states quickly submitted names to the national IWY Commission
of committee members who either did not run or who did not win election as
delegates at the state meetings, in the hope they would be appointed as
delegates-at-large. So, too, several national IWY Commissioners, familiar
with who lost in the election at their own state meetings, submitted names of
state committee members who had not won delegate seats.

It is not the case that all the delegates who reported having served on their
state coordinating committee had the support of the committee as nominees
at the state meetings. The reader may recall from Figure 1.3 in Chapter 1 that
four types characterize the relation between state committee membership and
endorsement by the committee. *Insiders* were committee members who had
such support, whereas *Rejects* were committee members who did not appear
on the committee's slate of nominees but won nonetheless. In some states,
there was clearly a public relations factor at work: It would look entirely too
self-serving for any state coordinating committee to propose all of its members

Table 5.1

State Coordinating Committee Membership by Conference Status

Conference Status	Percent Member of State Committee	N
Elected Delegate	40.8%	(699)
Elected Alternate	31.8%	(110)
Appointed Delegate at Large . .	35.5%	(121)
Carter Commissioner	57.9%	(19)
Ford Commissioner	72.7%	(12)
Secretariat Staff	0.0%	(17)
Total	39.1%	(977)

as nominees, particularly in the smaller states with only 12 or so delegates to elect.

The third type, *Recruits,* were women who did not serve on the committees but had their backing in the nomination process. Particularly in high-population states, coordinating committees had to seek outside their own ranks for nominees, since their allotment of delegates far exceeded the number serving on the coordinating committee. In still other states, the committees sought new faces for their slates in compliance with the requirement for diversity in delegation composition on age, race, or ethnic grounds.

The fourth type, the *Newcomers,* were women who neither served on nor had the support of the state committees. This is a very diverse type in terms of motivation and political orientation. Some entered their names in nomination to oppose the conference and its Plan. Others wished to apply political pressure on one or two issues of special concern to them, such as NARAL members on abortion, radical feminists on sexual preference, or local activists concerned with women's health, battered wives, or rape victims.

As reported earlier, the distribution of the four types among the elected delegates and alternates were as follows: 35% were Insiders; 30% were Recruits; 29% were Newcomers, and 6% were Rejects.

Characteristics of State Committee Members

The first step in the analysis was to explore what differentiated delegates who were state committee members from those who were not members.

Committee members had the longest involvement with the work of the IWY Commission since most had served on the state committees since they were established by the Ford Commission. Hence it is of some interest to inquire whether they had any cluster of status, political, or organizational characteristics that distinguished them from the "new blood" brought into the delegations through the election process at the state meetings.

The technique used in this analysis is multiple regression, which permits us to establish which characteristics made independent contributions to whether a delegate was a member of a state committee or not. Since this is the first presentation of regression results in this study, a few words are appropriate concerning the procedure and the manner in which results will be reported. I shall present regression results in terms of standardized beta coefficients rather than the unstandardized metric or raw coefficients. There is considerable methodological disagreement among researchers and statisticians on this issue. The purist position argues that cause and effect are better represented in the metric coefficients, and scientists should state their findings in hard metric terms rather than the loose, sample-specific, relative terms implied by using standardized beta coefficients. A purist would argue, for example, that income in dollars may be a function of education in years, best expressed in metric terms rather than income measured in standard deviation units as a function of education measured in standard deviations. But the measures used in this study, as in most contemporary sociological research, are not true or standardized measures of the variables involved; the zero point is arbitrary and the intervals are not necessarily equal. Hence the metric coefficient is not *prima facie* closer to the real world than any of a variety of other transforms of the variables. One statistician, Andy Anderson (Personal communication, 1981) has argued that since the betas can be thought of as the raw regression coefficients one would have obtained had we first converted all scores to z-scores and then done the regression, the beta coefficient does little more violence to the underlying phenomena than does the original flawed measurement. I do not assume, as many metric purists do, that the scores used are true or pristine reflections of the concepts they purport to represent.

Then, too, I shall not examine the beta coefficients in any fine detail nor make much of minor differences among them. My concern is with patterns and trends in the data, for which the use of beta coefficients is justifiable. Wherever beta coefficients are compared across equations, as I shall do in the change analysis reported in later chapters, I will take care to indicate whether there is any major discrepancy in comparisons of betas across equations versus comparisons of the metric coefficients across the same equations. Further, since the beta coefficients are a function of both the real effects as measured by the metric coefficients and sample variability, I shall also report any instances in which the variances on the dependent variables measured at two time points differ significantly from each other. Where they do not, and the metric coefficients differ in the same direction as the beta coefficients, there is no reason to believe a comparison of beta coefficients is misleading.

In subsequent uses of the regression technique, only a final best predictor set of independent variables will be shown. But in this first presentation of a regression analysis, on what predicts whether a delegate was a member of a state coordinating committee or not, I shall trace the three steps through which the analysis moved in the effort to test different sets of predictor variables and gradually to specify them further, where the data permit, through the use of more refined subscores.

The first equation, shown in the first column of Table 5.2, includes as predictor variables a set of five status variables and three organization variables. Status variables include age, household income, educational attainment, minority group status, and religious-group affiliation, with the latter two variables defined as dummy variables. In order to highlight minority status on the grounds of race and religion as a predictor of committee membership, these variables are defined with "1" equal to nonwhite and non-Protestant. Under organizational variables, Eq. 1 includes total organizational membership and the number of traditional women's organizations the delegates belonged to as indices to visibility in the associational life of the state, and the number of feminist organizations the delegates belonged to as an index of visibility in movement politics in the state.

Table 5.2 shows that six of the eight variables make significant independent contributions to state coordinating committee membership. Status characteristics are clearly more important than the organizational variables: Being older, nonwhite, living at higher income levels, and being Protestant (a negative sign to the coefficient for this religious affiliation dummy variable means being Protestant) are the major predictors of membership on the state committees. Only one of the three organizational measures contributes any significant effect over and above the status characteristics: membership in traditional women's organizations. Although the coefficient is positive in sign, membership in feminist organizations only hovers on significance.

Hence the image of the state committee member is reminiscent of earlier profiles of the state commissions on the status of women: She is an upper-middle-class, middle-aged Protestant woman who has been active in organizations like the League of Women Voters or a business and professional women's club, but not conspicuously involved in feminist organizations. The only difference is a notable one, for the strongest predictor was membership in a minority group, suggesting the felt importance, in light of the thrust of the public law that funded the conference, for significant outreach to embrace racial and ethnic diversity in the appointments to the state committees. (Of course this must be a qualified interpretation, since I have not sampled *all*

Table 5.2

Regression on State Coordinating Committee Membership of Social Status,
Organizational Membership, and Political Experience

VARIABLE	EQUATION #1		EQUATION #2		EQUATION #3	
	Beta Coef.	Signif. Level	Beta Coef.	Signif. Level	Beta Coef.	Signif. Level
SOCIAL STATUS						
Racial/Ethnic Minority[a]	.111	***	.116	***	.088	*
Age	.106	**	.073	*	.053	
Household Income	.091	**	.079	*	.077	*
Religious Group Minority[a] . . .	-.064	*	-.045	+	-.053	+
Education	.008		---[b]		---	
ORGANIZATIONAL MEMBERSHIP						
# Traditional Women's Organizations	.095	**	.073	*	.075	*
# Feminist Organizations . . .	.063	+	.052		.073	*
Total # Organizations	.047		---		---	
# Political Organizations . . .	---		.001		---	
POLITICAL EXPERIENCE						
Mainstream Political Activity Level	---		.091	*	.097	**
Democratic Party Preference[a]. .	---		-.028		---	
Held Public Office	---		.145	***	---	
Appointive Office	---		---		.131	***
Elective Office	---		---		.011	
Feminist Political Activity Level	---		.057		---	
Gender-Linked	---		---		.102	*
Sex-Linked	---		---		-.072	+
R^2 =	.070	***	.109	***	.112	***
F =	8.525		9.200		9.444	
N =	(938)[c]		(919)[c]		(919)[c]	

[a]Dummy Variables: Nonwhite and Non-Protestant have value of 1.
[b]Not entered in equation.
[c]The N shown is the minimum N in the covariance matrix the regression equation is based on. This practice is followed throughout the volume.

+ $p \leqslant .10$
* $p \leqslant .05$
** $p \leqslant .01$
*** $p \leqslant .001$

state committee members but only those who won elections at the state meetings).[2]

It should also be noted that educational attainment showed no direct effect on committee membership. This may come as a surprise to anyone familiar with surveys based on national probability samples, but it underlines the unique nature of the sample: As seen earlier, educational attainment is very high in the sample as a whole, so there is less room for education to play a part in the analysis. In addition, educational attainment, although not contributing an independent effect as a predictor of committee membership, may work through the intermediary of organizational visibility. Most members of the League of Women Voters and, by definition, the members of AAUW, are college-educated women. Since a large proportion of the sample are members of these two traditional women's organizations, such membership may be serving as a proxy for educational attainment.

It is also relevant that the task of appointing the state committees was managed from Washington, D.C. and that Secretariat staff members who served as regional coordinators had to work with the networks most likely to include experienced and interested women. Since it was a *state* committee, those organizations with visible headquarters and officers at the state level were obvious contact points. This, too, would contribute to the fact that membership in traditional women's organizations is a significant predictor of state committee membership.

In Eq. 2 (second column in Table 5.2), those variables that showed no significance in the first equation (education and total organizational membership) are dropped, the remaining six significant variables are retained, and five new ones are added that tap political experience: the number of political organizations belonged to, Democratic party preference, level of mainstream and of feminist political activity, and experience in holding public office. A glance down the column of beta coefficients for Eq. 2 shows we have picked up a powerful predictor in experience in holding public office ($\beta = .145$). Less powerful, but still statistically significant, is activity level in mainstream politics ($\beta = .091$). Surprisingly, the counterpart measure of activity level in feminist politics does not contribute a significant independent effect, though the sign is positive. Note, too, that the inclusion of direct measures of political experience and office-holding has had the effect of reducing the strength of most of the social status predictors: Age, for example, is less powerful, perhaps because in

[2]This is an important point. It was our impression that the state committees themselves tended to sponsor their minority-group members as nominees on their slates, precisely to conform to the requirements of the public law. Hence the significance of minority-group membership may apply to the slates and to successful election rather than as a true predictor of membership on the state committees from their origin in 1976.

the first equation it served as a proxy for political experience (which is positively related to age).

From the data provided in Eq. 2, however, it looks as though explicitly feminist activity played no role in predicting state committee membership: Feminist organization membership has slipped below the .05 significance level, and level of feminist political activity is not important. What seems to matter is mainstream politics, public office-holding, being relatively well-to-do, Protestant, and nonwhite. (Party preference shows no significant effect.)

The third and final step in the analysis specifies certain of the variables in Eq. 2 that seemed puzzling. This specification is of particular importance on two measures: public office-holding and movement political activity level. When holding public office is divided into elective and appointive office, it is clearly appointive office that predicts state committee membership, not elective office. Unfortunately, I did not specifically ask the respondents whether they had served as appointed members of a state or a local commission on the status of women, but the suspicion is that this is a major type of appointment in the variable on holding appointive office. It is not likely, in other words, that having served as an elected city council member predicts membership on the state committees; having served as an appointed member of a status of women commission may.

A specification of the feminist political activity index helps to explain why it was not a significant predictor in Eq. 2. Once the general index is replaced by the two subscores that differentiate between gender- and sex-linked feminist activity, it becomes clear that feminist activity played a role in the appointment to and election of state committee members: It is state visibility due to political efforts to expand women's economic and political rights, rather than private rights in the areas of sex, abortion, sex preference, or family planning, that predict appointment to the state committees and subsequent nomination and election as a delegate to Houston. In fact, having been active on sex-linked issues hovers on significance as a *negative* predictor of state committee membership (thus effectively cancelling out the influence of gender-linked activism in the overall composite score used in Eq. 2).

Although it is still a significant predictor, there is a sharp reduction in beta size and significance level of racial or ethnic minority status in Eq. 3 compared to Eqs. 1 and 2. Just as age was seen to be a proxy variable for political experience, minority-group status may be a proxy for specific kinds of political activity and concerns. Consistent with this is the fact that racial or ethnic minority status is positively correlated with gender-linked feminist activity ($\beta = .188$) but negatively correlated with sex-linked feminist activity ($\beta = -.122$). At this stage of their involvement in feminism, Black, Latina, and Native-American women support economic and political rights for women, but many withhold their support on issues that threaten their more traditional family, church, and community relationships.

Hence the final profile of state committee members that emerges from the third and last equation is of women who have been visible in their states through political activity on the rights of women in economic and political areas as well as in mainstream politics in both parties, who have served in appointive posts at state or local levels, belonged to a variety of women's organizations (more traditional than feminist), were somewhat better-off financially, were minority-group members, and were more likely to be Protestant than Jewish or Catholic.

Overall, the amount of variance explained in these equations is not large, as indicated by the R^2s shown at the bottom of Table 5.2. Although all three are highly significant in a statistical sense, they increase only from $R^2 = .07$ in Eq. 1 to $R^2 = .112$ in Eq. 3.

Insider versus Newcomer Delegate Types

One additional step will help sharpen the focus of the analysis. In the predictive equations thus far, the use of a dichotomous variable on state committee membership means the nonmembers include two very different groups of delegates: the *Recruits,* people whose nominations were supported by the committee (223 delegates), and the *Newcomers,* people who were neither members of the committees nor supported by them (255 delegates). Less critical, but possibly blurring some of the results, is the presence of the 48 *Rejects,* the delegates who had been members of, but not supported by, the committees on the official slate of nominees. The next step, then, is to refine and contrast the dependent variable and use the final best set of predictors (those in Eq. 3) to explore whether the significant predictors of Insider status differ from the predictors of Newcomer status, a comparison one can describe as old timers versus new blood. The results are shown in Table 5.3.

On most of the variables in these two regression equations there is a reversal of signs between the two delegate types: Thus, for example, high income and Protestant religious affiliation predict an Insider delegate type, whereas low income and being Catholic, Jewish, agnostic, or Mormon predict a Newcomer delegate. Interestingly, it is having been highly active on sex-linked feminist issues but *not* a member of feminist organizations that provides an important pair of characteristics predictive of the Newcomer delegate type. The Newcomers, in other words, were not conspicuous joiners as the Insiders clearly are, nor were they very visible through appointments to public office as the Insiders are. Rather, they are either conservative or liberal-to-radical white women whose political energies had centered on one or the other side of issues that were controversial in the women's conference, such as abortion and sexual preference.

Not shown because the R^2 fell short of a .05 alpha level, but worth reporting, are findings concerning the predictors of who are classified as Recruits

Table 5.3

Regression on Elected Delegate Type of Social Status, Organizational Membership, and Political Experience

VARIABLE	Delegate Type [a]			
	INSIDERS		NEWCOMERS	
	Beta Coefficient	Signif. Level	Beta Coefficient	Signif. Level
SOCIAL STATUS				
Racial/Ethnic Minority	.090	*	-.075	*
Age	.083	*	.006	
Household Income	.094	*	-.124	***
Minority Religious Group	-.056	+	.061	*
ORGANIZATIONAL MEMBERSHIP				
# Traditional Women's Organizations	.064	+	-.057	+
# Feminist Organizations	.110	**	-.137	***
POLITICAL EXPERIENCE				
Mainstream Political Activity Level	.044		.023	
Held Appointive Office	.137	***	-.141	***
Held Elective Office	-.001		-.012	
Gender-Linked Feminist Activity Level	.084	*	-.120	*
Sex-Linked Feminist Activity Level	-.075	+	.113	**
R^2 =	.097	***	.099	***
F =	7.099		7.207	
N = (735)				

[a] Insiders are state committee members who were on their committees' slate of nominees at the state meetings. Newcomers are delegates who neither served on the state committees nor had the support of the committees in the state elections.

+ $p \leqslant .10$
* $p \leqslant .05$
** $p \leqslant .01$
*** $p \leqslant .001$

(nonmembers who were endorsed by the state committees). These tended to be young, non-Protestant women inexperienced in mainstream politics, suggesting that the state committees attempted to diversify their slates on such conspicuous status variables as religion and age, and to seek nominees with less political experience than themselves. That sex-linked feminist and antifeminist activists made their way into the delegate body had little encouragement from the state committees: These were the "new blood" whose own interests in such issues motivated them and their supporters to seek nomination and election as delegates to Houston.

Table 5.4 provides at least partial support to the interpretation given concerning the diverse nature of the issues the Newcomers brought with them into the delegation and conference deliberations. It shows the contrast, by delegate type, in the groups supporting their nomination at the state meetings. Only a tiny percentage of the Insiders and Recruits report support by antiabortion (4%) or anti-ERA (2%) groups, but 18% of the Newcomers had support

Table 5.4
Groups Supporting Nomination of Elected Delegate Types

| | | Delegate Type | |
GROUP SUPPORT[a]	INSIDERS	RECRUITS	NEWCOMERS
1. PERCENT HAD SUPPORT OF:			
Women's rights	73.0	70.5	50.0
Pro-ERA	71.4	68.0	47.6
Racial/ethnic	39.4	40.5	26.2
Lesbian	21.4	24.1	30.3
Anti-Abortion	4.0	3.8	18.0
Anti-ERA	2.0	3.4	16.6
2. NUMBER OF GROUPS SUPPORTING NOMINATION:			
None	0.0	0.0	38.6
1 or 2	29.7	29.1	30.0
3 or 4	46.7	43.8	25.2
5 or more	23.7	27.0	6.1
N =	(271)	(223)	(255)

[a]Question specified "any organization, caucus or coalition of the following types?" (Q.11, October survey.)

from antiabortion groups, 17% from anti-ERA groups.[3] So one can simply say that the Newcomers are a more diverse group of delegates with a wider array of political views on women's issues than the Insiders or Recruits. Note, too, that there were a great number of Newcomers who reported no group support at all (39%); they simply sought out and won election as individuals, without formal endorsement from any organization, caucus, or coalition.

Since the Insiders had a longer association with the work of the IWY Commission and were a less diverse group of delegates than the Newcomers, I expected these two delegate types to differ in both their motivation in seeking the nomination in the first place and in their expectations concerning which groups they would work with at the national conference. The results were disappointing on both counts. There were no significant differences between Insiders and Newcomers in the extent to which they sought election in order to influence an issue, represent an organization, improve their position in party politics, or help their own political career (data not shown).[4]

The only significant difference in motivation between the Insiders and the Newcomers concerned "participation in an historic event": Seventy-one percent of the Insiders, versus only 50% of the Newcomers, stressed this as an important factor in their seeking election as a delegate. Perhaps, having already spent a year working on the state committees and having been exposed to materials from the national IWY Commission that stressed its continuity with past political efforts of feminists in American history may have impressed the Insiders with the historical significance of their own participation in Houston. By contrast, many women among the Newcomers would be as unsympathetic to the goals of nineteenth-century suffragists as they are to contemporary feminists, whereas others in their ranks who have worked on such issues as abortion reform, health centers, gay rights, and retreats for displaced homemakers may also feel little empathetic linkage to the vote-seeking suffragists of the past on the grounds that the latter were too moderate in their political goals.

There were sharp differences in the role expectations of the delegate types as they looked ahead to participation in Houston. Insiders, who gained a head-start on collective *esprit* from serving on the state committees, were far

---

[3]This is a conservative estimate of support from anti-abortion and anti-ERA groups, since the Newcomers include many delegates from among the Pro-Life and Moral Majority political groups that sought and won a number of delegate seats despite having no prior ties to the state committees nor endorsement by them. As seen in Chapter 2, refusal rates were particularly high from such delegates.

[4]I also expected the Insiders to show higher levels of expectation concerning working with the state delegations and the Newcomers to give greater stress to working with caucuses and organizations when they reached Houston. But here, too, there was little difference between the two delegate types.

Table 5.5

Expected Role in Houston of Insider and Newcomer Delegates (in percent)

EXPECTED ROLE	D e l e g a t e T y p e	
	INSIDERS	NEWCOMERS
Team Member	58.3	39.5
Representative	23.5	32.7
Issue Caucus	18.2	20.6
Organization	5.3	12.1
Solo	17.0	27.0
Don't Know	1.1	.8
N =	(264)	(248)
Significance Level: **		

** $p \leq .01$

more likely than the Newcomers to define their roles in advance as *Team members* (members of a delegation), whereas the Newcomers tended to view their anticipated roles as *Solo* (as an individual delegate), or *Representative* roles (issue caucus or organization representatives) (see Table 5.5). I shall return shortly to a more extended analysis of the structural determinants of these three conference roles.

Organizational Membership and Delegate Role Expectations

There are strong suggestions in the analysis that members of feminist organizations brought rather different expectations rooted in different backgrounds and motivations to the national conference than did members of traditional women's organizations. Two of the indices on organizational membership are used to highlight these differences. The code on feminist organizations is based on membership in three specified organizations: the National Organization for Women (NOW), the National Abortion Rights Action League (NARAL), and the National Gay Task Force (NGTF). The code on traditional women's organizations is similarly based on three specific or-

ganizations: The League of Women Voters (LWV), the American Association
of University Women (AAUW), and a Business and Professional Women's
Club (BPW).

There are several sharp differences between delegates high in feminist
organizational membership and those who are high in traditional women's
organizations. The motivations guiding their seeking nominations as delegates, what groups they expected to work with in Houston, and the general
roles they expected to play in Houston vary (see Table 5.6). The higher the
level of membership in feminist organizations, the more focused the delegates
were in seeking delegate status in order to influence an issue, represent an
organization, and even (though slightly) to help their own political career. By
contrast, membership level in traditional women's organizations shows no
strong relation to motivational profile. Delegates who belong to the League of
Women Voters, AAUW, and a Business and Professional Women's Club are
no more likely than nonmembers to have sought election as a delegate in
order to influence an issue or represent an organization, though they are
slightly more apt to be concerned with helping their own political careers.

A similar pattern is shown on the extent to which the delegates expected to
work with an organization, an issue caucus, or the delegation itself once they
reached Houston. Feminist organizational membership is significantly related
to the expectation of representing their organizations in Houston and of working with issue caucuses there. Membership in traditional women's organizations shows no relation to issue or organizational involvement in Houston,
whereas it does relate to an increased expectation of working with the delegation itself. Consistent with this contrast, the bottom third of Table 5.6 shows that
the higher the membership profile in feminist organizations, the less the delegates saw themselves as Team members, and the more they saw themselves in
Representative roles on the Houston scene.

I suspect these results reflect the different social and psychological meaning
of membership in these contrasting types of organizations. Traditional wom-
en's organizations have a long history in the United States, and many older
women in the sample have been members for several decades. Such life-long
organizational membership is apt to gratify a diverse set of needs for friendship, ties to the community, and professional advance, as well as purposive
action in pursuit of political goals of significance to them as women, employees, or citizens. By contrast, feminist organizations have a short history,
and their members are more likely to seek social and political change on
issues with a high priority on a feminist agenda. Whereas the League of
Women Voters may recruit new voters in a registration campaign, NOW
members will exert pressure on how the new registrants vote. Another way of
putting this is to suggest that, for many members of traditional women's

Table 5.6

Motivation in Delegate Election, Groups Expected to Work with in Houston, and Expected Role in Houston, by Membership Level in Feminist and Traditional Women's Organizations (in percent)

VARIABLE	No. Feminist Organizations				sign. level	No. Traditional Women's Organizations				sign. level
	0	1	2	3		0	1	2	3	
MOTIVATION IN SEEKING ELECTION AS DELEGATE:[a]										
To represent an organization	56.9	57.4	62.7	86.7	**	63.2	54.0	47.4	61.5	
To influence an issue	63.5	68.1	76.4	80.0	*	68.0	66.8	72.7	55.3	
To help own political career	19.2	19.2	21.4	28.5	+	16.1	22.4	28.4	28.3	*
EXPECTATION OF WORKING WITH SPECIFIED GROUP:[a]										
State Delegation . . .	80.5	83.9	84.5	60.0		77.2	86.6	84.8	92.3	**
Issue Caucus	54.0	57.4	72.7	73.3	*	61.0	53.9	58.8	59.0	
Organization	41.8	49.2	67.7	73.3	**	48.4	50.4	44.4	51.3	
EXPECTED ROLE:										
Team Member	52.2	48.0	46.5	20.0	**	45.1	51.5	59.0	48.6	
Solo	25.6	22.8	11.8	26.7		22.7	23.6	21.0	21.6	
Representative	21.1	26.8	40.9	53.3	**	30.1	23.7	20.0	29.7	
N =	(387)	(250)	(127)	(15)		(401)	(237)	(100)	(37)	

[a]Percent who respond a "great deal" on extent to which each of the specified factors played a role in their desire to be a delegate, or a "great deal" in how closely they expected to work with each specified group.

+ p ≤ .10
* p ≤ .05
** p ≤ .01

organizations, membership is an end in itself; for most members of feminist organizations, membership is a means to an end.[5]

---

[5]Chapter 6 will provide a more detailed analysis of organizational contrast. In particular, I will explore how members of NOW and the League of Women Voters differ in their attitudinal and belief systems.

Structural Characteristics of Delegations

Level of Political Consensus in Delegation

Thus far it has been the personal attributes of the delegates themselves that have been explored. There are also structural differences among the state delegations that may influence the tendency to emphasize a Team member or to depress a Solo or Representative role. Some of this structural variation among the delegations can be inferred from information provided by the delegates themselves. For example, when asked in October to characterize their delegation as a body, 66% of the delegates said it was "largely feminist," another 24% "mixed feminist and antifeminist," and only 7% "largely antifeminist." In February, they were asked to characterize their delegation on two dimensions: One concerned the extent to which the respondents felt members of their delegation shared their political views. Some 44% described their delegation as "very high Pro-Plan consensus," another 41% "high Pro-Plan consensus, with most delegates supporting all but a few resolutions." Only 6% said their delegations were "split on most resolutions," another 6% that their delegations were either largely or totally Anti-Plan in their voting pattern on the resolutions.

The perceived political consensus of the delegations shows a decided relation to the willingness of the delegates to define their Houston role as team members. A delegation is defined as having *high political consensus (relative to the responding delegate, of course) if 80% or more of the delegates shared the respondent's political views on women's issues: This was true for 45% of the delegates. Another 30% reported a range of shared political views of 50–79%; these are labeled moderate political consensus.* The remainder, some 25% of the delegates, reported agreement with their political views on the part of less than 50% of the delegates from their state; these are labeled *low political consensus.*

Table 5.7 summarizes the effect of variation in the level of political consensus in the delegation on the role expectation of the delegates (top half) and the extent to which these early role expectations were maintained by the time they reported their actual role in February (bottom half). As hypothesized, identification as a Team member is positively related to the extent of political consensus in the delegation: The proportion stressing a Team member role increases from about one-third (36%) where there was *low* political consensus in the delegation to well over one-half (58%) where there was *high* political consensus. Stress on a Solo or Representative role shows a reverse pattern: Standing alone as an individual delegate or serving as spokesperson for an issue caucus or organization is most prevalent when political consensus is low, least prevalent when political consensus is high.

Table 5.7
Expected and Actual Conference Role by Level of Political Consensus in the State Delegation

Expected Role & Role Retention	Level of Political Consensus in Delegation		
	HIGH	MODERATE	LOW
EXPECTED ROLE (October)			
Team Member	57.8	48.7	36.0
Solo	18.0	26.6	30.0
Representative	24.2	24.8	33.1
N =	(339)	(222)	(172)
ROLE RETENTION (Percent actually filled role they expected)			
Team Member	77.5% (196)	70.0% (108)	63.7% (62)
Solo	65.6% (61)	57.6% (59)	50.8% (53)
Representative	32.7% (82)	48.1% (54)	55.9% (54)

The data shown at the bottom of Table 5.7 suggest that high political consensus was conducive to the retention of Team member and Solo roles but to a reduction in Representative roles. Of those who expected to play a Representative role, only 32.7% reported 4 months later that this was the role they in fact played if they had served in a delegation of like-minded delegates. If they were a minority and felt the rest of their delegation held different political views, 56% reported they played the Representative role. The highest role retention is shown by the delegates in high consensus delegations who expected to play a Team member role (a full 78% retained this choice 4 months later). It appears that representing an issue or organization may fade and be replaced by a team spirit when the group itself is very high on political consensus.

Many of the comments respondents made give a close-up view of what it was like to be a member of delegations varying in the extent of shared political views with the respondent. One Anti-Plan delegate from a state delegation she saw as largely opposed to her views (low political consensus in our terminology) wrote:

> I had a sense of triumph when I was elected and thought I would go to Houston as a fighter for things my delegation was against. We had a long flight to Houston . . . lots of time to talk. A woman I thought my absolute enemy had a daughter going through the same things mine was, and we ended up liking each other. . . . We talked about our differences for a long time. I voted for things I was against only a month before. I think deeper about things now.

The delegation in question had a very high level of support for the national Plan; its chairperson was, in fact, one of the Pro-Plan coordinators at the conference. The delegate quoted above clearly felt very much a minority of two women, and she seems to have softened her views through personal familiarity with several of the Pro-Plan supporters in her delegation. Although she spoke up for what she believed on a few issues of deep concern to her, she was influenced to shift perspective toward the delegation's position on issues less salient to her.

A very different note was struck by a woman from a state delegation in which conservative views were held by a large minority of the delegates. She wrote, in part, "I sure was glad to have real friends with me. It would have been awful hard to hold tight to our position otherwise."

The development of a collective *esprit* was cited by many women in delegations with very high political consensus—a consensus that was sometimes only won after heated debate at delegation meetings prior to the conference. Thus one woman wrote:

> We had a lot of differences among us that we fought over at meetings of the delegation back home. But at the opening session, our entire delegation stood with tears in our eyes, bursting with pride for all the women of America. I think we all felt that those months of work and battling behind us were worth it. We ended up strongly Pro-Plan.

Another woman wrote, "Nothing gave more pleasure than seeing and being a part of the whole California delegation, waving our yellow scarves in a united vote." This collective identification is what being a Team member means, but it does not depend on anyone changing their views or their votes; it can simply involve a deepened understanding of their differences, or playing down those differences while working in the larger collectivity that has meaning to them. A delegate from Georgia caught this view in her report:

> I was real proud of our delegates. We experienced sisterhood and sharing of concern for all women in the Georgia delegation, including our Stop ERA members. They actually stayed with the delegation when the "Stop ERA" people walked out. They voted against the resolution, in keeping with their views, but we were all very moved by their remaining with the delegation when the pressure got tough.

Although not herself from Ohio, one delegate made the following comment from her observations of that delegation:

> Most memorable to me was a lone black Ohio delegate who was kissed and hugged by fellow Ohio delegates when the Minorities resolution was passed. She "praised the Lord." These were the same white women who voted strongly against ERA, abortion, etc. Barbara Jordan was right—we need to learn to compromise, and one way to do that is to first make contact with those we disagree with.

There were also many examples of how sharing the same sex contributed to the Team member role. For one very politically experienced woman, the lesson has persisted well beyond the 1977 conference:

> I have been a politician for over 20 years, but working on the state delegation taught me something, a new realization: a sense of oneness, and the depth of just being a woman and a feminist. This winter, I found I began asking people where they stood on women's issues when I first met them. In 20 years in politics, I never thought to ask what someone's political party preference was when I met them, despite being very much involved with one party myself! Now I know how much deeper involvement in the women's movement cuts than ordinary politics.

Delegation Size and Conference Role of Delegates

There was some suggestion in the qualitative comments the delegates made about their experiences in Houston that the sheer size of the delegation might be a relevant variable in a number of respects. To serve in a small delegation of 12 people is a very different experience from serving on one of 50 or, as in the case of California, 96 people. For one thing, it is much harder to get acquainted with a very large number of people than with a dozen or so, which suggests that those serving on small delegations might have had an easier time developing a collective identification that encouraged a role choice as a Team member. By contrast, a large delegation had room to tolerate a good deal of diversity, perhaps encouraging, by the greater anonymity and impersonality of meetings, the retention of identification with the organizational or caucus commitments brought into the delegation when it was formed.

Table 5.8 suggests a tendency in this direction, for those who served in small delegations (defined as between 12 and 20 members) are more likely to anticipate playing a Team member role than those who served in large delegations (defined as between 36 and 96 members). No pattern is shown on Solo role expectations (which tend generally to be rather idiosyncratic), but there is an increase in Representative role expectations among those on large delegations.

Table 5.8
Expected Role by Size of State Delegation (in percent)

EXPECTED ROLE	Size of State Delegation		
	SMALL	MEDIUM	LARGE
Team Member	54.1	51.3	42.2
Solo	21.1	25.9	22.0
Representative	25.0	22.6	36.0
N =	(244)	(261)	(256)

What is not clear from these data is whether the role expectations are genuine reflections of delegation size or a spurious effect because delegation size is related to some other, more relevant, variable. The larger the delegation, the greater the tendency for more delegates to be from large cities, for example, in the highly urbanized industrial northeastern or midwestern states. Table 5.9 confirms the high association between city size and delegation size: More than 50% of those in large delegations lived either in large cities or their suburbs (defined as over 300,000 residents), which is true for only 13% of those on small delegations. Table 5.10 shows that expectations of serving as Team members is not as much a reflection of delegation size as of city size: People from farms, rural areas, or small towns were more likely to report having played the Team member role, whereas those from large cities tended to play Representative roles, a pattern found within both small and large delegations. Highly urban delegates, then, seem to have brought more dif-

Table 5.9
Size of City of Residence by Size of State Delegation (in percent)

Size of City of Residence	Size of State Delegation		
	Small	Medium	Large
Farm or Town	40.2	25.3	17.2
Medium Size City	47.1	39.8	27.3
Large City	12.7	34.9	55.5
N =	(243)	(263)	(256)

Table 5.10

Expected Role by City Size and State Delegation Size (in percent)

Expected Role	Delegation: City:	Small Small	Medium	Large	Medium Small	Medium	Large	Large Small	Medium	Large
Team Member . . .		60.2	52.2	37.5	50.0	49.0	52.7	53.3	41.4	43.0
Solo		16.3	28.0	19.1	32.8	25.0	19.8	19.2	32.9	16.2
Representative .		23.4	20.0	42.9	16.7	26.0	27.4	27.2	25.7	40.8
N =		(98)	(115)	(31)	(66)	(106)	(91)	(44)	(70)	(142)

ferentiated views into their delegations, and perhaps more sophistication in knowing how to press for those views from previous work with issue caucuses and organizations in their cities. The greater ease of accepting a collective identification as a Team member on a state delegation may grow out of the small town or rural person's experience of living in a cohesive, long-known community. This is of course only a speculation, though consistent with sociological thought about the nature of metropolitan political life compared to rural and small-town America. This speculation can be put to an empirical test and at the same time bring together several threads of the analysis through a multiple regression on the roles the delegates actually played at the conference. This is the focus of the following section.

Actual Roles Played in Houston

By dichotomizing each of the three roles as dummy variables, one can investigate the determinants of each actual role type as reported in the February survey, using both structural and individual attribute variables. Three variables refer to structural characteristics of the delegation: size, political consensus, and the number of times the delegation met (an exposure variable). I assume that the more times a delegation met, the greater the probability that a collective Team member role will be reported. In keeping with previous findings (Table 5.10), I also assume that the larger the city of residence, the more the delegates will report Representative rather than Team member roles. Three additional variables are personal attributes: formal responsibility for the delegation through service as an officer or chairperson of a task force or committee, which might encourage a Team member role choice; membership on the state coordinating committee, which would similarly predispose the delegate to team identification; and age, on the assumption that younger women may be more attracted to the more assertive Representative role, whereas older women may gravitate to the Team member role.

Table 5.11 shows the results of this regression test. A very decided profile of the Team member emerges from the first column: The most significant and independent predictors of actually playing a Team member role in Houston were the number of times the delegation met; high levels of perceived political consensus in the delegation, presumably predisposing the delegate to identify readily with others on the delegation; long-standing association with the IWY Commission's work through service on the state committee; and being older. City size shows a negative coefficient, meaning that residents of large cities were less likely than those from small cities to have reported a Team member

Table 5.11

Regression on Actual Conference Role Type of Status, Opportunity, and Contextual Variables (Beta Coefficients)

Predictor Variables	Actual Conference Role Type		
	TEAM MEMBER	SOLO	REPRESENTATIVE
No. Times State Delegation Met . .	.186 ***	−.110 **	−.074 *
Political Consensus Level of State Delegation	.120 **	−.046	−.054
State Committee Member[a]	.110 **	−.066 +	−.053
Age	.106 **	.027	−.172 ***
Size of City of Residence	−.053	−.057	.057
Size of State Delegation	.052	−.095 *	.078 *
Level of Formal Responsibility in State Delegation	.038	−.058	.027
R^2 =	.083 ***	.037 ***	.053 ***
F =	8.963	3.749	5.501
N = (700)			

[a]Dummy variable.

+ p ⩽ .10
* p ⩽ .05
** p ⩽ .01
*** p ⩽ .001

role, but this is not a statistically significant coefficient. Delegation size or formal position on the delegation have no independent effect.

The predictors of a Representative role in Houston are in sharp contrast to the profile shown for Team member: The single most important predictor here is the youthfulness of the delegate. Infrequent meetings and large delegation size also contributed significantly to whether a delegate actually played a Representative role in Houston. The signs are in the predicted direction for political consensus and committee membership, both of which reduce the tendency to a Representative role, but the coefficients are not statistically significant. Thus, the profile of a delegate who played a Representative role in Houston is a young, highly urban delegate serving on a large delegation that rarely met. It is highly likely that they were among the "new blood" (Newcomers) elected at state meetings and dedicated to work on a few resolutions of keen interest to them.

Throughout the analysis, the Solo role seems to be more idiosyncratic: The variables in the question explain much less and are limited to infrequent delegation meetings and small delegation size.

Development of Personal Familiarity with Home-State Delegates

The delegates were asked to estimate what proportion of their delegation they knew personally at three points in time: before the state meeting was held; after the state meeting but before the national conference; and by late winter, 3 months after the conference. These data on extent of personal familiarity with home-state delegates permit an investigation of what determined both level and change in the extent of personal familiarity over the time period from the formation of the delegation to its demise or transformation into a newly constituted organization by the spring of 1978.

Table 5.12 shows that most of the change in the extent of personal familiarity with home-state delegates took place before the delegation left for Houston: Only 15% of the delegates reported knowing at least 80% of their sister delegates before the state meetings, but by October this had tripled, to 45%. By 3 months after the national conference, the increase is only another 10% (to 55%).

What happened between the three points in time, of course, was that a number of meetings of the state delegations or of committees the delegation set up at its first meeting took place. The typical profile of delegation meetings is suggested in Table 5.13, where it can be seen that most delegations met more than twice before the conference, two or three times during the conference, and one to three times after the conference. On average, then, the

Table 5.12

Personal Familiarity with Delegation Members over Time (elected delegates and alternates only)

Proportion of Delegates Known Personally	Timing of Meeting		
	BEFORE State Meeting	AFTER State Meeting but BEFORE National Conference	AFTER National Conference
80% or more	15.1	45.1	55.0
50% – 79%	20.0	19.6	15.6
25% – 49%	21.9	19.7	15.9
Less than 25%	36.1	15.6	12.6
None	6.9	1.2	.8
	100.0	100.0	100.0
Base N	(872)	(888)	(883)

delegations met between four and five times between the state meetings in the summer of 1977 and late winter of 1978, when the delegates responded to the second survey. The range was from only one meeting to more than twelve. Of course, not all the delegates attended all the meetings of their delegations. In fact, we can only be confident of attendance before the national conference, because only the October survey asked if the delegates had themselves attended. Of those who reported that a meeting had already taken place, 86% said they had themselves attended. I did not ask about personal attendance concerning meetings during and following the conference, though it seems reasonable to assume a high level of attendance in Houston and probably some drop-off in attendance when the delegates returned to their home states.

The rapid rate of increase in personal familiarity with sister delegates over the 6-month period can be seen in Table 5.14, where state committee membership and frequency of delegation meetings is introduced, where appropriate, for the three points in time. Before the state meetings, if the delegates had not served on the state committee, only one-fifth knew one-half or more of their state delegates; by the winter after the conference, if the delegation had met a number of times, four-fifths of the delegates knew one-half or more of their home-state delegates.

Delegation membership and conference participation clearly expanded the number of personal acquaintances the delegates enjoyed. Such personal familiarity is a minimal base for the development of contacts that may prove useful for specific political efforts or for the development of a personal political career. Clearly, there are many things, both personal and structural, that affect the size of a personal network apart from delegation membership, noted previously. Even those with no previous contact with the state coordinating committees knew a significant number of the delegates who shared their success in the elections at the state meetings. Which factors besides state committee membership are independent contributors to the proportion of elected delegates known before the state meeting is explored in a regression mode in Table 5.15. It was assumed that involvement in organizations, state mainstream politics, and feminist political activity would pave the way for high levels of personal acquaintance in the state. In addition, I test whether participation in the liberal causes of the 1960s and early 1970s increased acquaintanceship levels and whether membership in a minority racial or religious group depressed such acquaintanceship.

Three factors show significant independent contributions to the level of personal acquaintance. Long-standing association through state committee membership shows an expectedly high coefficient of $\beta = .290$. Almost equal in strength is activity in mainstream politics at the state level ($\beta = .200$), presumably through travel, correspondence, and involvement with state party organizations. Level of feminist political activity contributes a significant, but

Table 5.13
Frequency of State Delegation Meetings before, during, and after the National Conference (in percent)

Frequency of Meetings	Time of Delegation Meetings		
	BEFORE Conference	DURING Conference	SINCE Conference
None	7.8	3.4	42.7
Once	25.3	21.1	28.4
Two or Three Times	41.0	52.9	20.9
Four or More Times	25.9	22.6	8.0
N =	(875)	(845)	(805)
Don't Know	1.6	2.6	6.2
N =	(889)	(868)	(856)

Table 5.14

Effects of State Committee Membership and Frequency of Delegation Meetings on Personal Familiarity with Homestate Delegates (in percent)

Time	Intervening or Conditional Factor	Proportion of Delegates Personally Known				
		80% or more	50% to 79%	26% to 49%	Less than 25%	N
A. BEFORE STATE MEETING						
	Not State Committee Member	7.4	15.9	22.7	54.0	(485)
	State Committee Member	27.0	27.3	21.9	23.8	(319)
	Chi.Sq.Signif. ***					
B. AFTER STATE MEETING BUT BEFORE CONFERENCE						
	No Delegation Meeting	27.2	21.7	22.4	28.8	(254)
	At Least One Meeting	53.1	18.9	18.1	9.9	(525)
	Chi.Sq.Signif. ***					
C. AFTER CONFERENCE						
	Low Meeting Frequency	45.9	20.2	17.4	16.5	(242)
	Medium Frequency . . .	55.5	11.4	19.9	13.3	(272)
	High Frequency	66.0	14.4	11.6	8.0	(250)
	Chi.Sq.Signif. ***					

*** $p \leqslant .001$

Table 5.15

Regression on Proportion of Delegates Known Personally before State Meeting

PREDICTOR VARIABLE	Beta Coefficient	
Member, State Committee[a]	.290	***
Political Activity on STATE Level	.200	***
Racial/Ethnic Minority Group Member[a]	-.102	**
Feminist Political Activity Level	.081	*
# Groups Supported Nomination	.056	+
Total # Organizations	.028	
Catholic[a]	-.020	
# Liberal Causes	.005	
R^2 =	.207	
F = 22.383		
N = (695)		

[a]Dummy Variables.

+ $p \leqslant .10$
* $p \leqslant .05$
** $p \leqslant .01$
*** $p \leqslant .001$

more modest, influence ($\beta = .081$), whereas involvement in liberal causes or extensive organizational membership did not contribute any independent influence on level of personal acquaintance with members of the delegations before their election. Racial or ethnic minority group membership significantly reduced the extensiveness of personal acquaintance, as did a Catholic religious affiliation, though in the latter case not significantly so. The number of groups that supported the delegates' nomination at the state meeting also encouraged a wider net of personal acquaintance with sister delegates; this verged on statistical significance. Together these predictors produced a highly significant R^2 of .207.

The level of personal acquaintance when the state delegations were formed

Table 5.16

Regression on Proportion of State Delegation Known Personally after National Conference (Beta Coefficients)

Predictor Variables	Beta Coefficient	Significance Level
Proportion of State Delegation Known Before State Meeting	.353	***
Size of State Delegation	-.262	***
Political Consensus Level of State Delegation	.191	***
Pre-Conference Expectation of Working with State Delegation	.176	***
Plenary Session Activity Level	.068	*
No. Times State Delegation Met	.068	*
Level of Formal Responsibility in State Delegation	.062	*
Size of City of Residence	-.016	
R^2 =	.441	***
F =	68.15	
N = (700)		

   * $p \leqslant .05$
*** $p \leqslant .001$

in the summer of 1977 is therefore seen to be more extensive for white, Protestant members of the state coordinating committees who had been active in state mainstream politics and, to a more limited degree, in feminist politics. What happened from that point forward, in terms of enlarging personal acquaintance, and hence of potential future political network size, can be explored by including the baseline variable of previously known delegation members in an equation dealing with the extent of personal acquaintance by late winter, when the national conference was already receding into history. A variety of predictor variables are entered into the regression equation on postconference personal acquaintance level shown in Table 5.16. Three variables tap structural characteristics of the delegation (size of delegation, size of city of residence, and political consensus of delegation); two variables tap opportunity or exposure (number of times the delegation met and level of formal responsibility in the state delegation); one variable serves as an index of motivation (high preconference expectation of working closely with the state delegation); and the last variable measures the level of activity the delegates report during the plenary sessions in Houston.

The size of the delegation is second only to the baseline measure of previous personal acquaintance in affecting an expansion of the personal networks of the delegates: Those on small delegations got to know proportionately more of the members of their delegations than women serving on large delegations (hence the negative sign for this coefficient). So, too, delegations perceived to be high on political consensus encouraged further increases in personal acquaintance, and delegates who expected to work with the state delegation in Houston apparently enlarged their acquaintance level in the course of their political effort. Opportunity (through frequent delegation meetings), formal responsibility within the delegation, and visibility during the conference (through high levels of plenary session activity) added more modestly to the expansion of personal acquaintance by the postconference survey. Together, the variables go a long way to explaining the level of personal familiarity the delegates reached by the late winter of 1978, with a highly significant R^2 of .441.

Survey data and regression equations cannot capture the actual processes of contact and friendship formation, to say nothing of the emotional tone and personal significance of the many contacts the delegates made during the months they served on state delegations and the days they spent in Houston. These are observant, outgoing, and gregarious women, thrown into socially dense and politically intense situations during the national conference. It was our observation that the patience the delegates showed in Houston as they spent precious time on lines to register, obtain their badges, use an elevator, or eat at crowded facilities was made easy precisely because they are outgoing and gregarious women. They used all that time they spent on lines talking to each other, not only with people they knew but with people they were meeting for the first time. First encounters were undoubtedly eased by the political symbols the delegates wore: A quick glance at the badges, ribbons, buttons, armbands, and hats provided a profile of the political affiliations of the delegates, profiles rounded out and personalized through conversations.

A society stratified by social class and race, with considerable regional variation in the distribution of ethnicity, provides little opportunity to become personally acquainted with people from groups different from one's own, whether that difference is rooted in occupation, age, race, religion, or ethnicity. I have already noted that some of this diversity was built into the state delegations themselves, providing an opportunity to establish personal connections that crossed racial and ethnic lines. It was striking how frequently the delegates pointed to these cross-ethnic encounters as the high points of their experience at the national conference. Thus, at least a dozen delegates pointed to contact with Native-American women in their delegations as among their most memorable Houston experiences. One woman from the southwest commented, "Several long conversations with a member of my own delegation, a native-American, helped me undo a lifetime of misunderstanding." Another woman from Arizona wrote, "Though I am from Arizona, I had never known any native Americans close up. I had lots of opportunity for long intimate talks with two native-American women in my delegation, and just felt like a student at the feet of two great teachers." A woman from New York City had dinner with a cousin of hers who was in the California delegation, and gave an indirect account of her cousin's contact with Asian-American women in her delegation:

> She told me about the problems Asian wives of American servicemen have in this country, how isolated they are, how dreadful the sweatshops they work in out there. I had never known such problems still exist in this country. I thought they passed with my parents' generation—those awful sweatshops we knew as children in New York.

Another encounter involved a shift of vote on controversial issues:

> We were a small delegation of twelve persons, three of whom were native-Americans. I was seated next to them and developed a deep level of intimacy with them as the hours went on. We grew to respect each other's opinions and ended up influencing the delegation on issues, such as reproductive freedom and lesbianism, which the native-Americans had previously been against. When the Minorities resolution passed, we all danced in the aisle and cried tears of joy.

The encounters referred to in the quotes above could just as readily have occurred during a delegation meeting back in their home states, though it is also probably the case that being one of 56 delegations in Houston helped to cement ties within each delegation. Far more frequently, among the most memorable experiences the delegates reported were encounters with delegates from *other* states, most often as a consequence of the seating arrangement on the floor of the plenary sessions. Over 200 of the comments the delegates made were based on either observations of, or conversations, with people from other states who were seated in front of, behind, or across the aisles from their own delegation. Many of these cross-state contacts and observations concerned women from ethnic, religious, or political groups very different from their own. To share the flavor of these encounters, what follows are the most "memorable" ones to this privileged reader of their comments:

We sat near a delegation with a number of native-American women. I was amazed by the kinds of problems they told me they experienced. As an upper middle class eastern Jew, my eyes were opened to our diversity and the different problems other groups encounter. Before this conference, I thought my greatest handicap was being Jewish. Not any longer. It's being a woman.

I'd been watching the Alabama delegation that was seated near us. As a black woman, to walk across that aisle and explain parliamentary procedure to them was one of the most difficult but best steps in my life. I could not enjoy seeing "my" resolutions passed when the opposition didn't even know how to function.

We sat behind a delegation with a lot of Mormon women. It was most gratifying to succeed in persuading a few of them to separate themselves from the anti-plan bloc, to put women above the differences and then watch them vote "yes" on a few issues the rest of the antis voted against.

My delegation was pretty much in agreement and solidly pro-plan. I talked a lot with women seated near me from another part of the country. By the time the sexual preference plank came up, one of these women (anti-plan, anti-abortion) smiled and said "don't worry, it will pass." After the vote she shook hands and said "see, I told you." The last day, we shook hands again and agreed that we were awfully glad we had met, and that women like us, on opposite sides and opposite parts of the country, to meet and talk and feel good about each other was what Houston was all about.

I sat near and watched the majority delegates in the Indiana delegation (I was in the Tennessee alternate section) vote solidly anti-everything, no on every resolution. When I encountered one of them in a line at the coffee concession, I asked why they had chosen yellow as the color of their "majority" ribbons (not combatively, just from real curiosity). Did they know yellow was the color the suffragists had worn when struggling to win votes for women? This led to real conversation between us, open, honest, thoughtful. We found (to her and my amazement) that we agreed on a lot of things. Imagine my pleasure, in succeeding votes after we returned to our seats, to see this woman on several occasions, break with her own delegation and vote in favor of certain resolutions. I felt our talk had made a difference, that women can reach other women.

Many of the Pro-Plan delegates wrote comments similar to the last quote above, projecting the idea that they had been persuasive in changing the views and hence the votes of Anti-Plan delegates either within their own delegation or from delegations seated near them. There is at least some element of wishful thinking in these views, since a great number of the Anti-Plan delegates did not come to Houston with an intention of voting against every single resolution in the agenda, as so many Pro-Plan delegates believed. A few Anti-Plan delegates hint at this in their own comments in the survey. One who reported that the high point for her was the passage of the Minorities resolution, went on to explain, "Before going to Houston I had studied the issues and was prepared to vote for the minority resolution as well as several others."

It is interesting that the Pro-Plan delegates, so quick to report any evidence of bloc-voting on the part of the Anti-Plan delegates, did not see their own behavior as similar when they or their friends swallowed their reservations and voted with the Pro-Plan majority on some controversial resolutions. Because they were convinced the Anti-Plan delegates were united in opposition to the entire Plan of Action, the Pro-Plan delegates who made personal contacts with Anti-Plan delegates and then observed the latter voting for a few resolutions were quick to attribute such votes to their own political persuasiveness during friendly conversations. Chapter 6 will explore further the contrast between perception and reality in the views of the polarized groups of Anti- and Pro-Plan delegates. The point here has been to provide some close-up view of the variety of relationships and the emotional flavor of the encounters experienced by the delegates that are hidden behind the statistics on the formation and expansion of personal acquaintance with members of their delegations. New acquaintances from their own delegations were only one source of network-building. Houston itself, as illustrated in the quotations above, provided an even greater variety of potential new contacts, and it is to these that we turn for the last step in the analysis of this chapter.

Network Formation in Houston

Houston was fertile ground for the cultivation of new relationships that may have importance to network building and future political activity by the delegates. Already noted for their gregarious "joiner" quality where organizational membership is concerned, the delegates responded to the people and event-packed days in Houston in a predictable fashion: The average delegate developed 22 new contacts with people she met for the first time in Houston with whom she planned to keep in touch. As noted in Chapter 4, the elected delegates and alternates reported the highest mean level of new contacts with women from their own states ($M = 9.5$), somewhat lower means for new contacts that crossed state lines ($M = 7.5$), and a mean of 5.2 new contacts with people from their own towns and cities. Those whose duties and official responsibilities were extensive, like the national IWY Commissioners and members of the Secretariat staff, reported not only higher average levels of new contacts but a predominance of contacts that crossed state boundaries.

Since there was a wide range to the number of new contacts made in

Houston, there was considerable room for the influence of many variables on contact formation in Houston. Since I asked the delegates to estimate their new contacts separately for the three units of their own city, own state, and other states, it is possible to explore differences in the influence of a particular variable for contacts of these three types. Thus, for example, women from a large city like New York were far more likely to meet other New Yorkers in Houston for the first time (either sister delegates from their own delegation, observers, or appointed delegates-at-large), than were women from a small town in Florida. By the same token, one would expect a woman from a small town like Elmira, New York, to develop a lot of new contacts from other parts of her state, both because few Elmirans would be in Houston and because her delegation itself is very large.

Table 5.17 brings the same set of predictor variables into three regression equations on new contacts to show what differentiates network formation by city, within states, and between states. It shows that new contacts with hometown people is largely a function of the size of that city; no other variable

Table 5.17

Regression on Network Formation of Contextual and Activity Variables (Beta Coefficients)

Predictor Variables	New Contacts Made		
	OWN CITY	OWN STATE	OTHER STATES
Size of City of Residence . .	.175 ***	−.103 **	.044
Size of Delegation	.061	.181 ***	.033
No. of Groups Worked with in Houston	.054	.143 ***	.193 ***
Plenary Session Activity Level	.029	.041	.097 *
No. of Events Attended in Houston	.011	.031	−.049
Age	.015	.039	.023
R^2 =	.049 ***	.065 ***	.070 ***
F =	5.89	8.05	8.71
N = (700)			

```
  * p ≤ .05
 ** p ≤ .01
*** p ≤ .001
```

shows any significant effect, though all are positive in sign. Contacts outside the hometown but within the state show a more interesting profile. Size of delegation is the strongest predictor: Clearly, the larger the delegation, the more opportunity there was during the days in Houston to become acquainted with delegation members in more than a distant and casual way. Within state, new contacts are also affected by the size of the city of residence, but in the opposite direction: The smaller the hometown size, the more new contacts are made with people from other parts of the state, like the woman from Elmira described above. Thus the national conference seems to have contributed to ties between country and city and between small-town and big-city within the states. Home state contacts are also affected by the number of groups the delegates worked with in Houston, since the groups involved purposeful contact not only with members of the delegation but with those from organizational chapters, observers, or appointed delegates-at-large from one's home state.

New contacts with people from other states show yet a third profile: The strongest predictor is working with a number of groups (caucuses, organizations, other delegations), with their rich potential for new acquaintance formation around shared interests. The second, though less significant, predictor of out-of-state new contacts was the activity level of the delegates during the plenary sessions: Any involvement in persuading others to change their votes, like the examples given earlier of women befriending and talking to delegates from another state seated near their own, or passing messages along from Pro-Plan or Anti-Plan floor coordinators, would contribute to new connections of this sort.

Age played no part in the extensiveness of the new contacts formed in Houston; apparently young women were just as likely as older women to meet new people and plan to keep in touch with them. Nor was the level of attendance at such events as the torch rally, receptions, exhibit halls, or workshops related in any influential way to contact formation. Most of these events were of a spectator variety, where attention is concentrated on a podium, parade, or stage, in sharp contrast to the Coliseum, where the floor, rather than the podium, was where the action took place.

Conclusion

There is no way to tell whether the extensive profile of personal acquaintance and new contacts the delegates formed through their involvement with the state delegations and the national conference itself has been utilized in the years since the IWY Commission submitted its report to former President Carter in March 1978 and closed its books and headquarters. At the national level, a large and committed core of people have continued the work of the IWY Commission in the form of a Continuing Committee of the National Women's Conference, co-chaired by Sarah Harder and Anne Turpeau. At this writing, the Continuing Committee had launched a 5-year program of action for 1981 through 1985, plans for a second conference are already underway, and an Advocacy Network is in place for the purposes of outreach, activation, and collaboration on behalf of the Plan of Action endorsed in 1977 in Houston.

Whether there are viable continuing committees on the state level to carry forward the state plans of action many states adopted, I do not know. But clearly, the spirit of Houston enlarged and reinforced the invisible web of contacts among American women that events may activate in the coming years. As and when that happens, what may loom again in public visibility are the acquaintances whose formation has been charted in the course of this chapter. I hope that, for some of the delegates, these acquaintances and new contacts will become political constituents as the former delegates become candidates for and win elections to office in mainstream and movement politics.

6

The Structures of Affect and Belief

Introduction

Until 1970 or so, the predominant paradigm in the social sciences for interpreting social and political movements was psychological; a social scientist would search out the motivation for movement participation in early family histories, expecting to find elements of psychological pathology and social deviance lurking there (Davies, 1962; Feuer, 1969; Gurr, 1970). Since 1970, the emphasis has shifted to treating social movements as an extension of mainstream social and political life by investigating the development of networks of individuals and of organizations that come together to achieve some social and political change outside of mainstream politics and existing community institutions. The shift from psychological to organizational explanations of social movements has tended to bypass direct inquiry concerning belief systems or their psychological underpinning, as Ferree and Miller (1978) have pointed out, and as Mueller and Judd (1979) have begun to explore empirically.

The analysis reported in Chapters 4 and 5 was in keeping with this recent tendency in the literature on social movements to focus on network building, tables of organizations, coalitions of organizations. It was in that framework that I explored the differences between delegates, IWY Commissioners and Secretariat staff members. The official IWY Commission report and most press accounts of the conference were similar in their emphasis on organizational behavior such as the effort of the various caucuses to amend or hammer out substitute resolutions. An observer of the plenary sessions could easily notice that at least 75–80% of the delegates stood in a final "aye" vote on all but one resolution. A vote, after all, is a clear behavior act that is easy to report since it permits only three clear options: One can vote for, against, or abstain from a motion. There is no room for qualification, no chance to register ambivalence.

But it is not likely that all the delegates who voted "aye" to a particular resolution shared the same level of enthusiasm for it. Some would have preferred to qualify a resolution, others to extend it more boldly. On at least two resolutions, Reproductive Freedom and Sexual Preference, not only was there much sharper polarization of views and feelings between those who voted for or against them but many people who voted the same way did so with very different feelings, some with a sense of elation, others with deep personal sorrow.

Many delegates reported either their own inner conflict or their observations of the pain or joy of other delegates when certain of the resolutions passed in Houston. On the Reproductive Freedom resolution, one woman observed, "Seeing women who were personally and morally opposed to certain issues stand and vote for them to help all women impressed me more than anything else. I saw many Catholic women stand up and vote for abortion, crying all the while." Another woman shared her own inner turmoil and the very great pain involved for her to publicly support the resolution because it was so strongly against the values of her family:

> As a Catholic and a member of a staunch anti-abortion family, my vote for reproductive freedom was made, in conscience, at great personal sacrifices to me. But I felt it was a grave and solemn decision, soberly made, and I could not join in the cheering.

Another reaction catches not only the ambivalence behind the public act of voting for the reproductive freedom resolution but the remarkable empathy and support of her sister delegates:

> As an ordained minister and former chaplain in a large county hospital, the vote on reproductive freedom was extremely difficult emotionally for me, though I am committed to pro-choice. As the anti-choice banners went up, it choked me up and I stood up to vote yes, crying all the while. Unexpectedly, there came from at least six fellow delegates from my state, gestures of such wonderful support, silent gestures of support for me: a hand clasp, a hug, strong hands on my shoulders. It made all the difference in the world to me at that time.

It was this issue above all others that the Anti-Plan delegates wrote about in describing what stood out in their memories of the conference. One wrote:

> It is not a positive memory, but a vivid and sobering one. It occurred as the
> resolution on reproductive freedom was passed on the Sabbath. A demonstration
> was mournfully staged by Pro-Life people. Pro-abortion delegates doubled their
> fists, thrust them into the poster of the baby Pro-Lifers carried, ripping it. They
> shouted "choice, choice." But to me it sounded like "crucify, crucify."

Another woman wrote: "Two things stand out. One was the feeling of horror
that women were willing to have their unborn children killed to advance
themselves, and the second, the hope the conference gave me that women
can work together for their betterment." In a last example, a woman wrote in
a vein that runs through many comments on the controversial issues at the
conference, that is, that for the first time they appreciated the depth of commitment and feeling among those they disagreed with:

> Immediately after the reproductive freedom resolution had passed, during the
> anti-demonstration, the woman beside me broke down and wept. When the dem-
> onstration ended I asked her why she had cried, since I had seen that she voted in
> favor of the resolution. She said it was not that she shared the anti-abortion views,
> but that for the first time she comprehended the depth of their emotional commit-
> ment to their position; so she wept with them for their defeat.

As some of these quotations illustrate, private belief can be out of joint with
public behavior. One can vote for a resolution but feel pain in doing so. We
can act under pressure from an organization or movement we belong to and
espouse a belief about which we privately feel a good deal of ambivalence.
Nor does this apply only to issues publicly acknowledged to be controversial,
like reproductive freedom and sexual preference. Most women in the feminist
movement today support child-care centers, typically as an aide to employed
mothers, increasingly to meet the developmental needs of children. Yet,
many who support child-care centers have serious reservations about using
such centers themselves, either out of preference for keeping a preschooler in
a familiar and familial environment or out of sober realization of how far short
from ideal most child-care centers are in a country that provides so little
funding for this human service.

It is to these questions of ideology and feeling or, as I shall refer to them,
belief and *affect,* that this chapter is addressed. We have already seen in
Chapter 3 that, compared to any national sample of American women, the
delegates show a skewed distribution of response to attitude items dealing
with economic rights, marital equity, abortion, and child care. Yet, there is
sufficient variance on the indices that measure these dimensions to permit an
exploration of its determinants. This will be the first topic of the chapter.

The second topic focuses on a set of affect scales that tap the more free-
floating feelings people have toward a variety of groups in American society.
The groups in question were largely tailored to the circumstances and issues

of concern to the national women's conference: groups supporting or opposing the ERA and abortion; political groups like liberals, conservatives, and
radicals; the two predominant racial or ethnic groups represented in the sample, Blacks and Latinas; several occupational groups, that is, business/
professional, farm/rural, and labor unions; and three groups of special interest
to the study, NOW, the National Women's Political Caucus (NWPC), and the
IWY Commissioners. These affect scales were included in both surveys in
order to explore whether any change took place in the structure of affect
within the delegates as a consequence of participation in the conference. This
is the second topic covered in the chapter.

The third and fourth sections of the chapter build on the first two. Drawing
on the analysis of beliefs and affect toward groups, I shall explore whether
there are pressures toward consistency of belief and affect as a result of
organizational commitments the delegates brought with them to Houston. To
explore the issue of constraint toward belief consistency, members of two
specific organizations well represented among the delegates are compared:
the National Organization for Women, as the prime example of a feminist
organization, and the League of Women Voters, as an example of an
equally sophisticated political organization, but one with no wide range of
feminist belief commitments. The hypothesis to be tested in this analysis is
whether individuals show less variance across a number of belief domains if
they belong to a feminist organization than if they belong to a nonfeminist but
equally political organization like the League. This is the third topic of the
chapter.

The fourth and last section narrows attention to the two key caucuses that
stood in opposition to each other at the national conference: the Anti-Plan
and the Pro-Plan activists. Here I shall explore the respects in which they
differ most and least in belief and affect and how they changed as a consequence of their encounter in Houston.

Belief Structure

The major dependent variables in this analysis are the five belief indices
introduced in Chapter 3. They tap beliefs on equity in marriage, child-care,
economic rights for women, abortion, and what I have called *bottom-line
feminism*. A brief summary sketch of the composition of these five indices
follows (see Table 3.9 and the text in Chapter 3 for further details).

Abortion Index: The abortion index is based on items indicating approval
of access to legal abortion under five circumstances: the mother's health is
endangered; the chance of fetal defect; no desire to marry the man responsi-

ble for the pregnancy; the family income is too low; and no desire for more children. The last three social conditions received less approval than the two health conditions, which is consistent with the ranking shown, (at lower levels of endorsement), in public opinion polls since the mid-1960s. The index is a simple one, from zero to 5, indicating the number of conditions approved by the respondent for access to legal abortion.

Marital Equity Index: The marital equity index consists of three items tapping views on men sharing housework equally with their wives, whether it is more important for a wife to help a husband's career than to have her own, and whether it is better if the husband is the achiever and the wife the homemaker. The last two items have been in use in national surveys since the mid-1960s.

Economic Rights Index: The economic rights index consists of three items tapping views on whether women should have the same job opportunities as men, whether the job should be kept for her if a woman has a baby, and whether women should be considered as seriously as men for posts as executives, politicians, or U.S. President.

Child-Care Index: There are five items in the child-care index, two of which have been used in polls since 1964 and deal with working mothers and their children: Whether an employed mother can have just as warm a relationship with a child as mothers at home, and whether preschool children suffer emotionally if mothers work. Three new items were added to these, specifically tapping use of child-care centers: One deals with benefits to the child of attendance at a child-care center, and two deal with personal attitudes toward child-care centers, that is, opposition to personal use even of a good center, and preference for a relative to care for a child rather than a child-care center.

Bottom-Line Feminism Index: The last index, the bottom-line feminism index, is based on four items, three of which tap the definition of a feminist, that is, whether a person is not a feminist if he or she opposes the ERA or abortion or does not work for lesbian rights. The fourth item asks if the lesbian issue does more harm than good to the women's movement. A high score on the index means the respondent rejects the "harm" notion and accepts the view that people cannot be considered feminists if they oppose the ERA, abortion access, or lesbian rights.

The means on these belief indices are at the high end of the score range, with the exception of the bottom-line feminism index, on which the mean is only slightly higher than the midpoint on the score. On the other hand, the standard deviations are quite large on all five indices. With the scores converted to a 0–100 range, one standard deviation varies from 14 points on the economic rights index to 23 points on the abortion as well as the bottom-line

Table 6.1

Pearson Correlation Coefficients between Belief Indices[a]

Index	Marital Equity	Child Care	Economic Rights	Abortion	Bottom-Line Feminism
Marital Equity	–	.605	.541	.448	.396
Child Care		–	.421	.394	.338
Economic Rights			–	.273	.213
Abortion				–	.396
Bottom-Line Feminism					–

[a]All coefficients statistically significant at the .001 level.

feminism indices. The five indices are all significantly correlated with each other, as shown in Table 6.1, but at a magnitude low enough to heighten the expectation that some different determinants may be at work in each of the five belief domains. This is particularly the case for the indices that tap abortion and sexual preference, which show the lowest correlations with the economic rights index.

Determinants of Belief Structure

There are advantages to an analysis of the determinants of the five belief domains with this particular sample, for the reason that the respondents have had a longstanding concern for the issues involved and are not as likely to give casual responses to the questions, as many respondents do in general population surveys on issues of low salience to them. Many have given long and thoughtful attention to the beliefs they now hold. They are also a very heterogeneous sample of women in age, educational attainment, religious affiliation and salience, race, ethnicity, and family status. Precisely because of the expansion of issues the feminist movement has become concerned with since 1970, significant differences may be found on these belief measures according to the age and religious affiliation of the woman. It is not easy to change a lifetime of convictions; decisions and commitments made a decade or more ago have structured many lives in ways that resist belief changes later in life. Hence older women, or those with deep religious commitments, may be less able or willing to accept feminist ideas about sex and family than about economic and political rights for women.

Table 6.2 brings together the results of a regression analysis of the five belief indices with eight predictor variables: general political orientation, religiosity as measured by church attendance, age, family size, educational attainment, level of own earnings, and two dummy variables on minority religious and racial or ethnic membership, that is, Catholic and minority group member.

A very liberal or radical political orientation and low religiosity are highly significant and independent contributors to endorsing feminist beliefs on all five indices. Political orientation is the stronger of the two predictors on all but the abortion index, where religiosity contributes slightly more ($\beta = -.238$) than political orientation ($\beta = .215$). Beyond these two significant predictors, there are different clusters of determinants that vary from one belief measure to another. Being Catholic contributes independently of religiosity to three of the measures: economic rights, abortion, and bottom-line feminism. Indeed, being Catholic is the strongest predictor of attitudes toward abortion ($\beta = -.290$). On the other hand, Catholic women take a more feminist position on the economic rights index than non-Catholic women, the only belief domain on which this is the case. Minority group members are less supportive of the feminist position on all five indices, though this is statistically significant only for marital equity, abortion, and bottom-line feminism. Additional analysis, not reported here, showed that both Blacks and Latinas were less apt to score at the feminist end of all five belief measures than majority women did. Feminist beliefs concerning abortion, sexual preference, and marriage may be viewed as too threatening to traditional values of continuing importance to rural women, Blacks, and Latinas at this stage of their affiliation with the feminist movement.

Number of children is an indirect measure of the degree to which women have in the past invested heavily (or not) in the world of the family and childrearing. In keeping with this, number of children shows a significant effect on attitude toward marital equity, child care, and abortion, independent of age, religion, or political orientation. Women with large families of their own are less supportive of child-care away from the family, less permissive toward abortion, and less egalitarian in their conception of the marital relationship.

Older women are less apt than younger women to show high scores on these feminist belief measures, but the coefficients are significant only for marital equity and bottom-line feminism, suggesting a generational barrier toward change either in the marital style they have evolved and accepted in their own marriages or in their definition of someone as feminist. Many older feminists support the ERA and educational and economic opportunities for

Table 6.2

Regression on Feminist Belief Indices of Political and Religious Orientation and Personal Attributes (Beta Coefficients)

PREDICTOR VARIABLES	Belief Indices				
	Marital Equity	Child Care	Economic Rights	Abortion	Bottom Line Feminism
Political Orientation (High=Conservative)	-.331 ***	-.321 ***	-.215 ***	-.215 ***	-.392 ***
Religiosity	-.180 ***	-.122 ***	-.147 ***	-.238 ***	-.137 ***
Catholic [a]	-.006	-.056 +	.081 *	-.290 ***	-.121 ***
Minority Group Member [a]	-.076 **	-.016	-.043	-.066 *	-.133 ***
Age	-.224 ***	-.035	-.063 +	-.030	-.106 ***
# Children	-.084 **	-.108 ***	-.021	-.065 *	-.025
Education	.076 **	.046	.031	.058 *	.016
Own Earnings	.056 *	.084 **	.047	.038	.002
R^2 =	.347 ***	.226 ***	.110 ***	.355 ***	.321 ***
F =	60.08	33.03	13.99	62.35	53.41
N = (913)					

[a] Dummy variables.

+ $p \leqslant .10$
* $p \leqslant .05$
** $p \leqslant .01$
*** $p \leqslant .001$

women but have reservations about egalitarianism in marriage and feel that the lesbian issue has done more harm than good to the women's movement. The fact that the coefficient for age on abortion attitudes is negative but not significant suggests it may be the greater salience of religious beliefs among older women, rather than age per se, that is involved in this belief domain.

Educational attainment shows a positive relation to all five belief measures, though it is significant only for marital equity and abortion attitudes. Level of own earnings is an interesting variable that may be a disguised measure of work salience (a variable I regret not to have included in the survey), a pattern consistent with the finding that most significant coefficients on own earnings are on the child-care and marital equity indices. Few women who earn more than $25,000 a year can care for their own children themselves; work obligations necessarily have priority. Still other high-earning women either never married or never had children of their own, and hence can espouse strong feminist beliefs on marital equity and child-care with no inner conflict or counter experience to contend with. (The correlation between family size and own earnings is negative, $r = -.261$.)

To find considerable variation in which predictor variables most strongly determine belief pattern among the five domains suggests a lot more diversity under the feminist banner than the high level of endorsement of the resolutions in Houston would suggest. Many beliefs may be held in a moderate or lukewarm manner simply because so many women have lived a long portion of their lives untouched by the recent views of the feminist movement. Religious training and family commitments may preclude any radical change in belief during the second half of one's life. That there is a lot of diversity in the extent to which the five belief domains are endorsed, even among feminists, can be demonstrated by including in the regression equations a measure of feminist self-concept. To the extent other predictor variables, like age or religiosity, continue to show significant independent coefficients even when a measure of feminist self-concept is in the equation, would then support the interpretation of individual variation in feminist belief structure, tailored to the special circumstances of women's biographies.

The measure of feminist self-concept is a single item asking the respondents to rate themselves on their general position concerning sex equality, from "strongly feminist" to "strongly anti-feminist" (Q.40A, October survey). In Table 6.3, four predictor variables are carried forward from Table 6.2 (religiosity, political orientation, age, and education), together with the feminist self-concept measure. Even a glance at Table 6.3, with its predominance of statistically significant coefficients, shows that there is a great deal more involved in personal belief structures than feminist self-concept: General political orientation and religiosity contribute significantly to all five belief domains, independent of feminist self-concept.

Table 6.3

Regression on Belief Indices of Political and Religious Orientation and Personal Attributes, Controlling for Feminist Self-Concept (Beta Coefficients)

PREDICTOR VARIABLES	Belief Indices				
	Marital Equity	Child Care	Economic Rights	Abortion	Bottom-Line Feminism
Feminist Self-Concept [a] . .	.381 ***	.338 ***	.261 ***	.240 ***	.082 **
Religiosity [a]	-.185 ***	-.149 ***	-.116 ***	-.346 ***	-.240 ***
Political Orientation [a] (High=Conservative) . .	-.193 ***	-.182 ***	-.117 ***	-.125 ***	-.277 ***
Age	-.246 ***	-.062 *	-.076 *	-.016	-.101 ***
Education	.094 ***	.083 **	.032	.102 ***	.054 +
R^2 =	.443 ***	.281 ***	.154 ***	.308 ***	.244 ***
F =	144.53	70.85	33.15	80.71	58.51
N = (913)					

[a] High scores on these three variables mean Strongly Feminist, high religious attendance, and conservative political orientation.

+ $p \leqslant .10$
* $p \leqslant .05$
** $p \leqslant .01$
*** $p \leqslant .001$

Second, the self-concept variable is less significant in attitudes toward abortion and bottom-line feminism than for the three measures of marital equity, child care, and economic rights. On abortion, religiosity is more important than feminist self-concept; on bottom-line feminism, age as well as political orientation and religiosity are more important predictors than self-concept. Many women defined themselves as strong feminists who have reservations about abortion, worry that the lesbian issue may do more harm than good to the women's movement, and reject the view that opposition to abortion or working for lesbian rights is sufficient to deny the label of feminist to someone like themselves.

From this analysis, it appears that there was more variation among the delegates in their attitudes toward issues on which they voted in Houston than one might have expected from observation of their voting behavior. Another approach to private feeling and belief is taken in the next section, on subjective feelings toward a variety of groups, most of which were represented at the conference itself.

Affect Structure

The affect scales are 7-point ratings in response to the question:

> For each of the following groups, indicate your feeling toward it on what can be called a "feeling thermometer" or "feeling scale," where "1" means NEGATIVE or COLD, a "4" means NEUTRAL (neither cold nor warm) and "7" means POSITIVE or WARM.

Ratings were obtained for 16 groups in the October survey, and again in the February survey (Question 8, October; Question 45, February). These ratings provide the data with which to explore the more subliminal, subjective responses of the Houston delegates toward the variety of groups represented in their midst: specific organizations like NOW and the NWPC; the IWY Commissioners; groups differentiated in general political terms; ethnic and occupational groups. I first present the ranking of the responses to the 16 groups by the mean affect scores shown by the sample, then explore them with a control on the delegates' own political orientation, probe the determinants of the affect scores for a selected number of the groups on the list, and, last, show what determined change in the affect scores between the two surveys.

Figure 6.1 shows the ranking of the mean affect scores toward all 16 groups. That the majority of the delegates represent a liberal Democratic coalition is apparent in this ranking, with pro-ERA, NWPC, Blacks, Latinas, NOW, and pro-abortion groups at the top of the affect barometer. Lesbian and radical groups hover in the neutral range of the scale, and conservative,

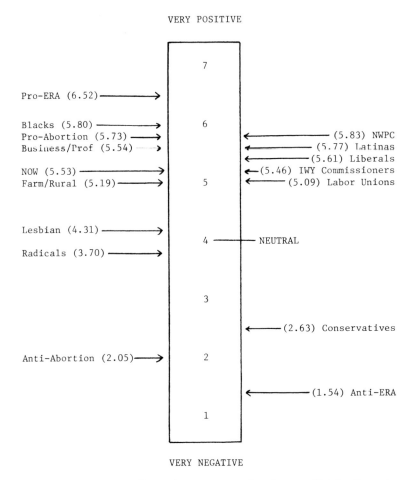

Figure 6.1.   Mean scores on affect scales concerning selected groups (October Survey).

anti-abortion and anti-ERA groups at the negative end. On average, the standard deviation around these means was 1.6 points, with the lowest standard deviations for affect toward Blacks and Latinas ($SD = 1.2$) and the highest standard deviation toward radical and lesbian groups ($SD = 1.9$).

The delegates' own political orientations are of obvious importance to variation in the ranking of affect toward the 16 groups. Figures 6.2 and 6.3 use the same graphic presentation of ranked mean affect scores separately for the five categories of general political orientation, from radical to conservative. It can readily be seen from this visual mode that radical delegates hold to a sharply polarized affect pattern, whereas conservative delegates do not. For the radical and very liberal delegates, there is a sharp polarization of affect, with conservative, anti-abortion and anti-ERA groups at the extreme negative end of the feeling scale, and their opposites—pro-ERA, pro-abortion, NOW, radical, lesbian, and liberal groups—all at the very positive end of the affect scale. For the radical delegates, only the IWY Commissioners appear in the neutral range of the scale.

By contrast, the conservative delegates tend to show mean scores in the middle range of the scale, with very negative affect only toward Lesbian and radical groups. This suggests a good deal of variation among the conservative delegates in their feelings toward the relatively liberal groups that predominate among the 16 groups they rated. This can be illustrated in terms of the standard deviation around the mean score of affect toward anti-ERA groups: Among conservative delegates, the standard deviation is 2.8, whereas for liberal delegates it is only 1.1, a contrast that was found for 13 of the 16 groups. It is also of interest (data not shown) that conservative delegates differed among themselves in affect toward abortion groups (both pro and anti) more than they did toward ERA groups (both pro and anti), a pattern consistent with findings in the first section of this chapter, which suggested religiosity is a critical factor, independent of political orientation, in attitudes toward abortion, but probably much less so, if at all, in affect and belief concerning the ERA.

Affect toward the IWY Commissioners is the only instance in which radical and conservative delegates were like each other (mean scores of 4.7 and 4.2, respectively): Neither end of the political continuum felt as warmly toward the IWY Commissioners as those who defined themselves as very liberal to moderate in political perspective. Note that these data are from the October survey, for the pattern shifted by February, by which time radical delegates showed an increase (that is, more positive) and conservative delegates a decrease (that is, more negative) in their affect scores toward the IWY Commissioners.

Figure 6.3 presents the mean scores on affect toward ethnic and occupational groups by the delegates' political orientation, with a few interesting results. For one, Black and Latina groups head the rank order for liberal and radical delegates, with mean scores decidedly on the positive side (e.g., 6.3 on the 7-point scale for radical delegates' feelings toward Blacks). By contrast, conservative delegates show much less positive affect toward racial and ethnic groups, with the means toward Blacks ($M=4.8$) and Latinas ($M=4.7$) hovering at the moderate neutral position on the scale. This is of particular interest in light of the considerable stress at the conference itself that here at least was one broad issue, caught by the Minorities resolution, on which there was consensus shared by both the liberal Pro-Plan and the conservative Anti-Plan

Figure 6.2. Mean scores on affect scales on political and conference-relevant groups by political orientation.

AFFECT SCALE		RADICAL		VERY LIBERAL		LIBERAL		MODERATE		CONSERVATIVE
						Political Orientation				
VERY POSITIVE 7	7	Pro-ERA...6.8 Pro-Ab...6.5	7	Pro-ERA...6.9	7	Pro-ERA...6.6	7	Pro-ERA...6.2	7	
6	6	Radical...6.1 NOW,Lesb...6.0 Liberal...5.9	6	Pro-Ab...6.5 Liberal...6.4 NOW...6.1	6	Liberal...5.7 IWY...5.6 Pro-Ab...5.5 NOW...5.4	6		6	
5	5	IWY...4.7	5	IWY...5.6 Lesbian...5.1	5		5	IWY...5.5 Pro-Ab...4.9 NOW...4.9 Liberal...4.3	5	Conserv...5.3
NEUTRAL 4	4		4	Radical...4.5	4	Lesbian...3.8	4	Conserv...3.4	4	Anti-Ab...4.6 Pro-ERA...4.3 IWY...4.2 Anti-ERA...3.8
3	3		3		3	Radical...3.1	3	Lesbian...3.1 Anti-Ab...2.8	3	NOW...3.2 Pro-Ab...3.2 Liberal...3.0
2	2	Conserv...1.9 Anti-Ab...1.4 Anti-ERA...1.2	2	Conserv...2.1 Anti-Ab...1.5 Anti-ERA...1.2	2	Conserv...2.6 Anti-Ab...2.1	2	Radical...2.3 Anti-ERA...1.8	2	Lesbian...2.2 Radical...1.9
VERY NEGATIVE 1	1		1		1	Anti-ERA...1.4	1		1	
N =		(76)		(367)		(320)		(137)		(59)

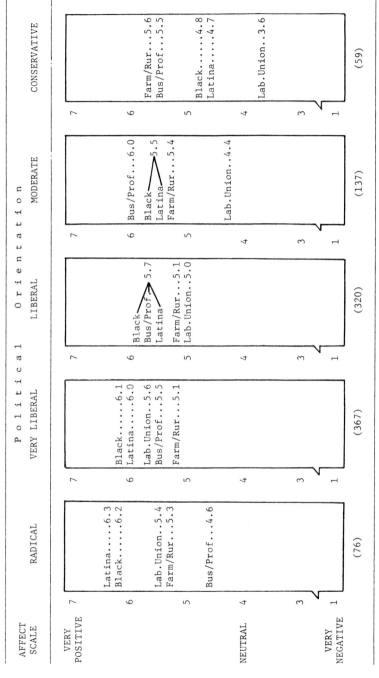

Figure 6.3. Mean scores on affect scales on ethnic and occupational groups by political orientation. (Note that the affect scale is truncated at the negative end.)

199

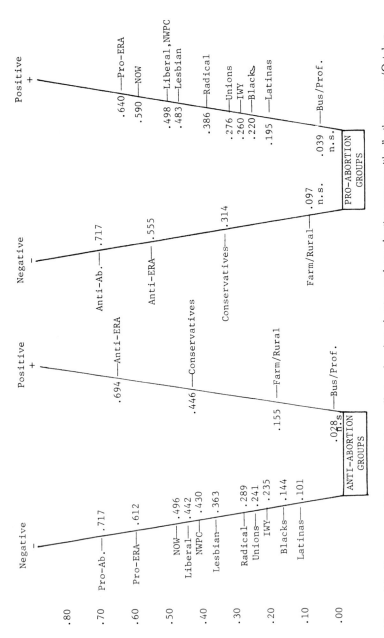

Figure 6.4. Pearson correlation coefficients on affect scales: Anti-abortion and pro-abortion groups with all other groups (October Survey; all correlations are significant except as noted).

delegates. Only a few radical delegates showed affect scores toward Blacks below 5 on the 7-point scale, whereas the range represented by one standard deviation for conservative delegates' feelings toward Blacks was 3.4 to 6.2, with a comparable range for their affect toward Latinas.

Affect toward the three groups classified as occupational groups—Business/professional, farm/rural, and labor unions—shows yet another pattern. Affect toward rural/farm groups is not differentiated by political orientation of the delegates, which hovered around 5 on the 7-point scale (slightly toward the positive end). Labor unions showed a predictable pattern, ranging from 5.3 among radical delegates to 3.6 for conservative delegates. Business/professional groups received the lowest mean score from radical delegates, the highest scores from those with a moderate political orientation. Apparently, conservatives have some reservations here, too.

Abortion was perhaps the most controversial issue at the national conference, with more people intensely involved on one side or the other of this issue than on any other. The frequency with which this resolution was spontaneously mentioned by the delegates in their questionnaire comments, and the strong relation between the affect scores toward activist groups dealing with abortion and the political orientation of the delegates, give further evidence of this. But there is also a meaningful patterning to the way the affective ratings hang together. This can be illustrated by examining the negative and positive correlations between affect toward anti- and pro-abortion groups and each of the other 14 ratings. Figure 6.4 shows these Pearson correlation coefficients, ranked by their magnitude, with all the negative correlations on the left of the two figures and the positive correlations to the right of the figures. From observations in Houston, one might have expected less strong correlations in the reported affect toward pro-abortion and pro-ERA groups than appear here (correlations between $r=.640$ and $r=.717$). But one can more generally note the strong clustering of positive affect toward pro-abortion groups with the whole cluster of liberal groups such as NOW, NWPC, liberal, radical, and lesbian groups; it has a mirror image, to the left of Figure 6.4, in the level of intercorrelations with the anti-abortion groups. Note too, that positive affect toward anti-abortion groups is significantly correlated with affect toward Blacks and Latinas: Those who are warmly predisposed toward anti-abortion groups feel less positively toward Blacks and Latinas than do the opponents of anti-abortion groups.

Determinants of Affect Structure

It is a tribute to the thoughtfulness and political experience of the delegates that the analysis of the determinants of the affect scores yields as clear a pattern of results as it does. Table 6.4 brings together the results of a regres-

Table 6.4

Regression on Selected Affect Scales of Political and Social-Demographic Characteristics (Beta Coefficients, October Survey)

Predictor Variables	Affect Scales						
	CONSERVATIVE Groups	LIBERAL Groups	RADICAL Groups	NWPC	IWY Commissioners	LESBIAN Groups	PRO-ABORTION
POLITICAL							
Political Orientation (High=Conservative)	.437 ***	-.471 ***	-.392 ***	-.202 ***	-.044	-.320 ***	-.245 ***
# Liberal Causes	-.047	.091 **	.154 ***	.005	.008	.063 *	-.008
Mainstream Political Activity Level	-.111 ***	.021	-.053 +	.052	-.019	-.060 *	.006
Sex-Linked Feminist Activity Level	.068	.046	.142 ***	.017	-.028	.275 ***	.121 ***
Gender-Linked Feminist Activity Level	.091 *	-.007	-.092 *	.031	.151 ***	-.104 **	-.019
# Feminist Organizations	-.079 *	.039	.069 *	.162 ***	.039	.101 ***	.106 ***
SOCIAL-DEMOGRAPHIC							
Age	-.010	.005	-.126 ***	.054	.141 ***	-.131 ***	-.025
Religiosity	.097 **	-.095 **	-.086 **	-.116 **	.028	-.122 ***	-.249 ***
Catholic[a]	-.000	-.044	-.019	-.084 *	-.117 **	.012	-.250 ***
Minority[a]	.102 **	.074 *	.062 *	.017	.036	.016	-.001
Unattached[a]	.027	.003	.064 *	.014	.073 *	.078 **	.027
R^2 =	.291 ***	.357 ***	.412 ***	.168 ***	.068 ***	.423 ***	.412 ***
F =	29.54	39.82	50.33	14.45	5.24	52.71	50.28
N = (801)							

[a] Dummy Variables: Catholic=1, Non-Catholic=0; Ethnic/Racial Minority=1, Majority=0; Single, Divorced, Separated and Widowed=1, Married=0.

* $p \leqslant .05$
** $p \leqslant .01$
*** $p \leqslant .001$

sion analysis of the October affect ratings on three kinds of groups: the three general political-orientation groups (radicals, liberals, and conservatives); two quite specific political categories (IWY Commissioners and the NWPC) and the two most controversial groups (pro-abortion and lesbian groups), for a total of seven regression equations.

A variety of predictor variables were used in this analysis. There already is strong evidence from previous tables that political orientation of the delegates is an important determinant. In addition, several other political variables were included that may contribute independent effects to the affect scores: the number of liberal causes the delegates have been involved with in the past; the three major political activity measures (mainstream politics, feminist politics of both a sex-linked and gender-linked variety); and the number of feminist organizations the delegates belonged to. On the social-demographic side, it was predicted that age, religiosity, and membership in minority religious and ethnic groups would relate significantly to the affect scores. Last, it was specifically predicted that being in an unattached marital status (i.e., not living in a heterosexual relationship because of separation, divorce, widowhood, or never having married) would be associated with positive feelings toward both lesbian and radical groups (the latter because of the consistency with which lesbian and radical issues seem to be closely linked in the structure of belief and affect in the sample).

Since there is both internal consistency in the determinants of affect toward specific groups and considerable contrast across the various groups, the results are discussed separately for each of the seven regression equations shown in Table 6.4. Affect is warm and positive to conservative groups among those with the following characteristics (apart from and independent of the linkage between political orientation as conservative and positive affect to conservative groups, which shows an expectably high beta coefficient, ($\beta = -.437$): low levels of activity in politics generally and feminist organizations specifically, membership in a minority group, high religious observance, and a slight tendency to have been involved in gender-linked feminist activity. At least in the delegate body in Houston, those predisposed to conservative groups are not very experienced in politics of either a mainstream or feminist variety. Ethnic-group membership is difficult to interpret here since significant beta coefficients are found in the affect scores of minority group members toward all three political groups, though none as strongly as toward conservative groups. On the zero-order correlations, minority-group membership is significantly related only to affect toward conservative groups, but at a modest positive level of $r = +.153$.

Affect toward liberal groups shows only two significant predictors: having been involved in a number of liberal causes in the past and a low level of religious observance. Positive affect toward liberal groups apparently cuts across all levels of political activity, both mainstream and feminist.

Affect toward *radical groups* shows a sharply etched profile: being young, unattached, and low in religiosity; having had involvement in liberal causes in the past; and having been active on sex-linked issues but, significantly, *not* active on gender-linked issues, all predispose to positive feelings toward radical groups. It is of special interest that the signs reverse on the two measures of feminist activity in an equation that includes age as well, for younger women generally show higher levels of political activity on sex-linked issues and older women on gender-linked issues.

Favorable feelings toward the *NWPC* are most typical of those with a liberal political orientation but with no independent effect of involvement in liberal causes in the past, as in the case of affect toward liberal groups. Rather, it is a high level of involvement in feminist organizations plus a low level of religiosity that tips the balance toward positive affect toward the NWPC. An urban, liberal, secular cluster is suggested by this profile. Maybe a "check-writing" endorsement is showing as well, for involvement in the NWPC involves neither attending meetings nor a past profile of direct political activity in either mainstream or feminist politics, neither of which show any significant coefficients in the affect scores toward NWPC.

Affect toward the IWY Commissioners provides yet another profile. Here, general political orientation does not influence the affect scores. (As noted earlier, political orientation shows a curvilinear pattern here.) The primary determinants are being older, non-Catholic, and having been very active in gender-linked feminist politics, an image consistent with the profile of many feminists who pioneered the movement in the 1960s, served on state commissions on the status of women, and worked in organizations and political caucuses to improve the status of women in higher education and the economy. Yet, together, these variables do not capture very much of the variance in affect toward the IWY Commissioners, as suggested by the fact that the R^2 in this equation, though statistically significant, is the lowest ($R^2 = .068$) of the seven equations.

Affect toward lesbian groups, by contrast, is more adequately predicted by the variables in the regression equation ($R^2 = .423$), six of which are highly significant. The profile provides a striking contrast to that for the IWY Commissioners: Whereas positive affect toward the IWY Commissioners was strongly related to gender-role activism, positive affect toward lesbian groups is highly associated with sex-linked feminist activity and a *low* level of activity on gender-linked feminist issues or mainstream politics. Youthful age, low religiosity, unattached marital status, and a high level of membership in feminist organizations round out the picture of the major predictors of positive affect toward lesbian groups.

Affect toward pro-abortion groups is similar in many ways to the affect structure where lesbian groups are concerned, with two notable exceptions:

Age is not relevant here, and being Catholic is. Those with positive affect toward abortion reform groups are decidedly non-Catholic liberals, low in religiosity, active on sex-linked issues, and members of feminist organizations.

Impact of the Conference on Affect Scores

All the variables that entered the equations on the affect scores were obtained in the October survey, and most relate to past events or personal status characteristics. If the conference experience itself had an impact on the delegates in how they felt toward the diverse range of groups on the rating list, one would expect the R^2 to be lower for the affect scores obtained in February regressed on the same background variables used in the regressions on the October ratings.

Table 6.5 shows a slight tendency in this direction, though the drop in R^2 is no more than 7% (pro-abortion groups). Only for the NWPC and the IWY Commissioners is there an increase (3 and 4%) rather than a decrease in the R^2. There is overlap in composition between these two groups, because many who served as Commissioners have also been active in the NWPC. In turning

Table 6.5

R^2 in Regressions on Selected Affect Scales with Same Set of Political and Demographic Predictor Variables: October versus February

Affect Toward Groups	October 1977	February 1978
Conservative Groups	.291	.274
Liberal Groups	.357	.343
Radical Groups	.412	.389
NWPC	.168	.201
IWY Commissioners	.068	.131
Lesbian Groups	.423	.416
Pro-Abortion Groups	.412	.342

[a]Predictor variables are those shown in Table 6.4: political orientation, # liberal causes, mainstream political activity level, sex-linked feminist activity level, gender-linked feminist activity level, # feminist organizations, age, religiosity, Catholic, Minority, and Unattached marital status.

Table 6.6

Regression on Affect toward IWY Commissioners of Political and Demographic
Variables: October versus February (Beta Coefficients)[a]

Predictor Variables	Affect Toward IWY Commissioners	
	October 1977	February 1978
POLITICAL		
Political Orientation . . . . . . (High=Conservative)	-.044	-.166 ***
# Liberal Causes	.008	.072 *
Mainstream Political Activity Level	-.019	.041
Sex Linked Feminist Activity Level	-.028	-.032
Gender Linked Feminist Activity Level	.151 ***	.160 ***
# Feminist Organizations	.039	.070 *
SOCIAL-DEMOGRAPHIC		
Age	.141 ***	.095 *
Religiosity	.028	-.027
Catholic	-.117 **	-.093 **
Minority	.036	.050
Unattached	.073 *	.018
R^2 =	.068 ***	.131 ***
F =	5.24	10.86

[a] The direction of change is the same for both the metric coefficients and the standardized beta coefficients between the two equations for all 11 predictor variables. Further, there is no significant difference in the variances of the dependent variable on Affect toward IWY Commissioners in the two equations (S.D. = .155 in preconference and .154 in the postconference survey.

* $p \leqslant .05$
** $p \leqslant .01$
*** $p \leqslant .001$

to the question of change in affect structure over time, I first select the IWY Commissioners for special attention, because the results provide an interesting example of change that is easily interpreted.

Table 6.6. shows the profile of the same predictors of affect toward the IWY Commissioners for both before and after the conference. The most significant change between surveys is on age and general political orientation. Before the conference, there was no relation between political orientation and affect toward the IWY Commissioners, but there was a strong tendency for older delegates to have more favorable feelings toward the IWY Commissioners than younger delegates did. After the conference, political orientation became a strong predictor of affect toward the IWY Commissioners, and age dropped in significance, suggesting that the performance of the IWY Commissioners (or, perhaps, of only the most visible among them in Houston) changed the views of younger, less religious women, and, perhaps, those at the opposite ends of the political continuum, radicals and conservatives.

Also consistent with this shift is the fact that membership in feminist organizations and past involvement in liberal causes have shifted from nonsignificant to significant predictors of affect toward the IWY Commissioners in the second survey. Closer inspection shows that radicals and conservatives, who showed roughly the same mean score of affect toward the IWY Commissioners in October, changed considerably by February: Radicals moved toward more positive affect (from $M=4.7$ to $M=5.2$), whereas conservatives shifted to more negative feelings toward the IWY Commissioners (from $M=4.2$ to $M=3.6$). It is this change at the two ends of the political orientation measure that explains why the beta coefficient is significant in the February rating ($\beta=.166$) but not in October ($\beta=.044$).

The sheer amount of change in the scores given in February compared to October, and the extent to which such change varied by the group being rated, can be seen in Table 6.7. The groups are ranked here by the extent of stability in the affect scores given by the delegates; hence it is readily seen that affect toward pro- and anti-ERA and pro- and anti-abortion groups are the most stable, that is, the least affected by any intervening experience, between October and February. There was much more change in affect toward lesbian, radical, conservative, and the three occupational groups between the two time points. By comparing the last two columns in Table 6.7, we can gauge whether the direction of change was tipped more toward positive or toward negative feelings after the conference, compared to before the conference. In many cases, there was just about the same level of positive as of negative change (the pro- and anti-abortion groups, the NWPC, ethnic groups, radicals, and lesbians). The ratio is tipped to more positive than negative change in the feelings toward pro-abortion groups, NOW, and the IWY Commissioners, and the reverse (more negative than positive change),

Table 6.7
Affect Scales: Change between October 1977 and February 1978 (in percent)

Extent of Change	Group	NO Change	C h a n g e P a t t e r n	
			More POSITIVE in February	More NEGATIVE in February
LOW	Anti-ERA	82	10	8
	Pro-ERA	81	9	10
MODERATE	Anti-Abortion	68	12	20
	Pro-Abortion	61	26	13
	NWPC	56	23	21
	NOW	52	27	21
	Blacks	51	25	24
	Latinas	50	24	26
	Liberals	50	23	27
HIGH	Lesbians	49	27	24
	Radicals	46	27	27
	IWY Commissioners . .	46	31	23
	Labor Unions	45	24	31
	Conservatives	44	23	33
	Business/Prof.	43	25	32
	Farm/Rural	42	25	33

N = (939)

toward anti-abortion groups, conservatives, and the three occupational groups.

What happened to bring about a change in the affect scores over time? The fact that there is variation in affect stability across the groups rated, and that the direction of change also varies from one group to another, suggests there must have been something at work beyond personal mood the day the delegates filled out the questionnaires. Although one does not know the extent to which either general instability of affect ratings or personal mood played a part in the ratings, one *can* test the extent to which experience in Houston and assessment of the conference explains variation in the affect ratings.

Since the procedures in this test will be followed in other change analysis in subsequent chapters, it is useful to be explicit about the logic of the analysis.

There are three steps to a change analysis of the panel variables. The first step involves establishing the best set of predictor variables on which a panel variable is regressed at Time I, the October survey. The second step of the change analysis uses the same set of predictor variables for the panel factor reported at Time II, the February survey. If the R^2 is lower for the Time II equation than for the Time I equation, it increases the probability that the intervening experience of attending the conference had an effect upon the participants. If the R^2 is higher, it is possible that subgroups in the sample were differentially affected by the conference experience. Thus, for example, in the second step analysis concerning the IWY Commissioners, the delegates' age was a significant predictor at Time I but not at Time II, suggesting that older women became more critical and younger women more positive toward the IWY Commissioners as a result of the conference.

The third step of the analysis attempts to pinpoint what it was about the conference that might have had such an effect. But the criterion now becomes whether these intervening conference variables contribute to the affect scores at Time II *over and above the scores given at Time I*. Using the IWY Commissioners analysis as an example, the three steps and their findings may be summarized as follows:

Step 1: Determinants of affect score at Time I. Older, non-Catholic women who had been active on gender-related issues were the most positive in their feelings toward the IWY Commissioners in October.

Step 2: The same set of determinants, used now as predictor variables for affect scores at Time II. Age became less important and past feminist activity more important, and political orientation emerged as an important predictor of affect toward the IWY Commissioners after the conference. Younger women, radical and very liberal delegates appeared more positive, conservatives less positive, in February than they had been in October.

Step 3: Conference variables as predictors of affect score at Time II, controlling for affect score at Time I. As we shall see, two variables relevant to the conference itself made significant contributions to how the delegates felt about the IWY Commissioners by Time II: the number of groups the delegates worked with in Houston and their assessment of how the conference was run. Those who worked with a number of caucuses (in which several IWY Commissioners were conspicuous participants) and those who rejected the view that the conference was a tightly managed or highly controlled affair tended to show positive affect change toward the IWY Commissioners, independent of how they had regarded them before the conference.

A final test is a check whether the combined effect of the significant beta coefficients on conference variables contributes significantly to the multiple regression R^2 over and above the correlation between the panel variables measured in the two surveys. This is shown as the last row in a change table, $R^2 - r^2$, in which the r^2 (square of the correlation between the affect scores at Time I and Time II) is subtracted from the Time II regression R^2. In the case of change in affect toward the IWY Commissioners, there was a very positive result of $R^2 - r^2 = .082$. This is a very conservative estimate of the amount of variance explained by the exposure variables, since it is a net effect over and above the correlations of the preconference dependent variable with all the exposure variables in the equation. Hence in the analysis of affect toward the IWY Commissioners, one can say that *at a minimum,* 8% of the variance in postconference affect is explained by the exposure variables in the equation.

The third step of the change analysis on the affect scores is reported in Table 6.8 and concerns 7 of the 16 groups: the three political groups, the NWPC, the IWY Commissioners, lesbian groups and pro-abortion groups (the same groups previously focused on in the regressions predicting affect scores in October, Table 6.4). A variety of predictor variables was included in the equations. Five are based on reports of actual behavior at the conference: the general active plenary role index; the number of groups worked with during the conference; the number of meetings attended of the Pro-Plan, Anti-Plan, and lesbian caucuses. Note that the latter two caucus-attendance measures are entered only in the most relevant equation, that is, Anti-Plan caucus attendance in the conservative group affect equation, and lesbian caucus attendance in the lesbian group equation. In addition, the bottom-line feminism index is included, on the expectation that whether the delegates defined feminism in a narrow or more inclusive way might affect their tendency to show a change in feelings toward the specified groups, that is that high-scorers who believe it is necessary to support the ERA, abortion access, and lesbian rights to be considered a feminist might show more shift toward positive affect toward lesbian and radical groups as a result of favorable experiences at the conference.

The index on conference control is a measure of the extent to which the delegates saw the conference as an open, democratic one or as a tightly managed one in which it was difficult to gain access to a microphone, control was in the hands of urban eastern Democrats, and resolutions were "railroaded through." (A high score on the index indicates the delegates felt the conference was tightly controlled.) This was an assessment given in the February survey, and our expectation was that high-scorers would tend to show negative affect toward those groups conspicuously active at the plenary sessions. The last predictor variable was membership in NOW, on the assumption that this was a facilitating basis for positive affect change all told, in light of the conspicuous presence of NOW members, the fact that their President was an IWY Commissioner, and their involvement in the Pro-Plan caucus. Although not a conference or exposure variable per se, NOW membership

Table 6.8

Impact of Conference on Affect toward Selected Groups: Regression on February Affect Scales of Conference Participation, Controlling for October Affect Score (Beta Coefficients)

Predictor Variables	February Affect Scales						
	CONSERVATIVE Groups	LIBERAL Groups	RADICAL Groups	NWPC	IWY Commissioners	LESBIAN Groups	PRO-ABORTION Groups
October Affect Score (same group)	.536 ***	.654 ***	.643 ***	.606 ***	.532 ***	.636 ***	.650 ***
Bottom-Line Feminism	-.078 *	.049 +	.103 ***	.016	-.008	.129 ***	.041
Conference Control	.046	-.078 **	-.084 ***	-.196 ***	-.250 ***	-.101 ***	-.150 ***
Active Plenary Role	-.014	.003	.040	-.032	-.001	.065 **	.030
# Groups Worked With	-.005	.049	-.021	.045	.063 *	-.050	.024
NOW Member	-.058 *	.043	.058 *	.071 **	.058 *	.049 *	.017
Attended Pro-Plan Caucus[a] Meeting(s)	-.014	.023	-.018	.045	.009	.009	.021
Attended Anti-Plan Caucus[a] Meeting(s)	.107 ***	—[b]	—	—	—	—	—
Attended Lesbian Caucus[a] Meeting(s)	—	—	—	—	—	.054 *	—
R^2 =	.418 ***	.548 ***	.566 ***	.572 ***	.463 ***	.654 ***	.597 ***
$R^2 - r^2$ =	.036	.019	.026	.081	.082	.038	.029

[a] None, one meeting, or two or more meetings.

[b] Not included in equation.

* $p \leq .05$
** $p \leq .01$
*** $p \leq .001$

seemed more important in this third step in the change analysis, since its contribution would have to be independent of the earlier affect scores.

In examining the results of this regression analysis, I shall first note which of the predictor variables tends to provide a significant increment over the earlier affect score and then discuss the cluster of characteristics associated with change in the feelings toward the seven groups covered by these equations. In light of the relatively high level of stability between the two surveys already shown in Table 6.7, there is no surprise in noting that the earlier affect scores are the strongest predictors in all seven equations. What is of interest is that the beta coefficients differ in how much they contribute to the Time II affect score across the groups, for this is one indication of the extent to which other factors played a role in the change profile. The lowest beta coefficients associated with the earlier affect score are for conservative groups and IWY Commissioners, whereas the highest are for liberal and pro-abortion groups, which is consistent with the previous finding of greater change in the affect toward liberal and pro-abortion groups.

The second strongest predictor of change in affect is the conference control index: In six of the seven equations, the beta coefficients are significant and negative, suggesting that those who assessed the conference as highly controlled and managed, changed toward more negative feelings toward all the groups except conservative groups (on which the beta coefficient is positive, though not significant).

Bottom-line feminism shows a more varied pattern. Those who held very strict criteria for defining a feminist tended to shift to more negative feelings toward conservative groups and more positive feelings toward radical and lesbian groups, suggesting that the contacts they made with radical and lesbian delegates in Houston lent further support to their convictions that the lesbian rights issue had not harmed the women's movement and that a feminist ought to be active in seeking abortion reform and lesbian rights.

An active role during the plenary sessions contributed to positive change in affect toward lesbian groups, consistent with the observation of many that lesbian delegates and floor personnel played an important role in floor management and in the Pro-Plan caucus. Those who were themselves active therefore had the experience of working as part of a team with lesbian delegates, and came away with more positive affect toward lesbian groups in general.

Women who worked with a large number of groups during the conference probably held strong convictions on a number of issues coming to a vote in Houston. A high score on this index means having worked with issue caucuses, state delegations, observers, IWY Commissioners, Secretariat staff members, and delegates from their own organization or political party. Such high scores are associated with positive change toward the IWY Commissioners (who were also working in diverse ways with the same broad range of groups at the conference) and with negative change in affect toward lesbian groups, who tended to be more single-issue in focus and as a consequence were perhaps perceived as handicaps to the successful passage of resolutions dealing with other issues.

NOW membership shows a positive coefficient in five of the seven equations and a negative coefficient on one (toward conservative groups), suggesting that NOW members experienced favorable and reinforcing encounters at the conference, which stimulated an increase in their already positive feelings toward radical groups, the NWPC, lesbian groups, and an improvement in their perception of the IWY Commissioners (or, at least, that portion of the IWY Commission with whom they had political contact in Houston). The intensity with which conservative delegates expressed their views during the conference may similarly have stimulated NOW members toward even more negative feelings toward conservative groups generally. If outgroup antagonism is a necessary motivator in a social movement's vitality, this can be viewed as a positive consequence of the conference on members of NOW.

Attendance at Pro-Plan caucus meetings had no significant impact on affect change, perhaps because so many delegates attended such meetings (60% attended at least one) and because the very general purpose of the Pro-Plan caucus was to effect the successful passage of the whole national Plan.

By contrast, attendance at Anti-Plan caucus meetings contributed a significant increment in positive affect toward conservative groups, as attendance at lesbian caucuses did toward lesbian groups. Such attendance may have reinforced, through new contacts, an already existing favorable predisposition toward the groups involved, much as NOW membership did.

A look at the profile of predictors associated with each of the seven groups suggests a few general tendencies in these findings. It seems to be the more extreme groups and the highly specialized ones toward which affect changed more significantly as a consequence of the conference. Thus, none of the predictors except conference control affected feelings toward liberal groups: As shown by the $R^2 - r^2$ value, there is the lowest increment to affect change toward this group (.019). By contrast, affect was changed by the conference toward conservative and radical groups, the very specific issue groups represented by lesbian and pro-abortion groups, and, even more so, toward the NWPC and the IWY Commissioners. The pattern of predictors toward the latter two groups is quite similar, partly because of the overlap between the two in membership. Women like Bella Abzug, Ellie Smeal, Liz Carpenter, Mary Ann Krupsak, Mildred Jeffreys, Gloria Steinem, and Audrey Colum were nationally prominent as both IWY Commissioners and as activists associated with the NWPC.

Last, it is of interest that conference control played a larger part in affect change where IWY Commissioners were concerned than for any other group ($\beta = -.250$), the next closest large beta coefficient being on affect toward the NWPC ($\beta = -.196$). IWY Commissioners had more to say than any other group about what went on during the conference, through the advance plans they drew up for the conference and through their actual roles at the conference. Thus, if the delegates thought the conference was tightly controlled, they became more negative toward the IWY Commissioners; if they rejected the view that the conference was overly managed and controlled, they became more positive in their feelings toward the IWY Commissioners.

Belief and Affect Consistency

In this analysis of both belief domains and affect, the focus has been on the political and personal attribute determinants of discrete domains of belief and affect, that is, on the particular clusters of variables that are the most significant predictors of the five belief indices and the 16 affect scores. Despite the skewed nature of the measures in this largely feminist sample, the analysis has shown that a considerable diversity of factors determined belief on one issue as compared to another, or affect toward one group as compared to another group.

In this section, the analysis shifts to variation in the *level of consistency across the belief and affect domains*. To do this builds on the assumption that a social movement is a complex coalition of formal organizations and informal groups that share a commitment to change and that use a variety of tactics involving shifting coalitions depending on the specific issue at stake. To rid textbooks of sexist illustrations might involve the media task force of NOW and a coalition of teachers, writers, and women in the publishing industry. To establish a local retreat for displaced homemakers might involve a coalition of social workers, women's advocates on a city council, a local feminist law firm, and a group from a Parents without Partners club. The particular organizations that come into such coalitions vary in the extent to which feminist issues are salient on their organizational agendas. An organization like NOW is at the center of the feminist movement and presumably would self-destruct when and if its goals for sex equality were reached. An organization like NWPC would, similarly, have little purpose if and when women were represented in all state and national legislative bodies at a 52% level, equal to their proportion in the total population. The League of Women Voters, under such circumstances, might reconstitute themselves simply as a League of Voters for the continuing purpose of political education and action, involving as many men as women in the membership of the organization.

Of course, American society is a long way from attaining such a goal, and in the interim the organizations that are associated with the feminist movement have become more diverse as the movement has grown. For the League of Women Voters, the AAUW, and the Federation of Business and Professional Women's Clubs to form a coalition with NOW, ERAmerica, and the NWPC to secure the passage of the ERA is a development of recent years. None of these traditional women's organizations has any wide-ranging agenda that embraces the diversity of issues to which NOW has been dedicated. Although AAUW and NOW members may agree on the ERA, there is no assurance that they would do so on marital equity, child care, or abortion. This is, of course, an assumption; the next section will attempt to establish the extent to which this is the case.

Consensus and Constraint:
NOW versus the League of Women Voters

The question raised here is whether there is consistency across the domains of affect and belief, and whether that consistency varies between members of the National Organization for Women and members of the League of Women Voters. NOW is the most representative feminist organization, with a very broad agenda of feminist commitments, whereas the League is a good representative of an equally sophisticated political organization of women that has no central feminist ideology or commitment to work for increased sex equality. At issue in the analysis is whether NOW members show a greater degree of belief and affect consistency than League members do.

There are several ways one could show consistency of affect and belief. First, one can predict that NOW members should show higher mean scores on any given set of indices or scales tapping feminist beliefs than League members. Second, one can predict that the variance around those means should be less for NOW members than for League members, on the assumption that members of an explicitly feminist organization will feel pressure to subscribe to their organization's position even if they are not personally committed to action on every issue on which the organization has taken a public stand. In both these measures of consistency, the emphasis is on the level of agreement of a group across a set of belief measures.

The third measure of consistency is different. Mueller and Judd (1979) have argued that it is not sufficient in studying belief systems to only demonstrate consistency across items or indices. If the idea of consistency is important, there should be pressure at the *individual level* for such consistency, not simply at the aggregate group level. Applied to the present analysis problem, this means that NOW members should show less variance across the belief measures as individuals. To differentiate between the individual and group level, Mueller and Judd proposed the concepts of *constraint* and *consensus:* *Constraint* is indicated by low within-individual variance across items, and *consensus* by low group variance across individuals. They argued that most studies of social movements fail to make this distinction and concentrate only on consensus, the degree to which specific beliefs are shared by members of the movement, rather than the degree of constraint or coherence between items (or belief domains, in my data) held by individuals.

Three indicators of consensus and one of constraint are used in the analysis to follow, with the following four predictions: In the *consensus analysis* (*a*) higher mean scores on all affect and belief measures for NOW members than League members; (*b*) lower average variance of index scores across individuals who belong to NOW than those who belong to the League; and (*c*) lower coefficients of variation for NOW than League members on the individual measures, and a lower average coefficient of variation when the individual measures are pooled. The *constraint analysis* will explore within-individual variance across a set of affect and belief domains and (*d*) it is predicted that there is lower within-individual variance for NOW members than for League members.

Specification of Organizational Membership Types

The delegates were asked whether they were members of five specific organizations: Forty-three percent reported that they belonged to NOW, 31% that they belonged to the League of Women Voters. These were, in fact, the two organizations with the highest proportion of members in the delegate body. By comparison, 21% reported membership in NARAL, another 21% in AAUW, and 18% in a Business and Professional Women's Club. There was a good deal of overlap in membership among these organizations, as shown in Table 6.9. Of those reporting membership in NOW, 34% belonged to the League as well. Of the women reporting membership in the League, 48% were also members of NOW. This is probably a reflection of the nature of the sample. It is highly unlikely that such high levels of dual membership would be found among a full roster of either NOW or League members.

To refine the comparative analysis of organizational membership impact upon belief and affect consistency, I shall use a four-way classification of membership in NOW and the League: *NOW only* are women who belong to NOW but not to the League; *LWV only,* those who belong to the League but not to NOW; *Joint* members, those who belong to both organizations; and *Neither,* those who do not belong to either organization. This typology yields a reasonable distribution of cases in the four membership types: 276 Now only members, 150 LWV only members, 141 Joint, and 375 neither.

Table 6.9

Membership Level and Overlap in Five Specified Organizations

Organization	Total Sample[a] Percent Members of...	Percent of NOW Members Who Belong to...	Percent of Other Organization Members Who Belong to NOW...
National Organization for Women (NOW) . . .	42.6%		
League of Women Voters (LWV)	31.1%	34.3% (426)	48.2% (303)
National Abortion Rights Action League (NARAL)	20.9%	37.7% (427)	77.0% (209)
American Association of University Women (AAUW)	21.3%	23.6% (428)	48.1% (210)
Business & Professional Women's Club (BPW)	17.8%	13.7% (423)	34.5% (168)
N =	(1187)		

[a]Question 46g-j, February survey.

Affect and Belief Measures

Thirteen measures of affect and belief are used in the analysis: The five indices on belief domains now familiar from the first section of the chapter—abortion, marital equity, child care, economic rights, and bottom-line feminism—and a second set of measures selected from the 16 affect scales. Since social movements typically take strong positions toward groups consistent with their ideology and equally strong positions in opposition to groups that reject their ideology, we used two pairs of groups from the affect scale set: Pro- and anti-ERA; pro- and anti-abortion. To provide a counterpart to affect to lesbian groups, I have included conservative groups, for a total of 6 affect scales. The third set of measures are the feminist ratings on self and closest friend. All scores were transformed so that high categories represent strong profeminist affect and belief. Thus, the profile of a top scorer on all 13 measures would be as follows: Women who define themselves and their closest friend as "strongly feminist"; who favor access to legal abortion under all five specified conditions, including being married and not wanting additional children; who favor full economic equality of women with men; who take a strong stand on equity in marriage; who feel no harm comes to children of working mothers and who would use child-care centers in preference to relatives; who do not consider anyone a feminist unless he or she supports the ERA, lesbian rights, and abortion access; who feel very positive toward pro-ERA, pro-abortion and lesbian groups and very negative toward anti-ERA, anti-abortion and conservative groups. This profile is consistent with the ideology endorsed by NOW.

NOW has adopted positions on the issues involved in the affect and belief measures at different points in its short history, and women in the delegate body have become involved in the feminist movement at different stages of their personal lives and at different stages of the movement's development. Hence, in addition to predictions of greater consensus and constraint in the affect and belief structure of NOW members compared to League members, I also predict variation by the domain involved among all organizational membership types, NOW included. Since ERA and economic rights were part of the original ideological mandate of the founding members of NOW, less variance is expected on these measures than on indices that tap issues that loomed only in more recent years on the NOW agenda. Abortion was an issue that almost split the organization a few years after its founding and only gradually became a major focus of NOW political efforts. Lesbian rights threatened a comparable split within the organization and has only emerged in recent years as a priority on the NOW agenda. Indeed, it is an issue still in the process of acceptance within the feminist movement. As a reflection of this recency and the ongoing process of consensus-building, I predict the greatest amount of variance on this issue, as tapped by the affect ratings toward lesbian groups and the bottom-line feminism index.

Consensus Analysis

Figure 6.5 presents the results of the analysis of affect and belief consensus by membership type. As indicated at the extreme left of Figure 6.5, there are significant differences between the membership types in the analysis of variance on all 13 measures. The most general pattern shown by the detailed results, as indicated by the Duncan subset procedure, is for NOW only members to show the highest mean score, that is, the most feminist position, on the measures. Although the score means are slightly higher for Joint members

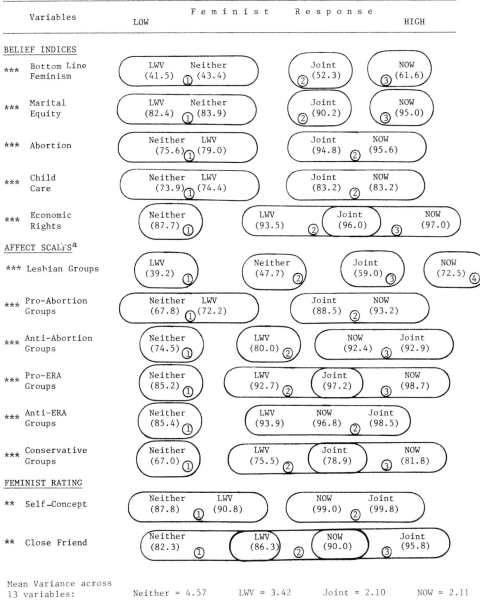

Variables	Feminist Response		
	LOW		HIGH

BELIEF INDICES

*** Bottom Line Feminism
LWV (41.5) Neither (43.4) ①   Joint (52.3) ②   NOW (61.6) ③

*** Marital Equity
LWV (82.4) Neither (83.9) ①   Joint (90.2) ②   NOW (95.0) ③

*** Abortion
Neither (75.6) LWV (79.0) ①   Joint (94.8) NOW (95.6) ②

*** Child Care
Neither (73.9) LWV (74.4) ①   Joint (83.2) NOW (83.2) ②

*** Economic Rights
Neither (87.7) ①   LWV (93.5) ②   Joint (96.0) ③   NOW (97.0)

AFFECT SCALES[a]

*** Lesbian Groups
LWV (39.2) ①   Neither (47.7) ②   Joint (59.0) ③   NOW (72.5) ④

*** Pro-Abortion Groups
Neither (67.8) LWV (72.2) ①   Joint (88.5) NOW (93.2) ②

*** Anti-Abortion Groups
Neither (74.5) ①   LWV (80.0) ②   NOW (92.4) Joint (92.9) ③

*** Pro-ERA Groups
Neither (85.2) ①   LWV (92.7) ②   Joint (97.2) NOW (98.7) ③

*** Anti-ERA Groups
Neither (85.4) ①   LWV (93.9) NOW (96.8) Joint (98.5) ②

*** Conservative Groups
Neither (67.0) ①   LWV (75.5) ②   Joint (78.9) NOW (81.8) ③

FEMINIST RATING

** Self-Concept
Neither (87.8) LWV (90.8) ①   NOW (99.0) Joint (99.8) ②

** Close Friend
Neither (82.3) ①   LWV (86.3) ②   NOW (90.0) Joint (95.8) ③

Mean Variance across
13 variables: Neither = 4.57   LWV = 3.42   Joint = 2.10   NOW = 2.11

[a] High scores are _positive_ affect toward lesbian, pro-abortion and
pro-**ERA** groups and _negative_ affect toward anti-abortion, anti-ERA
and conservative groups. All scores converted to a 0–100 range.

** p ≤ .01
*** p ≤ .001

Figure 6.5.   Belief and affect consensus by organizational membership type: Subsets and mean scores.

than for NOW only members on four measures, both types share the same subset where this is the case, hence the general pattern holds on all 13 measures. The most typical pattern, when a subset includes more than one membership type, is for a link between Joint and NOW only types on the one hand and between the LWV only and Neither types on the other.

The relative grouping of Joint members with NOW only compared to Joint and LWV only types provides an interesting contrast: In 10 of the 13 measures, Joint and NOW only types are in the same or a shared subset, which is true for only 5 of the 13 measures where Joint and LWV only types are concerned. NOW membership seems to have a stronger pull than the League for commitment on the issues covered by the 13 measures, suggesting that NOW members who belong to both organizations may stimulate more dissent in League meetings than League members who belong to NOW do at NOW meetings!

NOW only members represent a distinct and separate subset on only three of the measures: affect toward lesbian groups, marital equity, and bottom-line feminism. On these three measures, League members who also belong to NOW seem to retain some differentiation from their friends in NOW, showing greater reservations on the private issues of marriage, sexual preference, and strict versus open definitions of feminism.

The bottom of Figure 6.5 provides a second bit of evidence of greater consensus among NOW members than League members: Both NOW only and Joint membership types show much less variance across the 13 measures in Figure 6.5; indeed, NOW only members show only one-half the average variance (2.11) that is shown by women who belong to Neither organization (4.57), and only slightly less sharp a contrast from LWV only members (3.42).

A second, more detailed way to inspect variance as a measure of consistency across the four membership types is the coefficient of variation for each of the 13 measures and the mean coefficient of variation across the measures (shown in Table 6.10). On all 13 measures, NOW only members show lower coefficients of variation than LWV only members, and on 10 of the 13 measures, NOW only members show less variance than those who belong to both NOW and the League. As shown in the last row, the mean coefficient of variation is lowest for NOW only and Joint members (15.2 and 17.6, respectively), much higher for LWV ONLY members (26.5), and highest of all for those who belong to neither organization (31.4).

The data in Table 6.10 are also of interest from the point of view of variation in the size of the coefficients across the 13 measures. They have been ranked by coefficient size for the NOW only members to facilitate this comparison. An inspection of this ranking is an invitation to a historical tour of the development of the NOW agenda since the mid-1960s. The longer an issue has been the focus of a movement or an organization's concerns, the greater

Table 6.10

Belief/Affect Consensus: Coefficients of Variation (in percent) of Feminism Measures by Organizational Membership Type[a]

Belief/Affect Measure	Organizational Membership			
	NOW ONLY	JOINT	LWV ONLY	NEITHER
Pro-ERA Groups	4.2	10.5	7.5	28.2
Economic Rights	7.1	7.7	8.4	8.3
Marital Equity	8.0	9.3	14.0	17.6
Feminist Self Concept . . .	10.3	17.6	19.7	27.7
Child Care	10.8	10.7	15.8	18.8
Anti-ERA Groups	11.3	9.8	18.8	29.9
Pro-Abortion Groups	14.0	19.5	36.4	41.6
Anti-Abortion Groups	16.2	17.2	31.2	37.7
Abortion	17.6	19.4	42.8	46.8
Conservative Groups	22.2	23.9	28.2	36.5
Feminist Rating of Closest Friend	22.8	26.7	28.5	35.2
Bottom Line Feminism	23.6	22.3	28.1	28.3
Lesbian Groups	29.3	34.6	54.9	52.1
Mean Coefficient of Variation	15.2	17.6	26.5	31.4

[a]Coefficient of
Variation . . . . = $\dfrac{\text{Standard Deviation}}{\overline{X}} \times 100$

one may assume the pressure is for high consensus among members on an issue or, if there is no pressure, at least time for the gradual process of belief change in all its particularity. Issues that have emerged only in recent years are still being debated by members in the process of reaching their own position, often lagging behind the adoption of that issue by the leaders of an organization. Greater consensus translates into lower variance, and an inspection of the ranking in Table 6.10 is consistent with this historical development of feminist beliefs. The issues that first sparked the formation of NOW are precisely the issues on which NOW members show the *least* variance—ERA, economic and political rights for women, and marriage as a partnership (shades of NOW's statement of purpose in the year NOW was formed, 1966).

NOW members show *moderate* levels of variance on issues that began to loom in the late 1960s and early 1970s as NOW gained a reputation as the leading feminist organization and had identified the social and political forces working against women: Hence on abortion, anti-ERA groups, and conservative groups generally, the variance shown by NOW only members is at a moderate level. The *highest* level of variance is shown for the affect ratings NOW only members gave toward lesbian groups and the bottom-line feminism index, which has two items concerning lesbian rights in it. On this issue, consensus has not yet been reached. In fact, the Houston conference was probably itself part of the process of consensus formation.

It can also be seen that the difference between NOW only and LWV only members increases, the more recently the issue became part of NOW's agenda. There is very low variance among both LWV only and NOW only members on economic rights, marital equity, and affect toward pro-ERA groups, but this difference increases as one moves toward the contemporary, still controversial issues of lesbian rights and abortion. On these two issues, League members show as much variation as people who belong to neither organization.

Constraint Analysis

The results of the analysis of belief and affect constraint parallel those reported previously for belief and affect consensus. NOW members show much more consistency at the individual level across the 13 feminism measures than League members, as shown by the lower average within-individual variability in Table 6.11 for NOW only and Joint members than for LWV only or for those who belong to Neither organization.

Individual Variability over Time

Since the affect scales had been repeated in the February survey, we explored the questions of whether there was any trend toward less individual variability in February than in October and whether any of the membership types showed greater reductions in that individual variability than others. This affect constraint analysis, based on seven affect scales, did not show any significant trends over time. NOW only members have the least within-individual variability and the lowest variance around average individual variability, and LWV only members show the highest variability and variance, but the pattern remained the same in February as it was in October (see Table 6.12).

An affect consensus analysis of change over time showed a slight, but not

Table 6.11

Belief/Affect Constraint: Average within-Individual Variability across Thirteen Feminism Measures, by Organizational Membership Type

Organizational Membership Type	Average Within-Individual Variability[a]	N
NOW ONLY	27.14	(262)
JOINT members	26.62	(129)
LWV ONLY	38.94	(143)
NEITHER NOW nor LWV	44.00	(340)
F Ratio =	9.53 ***	

[a]A variable was first computed for individual variance across the 13 feminism measures, then averaged within each organizational membership type.

*** p ⩽ .001

Table 6.12

Affect Constraint by Organizational Membership Types: October versus February Surveys

Organizational Membership Type	Average Within-Individual Variability[a]		Variance of Individual Variability[b]	
	October	February	October	February
NOW ONLY	1.56	1.53	1.56	1.60
JOINT Members	2.30	2.28	1.79	1.82
LWV ONLY	3.50	3.51	2.13	2.27
NEITHER NOW nor LWV .	2.65	2.61	2.04	2.16

[a]Individual variance across 7 affect scales, averaged for each organizational membership type.

[b]Standard deviation of average within-individual variability.

significant, trend toward more polarized affect toward feminist and anti-feminist groups, but this held among all four membership types, and hence is not reported in any detail here. NOW only members, despite their already skewed average affect scores in October, shifted slightly on all seven measures toward even more positive affect toward lesbian, radical, pro-abortion, and pro-ERA groups and toward more negative affect toward conservative, anti-abortion, and anti-ERA groups. These were not dramatic shifts, however: For example, NOW only members became somewhat more negative in affect toward conservative groups, while LWV only members became somewhat more positive in affect toward pro-abortion groups. By and large, whatever pressure organizational membership exerted seems to be relatively constant, impervious to major shifts in a short time span, even as a consequence of very intense political experiences like participation in the Houston conference.[1]

Consensus and Constraint:
Pro-Plan versus Anti-Plan Activists

It was noted in Chapter 2, during the response pattern analysis, that delegates who worked against the national Plan of Action were underrepresented in the study. Many refused to respond as a political act of rejection of the IWY Commission and its work, whereas others were instructed not to respond, at least to the first survey. But there are at least a small minority of delegates in the panel sample who report having worked closely with the "Majority" caucus and against the conference agenda. Since much the same type question was asked of Pro-Plan caucus activists, there are enough cases to explore how these two caucuses, so critical and visible in the plenary sessions and caucus meeting rooms in Houston, differ and how their conference participation affected them.

Specification of Activist Types

The activist types were defined on the basis of responses to the question "How much did you work with each of the following groups during the Houston conference?" [Q. 9, February survey]. *Anti-Plan* activists are defined as those who report any level of activity with the "Majority" caucus, whereas *Pro-Plan activists* are those who report the two highest activity levels in the response categories. *Nonactivists* are defined as those who did not

---

[1]This conclusion must be qualified by the possibility that the statistical methods used were not powerful enough to ferret out change, since NOW membership was shown to have had significant coefficients on affect change toward 5 of the 7 groups in the regression analysis in Table 6.8.

work at all with either caucus. (The Nonactivist type was not necessarily a passive participant; many of them may simply have been highly concentrated in work on a particular issue caucus rather than the Pro- and Anti-Plan caucuses).

Demographic Profile of Activist Types

Table 6.13 provides an overall profile of the three activist types across a number of social-demographic characteristics. There are significant differences between the Anti-Plan and Pro-Plan activists on almost all the characteristics shown. Most of these differences are consistent with informal observation and interviewing of delegates of each persuasion: Anti-Plan activists were overrepresented in delegations from the Midwest, West, and Southwest; 50% came from rural areas or small towns in their states, as compared to only 25% of the Pro-Plan activists. The Anti-Plan activists are almost all white, married women with rather large families; more are Catholic or Mormon and fewer report no religious affiliation than among the Pro-Plan activists. Close to 90% report very high religious attendance, compared to only 24% of the Pro-Plan activists. Fewer have attended college, more were not employed in 1977, and those who worked earned less money than Pro-Plan activists or Nonactivists.

The profile of socioeconomic indicators of the Anti-Plan and Pro-Plan activists suggests some intriguing differences in the routes to adult status these women have traveled. The Anti-Plan delegates are less educated and earn less money on their own if they are employed than the Pro-Plan delegates, yet both groups report the same percentage of high-income households. Despite this similarity of household income levels, fewer Anti-Plan activists rate themselves as upper-middle or upper-class than do the Pro-Plan activists (26% versus 47%, respectively). Yet another contrast between the two groups is found in what appear to be very different social mobility profiles, as suggested by the social class ratings they gave for their current families compared to those they report for the families they grew up in. Thus, a larger percentage of the Anti-Plan delegates (36%) say their families of origin were upper-middle or upper-class than report their present families to be at this class level (26%), whereas the reverse holds among the Pro-Plan delegates: Twenty-eight percent of their families of origin are reported as upper-middle or upper-class compared to 47% of their present families. This suggests that a larger proportion of the Anti-Plan delegates have been downwardly mobile and, reciprocally, a larger proportion of the Pro-Plan delegates have been upwardly mobile. Though highly inferential, there are hints in these data that many Anti-Plan delegates live in a small town, very traditional world with some yearning for lost status, while more of the Pro-Plan delegates live in an

Table 6.13

Social-Demographic Characteristics of Pro-Plan and Anti-Plan Activists at National Conference

Characteristic	ANTI-Plan Activists	Non-Activists	PRO-Plan Activists	Significant Inter-Type Differences
LOCALE:				
% reside in rural area or small town	50.1%	22.6%	24.6%	*
% reside in Midwest, West or Southwest	64.5%	42.8%	45.3%	*
FAMILY:				
% Married	87.1%	61.3%	55.7%	**
$\bar{X}$ Age	45.3	44.8	42.0	n.s.
$\bar{X}$ Number Children	3.65	1.86	1.77	***
RACE/RELIGION:				
% White	96.8%	72.8%	79.9%	*
% HIGH Religious Attendance .	86.5%	30.0%	24.0%	**
Religious Affiliation:				*
Catholic	44.8%	24.3%	14.4%	
Mormon	24.1	.9	.4	
Protestant	24.1	39.7	44.6	
Jewish	--	10.2	11.4	
None	3.4	16.6	17.3	
Other	3.4	8.3	11.8	
SOCIO-ECONOMIC STATUS:				
% Some college or less	42.0%	29.6%	23.3%	**
% Not currently employed . . .	32.3%	19.6%	13.4%	*
% Own income $20,000+	10.8%	19.9%	22.9%	*
% Family income $20,000+ . . .	68.9%	62.3%	66.2%	n.s.
% Upper middle/upper class . .				
Now	25.6%	40.9%	46.6%	*
Family of origin	36.3%	22.9%	27.8%	*
N =	$(47)^a$	(328)	(550)	

[a]This is an average base N; there is slight variation from one cross-tabulation to another.

    * $p \leqslant .05$
  ** $p \leqslant .01$
 *** $p \leqslant .001$

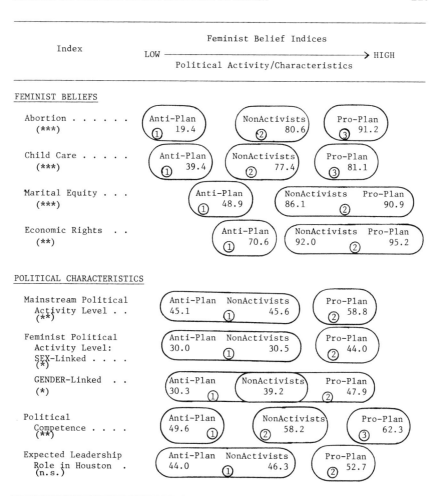

Figure 6.6. Feminist beliefs and political characteristics of Pro-Plan and Anti-Plan activists at national conference; * $p \leq .05$; ** $p \leq .01$; *** $p \leq .001$.

urban, cosmopolitan world they have gained access to by dint of their own educational and professional achievements.

Feminist Beliefs and Political Characteristics

Figure 6.6 uses the now-familiar device of mean scores by activist types, differentiated by the Duncan procedure into subsets wher. the mean scores are significantly different from each other, for a variety of measures of feminist

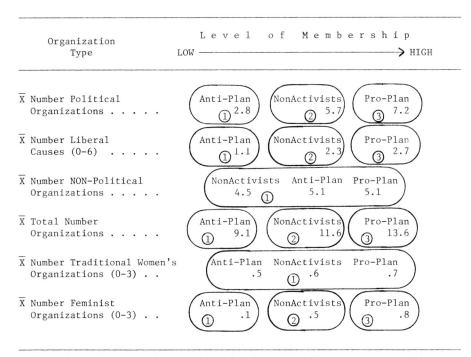

Organization Type	Level of Membership LOW ——————————————→ HIGH		

X̄ Number Political Organizations . . . . . — Anti-Plan ① 2.8 · NonActivists ② 5.7 · Pro-Plan ③ 7.2

X̄ Number Liberal Causes (0–6) . . . . . — Anti-Plan ① 1.1 · NonActivists ② 2.3 · Pro-Plan ③ 2.7

X̄ Number NON-Political Organizations . . . . . — NonActivists 4.5 ① · Anti-Plan 5.1 · Pro-Plan 5.1

X̄ Total Number Organizations . . . . . — Anti-Plan ① 9.1 · NonActivists ② 11.6 · Pro-Plan ③ 13.6

X̄ Number Traditional Women's Organizations (0–3) . . — Anti-Plan .5 · NonActivists ① .6 · Pro-Plan .7

X̄ Number Feminist Organizations (0–3) . . — Anti-Plan ① .1 · NonActivists ② .5 · Pro-Plan ③ .8

Figure 6.7. Organizational membership of Pro-Plan and Anti-Plan activists at national conference.

beliefs and political characteristics. It is hardly surprising to note that Anti-Plan activists uniformly score low and represent a separate subset on the feminist belief measures, but it was less expected that they would also show the lowest scores on level of past political activity or political competence. Their lesser involvement is not confined to feminist activities, but applies to involvement in mainstream politics as well. Except for competence rating, Anti-Plan activists are not differentiated from the Nonactivists on the political characteristic indices.

Nonactivists scored as high at the feminist end of the index as the Pro-Plan activists on marital equity and economic rights for women, but significantly less so in the case of abortion and child care. Pro-Plan activists are largely in the lead, too, in the level of activity they have had, both in mainstream and in feminist politics. Based, no doubt, on that past profile and the expectation of working closely with the Pro-Plan Caucus in Houston, they also show a distinct, high level of political competence and the expectation of being important at the Houston conference.

This does not mean, however, that the Anti-Plan delegates were nonjoiners. Figure 6.7 brings together a variety of measures on organizational participation, and it can readily be seen that low participation is typical only of general political and specific feminist involvement in organizational life: In traditional women's organizations and in a variety of organizations of a non-political nature (social, religious, and cultural), there are no significant differences among the three activist types. When all the organizations are put together in a summary code, the Anti-Plan activists still show a membership level above the general population ($M = 9.1$) although decidedly lower than the mean shown by Pro-Plan activists ($M = 13.6$).

Affect Consensus

The subjective level of affect toward one's own and other groups in society mirrors the profile shown on political behavior, organizational involvement, and background social characteristics. Table 6.14 shows the mean scores on the affect scales toward all 16 groups in the survey: In all but a few cases, the Nonactivists fall between the Anti-Plan and Pro-Plan activists, although they are uniformly closer to the latter than the former. The activists feel more strongly toward the groups they encountered in Houston, as their actions on the floor of the coliseum would predict. Like the earlier hints that conservatives feel less positively toward ethnic and racial minorities than do very liberal delegates, the more focused activist typology also shows significant differences between the Anti-Plan activists on the one hand and the Nonactivists and Pro-Plan delegates on the other. The Pro-Plan activists are clearly on the positive side of the affect scale toward Blacks and Latinas with a mean close to 6, whereas the Anti-Plan activists show a mean in the neutral range of the scale for both Blacks and Latinas. On the key issues of ERA and abortion, the two activist types are polarized at extreme opposite ends of the scales. By and large, affect consensus is high across the majority of the groups rated among both Anti- and Pro-Plan activists.

Affect Constraint

If attention is narrowed to the individual level, the question can be raised whether the activist types, precisely because of their greater investment of time and energy in the political activities at the conference, might show significant changes in their affect scores as a consequence of the conference. This question can be explored using the October and February affect scores for those groups most likely to be relevant to the roles the activists played in Houston. In this analysis of *individual affect constraint,* 10 scales were used (affect toward pro- and anti-abortion, pro- and anti-ERA groups, all three political groups—liberals, radicals, and conservatives, NOW, the IWY Commissioners, and lesbian groups). Several explicit predictions were made in

Table 6.14
Affect Consensus by Caucus Activity Types: Mean Scores, October Survey[a]

Affect Scale	ANTI-PLAN Activists	NONactivists	PRO-PLAN Activists	F-ratio[b]
Pro-ERA	1.90	6.52	6.78	394.5
Anti-ERA	6.35	1.55	1.25	348.8
Anti-Abortion	6.81	2.17	1.66	197.9
NOW	1.39	5.37	5.89	159.4
NWPC	2.13	5.68	6.15	149.9
Pro-Abortion	1.26	5.51	6.16	148.9
Liberal	2.48	5.50	5.88	100.7
IWY Commissioners . . .	2.48	5.40	5.67	72.2
Conservative	5.32	2.77	2.41	53.4
Lesbian	1.42	4.03	4.66	51.1
Labor Union	2.81	4.95	5.33	48.3
Radical	1.58	3.46	3.96	27.4
Black	4.42	5.83	5.89[c]	22.1
Latina	4.39	5.79	5.87[c]	21.8
Farm/Rural	5.59	5.27	5.09[c]	6.8
Business/Prof.	5.00	5.58	5.57[c]	2.9

[a] Scale range from 1(Negative-Cold) to 7 (Positive-Warm).

[b] All statistically significant.

[c] Except for these four groups, mean affect scores differentiate into three subsets on the Duncan procedure. On the scales toward Blacks, Latinas, farm and bus/prof groups, Nonactivists are in same subset with Pro-Plan activists.

anticipation of this analysis: Both the Anti-Plan and Pro-Plan activists would show lower individual variance across the 10 affect scales in the October survey than the Nonactivists would and, as evidence of conference impact, both activist types would show less individual variability and lower variance around the individual variability mean in the February ratings than they had in the earlier October ratings.

Table 6.15 gives evidence that these predictions were confirmed by the data. First, the Nonactivists showed the highest average within-individual variability in both surveys. Second, the average within-individual variability drops, over time, for both activist types, but not nearly as dramatically for the Pro-Plan as for the Anti-Plan activists: The mean individual variance for Pro-Plan delegates dropped from 1.96 to 1.68, but it dropped to less than one-half the October level for the Anti-Plan delegates (from 1.85 to .83). Third, the variance (standard deviation) around the individual variability also showed a dramatic drop in February, but only for the Anti-Plan activists (from 1.95 to .88), whereas there was a slight increase in the variance shown for Nonactivists and Pro-Plan delegates in the second survey.

As an embattled, tiny minority, the Anti-Plan activists seem to have become embittered. Their antagonism increased and the differences within their ranks narrowed as a consequence of their participation in the conference in Houston. Consistent with the findings from the constraint analysis reported earlier, the embittered aftermath for the Anti-Plan activists is suggested by an examination of specific changes in their affect scores toward a variety of groups. Though any one score shows modest changes between surveys, there was a consistent tendency for the Anti-Plan delegates to show more negative affect toward all the liberal and feminist groups by February, with a counter tendency to increase positive affect toward conservative groups, from a mean affect score of 5.3 in October to 5.8 in February (data not shown). Altogether, the change profile suggests not only the general tendency for people who

Table 6.15

Affect Constraint by Caucus Activity Types: October versus February

Caucus Activity Type	Average Within-Individual Variability[a]		Variance of Individual Variability[b]	
	October	February	October	February
Anti-Plan Activists	1.85	.83	1.95	.88
Non-Activists	2.51	2.43	1.72	1.88
Pro-Plan Activists	1.96	1.68	1.45	1.50
F-Ratio, (analysis of variance)	12.72***	21.76***		

[a]Individual variance across 10 affect scales, averaged for each Caucus Activity Type.

[b]Standard Deviation.

*** $p \leqslant .001$

work together to become more like each other but the tendency for losers in an intense political encounter to feel a bitter aftertaste that is generalized toward a wide array of individuals and groups.

The Pro-Plan activists, as the "winners" in Houston, show a general shift toward more polarized feelings toward the groups they rated: They became more positive toward liberal and feminist groups and more negative toward their opponents. Thus, their mean affect score toward pro-abortion groups, already a high 6.1 in October, rose, by February, to 6.5; toward radical groups, from 3.8 to 4.1; toward the IWY Commissioners, from 5.6 to 6.0. Their mean affect scores toward conservatives dropped from 2.4 to 2.1; toward anti-ERA groups from 1.3 to 1.1 (data not shown). It is interesting that, in this sample of activists, there is no trend toward regression to the mean: Even extreme mean scores became more, not less, extreme. This movement of their scores is consistent with the slight increase in variance between the two surveys (from 1.45 to 1.50), whereas the closing in to a more negative general assessment of the conference is clearly involved in the strong opposite tendency for the Anti-Plan activists to show one-half as much variance in February as in October (1.95 versus .88). The minority Anti-Plan activists emerged more united than the majority, Pro-Plan, activists.

Conclusion

It is of considerable political and sociological interest to have found that the conference stimulated individual constraint among the Pro-Plan and Anti-Plan activists, but did not do so for members of NOW and the League. To the extent that a social movement derives some of its energy from strongly held feelings of cohesion in the ranks of the movement and of hostility toward its opponents, large political events like the national conference may further intensify feelings that feed into and support the convictions that keep activity levels high in political efforts toward the goals of the movement.

There is also an interesting and important contrast between the quantitative results reported in this chapter and the tenor of the comments made by those delegates who responded to the open-ended question. The image projected by those qualitative comments was of women who went out of their way to speak to Anti-Plan delegates, if not to urge a change of vote, then at a minimum to increase the understanding between them. But the Pro-Plan delegates also report their surprise at finding how alike they were on issues and life experiences not directly relevant to the Houston agenda. In some ways, the Anti-Plan delegates showed more emotional honesty (others might say dogmatism): They made no claim to have influenced their opponents; it was rare for them to report even an increase in understanding the depth of feeling beneath the votes of the Pro-Plan majority, though they occasionally reported with the same surprise that they had undergone many personal life experiences similar to those of the Pro-Plan delegates.

It would be easy to be misled by the shared tears or congratulations that occurred when an opponent won on an issue, or by the human compassion that intense situations can stimulate. The colder instrument of a quantitative analysis is a healthy corrective to such self-delusion, for the profile that emerged from the statistical material suggests that Anti-Plan and Pro-Plan forces came away from Houston with a *sharpened* sense of their differences and an increased commitment to engage in political action that could only further widen, not close, the belief and affect gap that separates those who work toward, from those who work against, sex equality in American society.

It is even possible that many Pro-Plan delegates have had second thoughts about the gap between their public stand, when voting on some resolutions, and their private beliefs on those issues. Public displays of unity, in other words, may make for a flashy news story and provide short-run psychic boosts to participants but, in the long run, unless there is a deep and genuine consensus in the belief system involved, a seed of discomfort may remain. Those whose actions were free of any private–public discrepancy in beliefs, however, may then show not only a keen commitment to future political action, but a more unified sense of shared beliefs.

7

Paths to Political Competence and Action

Introduction

Some 20,000 people attended the Houston conference. Observers, invited guests, reporters, volunteers, and television crews represented close to 90% of this total. Only 2200 people were officially involved as delegates, alternates, IWY Commissioners, or Secretariat staff members, a mere 11% of those in Houston for the event. Respondents who reported that they had been "key persons" whose views "were sought out and taken into account," were therefore laying claim to very significant leadership roles indeed (Q. 5, February survey). In fact, only 10% of the sample said they had been a "key person." The modal response was that they had been an "interested participant," someone who tried to "make their views known," which was reported by 49% of the delegates. Falling between these two responses were 27% who said they were "important persons" whose views were "paid attention to." Only 15% felt they had been simply an "interested bystander" or "not much of a participant."

This chapter begins with an analysis of the leadership roles the delegates *expected* to play in Houston (from the October survey), compares them with the roles they *actually* played (as reported in February), and attempts to explain discrepancies between these reports as a consequence of specific activities engaged in during the conference. Many delegates were less important than they had expected to be, whereas others said they were more important than they had expected to be.

These gaps between expectation and reality are, of course, a common experience, hardly unique to the Houston conference. Expectations are rooted in personal biographies, in the variety of prior experiences, commitments, decisions that shape and change people in the course of their adult lives. With an average age of 42, most of the delegates had had many years to acquire such experiences. Various measures of organizational involvement and political activity will be used to explain expected leadership roles at the conference. With measures on specific activities engaged in at the conference (the exposure variables), one can explain some of the slippage between expected and actual leadership roles.

Leadership in the single event of the national conference is only the first step in the larger analysis of the chapter, which deals with the development of the political woman. The leadership role analysis is of intrinsic interest to understanding the Houston experience, but the issue of more enduring significance is the sequence of experiences that differentiate women of high or low political competence or high and low political aspirations. By pressing the analysis back into earlier phases of the lives of the delegates, one can unravel the development of political careers in ways that transcend the particularity of the Houston conference.

The effort to depict the political development of the women in the Houston sample must be done with caution. For one thing, the women vary in age from 16 to 81 and have lived their lives in particular historical periods that may affect the extent to which this retrospective analysis of their lives can be generalized to the political careers of women in the decades ahead. The age diversity of the delegates means the women moved through particular phases of the life span during very different historical periods. The average 42-year-old delegate was born during the Depression, left school in the 1950s, was just turning 30 when the current feminist movement began. A 62-year-old delegate 20 years her senior was an adult during the Depression, perhaps already a grandmother or well established in a career when the feminist movement began in the 1960s. By contrast, a 22-year-old delegate grew to adulthood during a period of ferment about gender roles in American society. Thus, being 22 in 1977 is very different from being 22 in 1957 or 1937. These differences will be even greater when there has been social change in the substantive area under investigation. The place of women in politics, like gender roles generally, is currently undergoing considerable change. Thus, the profile that emerges from the retrospective analysis, based on the past lives of the women in the sample, may have historical truth, but this is not necessarily truth generalizable to the future. It may be that what determined the movement of women into political life in the past, when it was very exceptional for women to gain significant positions in politics, is different from what will determine the movement of women into politics in the future. At a minimum, the findings must be assessed for possible historical limitations on their generalizability.

To attempt a sequential analysis of this sort, that is, to push back to earlier points in the personal histories of the delegates and to try to explain what determined some of those earlier involvements and political experiences, requires a careful ordering of the variables on a time dimension. The study is longitudinal only with respect to the conference itself, for the limited purpose of analyzing the impact of the intervening conference on those variables that were included in both surveys. The variables used in this chapter are almost all from the first survey. This requires that we specify a model for the sequencing of major life events and experiences. Some elements in that model have very little ambiguity: If there is a high correlation between ethnicity and organizational membership, no one would argue that joining organizations has an effect on ethnicity. In many other cases, however, there is considerable ambiguity concerning causal direction, and this requires an explication of assumptions about causal ordering. Thus, the section to follow introduces the analysis model and outlines the topics covered in charting the paths to political competence and action in the lives of the delegates.

The Analysis Model

Two aids are presented to illustrate the analysis model. The first is Table 7.1, which classifies the 46 variables used in this chapter by an underlying model of causal sequence. It is to be assumed that joining an organization and retaining membership in it by and large precedes political activity. A young lawyer eager for a political career cannot simply plunge into political activity in a vacuum: She will join organizations that mesh with her political interests and further her access to the political process. That network-building paves the way for future political constituencies. I assume, then, that it will be very exceptional for anyone who has not been deeply involved in organizations in her community to report high levels of political activity or office-holding.

Furthermore, the questions about political activity refer explicitly to the "last few years." Although organizational membership was given as a current profile (e.g., how many political organizations do you belong to *now?*"), it is assumed, since one-half the women are over 42 years of age, most such organizational memberships are of long standing. Many delegates have probably been members of a political party, an alumnae association, a union, or a church since their early adulthood, which could range from a few years in the case of very young delegates to several decades in the case of older delegates. More historically bound organizational memberships, like that in civil rights and feminist organizations, have a shorter potential history dating from the mid-1960s, but even here, I assume that for most delegates, well enough

Table 7.1

Variables in the Analysis Model

Time Classification (Past to Current)	Variables[a]
1. BACKGROUND ASCRIBED CHARACTERISTICS:	Age, Race/Ethnicity, Religious Affiliation, Educational Attainment, Hold Law Degree, POLITICAL ACTIVITY OF FAMILY OF ORIGIN, Social Class of Family of Origin.
2. ADULT FAMILY/PERSONAL ATTRIBUTES:	Marital Status, Religious Attendance, Educational Attainment of Husband, HUSBAND POLITICALLY ACTIVE, Current Social Class, Region of Residence, Size of City of Residence, Employment Status, Own Earnings, Total Family Income, Political Orientation, Employer.
3. ORGANIZATIONAL MEMBERSHIP:	TOTAL ORGANIZATIONS BELONGED TO, # POLITICAL ORGANIZATIONS, # FEMINIST ORGANIZATIONS, # NON-POLITICAL ORGANIZATIONS, # Traditional Women's Organizations.
4. POLITICAL ACTIVITY:	MAINSTREAM POLITICAL ACTIVITY, SEX-LINKED FEMINIST ACTIVITY, GENDER-LINKED FEMINIST ACTIVITY, HELD ELECTIVE PUBLIC OFFICE, HELD APPOINTIVE PUBLIC OFFICE, HELD ELECTIVE OFFICE IN POLITICAL PARTY, HELD APPOINTIVE OFFICE IN POLITICAL PARTY, # Liberal Causes, # Groups Supported Nomination, State Coordinating Committee Member.
5. OCTOBER RATINGS:	EXPECTED LEADERSHIP ROLE, POLITICAL COMPETENCE.
6. NOVEMBER CONFERENCE ROLE/ACTIVITIES:	ACTIVE PLENARY ROLE, Passive Plenary Role, # GROUPS WORKED WITH, # CAUCUS MEETINGS ATTENDED, # New Contacts Made in Houston, Delegation Responsibility, Size of Delegation.
7. FEBRUARY RATINGS:	ACTUAL LEADERSHIP ROLE, POLITICAL COMPETENCE.

[a]Capitalized variables are also dependent variables in the analytic sequence. Cf. Figure 7.1.

known in their states to have won election, such membership precedes the "last few years" of reported political activity levels. On these grounds, then, it is reasonable to categorize organizational membership in the analysis model as prior to recent political activity.

A second major assumption in the model is that adult family and work characteristics are meaningfully classified earlier in the time sequence than is organizational membership. It is assumed that family and job commitments determine the extent of organizational membership, not the reverse. One does not have a first child as a consequence of joining the PTA! Marital status, employment status, where one lives, and at what income level may set the parameters within which decisions are made about organizational and political activity. There are, of course, exceptions to this general tendency. Many of us know of marriages that have ended as a consequence of a spouse's excessive political involvement during the years of married life. Earnings may become depressed as a consequence of greater priority given to organizational than to job responsibilities. But, for the most part, for most people, I assume the time sequence runs from family and personal attributes to organizational involvement.

Most background variables present less ambiguity. They include ascribed characteristics like race, ethnicity, and social class of the family the delegates grew up in. Educational attainment has more timing ambiguity, of course, in light of the fact that many women have returned to school after a decade or more at home rearing children. Many middle-aged American women have earned advanced degrees 20 years after the birth of their children. But, again, this is not a typical pattern, and an analytic model and classification of variables in a time frame are designed for the typical, not the exceptional, life pattern.

Figure 7.1 provides an overview of the steps involved in the analysis, moving back in time in the lives of the delegates to explore six issues relevant to political development. From the analysis of (a) conference leadership, we move to (b) an analysis of political competence, then to (c) what determined activity level in both mainstream and feminist movement politics, and (d) holding elective and appointive office in government or political party, (e) the determinants of membership level in four types of organizations and, finally, to (f) political activity of husbands and of members of the families in which the delegates grew up.

The basic mode of analysis at these six steps is pairwise multiple regression. When the variables in question are panel items, I follow the logic of panel analysis already described in Chapter 6. This involves three major lines of investigation in the leadership and political competence analysis: a regression analysis of personal background, organizational, and political variables on leadership or political competence as tapped in first the October, then the February surveys, followed by a third regression of the February ratings on the exposure variables that measure conference roles and activities, while controlling for the October rating reported 5 months earlier.

As the analysis presses back in time, the range of variables drawn upon becomes more concentrated on a few types. Thus, to explain current ratings

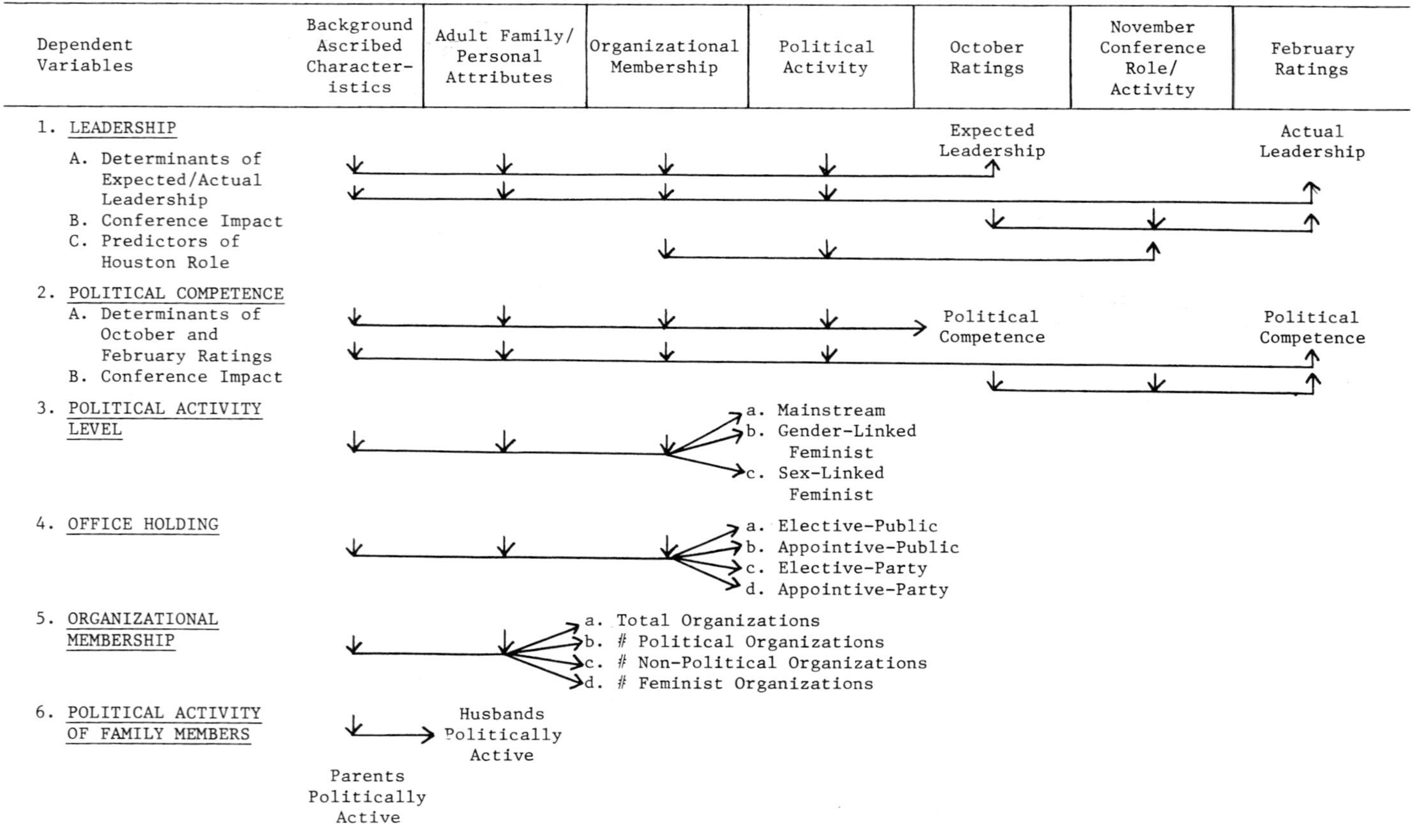

Dependent Variables | Background Ascribed Characteristics | Adult Family/Personal Attributes | Organizational Membership | Political Activity | October Ratings | November Conference Role/Activity | February Ratings

1. LEADERSHIP
   A. Determinants of Expected/Actual Leadership — Expected Leadership (October Ratings); Actual Leadership (February Ratings)
   B. Conference Impact
   C. Predictors of Houston Role

2. POLITICAL COMPETENCE
   A. Determinants of October and February Ratings — Political Competence (October Ratings); Political Competence (February Ratings)
   B. Conference Impact

3. POLITICAL ACTIVITY LEVEL
   a. Mainstream
   b. Gender-Linked Feminist
   c. Sex-Linked Feminist

4. OFFICE HOLDING
   a. Elective–Public
   b. Appointive–Public
   c. Elective–Party
   d. Appointive–Party

5. ORGANIZATIONAL MEMBERSHIP
   a. Total Organizations
   b. # Political Organizations
   c. # Non-Political Organizations
   d. # Feminist Organizations

6. POLITICAL ACTIVITY OF FAMILY MEMBERS
   Husbands Politically Active
   Parents Politically Active

Figure 7.1. Major dependent variables in the analytic sequence.

of political competence, I shall draw upon recent political activity and organizational membership as well as family and job experiences of the women and their social origins. By contrast, the analysis of organizational membership draws only on background and adult family and personal attributes. Since the model assumes organizational membership precedes political activity, this is necessarily so.

The chapter will close with an overview of the paths through which the political development of women seems to move and a discussion of the extent to which the results are either historically bound or applicable to the development of political careers among women in the 1980s.

Leadership at the Conference

Questions that ask about future plans produce responses that include fantasy as well as real intentions. If the question concerns something you expect to be doing a decade from now, one can expect more fantasy in the answer than if the question concerns next week. The question on leadership expectations for the Houston conference falls between these extremes of a few days and a decade ahead: Only a month intervened between the October survey and the November conference.

It is to be assumed, however, that there may be more slippage between expectation and actuality when the experience involved is a unique event rather than a familiar one. The first national women's conference was clearly a unique event, and hence there may be a sharp contrast in proportion and characteristics between those who expected and those who actually filled top leadership roles in Houston.

In addition, leadership roles at a large-scale conference are affected by the expectations of other participants. Had the majority of the delegates expected to be highly influential leaders, most would necessarily have had their hopes dashed, since no conference could use or sustain so top-heavy a leadership structure.

Both fantasy and realism were probably blended in the expectations reported in October when the delegates filled out their questionnaires in the quiet of their homes. A state legislator may have expected to *be* important at the conference as a simple extrapolation of the fact that she *is* important in her home state. An officer in a national organization concerned with women's issues could similarly expect to be important in Houston on the gorunds of her history as a responsible and experienced organizational leader.

There is no way to tell what the delegates' private thoughts were when they predicted whether they would be top leaders or just interested participants in Houston. We can only infer what may have gone through their minds from the statistical pattern revealed by regressing the same set of background characteristics on the leadership ratings before and after the conference. These results are shown in Table 7.2. A comparison of the two columns shows that some predictors became more important and others less important in the ratings given in February as compared to those given in October. The profile of women who *expected* to play important leadership roles before the conference includes high ratings of political competence, having served as an elective or appointive public official in the past, belonging to several feminist organizations, membership in a minority group, political activity on sex-linked issues, and a broad base of support from a number of groups in the state meeting elections. *Actual* leadership roles show a different profile: Here, the most significant predictors are still political competence, extensive group support, and minority-group membership, but experience in public office has been replaced by general political activity level in mainstream politics, and past activity on *gender*-linked issues has replaced *sex*-linked movement activity. Organizational membership was no longer significant, whereas coming from a large delegation became relevant to actual leadership role.

What is one to make of this shifting profile of predictors of actual, compared to expected, leadership? Why, for example, did holding public office predict leadership expectation, but not actual leadership experience? Serving as a public official may mean no more than having a local reputation as a mayor's appointee to a municipal commission or serving for a term on a school board. This no doubt contributed to political competence, but such highly specific political experience in office may not have been as important in Houston as previous activity in mainstream politics. High scores on the mainstream politics index means previous activity on the state or national level and, by inference, some network of contacts and ability to cultivate them at a national conference. It also involves previous experience as a delegate to party conventions, which would give a sense of familiarity in a first encounter with the Houston Coliseum. Hence important leadership experience may have been facilitated by extralocal ties from mainstream political activity and party conventions in a way that holding a local office did not.

It is consistent with this interpretation that group support shows increased significance as a predictor of actual leadership as compared to expected leadership. The groups represented at Houston had also been represented at the state meetings, so that delegates elected with a broad base of support could be more effective at the conference than could those who had a narrow base of support or who put their names forward without any organizational backing at all.

There is an interesting and probably interrelated set of factors involved in the drop in significance of membership in feminist organizations and the shift in the sphere of feminist politics that mattered to leadership roles. In October,

Table 7.2

Regression on Expected and Actual Conference Leadership Role (Beta Coefficients)[a]

Predictor Variables	EXPECTED Leadership Role (October 1977)	ACTUAL Leadership Role (February 1978)
Political Competence (October Rating)	.233 ***	.133 ***
POLITICAL ACTIVITY		
Held Elective and/or Appointive Public Office	.123 ***	.060
# Groups Supported Nomination . . .	.073 *	.108 **
Sex-Linked Feminist Activity . . .	.077 *	.053
Gender-Linked Feminist Activity . .	.050	.107 *
State Coordinating Committee Member [b]	.044	.003
Mainstream Political Activity . . .	.042	.075 *
ORGANIZATIONAL MEMBERSHIP		
# Feminist Organizations	.113 ***	.055
# Traditional Women's Organizations	-.030	-.003
BACKGROUND AND PERSONAL CHARACTERISTICS		
Minority Group Member [b]	.073 *	.094 *
Catholic [b]	-.031	-.027
Size of Delegation	.037	.081 *
Size of City of Residence	.026	.045
R^2 =	.198 ***	.155 ***
(N=722) F =	12.93	9.64

[a]
  Direction of change between the two equations is the same for both the
  metric and beta coefficients for all 13 predictor variables, but there
  is a slight increase in the variance of the actual leadership measure
  (S.D.=.842) over the preconference expected leadership measure (S.D.=.738)

[b]
  Dummy variables.

* $p \leqslant .05$
** $p \leqslant .01$
*** $p \leqslant .001$

sex-linked activism and high organizational membership were significant pre-dictors of expected leadership, whereas by February, neither were important; instead, the gender-activists reported that they actually played a more impor-tant leadership role than they had expected. The sex-linked activist tends to be a single-issue activist more often than the gender-linked activist. Almost everyone expected reproductive freedom and sexual preference to be con-troversial issues in Houston, so delegates with a particularly passionate in-volvement with either of these issues would expect to be quite important in the deliberations in Houston. But there were 24 other issues on the agenda, and the broader range of issues typical of the gender-linked activist's interests would then produce exactly the result shown in Table 7.2: more important roles in actuality than in expectation.

One last point in Table 7.2 is worth noting: Although delegation size played no role in leadership expectations, delegates from large delegations reported more important roles by February. Since the core leaders of the conference were themselves from large delegations (e.g., New York, Texas, California), delegates from large delegations had a higher probability of close ties to the core leaders than did delegates from small delegations, an edge they may not have expected would affect their roles.

That the total amount of variance in leadership role declined from October to February is seen in the drop of the magnitude of the R^2 from .198 in October to .155 for the February equation. This means that what the dele-gates actually did in Houston may have changed their leadership ratings. This can be demonstrated by regressing actual conference leadership on the indi-ces of conference activity and roles, while controlling for the expected leader-ship reported in October. By including the earlier leadership rating, we can be sure that any significant coefficient on any of the exposure variables is a contribution to actual leadership, independent of their expectations.

The regression results in Table 7.3 show that all six exposure variables did, in fact, contribute significantly to reported leadership role, independent of the earlier rating. The two most important contributions are the sheer number of groups the delegates worked with in Houston and the responsibility the dele-gates carried as chairperson, vice-chairperson, or committee member of their delegations: Both measures imply many points of contact with individuals and groups and hence an increase in the actual leadership role from earlier expec-tations. Factors with lesser effect, but still significant, are that the more caucus meetings the delegate attended, the larger the delegation she belonged to, and the more active she was during the plenary sessions, the more likely she was to achieve a significant leadership role. Although the indices for active versus passive plenary session roles are negatively correlated, this is a sufficiently moderate correlation for the passive role to show a significant negative beta coefficient in the equation. This means that leadership roles became more

Table 7.3

Regression on Actual Conference Leadership Role, Controlling for Expected Leadership Role: Impact of Activity in Houston (Beta Coefficients)

Predictor Variables	Actual Leadership Role
Expected Leadership Role	.391 ***
# Groups Worked with in Houston	.202 ***
Delegation Responsibility	.098 **
Active Plenary Session Role	.092 *
# Caucus Meetings Attended	.079 *
Size of Delegation	.077 *
Passive Plenary Session Role	-.076 *
R^2 =	.378 ***
F =	62.08
$R^2 - r^2$ =	.118

(N = 722)

* $p \leqslant .05$
** $p \leqslant .01$
*** $p \leqslant .001$

significant when behavior during the plenary sessions was consistently high on activity and low on passive responses or physical withdrawal from the floor.

The final R^2 is a high .378 but, more important, when this is adjusted by subtracting the correlation between the October and February leadership ratings ($r = .51$) there is still a highly significant residual: The exposure variables have contributed a minimum of 12% to the explanation of actual leadership reported in February.

Since the major exposure variables used in Table 7.3 will appear at several points in the analysis, this is an appropriate point to examine them separately in order to gain some illumination of why and how they affect change between the two waves of the panel analysis. Table 7.4 shows the most significant predictors for the three major exposure variables: active plenary role, number of groups worked with during the conference, and number of caucus meetings attended. Included in the equations are an array of predictor var-

Table 7.4

Regression on Role in Houston ("Exposure Variables") (Beta Coefficients)

Predictor Variables	Role in Houston		
	Active Plenary Role	# Groups Worked with in Houston	# Caucus Meetings Attended
Political Competence (Oct.) . .	.163 ***	.142 ***	.075 +
POLITICAL ACTIVITY			
Mainstream Political Activity Level	.113 **	.130 ***	.039
# Groups Supported Nomination	.079 *	.160 ***	.097 *
Feminist Political Activity Level	.075 *	.154 ***	.128 **
State Coordinating Committee Member[a]	.016	.019	.040
Issue-Focussed Delegate Role Concept[b]	.050	.094 *	.062
Team Member Delegate Role Concept[b]	-.024	.009	.028
Political Career Motivation in Delegate Role	.004	.007	-.077 *
ORGANIZATIONAL MEMBERSHIP			
# Political Organizations . . .	.129 **	.095 *	.084 +
# Non-Political Organizations	.006	.071 *	.049
BACKGROUND/PERSONAL CHARACTERISTICS			
Age	-.232 ***	-.232 ***	-.149 ***
Radical/Very Liberal Political Orientation[a]	.082 *	-.001	-.003
Conservative Political Orientation[a]	.062 +	.036	.021
R^2 =	.197 ***	.260 ***	.093 ***
F =	12.86	18.38	5.38
(N = 695)			

[a]Dummy Variables.

[b]Expected role, as individual delegate, member of delegation, issue or organizational representative, as analyzed in Chapter 4.

+   p ≤ .10
*   p ≤ .05
**   p ≤ .01
***   p ≤ .001

iables tapping relevant personal characteristics, political and organizational experience, and anticipated conference role type.

Age is the strongest predictor, with a highly significant negative coefficient in all three equations. This will come as no surprise to any older delegate who put in many hours every day of the conference. It took stamina and a good metabolism simply to attend plenary sessions and delegation meetings all day and long into the night. To go beyond sheer attendance to a more active role working with groups and organizations and attending caucus meetings, took an extraordinary amount of stamina. It is an interesting question whether a conference run at a more leisurely pace would facilitate more active roles by older women than the pressured pace of the 1977 conference permitted. It will be recalled from Chapter 3 that the delegates themselves would have preferred a longer conference rather than a shortened agenda.

Political competence and mainstream political activity were both important predictors of two of the three exposure variables: active roles in the plenary sessions and the number of groups worked with in Houston. Political competence and experience did not predict caucus attendance, no doubt because mere attendance does not differentiate between the passive spectator and the active participant. Activity level in feminist politics shows a highly significant coefficient with caucus attendance, reflecting both interest in and commitment to a broad range of feminist issues, and hence to more active participation in a variety of caucuses.

There is also a hint in the results that those who were most active during the plenary sessions tended to be from both ends of the political spectrum rather than the more moderate liberal position that characterized most delegates: Independent of all the more specific indicators of political activity, those with a very liberal or radical orientation or, to a lesser degree, those with a conservative political orientation, show higher activity levels during the plenary sessions than the more moderate liberals.

Of the three exposure variables, the number of groups worked with is associated with the most extensive networks in both mainstream and feminist politics, significant organizational membership, and a wide group-support base that, no doubt, precedes the state meetings. This is also the only exposure variable that shows a significant coefficient on the two measures of role concept: Those who had previously defined themselves as *representatives* of an issue or organization tended to work with more groups in Houston. Perhaps for this reason, political orientation does not relate to extensiveness of groups worked with: Women who are network-builders, joiners of issue-oriented organizations, and generally gregarious may be found at all points on the political spectrum and they may tend to work away from the limelight of the plenary sessions themselves.

On the other hand, there is quite a different balance to the size of the beta coefficients on feminist, as opposed to mainstream, political activity for the two exposure variables of plenary session role and number of groups worked with. The more conspicuous role in the tense spotlight of the plenary sessions drew *more* on experiences and skills gained through mainstream politics than feminist politics ($\beta=.113$ and $\beta=.075$, respectively), whereas working with a number of groups flows *less* from mainstream political experience than from feminist politics ($\beta=.130$ and $\beta=.154$, respectively). There is an echo here of the contrast between an elected official in the legislature and a NOW lobbyist on the hill: The legislator would be more effective on the conference floor, whereas the NOW feminist would excel in informal politicking off the floor.

An even stronger contrast can be seen in the relative contribution of mainstream, compared to feminist, political activity for the plenary activity index compared to caucus attendance. For plenary activity, skills from mainstream politics is the stronger of the two coefficients ($\beta=.113$ versus $\beta=.075$), whereas for the caucus-attender, the reverse holds: She is more likely to be an active feminist not significantly active in mainstream politics ($\beta=.128$ versus $\beta=.039$). This pattern is consistent with the atmosphere of the conference: Those experienced in party politics would feel very much at home on the Coliseum floor, so similar to a party convention, whereas the caucus meeting rooms would be more familiar political settings to those who had been most active in feminist politics.

There is an encouraging implication for the panel analysis of the data in the different profiles that predict the three exposure variables: They draw on a different balance of past experiences, which increases the likelihood that subsequent analysis using several exposure variables will tap a variety of channels through which the delegates participated in the events in Houston, and hence a greater probability that we can explain some of the change that took place between October and February.

A programmatic implication of this exposure variable analysis is also worth noting: If one wants to minimize the disadvantage of age and to encourage the same level of participation among older as among younger women, a conference with a very full agenda and a good deal of on-the-scene politicking should not be compressed into a mere $2\frac{1}{2}$ days. Had there been a 4-day conference with fewer hours spent each day in the plenary sessions, those with less stamina than the very youngest delegates might have had more opportunity for input and influence. Of course, the opposite message lies in the results as well, and it is one familiar from anti-war and New Left politics of the later 1960s: The sheer staying power of youth through endless hours of intense political meetings can contribute to political decisions to the left of the views held by older participants simply because final votes were taken long after the older people had left the meeting!

The next step in pursuit of the political development model is an exploration of the determinants of political competence, which emerged as one of the strongest determinants of leadership role. This topic is of more general impor-

tance than the historically unique and time-bound event of the national conference, since it is a fair assumption that a high level of political competence
will be just as important to political careers in the future as it has been in the
past.

Political Competence

The measure of political competence consists of self-ratings of how good
the delegates felt they were on specific skills typically used in political life:
debating, speaking before large numbers of people, knowledge of parliamentary procedures, and willingness to accept compromises. Although the
items refer to political behavior, there is a strong suspicion from the array of
topics in which the index was used, that the index carries a more generalized
component of self-confidence and self-esteem and is not merely specific to
the political area. Unfortunately, the questionnaire did not include any items
that could be construed as tapping general self-esteem, so this possibility
remains only a suspicion rather than an established fact. But it should be
borne in mind in the analysis of political competence that follows.

Table 7.5 shows the results of the regression analysis on the political competence ratings given in the two surveys. It is apparent that, unlike the counterpart analysis of leadership role (Table 7.2), there is relatively little change
between the two surveys in either the profile of predictor variables or the
magnitude of their contribution to the competence ratings the delegates gave.
The same three variables emerge at both time points as the most significant
predictors of political competence level: a high level of both mainstream and
gender-linked political activity and a high level of earnings by the delegates
themselves. Political skills are honed through political participation, which is
hardly a surprising finding, except that this relation is independent of the
considerable array of organizational membership variables, educational attainment, and general social status as measured by total family income.

It is particularly intriguing to find that a woman's own earnings is a strong
predictor of political competence, stronger in fact than educational attainment
(though the latter contributes a direct, independent effect on the competence
rating). "Total family income" is included in the equation as a control on
general socioeconomic status of the delegate's household.[1] That the woman's

---

[1]The alternative was considered, of using as an additional variable in the equation, "other
family income" rather than "total family income" (which includes the woman's own earnings).
This choice was rejected on the grounds that it was not the income earned by others in the
household but the general socioeconomic status of the household that could have an independent effect on the subjective political competence rating of the delegate. That "own earnings" is a
strong predictor over and above total family income strengthens the significance of economic
independence as a contributor to political competence level.

Table 7.5

Regression on Pre- and Post-Conference Political Competence (Beta Coefficients)[a]

Predictor Variables	PRE–Conference Political Competence (October)	POST–Conference Political Competence (February)
POLITICAL ACTIVITY		
Mainstream Political Activity Level	.178 ***	.134 ***
Gender–Linked Feminist Activity Level	.143 ***	.117 **
Held Elective a/o Appointive Public Office	.087 *	.099 **
Sex–Linked Feminist Activity Level	.020	.035
ORGANIZATIONAL MEMBERSHIP		
# Non-Political Organizations	.122 **	.123 **
# Traditional Women's Organizations	.052	.074 *
# Political Organizations . . .	.033	.062
# Liberal Causes	.018	.030
# Feminist Organizations . . .	.007	−.014
FAMILY/PERSONAL ATTRIBUTES		
Own Earnings	.149 ***	.143 ***
Husband Politically Active [b] . .	−.059 +	−.060 +
Total Family Income	−.001	−.016
BACKGROUND/ASCRIBED CHARACTERISTICS		
Education	.087 *	.053 **
R^2 =	.221 ***	.196 ***
(N=722) F =	16.78	13.31

[a] Direction of change between the two equations is the same for both the metric and beta coefficients for all 13 predictor variables, and there is no significant difference in the variance on the dependent variable: S.D. = 3.53 in the October measure and 3.51 in the February measure.

[b] Dummy variable.

+ $p \leqslant .10$
* $p \leqslant .05$
** $p \leqslant .01$
*** $p \leqslant .001$

own earnings is a highly significant predictor of her political competence, independent of the general socioeconomic status of her household, strongly suggests it is her own economic independence and self-sufficiency rather than the halo of general social status of her family, that contributes to her political competence. Women with high earnings are likely to have experiences at work that can be transferred to the political arena: skills of persuasion through meetings in connection with a job; knowing proper parliamentary procedures to chair or participate effectively at job conferences; defending a position in informal debate on a work issue; speaking before a large professional audience; and developing some grace and willingness to accept compromises when an impasse is reached between competing views on a work issue. And, of course, success at work can contribute significantly to a woman's self-confidence as well.

The transferability of skills developed on high-paying jobs to political effectiveness has interesting implications for the things that may facilitate the movement of more women into significant political careers, particularly in light of the finding, discussed in Chapter 8, that political competence level is a strong predictor of political aspirations. It may be short-sighted to believe that the route to national political visibility of more women is simply through expanded organizational involvement in political parties or feminist politics. Since economic independence and success contribute almost as much as does a high level of activity in mainstream politics, this means the removal of barriers to high-paying jobs and the recruitment to and promotion of more women to them has direct relevance not merely to the *economic* advancement of women but to their *political* advancement as well.

At the individual level, these findings have even more serious implications, for they suggest that a very difficult combination of experiences are needed to achieve a significant political career. High earnings do not come about except through high levels of training, a high motivation to succeed, and a great investment of time and energy in demanding careers. If, at the same time they are building a professional career, women must be politically active and belong to many organizations, it is difficult to see where much time is left for private lives as wives, mothers, homemakers. Jobs by day and politics by night and weekends is a draining combination, without family roles as a third competitor for finite amounts of time and energy. The most serious implication, then, is that the political woman would have not a dual-load from family and politics, but a triple-load of family, work, and politics. Little wonder that women who have reached national prominence in American politics have tended to be unmarried, married but without children, or latecomers to politics after the death of a husband or the launching of their children.

Another point of interest in the findings shown in Table 7.5 is the fact that sex-linked feminist activity contributes little to political competence ratings, whereas gender-linked activity is highly predictive. In fact, the latter is exceeded only by mainstream activity and the woman's own earnings as a predictor of political competence. There may be more in common between gender and mainstream politics than between sex-linked feminist activity and mainstream politics. Economic and political matters head the list of issues in both mainstream and gender politics. The political means are also similar: pressure on local, state, or federal government to change or draft new laws and regulations and to enforce them, and coalitions across groups and organizations to attain specific goals. By contrast, sex-linked feminist politics has been more local and state than national in focus and more concentrated in all-women networks than the general political arena, as illustrated by the establishment of rape hot-lines, women's health collectives, retreats for displaced homemakers, or counseling and therapy centers for women. Cooperative work among local groups of women is quite different from competitive work in mixed-sex political organizations. Both contexts may facilitate network formation and the acquisition of personal confidence, but the kinds of skills acquired differ in a way that reduces the relevance of the sex-issue activist's experiences for the kind of political competence needed for effectiveness in mainstream politics.

One caveat is necessary here. Sex-linked issues have a shorter history on the feminist agenda than gender-linked issues; as a consequence, activists on sex issues had had less political experience by 1977 than those with more than a decade of activity on gender issues behind them. A decade from now, the feminist who has worked on health, rape, or sexual preference issues may show political competence on a par with those who have worked on job discrimination and educational opportunity for women.

A final observation from Table 7.5 concerns the overall amount of variance in political competence accounted for by the set of variables in the two equations: That the R^2 is lower in the second survey ($R^2=.196$) than the first ($R^2=.221$) suggests that the conference itself may have affected the competence ratings by February. In light of the fact that the critical predictor variables in both surveys tap complex and ongoing factors like organizational savvy and economic success, we cannot expect more than a modest amount of change in competence ratings as a result of participation in the national conference. Nor will all the incremental change be in a positive direction, since the competence ratings of some women may have been lowered once they compared themselves with politically skillful women in Houston.

Table 7.6 shows the results of regressing the February political competence ratings on a set of exposure variables while controlling for the competence ratings given in October. A new and additional variable is also included in the equation, the number of new contacts the delegates made in Houston. This

Table 7.6

Regression on Post-Conference Political Competence Rating, Controlling for
Pre-Conference Rating (Beta Coefficients)

Predictor Variables	POST-Conference Political Competence (February)
Pre-Conference Political Competence	.721 ***
Passive Plenary Session Role	-.099 ***
Active Plenary Session Role	.112 ***
# Contacts Made in Houston	.066 **
# Groups Worked with in Houston	.032
# Caucus Meetings Attended	-.003
$R^2 =$	.646 ***
F	178.56
$R^2 - r^2 =$	.037

(N = 722)

** $p \leqslant .01$
*** $p \leqslant .001$

measure of network expansion may tap two factors important to the competence change analysis. First, the greater the number of new contacts, the more
likely it is that the delegate was in intense interaction not only in the formal
settings caught by the exposure variables on plenary, caucus, and organizational activity but in less formal settings in hotels, public events, and restau-
rants. Second, 3–4 months intervened between the conference and the
February survey, during which many delegates may have already used their
list of new contacts in working on political issues of concern to them, such as
the woman who said her list of 100 women she met in Houston "would be
helpful back home on my pet projects." That kind of effective use of new
contacts may add to the level of competence reported in the second survey.

The regression results show no significant impact on competence ratings of
either caucus attendance or working with a large number of groups: Both
these factors may simply involve more of the same kind of activities the
delegates engage in back home and hence do not change the more stable

quality of self-rated political competence. But three factors in the equation do show important effects. A directly active role during the plenary sessions has the most significant effect in raising the competence rating, one suspects because the conference itself was a unique event involving hundreds of women. To be active and visible in their midst gave a boost to the political competence rating of the women. In addition, having an active role in Houston meant practicing precisely the skills measured by the political competence index: Public debate, private dialogue, savvy concerning parliamentary procedure, and an ability to compromise were critical to success in amending the resolutions on the agenda. Second, a passive role during the plenary sessions was almost as strong a factor in depressing the competence ratings as an active role was in raising them, perhaps because those who assumed a passive role compared themselves unfavorably with the seemingly tireless, and politically skillful women on the floor and the podium of the Coliseum. Third, the number of new contacts made in Houston adds an increment to political efficacy, perhaps because the contacts have been successfully utilized in the months following the conference.

Although the overall R^2 is a high .646, this reflects the general stability of the competence ratings. The residual measured by subtracting the correlation (r^2) between the two competence ratings from the total R^2 is a modest 4% increment attributable to the influence of the exposure variables on the post conference competence rating.

There is an important implication in these results for the increased representation of women in the national political party conventions. If women delegates to party conventions are not among the floor activists, but sit back and merely observe men as the effective leaders on the floor, then their increased representation may not pave the way for more women aspirants for public office because the role of passive spectator seems to depress the subjective sense of political competence. In an ironic way, responsible roles in the old-fashioned party "ladies' auxiliary" may have as much or more potential for honing political skills and self-confidence than the greater on-stage visibility of serving as a delegate to a party convention.[2] In a similar vein, these findings should be borne in mind by planners of any second national women's conference. Once the show is over, the more enduring effects of such a conference on participants may depend on the role they played there: Too many stars may dim the confidence of other women in their own political competence, without which few women will aspire to public office.

[2]Of course, there is a general warning here as well: To the extent that political party conventions become television spectaculars devoid of any real political process because decision-making takes place off camera, all convention delegates, male and female, may come away with a deflated, rather than enlarged, sense of competence as political actors.

Holding Office

The image of the politician in American society tends to be of someone in an *elected* public office. It is far less common to think of a politician as someone whose office was attained through *appointment*. This tendency is reflected in research on women in American politics: In an extensive review of this literature, I found no study that examined the determinants or correlates of political *appointment* to public office. The emphasis was strictly on *election* to public office.

This is unfortunate, since a political appointment may be both an important step in the development of an eventual elective political career and an alternative to a career in elective politics. At the national level, appointments are rewards for party or candidate loyalty. Cabinet posts and ambassadorships, to say nothing of assistant secretaryships in the executive departments, go to those who have been active and loyal in support of the party and its successful candidates. The appointive route may have particular importance for the political careers of women since appointments are possible without large sums of money to run an electoral campaign and do not require a large constituency or a high order of combative skill in public debate. Appointive posts are often associated with knowledge of specialized fields and professional credentials and typically take less of a personal toll in time and energy than do elective offices. It is difficult to imagine a part-time mayor of a large city or a part-time U.S. Senator, but many appointive positions on agencies and commissions involve part-time work. Elected officials are subject to great pressure to fill their evening and weekend calendars with meetings, parties, speeches, rallies. Hence the appointive office may be more compatible with home life and child-rearing responsibilities than the elective office.

Appointive office was a more common political experience than elective office among the delegates in the sample: Twenty-nine percent had served in appointive public office, only 18% in elective public office. By contrast, the kind of office held within political party organizations was slightly more often elective (25%) than appointive (20%) (see Table 3.6, Chapter 3).

Since a sizable number of the delegates had held elective and appointive offices in political party organizations and in public administration, there was an unprecedented opportunity to explore the determinants of these four types of political positions. We could explore whether the determinants for elective office differ from those for appointive office and whether there are differences between holding office in political parties compared to public administrations. Of special interest is the extent to which activity in feminist politics facilitates or detracts from holding appointive or elective office compared to activity in mainstream politics, a crucial question if one is concerned with potential crossovers from feminist activity to mainstream politics in the future political careers of feminists.

The office-holding reported by the delegates may have taken place at any time in their lives; the question was not restricted to any particular time period. Consequently, I have enlarged the variety of background and status characteristics that may have affected their political visibility and hence their success in political appointments or electoral campaigns. Age is included as a control variable in all equations since the older the delegates, the greater their opportunity for having held office at some time in the past. Since the major predictor variables are the proximate and specifically political factors of organizational involvement and activity level in mainstream and feminist politics, any significant coefficients on the background and status variables are direct effects that underestimate the part these factors may have played in stimulating the intervening and proximate variables of political activity.[3] I will anticipate a finding that illustrates this point: Black women and Latinas are less apt than majority women to have held office of any kind. Since the equations include measures of organizational membership, political activity, education, earnings, and region of residence, this "direct" effect of minority-group membership on office-holding suggests either external barriers to the access of minority women to political office-holding on the grounds of race and ethnicity itself or a different subjective sense of political purpose among minority women.

Table 7.7 shows the four regression equations on elective and appointive public and party office-holding experience. In examining the results, we look first at the variables that show similar statistical strength and direction for all four types of office holding, then compare differences by elective versus appointive and public office versus party positions.

The strongest positive coefficients across all four equations are mainstream political activity level and number of political organizations the delegates belong to. The control variable, age, is positive in all four equations, though not significantly so in the case of elective office in political party organization, perhaps reflecting the pressure in both political parties to seek out and encourage more young people to advance within the party hierarchy, at least since the 1972 presidential conventions.

Although it is not always statistically significant, there is a general tendency for involvement in liberal causes, sex-linked feminist activity and membership in feminist organizations to be *negative* predictors of office-holding. Since this is net of age, it suggests that the mainstream political avenues represented by the four types of office-holding have not been traveled by very many feminist

---

[3]These indirect effects are explored in later sections of the chapter, as we press back further in time in the political development of the women delegates, in keeping with the analysis model presented in the introduction to this chapter.

Table 7.7

Regressions on Office-Holding Experience: Elective and Appointive Public Office and Political Party Office (Beta Coefficients)

Predictor Variables	Public Office Elective	Public Office Appointive	Political Party Office Elective	Political Party Office Appointive
POLITICAL AND ORGANIZATIONAL INVOLVEMENT				
# Political Organizations . . .	.231 ***	.213 ***	.189 ***	.186 ***
# Feminist Organizations . . .	-.177 ***	-.101 *	-.139 **	-.094 *
Mainstream Political Activity Level	.146 ***	.143 ***	.323 ***	.282 ***
Gender-Linked Feminist Activity Level	.111 *	.061	.015	-.003
# Liberal Causes	-.095 *	-.019	-.032	-.108 **
Sex-Linked Feminist Activity Level	-.069	-.097 *	-.094 *	-.003
ASCRIBED AND SOCIAL STATUS CHARACTERISTICS				
Age	.132 ***	.141 ***	.063 +	.139 ***
Southerner[a]	-.126 ***	-.069 *	-.058 +	-.039
Education	.068 +	.052	.016	-.027
Minority Group Member[a]	-.064 +	-.029	-.096 **	-.043
Catholic[a]	-.056 +	-.056 +	-.037	-.038
Political Activity Level of Family of Origin	.042	.062 +	.036	.023
Own Earnings	-.035	-.026	.017	.015
Husband Politically Active[a] . .	-.005	.025	.098 **	.050
Hold Law Degree[a]	-.001	.051	.050	.048
R^2 =	.148 ***	.147 ***	.214 ***	.178 ***
F =	9.15	9.02	14.29	11.40

(N = 903)

[a] Dummy Variables.

+ $p \leqslant .10$
* $p \leqslant .05$
** $p \leqslant .01$
*** $p \leqslant .001$

activists (or that the latter have been rebuffed when they sought attention by the party leaders).

Background predictors also show uniformly *negative* coefficients for women from the South, Catholics, and minority racial and ethnic groups and *positive* coefficients for those whose family of origin was politically active. This last characteristic is of considerable interest despite its lack of statistical significance since, like education, one assumes the major impact of a political family is an indirect one through organizational membership and the delegates' own levels of political activism, as we shall see later in the chapter. Another hint of interesting links to the family is the influence of having a politically active spouse, which contributes a significant boost to holding an elective office in a party organization. The full substantive implication of this will become clear at a later stage of the analysis, when we investigate the personal histories of the delegates more deeply.

A comparison of the size of the beta coefficients for elective versus appointive office-holding suggests that much more diversity results from taking the appointive route than the elective route: Both positive and negative coefficients are smaller for appointive office-holding. Thus, it seems to have taken less mainstream political activity to attain appointive office than elective office, and feminist organization membership is less negatively related to appointive than elective office, as is being Black, Latina, or a Southerner.

The contribution of feminist activity and feminist organizational membership to the equations dealing with public office are of special interest. Both appointive and elective public office show positive beta coefficients for gender-linked feminist activity and negative beta coefficients for feminist organization membership, but the pattern is less stark for appointive than for elective office. Delegates who have been elected public officials have been politically active on the gender issues of jobs, politics, and educational opportunities for women. The implication is they have done so as direct advocates on these issues, *not* through feminist organization membership. One can think of many examples on the national level of women in Congress who have never been members of a feminist organization but who have consistently worked for women's rights (Congresswomen Green and Griffiths to cite two prominent examples).

The same contrast tends to hold for political party versus public office: There is more room for women who are younger and southern in the party structure than in public office. In addition, membership in political organizations is much stronger than mainstream activity level for public office, whereas party office is more strongly associated with activity level than with extensive political organization membership. Indeed, these findings suggest that the party may reward the good political party activist, whereas those seeking public office are heavy joiners in political organizations in order to build the constituency-base necessary to launch a bid for nomination in an electoral campaign.

The general profile of the office-holder in mainstream politics in these equations does not encourage an expectation of an easy change in the flow of feminists into the mainstream of American political life. Having been at the Houston conference may have brought kudos and connections for the delegates in feminist circles when they returned home, but it is not clear that their reputation as a former delegate opened any political doors in those home communities any more than feminist activity, particularly on sex-linked issues, or membership in feminist organizations have done for these women in the past.

Mainstream versus Movement Political Activity

Perhaps that conclusion is too harsh; the experiences of the delegates may reflect the fact that the office-holding reported by the delegates could have taken place 20 years ago as well as 1 year before the national conference. A more direct investigation of the differences between mainstream and feminist political activity can be pursued with measures that refer to very recent years, during which considerably more than one-half of the delegates have been involved in politics. These measures are the three major indices of political activity level in mainstream politics and in gender- and sex-linked activity in the feminist movement.

The three political activity indices are positively intercorrelated, but at a modest level that allows for considerable difference in their determinants: The two measures of feminist activity are correlated at $r=.497$, whereas mainstream political activity is correlated somewhat more with gender-linked feminist activity ($r=.362$) than with sex-linked feminist activity ($r=.261$).

In keeping with the analysis model, the predictor variables are now limited to organizational membership indices and an expanded number of adult personal and status characteristics and demographic background factors. The three regression equations are shown in Table 7.8. Inspection of the statistically significant predictors shows there are different predictors for mainstream political activity than for feminist activity.

Mainstream Political Activity

Involvement in mainstream politics is most powerfully associated with high political organization membership, low feminist organization membership, and having a politically active husband. As we found with office holding, being Black or Latina shows a negative coefficient. If anything, holding a law

Table 7.8

Regression on Mainstream and Movement Activity Level and Ascribed and Status Characteristics, Personal Attributes, and Political and Organizational Involvement (Beta Coefficients)

Predictor Variables	Mainstream Political Activity Level	Feminist Activity Level	
		Gender-Linked	Sex-Linked
POLITICAL AND ORGANIZATIONAL INVOLVEMENT			
# Political Organizations . . .	.478 ***	.192 ***	.109 *
# Feminist Organizations . . .	-.217 ***	.005	.146 ***
# Liberal Causes	.064 +	.182 ***	.192 ***
# Non-Political Organizations	-.040	.109 **	-.012
# Traditional Women's Organizations	.029	.112 ***	-.072 *
PERSONAL AND FAMILY ATTRIBUTES			
Husband Active Politically[a] . .	.183 ***	.059 *	.042
Own Earnings	-.049	-.043	-.045
Employed Full Time[a]	.034	.160 ***	.071 *
Total Family Income	-.014	-.070 *	-.076 *
Religiosity	-.003	.045	-.043
Political Orientation . . . . (High=Conservative)	-.000	-.043	-.119 ***
ASCRIBED AND SOCIAL STATUS CHARACTERISTICS			
Minority Group Member[a]	-.065 *	.190 ***	-.088 **
Southerner[a]	-.046	-.017	-.070 *
Age	.029	.148 ***	-.106 **
Catholic[a]	-.016	-.004	-.062 *
Hold Law Degree[a]	-.042	-.001	.035
Education	-.004	-.038	-.049
R^2 =	.209 ***	.255 ***	.235 ***
F =	12.64	16.39	14.71
(N = 933)			

[a]Dummy Variables.

+ $p \leqslant .10$
* $p \leqslant .05$
** $p \leqslant .01$
*** $p \leqslant .001$

degree is a negative predictor, as is earning a high income of one's own. Clearly, the contribution of successful economic independence (that Table 7.5 showed to be highly predictive of political competence) does not contribute directly to higher levels of activity in mainstream politics. Women active in mainstream politics show the whole gamut of political and religious perspectives, as well as diverse levels of socioeconomic well-being (as measured by total family income), none of which has any independent effect upon mainstream activity level.

Gender-Linked Political Activity

Gender-linked feminist activity shows a decided contrast to mainstream political activism: No one predictor variable soaks up as much of the variance here as political organization membership did on mainstream activity. Instead, there are five factors that contribute to about the same degree (as measured by size of the beta coefficients): (a) involvement in political organizations, (b) involvement in liberal causes, (c) full-time employment, (d) being older, and (e) being a member of a racial or ethnic minority group. These most powerful predictors are followed by the somewhat lesser ones of membership in non-political and traditional women's organizations. That membership in feminist organizations contributes nothing independent of these other measures may simply mean that membership in one major feminist organization like NOW is a sufficient outlet for work toward the goals of expanded opportunity in education, the economy, and the polity for women who are wage-earners themselves and who live at modest income levels. The lack of significance on the measures of religiosity and political orientation suggests that women who have been active in gender-linked feminist politics have a considerable diversity of values though tending to the liberal side of the political continuum.

Sex-Linked Political Activity

Sex-linked activists share some characteristics with gender-linked activists, whereas others are uniquely their own. Their organizational profile is heavily tipped to liberal causes and feminist organizations, somewhat less to political organizations, and decidedly *not* to traditional women's organizations ($\beta = -.072$). They are also significantly younger, hold political values of a very liberal and radical persuasion, and are, significantly, *not* Catholic or southern.

The gender-issue activist may have been a feminist pioneer in the late 1960s and early 1970s, but by the late 1970s, these issues were endorsed by members of traditional women's organizations as well as NOW members. Since the mid 1970s, by contrast, the new pioneers have been younger women with a more radical feminist ideology, more secular values, and concern for women as the victims of violence rather than of societal discrimination.

Some people may see these results as an indication of fragmentation within the feminist movement, but they can just as readily be viewed as a functional differentiation of tasks and activities, with at least the older core of feminist views concerning sex equality now incorporated into the agendas of more traditional organizations.

Figure 7.2 summarizes, in a visual way, the major differentiating characteristics of the three types of political activity. Tracing a particular predictor variable across the three columns in this graphic presentation suggests that gender-linked feminist activity is the more moderate, middle ground, between mainstream politics and sex-issue politics. Thus, for example, high political organization membership is most predictive of mainstream politics, next of gender-issue politics, least of sex-issue politics. By contrast, feminist organization membership is negatively associated with mainstream politics and is a strong positive predictor of sex-linked feminist activity.

Minority-group membership shows a different profile: It is negative for both mainstream politics and sex-issue politics. Although it was transparent to everyone in Houston that feminists, indeed, antifeminists, rallied to the resolution from the minority group caucuses, it was much less obvious in the conference setting that minority women themselves did not subscribe wholeheartedly to the full range of resolutions considered at the conference. This is not simply a matter of political action, for we have already seen, in the preceding chapter, that minority-group women have a much less cohesive and consistent belief structure on feminist issues than majority women do. Black and Latina delegates are much less committed to the feminist agenda on abortion, sexual preference, and marital equity than they are to educational, economic, and political rights for women. For many women of color and minority ethnicity, race and cultural background are more pressing issues than those of sex and gender. Facing common problems with their men, they are more deeply embedded in traditional family, church, and neighborhood networks and do not subscribe to many of the beliefs now held by radical white feminists.

To some extent, minority women in the late 1970s may have been like the feminist pioneers of the 1960s, who first became involved and active on the issues of women's access to schools and jobs; many of the latter may turn to mainstream political activity or concern for sex issues for the first time in the 1980s. It is also possible that many minority women will subscribe to a feminist belief system concerning school, job, and political access for women but retain a preference for traditional lifestyles in marriage, family, neighborhood, and church. Nor should this surprise us, as evidence accumulates that many people in East European countries hold socialist beliefs concerning economic and political organization while subscribing to traditional views on family and church matters.

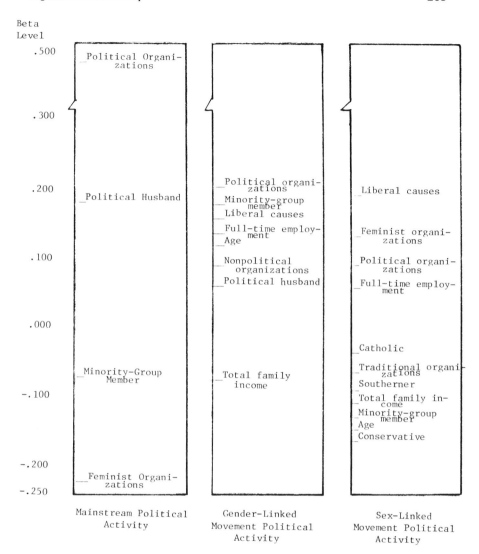

Beta
Level

Figure 7.2. Ranking of significant predictors of mainstream and movement political activity level. (See Table 7.8 for detailed results.)

Organizational Membership

The next step in tracing the development of the political woman is an exploration of organizational membership patterns. The delegates far exceed the nation at large in the overall level of their involvement in organizations, with a mean across all types of organizations of $M=12.6$ memberships.

The measure of total organizations was derived by summing across the estimates given by the respondents of how many organizations they belonged to for each of nine different types of organizations. Thus, for example, respondents were asked to enter in a box the number of educational groups or organizations they belonged to, with examples in brackets (e.g., PTA, Alumnae associations, AAUW, local school-improvement, or alternative education groups). In the analysis to follow, the nine organization types are dichotomized into *political* and *nonpolitical* organizations by the following classification:

> *Political* organizations (four types): Civic, civil rights, political, and feminist.
>
> *Nonpolitical* organizations (five types): Job-related, educational, religious, service, and social or cultural.

Since feminist organization membership is only one of four types in the political organization code, we shall also show the profile of determinants of membership separately for feminist organizations so that any unique aspects of organizational involvement in the feminist movement will be highlighted. It should also be noted that there is some overlap between the political and nonpolitical organizations since many unions, professional associations, and churches have been deeply involved in social and political action.

Thus, there are four dependent variables in the organizational analysis: total membership, political, nonpolitical, and feminist organizations. In keeping with the analysis model, only general value orientations, adult personal and family characteristics, and ascribed background or early family variables may enter the equations designed to predict membership level in the four types of organizations.

Total Organizational Membership

The profile of significant predictor variables on total organizational membership is a familiar one: The major predictors are similar to those found in national probability samples of the American population. Table 7.9 shows significant positive coefficients for age, education, total family income, and religiosity. Older women belong to more organizations than younger women: Like household furnishings, over the life span, people tend to accumulate more new ones than they drop (or throw away) old ones. Better educated adults at high income levels are the major support and provide the leadership for numerous organizations. And it has long been a characteristic of American religious life for high church attendance to be associated with embeddedness in an extensive array of nonreligious groups and organizations as well. Neither

Table 7.9
Regressions on Organizational Membership of Early and Adult Family and Socioeconomic Characteristics and Value Orientations (Beta Coefficients)

Predictor Variables	Total Organization Membership	Type of Organizational Membership		
		Non-Political	Political	Feminist
VALUE ORIENTATION				
Religiosity	.130 ***	.256 ***	-.024	-.133 ***
Radical/Very Liberal Political Orientation[a]	.042	-.057 +	.140 ***	.209 ***
Moderate/Conservative Political Orientation[a].	-.021	.010	-.074 *	-.048
ADULT FAMILY AND SOCIO-ECONOMIC CHARACTERISTICS				
Total Family Income	.158 ***	.152 ***	.146 ***	-.006
Education	.128 ***	.188 ***	.052	.059 +
Own Earnings	.071 *	.077 *	.036	.138 ***
Size of City of Residence	.044	-.028	.125 ***	.116 ***
Government Employee[a]	.040	.059 +	.005	-.009
Never Married[a]	-.037	-.040	-.024	-.005
Husband Politically Active[a]	.029	.038	.067 *	-.028
ASCRIBED OR EARLY FAMILY CHARACTERISTICS				
Age	.151 ***	.112 ***	.091 *	-.025
Political Activity Level of Family of Origin	.075 *	.047	.070 *	-.001
Minority Group Member[a]	.036	.040	.013	-.086 **
Catholic[a]	-.037	-.044	-.024	-.020
R^2 =	.150 ***	.218 ***	.129 ***	.182 ***
F =	10.48	16.53	8.77	13.19

(N= 846)

[a]Dummy Variable.
+ $p \leqslant .10$
* $p \leqslant .05$
** $p \leqslant .01$
*** $p \leqslant .001$

radicals nor conservatives show any higher organizational involvement than the large modal group of "liberal" delegates. On the other hand, women who draw large paychecks of their own, and those who grew up in highly politicized families, show a modest independent increment in total organiza-

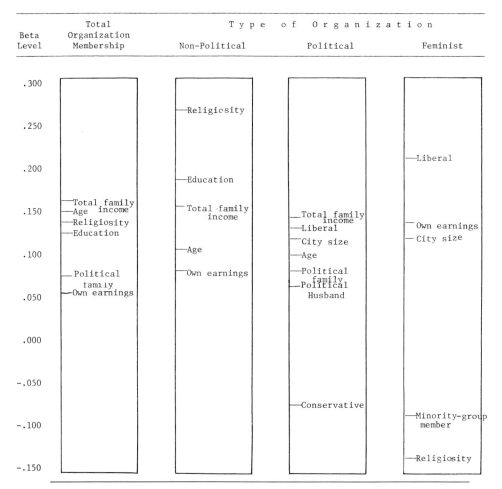

Figure 7.3. Ranking of significant predictors of membership level by type of organization. (*See* Table 7.9 for detailed results.)

tional involvement. (Figure 7.3 shows the major results in graphic form, with the significant predictors ranked by the magnitude of the beta coefficients for each of the four equations.)

Nonpolitical Organization Membership

The profile of predictor variables of nonpolitical organization membership is similar to that for total organizational membership. In some cases, the predictor variables are more strongly associated with nonpolitical organizations than with total organizations. Thus, for example, the coefficient for religiosity goes up from $\beta=.130$ for total organizations to $\beta=.256$ for nonpolitical organizations, as does educational attainment (from $\beta=.128$ to $\beta=.188$, respectively). On the other hand, a very liberal or radical political perspective shifts from being a positive predictor of feminist and political organization membership to being a negative predictor of nonpolitical membership level.

Political Organization Membership

This is clearly not the case when nonpolitical membership is compared with the political membership predictor profile (the second versus the third column in Table 7.9). The contrast is between more traditional, religious, service-oriented, small-town women (the major characteristics that predict *nonpolitical* membership level), and a more secular, large-city, liberal profile, plus growing up in a politically active family and having married a politically active man (characteristics that predict *political* membership level). Higher social status, as indexed by total family income, is a significant predictor of both types of organizations, but the women's own educational attainment plays a much lesser role in the level of political organization membership than of non-political organizational membership. Any interpretation of this profile is postponed to the next section.

Feminist Organization Membership

The last column of Table 7.9, on feminist organizational membership level, is a further exaggeration of the profile shown for political organization membership on several variables. A high membership level in feminist organizations is associated with a significantly lower level of religiosity, more liberal political orientation, and more urban residence. On the other hand, there are characteristics that are strongly associated with feminist, but not political, organization membership level: Family income no longer contributes any independent effect on feminist organizational membership level, but the effect of the delegates' own earnings dramatically increases to become one of the strongest predictors. But note, too, that politicized families of origin and a politically active spouse contribute no independent effect on feminist organizational membership such as they did for the overall political organization membership level.

Minority-group membership is significantly negative in the equation on feminist organization membership level. Whatever feminist goals minority women have sought, they have been less apt to pursue them through feminist organizations than majority women have. Once again, the implication is that minority women more often seek an expansion of rights for themselves through the rich tapestry of racial and ethnic organizations and civil rights organizations than through explicitly feminist organizations. It appears that Latinas have been as little inclined to focus their political efforts through mainstream feminist organizations as Black women have, when compared to majority group members in the sample (Rodriquez, 1981).

Last, marital status plays no role in any of the organizational types in the analysis. The dummy variable on marital status differentiated between single (never married) women versus all others, in the expectation that the lack of marital and family responsibilities might have facilitated high organizational membership. This is clearly not the case: On all four measures, being single shows a negative coefficient, though not a statistically significant one. Marriage in this sample, like the population at large, is associated with increased embeddedness in the institutional fabric of American communities.

Family Connections and Political Activity

Several findings reported in previous sections of this chapter have suggested a connection between a delegate's own political activity and that of significant figures in her personal life, through marriage to a politically active man or through having grown up in a family with politically active parents and siblings. Thus, for example, marriage to a politically active man was related to a woman's having held elected party office as well as to a higher level of activity in mainstream politics and gender-linked feminist politics. Although it only verges on statistical significance, we noted the curious finding that women with politically active husbands reported *lower* ratings of political competence than those whose husbands were not politically active.

There is a connection between growing up in a politicized family and marriage to a politically active man, a correlation of $r=.296$, in fact. This suggested the possibility that women may have absorbed some of their parents' interest in politics during their childhood and adolescence, perhaps carrying over that political interest into their own peer and community activities and eventually meeting and marrying a man who shared those political interests. The finding that such wives tended to hold party office suggests that at least some of these women may have played a supportive role in their husbands' careers in politics.

Unfortunately, I did not have the foresight to inquire any further into the nature of the husbands' political activity. All I know is whether or not the husband was active in politics. The same question was posed concerning the parents of the delegates. By drawing on other socioeconomic indicators of early family life and current family status, one can explore how these family connections affected the development of political interests and activities of the delegates during the course of their lives.

Table 7.10 provides a first set of analysis results on the part family connections have played in the political development of women. The results suggest a strong connection between a politicized early family life and a politicized marriage. The strongest determinant of such a marriage is having been reared by politically active parents, net of social class of origin, current adult status, and educational attainment of husband and wife. Second, one can infer that the politically active husbands are quite successful, as indicated by the significant positive beta coefficients for husbands' educational attainment and the current social class position reported by the wives. In light of these characteristics of the husband, however, there is an interesting twist: Both the women's own educational attainment and the social class of their families of origin are significantly *negative* predictors of politically active spouses.

Table 7.10
Regression on Husbands' Political Activity of Past and Current Status Characteristics (Beta Coefficients)

Predictor Variables	Politically Active Husband
Political Activity Level of Family of Origin	.238 ***
Education of Husband	.176 ***
Current Social Class	.120 **
Education of Wife	−.108 *
Social Class of Wife's Family of Origin	−.086 *
Catholic[a]	.066 +
Black[a]	.048
R^2 =	.101 ***
F =	10.29

(Base: Ever Married Respondents = 664)

[a]Dummy Variables.

+ $p \leqslant .10$
* $p \leqslant .05$
** $p \leqslant .01$
*** $p \leqslant .001$

The combination of these several factors is consistent with a profile familiar in American political history: The sons of lower-status parents with close connections to local political organizations are socially mobile through educational and job accomplishments, whereas daughters are socially mobile through marriage to well-educated, politically connected men. When such sons have interests in local party and electoral politics, marriage to women whose fathers are also involved in local politics can expand the husbands' networks of local political ties. Political connections of this sort may serve as the functional equivalent of a dowry, providing the husband with a knowledgeable aide, the helpful political wife. Though the coefficient only verges on statistical significance, the finding that Catholic women are more apt to report politically active husbands is consistent with the image of an ethnic, working-class political culture. The wife's political role is as an adjunct of her husband's political career, which may be why such women are less confident of their own political competence despite the fact that coming from a political family shows a positive correlation with the daughters' activity level in mainstream politics ($r=.219$). Marriage to politically active men is even more highly correlated with the women's activity in mainstream politics, with $r=.320$. We shall see in the next chapter that these wives report lower-than-average political aspirations of their own, which is consistent with their lower political competence ratings and further supports the interpretation that much of their mainstream political activity has been as political aides to their husbands.

The profile suggested by these data is a close fit to a family I knew as neighbors in a middle-sized Massachusetts city in the 1950s: Both husband and wife had grown up in an Italian, Catholic, working-class family, but the wife left high school before graduation and the husband worked in his father's construction firm, attending law school at night. Both families of origin were active in local political and church affairs, the wife's father more prominently so than the husband's father. When we met, the husband was the incumbent mayor of the city and the wife was rearing five children, carrying responsibilities for an intense organizational life in church and political party functions, and hostessing her husband's numerous political associates and legal clients at home. Her social skills and political connections served her husband well, and although she never entertained the idea that she herself could ever run for an elective office, she later became a delegate to the 1972 Democratic convention when the party was pressed sharply to increase the proportion of women in the delegate body.

A further hint of the political socialization some of the Houston women had received in their earlier years is found in Table 7.11, which specifies the political activity of the parents in relation to the incidence of politically active husbands. The family context most conducive to marriage to a politically active husband is one in which both parents were politically active: In this

Table 7.11

Husbands' Political Activity by Parental Political Activity (in percent)

Parental Political Activity	Percent Husbands Active in Politics
Neither Parent	17.0% (643)
Mother Only	15.4% (52)
Father Only	24.2% (128)
Both Parents	36.7% (90)
(Chi-Square 21.6***)	

*** p ≤ .001

case, 37% of the daughters married politically active men, in contrast to only 17% if neither of the parents had been politically active. When only one parent was politically active, the father was more important as a predictor of marriage to a politically active man (24%) than the mother (15%). One suspects that the "both parents" political pattern involved the mother playing the politician's-wife—adjunct role, much as the data suggest that the daughters who report having politically active husbands have done.

These findings were intriguing enough to take the analysis another step by examining the profile of parental political activity in relation to three background characteristics of the delegates: the social class of the family of origin, race, and age. Age is used as an indicator of cohort membership, on the assumption that the parental political activity refers to the years when the delegates were still living at home. This means that a 60-year-old delegate who reported that her parents were active in politics is referring to at least as far back as the 1930s, when she was an adolescent, whereas a 30-year-old delegate would have reference to the early 1960s.

First, let us examine the activity level of fathers, compared to mothers, at different social class levels. The results are presented in graphic form in Figure 7.4. Fathers' political activity shows a strong linear relation to social class, from a low of 10% in the lower-class to a high of 34% in the upper-class. Like the fathers, the mothers in the lower-class were rarely active in politics, but their activity level increases at a much slower rate than that of fathers, peaks in the upper-middle-class at 20%, and then drops to 12% in the upper-class. Hence the difference between fathers and mothers is sharpest at the highest class level and nonexistent in the lower- and working-class. To the extent that

Percent
Politically
Active

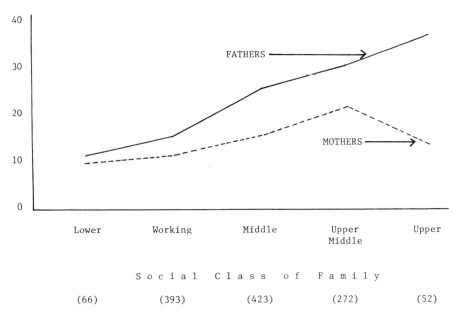

Figure 7.4. Political activity of mothers versus fathers by social class of family of origin (in percent).

same-sex parents serve as models for their children in this area, upper-class daughters would be far less likely than upper-class sons to develop an interest in politics.

There is also a highly consistent pattern of parental activity differentiated along racial and ethnic lines, even with a control for social class of the family of origin. (Case base size required a simple dichotomy of social class at this point.) Table 7.12 shows that, at both class levels, Black delegates report their mothers to have been as active as their fathers in politics. In fact, a slightly higher activity level is reported for the mothers of Black delegates than for their fathers. There was little difference in the level of fathers' political activity between white and Black delegates, but the mothers of Black delegates were twice as likely as mothers of white delegates to have been politically active.

This profile of racial differences is consistent with studies of Black families, which have found much more involvement in religious, civic, and communal institutions among Black women than among Black men. The family provides a powerful model of female competence and independence for the daughters of Black parents. Such a background makes more understandable the findings reported earlier in this chapter, that Black delegates, despite having had less political experience than whites, showed higher expected and actual leadership in Houston. This may draw on a generalized esteem and self-confidence rooted in family experience and maternal models to a greater extent than specifically political skills measured by the political competence index. That same strength of purpose may be reflected in the finding that Black women have been active on feminist issues from a base in nonpolitical, civil rights, and church organizations rather than feminist organizations. It could even be that respect and admiration for women comes more naturally through growing up female in a Black family than a white family, thereby making consciousness-raising and re-education unnecessary for Black women, as compared to white, and consequently lowering some of the motivation of Black women to join feminist organizations.

Social class and sex differences are far sharper in the reported political activity of parents among delegates from minority ethnic backgrounds.

Table 7.12

Parental Political Activity by Social Class of Family of Origin and Race/Ethnicity (in percent)

Social Class of Family of Origin	Race/ Ethnicity	Percent MOTHERS Politically Active	Percent FATHERS Politically Active	Base N
Lower/Working Class[a]	White	8.2%	16.8%	(197)
	Black	19.0%	17.2%	(58)
	Ethnic[b]	6.0%	6.0%	(66)
Middle/ Upper Middle/ Upper Class	White	18.5%	28.9%	(525)
	Black	34.6%	26.9%	(26)
	Ethnic	11.8%	35.3%	(34)

[a]
The relation between race/ethnicity and parental political activity is more significant among those from middle-class families of origin (Chi-Square = 21.5***) than among those from lower- and working-class families (Chi-Square = 12.5*).

[b]
Includes Latinas, Asian-American, Native-American and Pacific Islander women.

* p ⩽ .05
*** p ⩽ .001

Latinas predominate in the ethnic code here. The lowest levels of parental political activity are found in lower- and working-class families, where few fathers or mothers are politically active, whereas in upper-status families, mothers show no particular increase in political activity and fathers are very active indeed. The sharp class contrast can be seen from the percentage of ethnic minority women with politically active fathers: It ranges from 6% in the working-class to 35% in the middle-class, as compared to 17% versus 29%, respectively, among white delegates. Unlike Black women, today's Latinas will have to be on the pioneer edge of ethnic movement into political and organizational life, whereas Black women carry on the tradition of their mothers and, perhaps, of their grandmothers as well.

Table 7.13 shows an interesting cohort trend if we again control for social class of the family of origin. Parents of the oldest delegates, shown in the first column, were active in the 1930s, whereas parents of the youngest delegates, shown in the third column, were active in the 1960s. Hence comparisons across the rows depict changes in parental political activity from the 1930s to the 1960s. The pattern shown differs between fathers and mothers. There is

Table 7.13

Cohort Differences in Parental Political Activity by Social Class of Family of Origin (in percent)

Parent	Social Class of Family of Origin	Age 51–81[a]	31–50	30 or Younger
Percent MOTHERS Politically Active	Lower/Working	9.1% (77)	7.3% (193)	20.0% (50)
	Middle	14.2% (92)	18.5% (189)	22.6% (53)
	Upper Middle/ Upper	13.8% (87)	22.4% (125)	30.9% (42)
Percent FATHERS Politically Active	Lower/Working	14.3% (77)	12.4% (193)	24.0% (50)
	Middle	31.6% (92)	26.4% (189)	28.3% (53)
	Upper Middle/ Upper	32.7% (87)	29.6% (125)	33.3% (42)

a
  Chi-Square test shows no significant relation between social class and parental political activity for youngest cohort, but a highly significant relation (.001) for the two older cohorts.

no change in the activity level of fathers at the two higher social class levels (shown in the bottom two rows of the table), but for fathers of delegates from lower- and working-class families, there has been an increase in political activity in more recent years (from 14% in the 1930s to 24% in the 1960s).

Mothers' political activity has increased steadily over time at all three social class levels (the top three rows of Table 7.13). This means that the younger delegates grew up in homes in which mothers were as likely as fathers to be politically active, whereas the older delegates grew up in homes in which much sharper sex lines were drawn in parental political activity. I did not ask what kind of politics the parents were involved in, but it may be that at least some of the politically active mothers of the youngest delegates were among the older women who pioneered the surge of feminist political activity in the mid- to late 1960s. The average age of a delegate in our "under 30 years of age" category in 1977 was 25, which means she was born in 1952 and reached adolescence in the late 1960s. Her mother's generation had sparked the steady trend toward the increasing employment of women as their children entered adolescence, and it was from their experiences in the labor force that many older women in the mid-1960s discovered sex barriers to well-paying jobs or advancement and finally pioneered the renaissance of feminism.

These hints of early parental influence on the political development of daughters were intriguing enough to make us want to explore further the special influence of politically active mothers on their daughters. The question at issue was whether having a politically active mother was related to the daughter's level of political activity. Once again, an age control was introduced to test if there were any cohort trends consistent with the interpretation we have suggested concerning maternal political activity. There were too few cases of older delegates whose mothers, but not fathers, were politically active (only 9 cases) to permit a distinction between cases of "mother only" and of "both parents." Hence Table 7.14 shows only three types of parental political activity: (a) neither parent, (b) fathers only, and (c) mothers only *or* both parents.

With the three political activity measures (mainstream, gender- and sex-linked feminist politics) and three age groups, there are nine comparisons to test the effect of mothers' political activity on their delegate daughters' involvement in politics. In eight of the nine comparisons, delegates whose mothers were active in politics show a higher mean score on political activity than do delegates whose mothers were not active. Where fathers were the only parent involved in politics, their daughters show little difference from delegates who grew up in families where neither parent was active. If a 10-point difference in activity score is taken as a criterion of significance, none

Table 7.14

Mainstream and Movement Political Activity Level by Age and Parental Political Activity Profile (mean scores)[a]

Delegates Political Activity Level	Parents' Political Activity Profile	Age of Delegate		
		Under 35	36 – 50	Over 50
MAINSTREAM POLITICAL ACTIVITY LEVEL	Neither Parent . .	47.4 (187)	52.3 (238)	55.9 (160)
	Father Only	49.9 (35)	55.2 (45)	59.9 (39)
	Mother Only or Both Parents	57.1 (58)	72.6 (48)	69.6 (30)
	Total by Age:	49.6 (280)	55.5 (331)	57.8 (229)
GENDER LINKED FEMINIST ACTIVITY LEVEL	Neither Parent . .	37.6 (202)	43.7 (254)	49.2 (171)
	Father Only	40.2 (34)	48.5 (46)	49.2 (45)
	Mother Only or Both Parents	37.8 (59)	52.1 (52)	62.5 (33)
	Total by Age:	37.8 (295)	45.2 (352)	50.5 (249)
SEX LINKED FEMINIST ACTIVITY LEVEL	Neither Parent . .	37.8 (198)	36.0 (250)	32.4 (168)
	Father Only	44.7 (34)	34.4 (45)	36.2 (45)
	Mother Only or Both Parents	48.7 (58)	41.6 (51)	42.4 (32)
	Total by Age:	41.3 (198)	35.7 (347)	34.4 (245)

[a]All scores converted to 0–100 range.

of the nine comparisons between father-active versus neither-parent—active delegates are significant. In six of the nine comparisons, those whose mothers (or both parents) were active in politics are themselves more active in mainstream and feminist politics than delegates from politically inactive families. It may be inferred either that active mothers have stimulated their daughters' interest in politics, or that having two parents politically active provided a synergistic effect on the daughters' interest and activity in politics.

The maternal influence seems stronger for the older delegates than for the younger on gender-linked activity level. Comparing mother-active with neither-parent−active delegates, it can be seen that among the older delegates, the mean activity score is 62.5 for mother active versus 49.2 for neither parent active, whereas among the younger delegates, mother's activity plays no role at all ($M=37.8$ versus $M=37.6$, respectively). Mothers of the oldest delegates would have been politically active in the 1910−1930 period; many may have been involved in the campaign for women's suffrage. By contrast, younger women in 1977 grew into adulthood in the 1960s, when their own cohort was very active in civil rights, anti-war, and feminist activity, so that peers and the larger political climate at the time may have overridden any tendency for mothers' political activity to exert influence on the daughters. At least, this may hold for the traditional issues of schools, jobs, and political access for women: On sex-linked feminist issues, the younger delegates show the highest mean scores if their mothers were politically active ($M=48.7$), but relatively low scores if their mothers had not been active ($M=37.8$). At least some of the younger daughters of activist mothers may have drawn courage to deal with more controversial issues precisely from the fact of their mothers' involvement in politics. This is only a plausible interpretation, but the consistency of the results with these few indicators concerning parents and spouses suggests that family connections and maternal role models should be priority topics in future work on the early stages of the political development of women.

Paths to Political Activism: An Overview

This chapter began with an analysis of leadership roles at the Houston conference and, through a sequence of regression analyses, ended with an exploration of the political characteristics of the families the delegates grew up in. Some 46 variables played major or minor parts in the retrospective unfolding of the political development of the women respondents. In this overview of findings, I shall summarize the direct and indirect effects of past characteristics and experiences for contemporary levels of activity in mainstream and feminist movement politics. The emphasis will be on broad trends rather than fine detail. To provide such an overview, a summary set of path diagrams are presented, to bring together the major findings reported in the chapter. From the evidence summarized in these path diagrams, I will suggest that the data reveal four major routes to political activity, paths I have labeled the *Political*

Wife Route, the *Career Route,* the *Volunteer Route,* and the *Rebel Route.* The chapter will end with a discussion of whether the results can be generalized to the development of political women in the decades that lie ahead.

Paths to Mainstream Political Activity

Figure 7.5 brings together in diagram form the major significant beta coefficients in three regression analyses most relevant to unraveling the route to high levels of political activity in mainstream politics. Predictor variables are clustered in terms of the analysis model on paths to political activism; background characteristics are on the extreme left-hand side of Figure 7.5, moving to the right, through adult status characteristics and organizational membership, to the major dependent variable of mainstream political activity. The predictor variables with direct effects on mainstream activity level are shown in broken lines.

Also shown in Figure 7.5 are the significant beta coefficients from the regression analysis on level of political organization membership, the variable with the most direct effect on mainstream political activity. Variables with effects on political organizational membership are shown by solid lines.

The third regression result that contributes indirect effects on mainstream political activity level is the equation on marriage to a politically active spouse. The significant coefficients in this equation are shown in Figure 7.5 by dotted lines. In the interest of simplicity and felicity of phrase in discussing the patterns suggested by the path diagram, I will drop the continual specification that each predictor variable has a significant independent effect on the dependent variable at issue and describe the results simply in terms of direct and indirect effects on activity level in mainstream politics.

The major *direct* effects on mainstream political activity are a high level of political organizational membership, a low level of membership in feminist organizations, marriage to a politically active husband, and being white rather than a minority-group member. A major source of *indirect* effects on mainstream activity level consists of those variables that affect political organization membership on the one hand, or marriage to a political activist on the other. In the first instance (the predictors of political organization membership), the key variables are high family income, very liberal political orientation, residence in large cities or their suburbs rather than small towns, being older, having grown up in a politically active family, and marriage to a politically active husband—a profile of the middle-aged, well-to-do, cosmopolitan and liberal politician's wife.

The predictors of marriage to a politically active spouse suggest a less-well-educated woman who has been socially mobile from a politicized working-

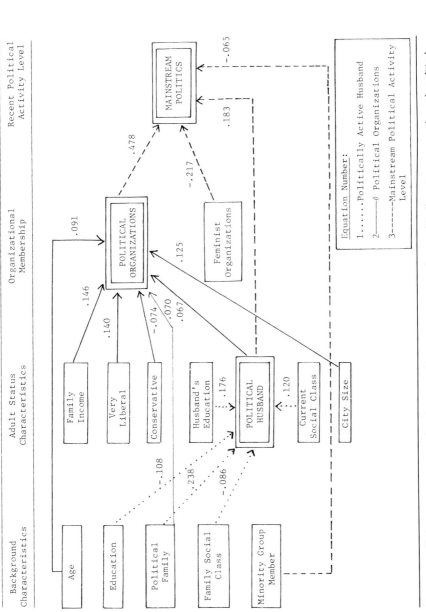

Figure 7.5. Paths to mainstream political activity: Regression sequence from politically active spouse through political organization membership to mainstream activity level (significant Beta coefficients only).

class family of origin (often a Catholic family). Her upward mobility comes through her marriage to a man who may have shared her class background and the political culture of urban working-class life, but who has made his ascent up the social hierarchy by dint of his own educational and occupational attainments. His occupational achievements, coupled with extensive political connections of his own and those of his wife's family, may then have been the social and political foundation on which he built a political career.

This political wife route to mainstream political activity among women is a familiar one in American political history. Only a minority of such women ever take off on political careers of their own; most remain adjuncts to their husbands' political careers. The most prominent exception to this pattern is exemplified by the widow who replaces her deceased husband in the public office he held at his death. Thus far in our political history, this pattern has held for the majority of women in the U.S. Congress and in governors' offices. Werner (1966) reports that of the 70 women who served in Congress in the period 1917–1964, one-half had relatives in Congress and more than one-half were appointed or elected to fill a vacancy typically caused by the death of a husband. Epstein (1981a) points out that the first two of five women governors came to office this way. It was only in the 1970s that women were elected to office in their own right at a nationally prominent level: Ella Grasso to the governorship of Connecticut in 1974, Nancy Kassebaum to the Senate in 1978.[4]

What is it about being a political wife that facilitates acceptance and occasional advancement in politics? Epstein (1981a) suggests that a critical barrier for women in American politics is the political party clubhouse. Women are active and useful aides during electoral campaigns, but to remain continuously active in party affairs *between* campaigns requires entry to and acceptance in the less public settings of party headquarters and clubhouses. The political wife may be more readily accepted in these settings than a woman acting on her own behalf. If not "one of the boys," the wife at least brings less status ambiguity, since there is no presumption of sexual availability to undermine the legitimacy of her presence in these informal settings. Such access and easy familiarity may facilitate general acceptance by the party of a woman who takes her deceased husband's place in an elective office.

Membership in feminist organizations is not a part of the political wife route, despite the fact that the political wives in the sample were themselves delegates to a women's conference. Like the women who have served as governors, senators, and representatives, many political wives are relative newcomers to the women's movement. They may have become active only in

---

[4]Even in this case, Nancy Landon Kassebaum grew up with family ties to a politically prominent man, Alfred Landon, a presidential candidate in 1936.

more recent years, as organizations and political parties endorsed the ERA and lent support to the increasing representation of women in the political party structures, and may never have joined a feminist organization. Their current support of feminism may mask rather superficial commitments to feminist goals of any broader variety (which I take to be the meaning of the negative coefficient of feminist organization membership on mainstream political activity level). The political wife route does not encourage the view that many women who travel it will move on to become effective feminist legislators or executives.

Gender- versus Sex-Linked Movement Politics

A number of variables showed significant direct effects on activity on gender- and sex-linked feminist issues. To simplify the graphic summary of these results, Figure 7.6 diagrams only the two equations showing direct effects on activity level in gender- and sex-issue politics.

First let us compare the determinants of activity in gender-issue politics (upper half of Figure 7.6) with mainstream politics (as seen in Figure 7.5). Where significant predictors are the same for these two spheres of political activity, it suggests some crossover to mainstream politics may occur in the years ahead among those women now active in gender-issue politics who share some characteristics with mainstream activists. Both spheres of political activity show strong direct effects associated with being older, being married to a politically active husband, and belonging to a number of political organizations. Unlike mainstream politics, however, the regression on gender-issue politics shows strong direct effects of high membership in nonpolitical organizations and traditional women's organizations, full time employment but low family income levels, past involvement in liberal causes, and membership in a minority group. There seem to be two routes implied here. The first, the volunteer route, is as familiar a pattern in the history of women's political participation as the political wife: It consists of involvement in extensive voluntary associations, often linked to church, civic, and cultural affairs or to broad political concerns represented by organizations like the League of Women Voters. Epstein (1981a) has pointed out that this seems to be a pattern unique to American political history, for voluntary associations have not been found to be a route to political careers in analyses of women in politics in West European societies.

Closely associated with the volunteer route through organizational involvement is a reform route, caught in the data by the significant beta coefficient of involvement in liberal causes for predicting high levels of activity in gender-issue politics. This route works through voluntary associations of long standing, such as those that took on civil rights issues in the 1960s, and

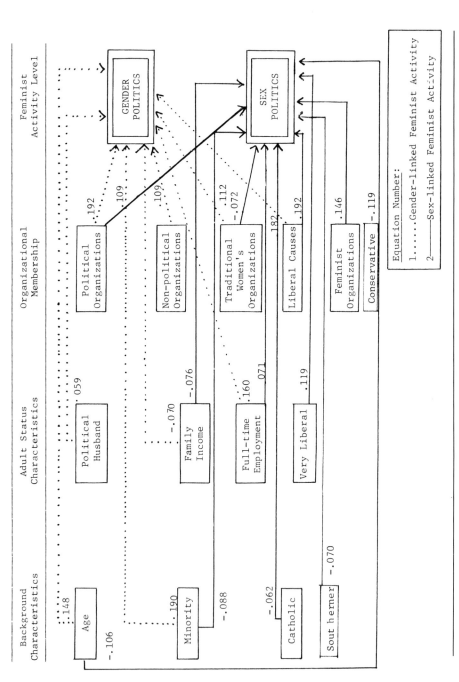

Figure 7.6. Paths to gender and sex-linked feminist activity (significant Beta coefficients only).

directly through reform efforts on issues affecting women. The particular manifestation of this reform route among the women in the sample is what I have labeled the career route. This is suggested by both the direct and indirect effects of economic characteristics on high activity levels in gender-issue politics. These include the direct effects of full-time employment but relatively low total family income (see Table 7.8 and Figure 7.6), and a set of indirect effects that work through membership in nonpolitical organizations (particularly job-related organizations). These indirect effects include high educational attainment, relatively high salaries (compared to those of other women), conventionality (as tapped by high religious observance), and relatively high family income (see Table 7.9). Together, they suggest a root in occupational self-interest, as older women attempted to break barriers against women's promotion and access to better-paying jobs. In the history of the National Organization for Women, such barrier-breaking in the job world was often linked to court efforts to expand the economic opportunities of poor women as well as professional women, as illustrated by NOW's Legal Defense Fund efforts to undo the negative impact of protective legislation restricting the weight-lifting and hours worked per day that could be done by female workers, which reduced their opportunity for being hired or promoted to better-paying jobs.

Thus, the volunteer route to political activity in gender-issue politics is a road traveled by many women. It draws on the extensive network of voluntary associations that has characterized American society throughout its history. The career route draws on the reform tradition, although it is focused on professional job advancement as well as on broad liberal impulses to benefit all women workers.

The cluster of major determinants of heightened activity levels in sex-issue politics (summarized graphically at the bottom of Figure 7.6) differs sharply from those associated with mainstream or gender-issue politics: It includes being young, white, non-Catholic, non-southern in residence, very liberal or radical in political orientation, and highly involved in feminist organizations. The latter is second only to involvement in liberal causes as a predictor of high levels of activity in sex-issue politics. Indirect effects through feminist organizational membership further illuminate the route to high involvement in sex politics: Highly urban residence, relatively high salaries, not being a member of a minority group, and low religious observance are the major predictors of feminist organization membership (see Table 7.9). It was of special interest to find that minority-group members are not pursuing this rebel route in feminist politics. Minority-group membership shows negative beta coefficients both as a direct predictor of sex politics (Table 7.8 and Figure 7.6) and as an indirect predictor through low involvement in feminist organizations (Table 7.9). Minority-group members are oriented to reform politics through more traditional organizations, church and civic participation, and mainline women's rights efforts that concentrate on economic issues. From this profile, it seems more likely that minority women will crossover from gender-issue to mainstream politics than from gender- to sex-issue politics in the years ahead.

Political Competence

The four routes traced in the political development of the women delegates is a reconstruction of their lives, discernible in rough outline through the statistical lens of regression analyses. It was somewhat surprising to find that the Houston delegate body, homogeneous, for the most part, with respect to at least some core issues on the feminist agenda, nonetheless showed similarities to American women in electoral politics in the past. The political wife or widow, the volunteer, the reformer, and the rebel routes that were suggested by this analysis have had their counterparts in American politics among women who had no connection at all with feminism. The life paths may be familiar ones, but the distinctly feminist motivation and goals are new.

Our reconstructed biographic history of the Houston delegates holds intrinsic interest in and of itself. But a more important question is what the future holds, as reflected in the skills, self-images, and aspirations the women had at our last contact with them in 1978, as they assessed themselves and looked to their futures. The political aspirations they hold will be the focus of the chapter to follow. Here I concentrate on the intervening measure of political competence, which provides a bridge between past political activity and political plans for the future.

The analysis of political competence reported earlier in the chapter is summarized in the path diagram in Figure 7.7. I bypass the change analysis in this summary and concentrate on the predictors of political competence reported in the February survey (Table 7.5). Two regression analyses are summarized in Figure 7.7: One deals with the direct effects on the political competence rating; the second equation, in which own earnings is the dependent variable, has not been reported previously. It is an important variable because it shows a very strong effect upon political competence ratings. Why own earnings have so strong an effect can be understood through the variables that themselves predict high earnings.

A word is necessary concerning the age variable in the regression equation on own-earnings. Earnings showed a curvilinear relation to age since pay increases with years of work experience until it reaches a plateau in the middle years and then declines. Women over 55 earn less than women between 40 and 55 because many in the oldest cohort were late returnees to the labor force or had lower levels of educational attainment and hence worked in lower-paying jobs than women in the middle-age cohort have. In addition, many employed women over 55 work part-time, which also reduces their

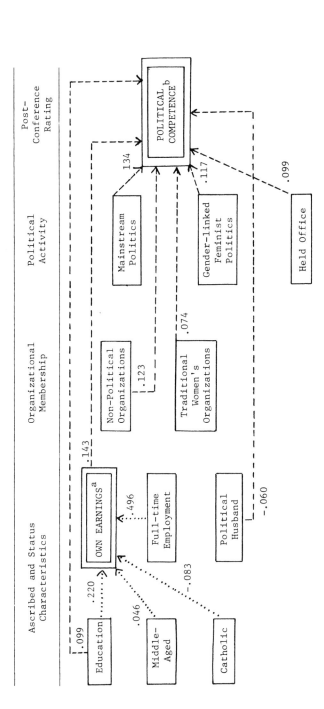

[a]The remaining variables in the equation were husband's education, minority group membership and private business employment, none of which were statistically significant. Age is dummy variable with 40–55=1, younger and older=0. Total R^2 on own earnings was .354.

[b]The other variables in the equation which contributed no significant independent effect on post conference political competence were: sex-linked feminist activity level, # liberal causes, # political organizations, # feminist organizations and total family income. Cf. Table 7.5.

Figure 7.7. Paths to political competence.

earnings level. Hence the age variable used in this equation is a dummy variable in which the middle years (40–55) are defined as "1," and both the younger under 40 and the oldest over 55 age groups are defined as "0."

Four of the seven predictor variables in the equation on own earnings were significant; they are shown by dotted lines on the left-most section of Figure 7.7. High earnings are a function of being middle-aged, employed full-time, having had high educational attainment, and being non-Catholic in religious affiliation—scarcely a surprising profile. What is of more interest is that education has both an indirect (through earnings level) and a direct effect on political competence rating. Clearly, there are skills acquired through higher education that contribute to political savvy, independent of the skills learned and the confidence gained through occupational efforts and success.

Beyond the educational and salary level contributions to political competence, political experience and organizational membership have direct effects on the competence ratings. Experience in both mainstream and gender politics, together with prior office-holding, are major contributors. But note that sex-issue politics *per se* has no direct effect on the competence ratings.

Marriage to a politically active spouse shows a strong negative relation to political competence. The political wife, we have seen, has had a good deal of involvement in both political organizations and mainstream politics; typically, she has served as an elected officer in a party organization. It is hard to imagine that her political role did not involve debating, public speaking, and chairing meetings; hence to find that marriage to a politically active spouse depresses the political competence ratings of the wives suggests some deeper level at which the political marriage depresses self-worth and self-confidence. Even the most public speech before a large audience by a political wife may contribute little to a feeling of personal competence because it is done as a part of a supportive, adjunct role rather than as part of an active, assertive role on one's own, such as competing against opponents in an electoral campaign. Expressive skills and personal loyalty, or media interviews that provide personal stories about a husband's tastes in food or hobbies, are no substitute for vigorous debate in defense of one's own ideas. For some of these wives, their roles as delegates in Houston may have been a first occasion on which they were largely political actors on their own rather than supporters of their husbands.

It is even possible that, although through very different routes, the political wife and the sex-politics rebel share some qualities in common. The political wife acquires a skill and taste for accommodation, loyalty, and cooperation since these are intrinsic to the supportive role she has played. Also, these are skills needed in politics to some extent. The rebel may also be loyal, solidary, and cooperative, but out of a radical ideological commitment to sex solidarity and a preference for cooperative, democratic decision-making rather than individual competition. But this also suggests that the major routes through which we may anticipate an increased flux of women into electoral politics in the future are the volunteer route and the career route. Those already embarked on these paths have acquired the necessary skills through organizational activities and the motivation from economic discrimination or heavy economic responsibilities on the one hand (the career route) or the general liberal concern for social issues and human justice on the other (the volunteer route) to have acquired a level of political competence that paves the way to aspirations for an elective office in the political system.

What is the likelihood that the patterns noted in the lives of the delegates provide a base for predicting feminist involvement in mainstream politics in the future? That even a sample such as this one included women like the political wife, already familiar in past political life in the United States, suggests that there has been no radical break with the past; rather, it is highly probable that older women who have been adjuncts to their politically active husbands will continue to enter state and national legislatures as replacements for their deceased spouses. It may take several decades before there will be any analogous pattern of men replacing their deceased wives in public office!

The dramatic increase in the professional attainments of women in recent years and, in particular, the entry of much larger numbers of women into the legal profession (Epstein, 1981b), has created the potential for a significantly enlarged pool of women to enter the electoral process. On the other hand, none of the analyses with this data-set has shown that a law degree contributes any special increment to either political activity level or competence ratings. The energies of most well-trained young women today are absorbed in building legal and other professional careers, not political careers. If they are also married, the combination of family and job responsibilities continues to press hard on available time and energy, and hence there is a great likelihood of late entry into politics, after professional status is secure or family responsibilities wane. Although the smaller family size prevailing today could enable women to enter politics at an earlier age, recent fertility trends showing an older maternal age at first birth works against this, at least for those women who might move into politics in the coming decade or so.

However, the greatly expanded proportion of women in the professions and business management augurs well for an increased representation of women in appointive posts in government at all levels. Appointive positions have the advantage of not requiring so large an interpersonal network to transform into constituencies as elective positions require. That women today are not withdrawing for long periods during the child-rearing years also allows them to become more experienced and able to compete with men by the early middle years when such appointments tend to be made.

One sobering limitation to the prospects of a greater influx of women into

public office through electoral politics is the shifting trend towards more conservative political forces in the nation at large. It has long been a pattern for
women in electoral politics to be more liberal and Democratic than conservative or Republican (Costantini & Craik, 1972; Johnson & Carroll, 1978). In a
conservative era, it is safe to predict that more women will run for office, but
fewer women will win the elections. The tendency in recent years for the
political parties to encourage women to run for office in campaigns the parties
do not expect to win only adds to the odds in favor of this unhappy prediction.[5]

But now it is time to let the women speak for themselves concerning their
political aspirations.

[5]Lipman-Blumen (1973) has suggested that women seem to have a greater chance of being
elected in times of social crisis than in periods of quiescence. It is an open question whether the
1980s will be a period of crisis comparable to the earlier periods on which her observation was
based.

8

Looking Ahead: Political Aspirations and Action

Introduction

By the late 1970s, women represented 53% of the voting population in the United States but only 8% of all public officials in the country. Against this standard of office-holding, the women delegates have already demonstrated considerable political interest, experience, and success in winning elections, for 18% have already held elective public office. If appointive office is also considered, then 37% of the delegates have served in public office, 31% in political party offices (see Table 3.6, Chapter 3, for details). On an assumption of continuity in the personal biographies of the delegates, future political activity and office-seeking should also exceed that in the total population. Indeed, such continuity of political involvement is not restricted to their own histories, for the delegates report high levels of office-holding by members of the families they grew up in: Eighteen percent reported that some member of their families had held office at a local level, another 9% at the state level.

The preceding chapter attempted to unravel the *past* political development of the delegates. This chapter looks to the future, through an analysis of the delegates' political aspirations for elective office in mainstream and movement politics. I will explore what predicts aspirations for elective office in mainstream politics compared to movement politics and what effect confer-ence participation had upon aspirations. I will also provide a typological sketch of what differentiates women who aspire to prominence in *both* mainstream and movement politics from those whose future aspirations are restricted to only *one* (mainstream *or* movement) political sphere.

The focus on *elective office* as a major dependent variable in the design of the study is a limiting factor that must be acknowledged at the outset. Were I analyzing a sample of delegates to the national political party conventions, plans to seek a nomination and run for office under a particular party banner would be far better as a measure of future political activity and aspirations. To "get ahead" in American politics requires affiliation with a party, building a reputation through local and national conventions, and expanding political networks that may become constituencies. But delegates to the national women's conference are a more varied group of political activists, with more varied modes of political tactics and preferences.

There are no doubt some women among them for whom a peak of political ambition would be reached if one day they win office as president of NOW or of the League of Women Voters, and this type of aspiration is measured by our *movement aspiration index.* But many other women may be just as committed to having a political impact on the world without ever running for public office or serving as an elected officer of a women's organization. Some will channel their political energies into paid employment and make their contribution to feminist goals through this less visible but nonetheless important route. Many such women will one day reach national prominence by appointments to state and national agencies or commissions. But there is no uniform career path to national prominence as a government appointee, and it was therefore not feasible to include any questions on aspirations for high appointive office.

Still other women may make less visible political contributions through less traditional routes such as organizational and coalition efforts to secure change in specific laws or policies that affect women: Thousands have done so in the ERA ratification campaign. In the 1980s, such contributions may include organized efforts to hold off the erosion of women's rights to legal abortion, welfare, or family planning facilities for teenagers; to expand child-care facilities or battered-wives shelters. Still others will be forming coalitions to have maternity leave written into disability clauses of union contracts or to change pension plans to assure that retired women receive the same returns as men. These kinds of political action are difficult to measure because they are less predictable; they have no stable organizational structure that permits us to measure "how much" prominence or success women seek through such actions.

It is even doubtful that "success" in these personal terms would have much meaning for such women. We have become so accustomed to the lack of ideological cohesion in American political parties that one forgets it is this lack of cohesion that underlies the view that politicians are committed more to their own personal advancement than to the collective goals or programs of their party. Many American feminists are more like European political party members than American political party members, for feminists are less motivated by personal ambition and more motivated by collective goals. Contemporary feminists are not unique in this respect; they are showing an important, long-standing characteristic of American women's political style, which involves political action through the relatively unstructured realm of volunteer organizations and issue-oriented coalitions rather than the political parties. In this parallel system of political activity, pressure is applied on parties and government alike. Women are very prominent in this parallel system, a point often missed by those who bemoan the conspicuous absence or low representation of women in the halls of legislatures, executive cabinets, or judicial benches.

With regard to an analysis of political aspirations, the implication of these comments is this: We cannot infer that delegates who reported no ambition to hold a high elective office are apathetic or will be uninvolved in politics in the 1980s. An absence of personal political ambition, as we are measuring it, may simply mask a preference for different political goals and different tactics.

Hence it is fitting that the last empirical analysis in the study will be an exploration of levels of commitment to the implementation of the resolutions passed in Houston. Some delegates, to be sure, will seek to accomplish that implementation by seeking public office; others will do so by working through appropriate private and public agencies; and still others will do so through a variety of organizations, coalitions, and campaigns that may be less visible or stable in duration, but nonetheless effective and politically significant.

This last analysis will explore the personal and political characteristics that predict high levels of commitment to specific resolutions passed in Houston, as well as to clusters of resolutions that carry a latent substantive focus. An important political question is implicit in that analysis: Is a social movement strengthened or weakened if movement members show specialization of political action along issue lines? Drawing from history, I assume that a political movement is strengthened if members align themselves differently on a multi-issue agenda rather than behind a single issue. This may be of special importance as a source of strength in the 1980s, as the feminist movement confronts growing organized political opposition from the Far Right. When political action draws on varied personal motivations as well as programmatic commitment by movement organizations, a movement is less likely to collapse when faced by well-organized opponents. With many issues, rather than one, on its agenda, political defeat can be more readily absorbed without crippling losses of morale or backing, and small successes can provide motivation to work on yet another issue on the movement agenda. If feminism survives the conservative backlash of the 1980s, it will be in no small measure because this third wave of feminism has developed a diverse, multi-issue agenda. It will not stand or fall on the outcome of even one great issue like ERA ratification.

Aspiration Measurement

The measure of political aspiration is a five-category question on how much interest the delegates have in holding an elective office in either mainstream or movement politics (from "none" to "extremely high" levels of interest). Mainstream political aspirations are therefore operationalized as interest-level in seeking an elected public office, whereas movement political aspirations are defined by interest-level in seeking an elected office in a women's rights organization. For each of these two primary spheres, three levels of elective office are specified: local, state, or national level.

Figure 8.1 profiles the delegates' political aspirations for the two types and three levels measured in both the pre- and postconference surveys. Predictably, high aspirations are more prevalent for local and state levels than for the national level, and for feminist movement politics rather than mainstream politics. The extremes are shown by the contrast between local movement versus national mainstream politics: One-half the delegates expressed moderate-to-high levels of interest in seeking office in a local women's rights organization, whereas only one-quarter showed similar levels of interest in seeking an office in national mainstream politics.

Some first hints of conference impact are suggested by the comparison of interest level before the conference and after the conference: In five of the six possible comparisons, there was a drop-off in high aspirations between the pre- and postconference surveys. The higher the level of office involved, the greater the decline in aspirations. Thus, on the level of the "net" effect, the conference seems to have dampened, rather than stimulated, the delegates' aspirations for office-seeking.

With political aspirations measured in terms of two types and three levels at two points in time, there were 12 potential dependent variables for the analysis of political aspirations. To reduce the scope of the analysis yet retain the core interest in movement and mainstream aspirations and conference impact, intercorrelations and multivariate cross-tabulations were inspected closely to determine the feasibility of constructing indices that combined the three levels of aspirations (local, state, and national). This inspection revealed a clear-cut hierarchic structure that justified data-compression from twelve to four composite indices of mainstream and movement aspiration for the pre- and postconference time points. Each hierarchic measure provides an index ranging from zero to 12, in which a score of zero means no aspiration for office at any of the three levels and a "12" means a high level of interest in

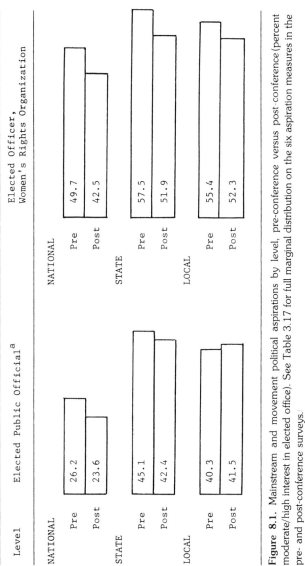

Level	Elected Public Official[a]	Elected Officer, Women's Rights Organization
NATIONAL		
Pre	26.2	49.7
Post	23.6	42.5
STATE		
Pre	45.1	57.5
Post	42.4	51.9
LOCAL		
Pre	40.3	55.4
Post	41.5	52.3

Figure 8.1. Mainstream and movement political aspirations by level, pre-conference versus post-conference (percent moderate/high interest in elected office). See Table 3.17 for full marginal distribution on the six aspiration measures in the pre- and post-conference surveys.

Table 8.1

Mainstream and Movement Political Aspirations: Composite Score Distributions, Pre- and Post-Conference (in percent)

Aspiration Score	MAINSTREAM POLITICS		MOVEMENT POLITICS	
	PRE	POST	PRE	POST
LOW (0 – 2)	33.0	34.2	23.8	29.9
MODERATE (3 – 10)	40.7	42.9	26.9	28.3
HIGH (11 – 12)	26.3	22.9	49.9	41.8
100% =	(957)	(938)	(945)	(939)
X̄ Score	6.4	6.1	8.1	7.2

holding office at the national level regardless of aspiration level in local or state politics. Only a few delegates who expressed high interest in national office-holding showed low interest in either local or state office, and they were largely older women who had already held political office at the local or state level. For most people, and even more so in a politically sophisticated sample such as this one, it is an implicit assumption that one does not seek office at a national level unless or until one has sought and held office at a state level; similarly, state aspirations tended to be preceded by experience or interest in local political office of some kind.

Table 8.1 shows the distribution of the delegates on the four composite aspiration measures. The pattern is essentially unchanged from that shown separately for the three levels in Figure 8.1. A larger percentage of delegates show high scores for movement aspirations than for mainstream aspirations: Thus, in the preconference survey, 50% of the delegates scored high on movement aspirations, but only 26% on mainstream aspirations. Similarly, the composite indices show, in both percentage and mean scores, that aspirations were lower after the conference than before. This is particularly the case for movement political aspirations, as indicated by the greater drop in mean aspiration score for women's rights organizations (from $M=8.1$ to $M=7.2$) than for public office aspirations (from $M=6.4$ to $M=6.1$).

Of course, the data in Table 8.1 show only the net change in political aspirations between the two periods. To show what happened on an individual level, change indices were constructed by subtracting the post-conference score from the pre-conference score for the two spheres of political aspirations (mainstream and movement). These score differences have been further collapsed in Table 8.2, where "stable or slight change" includes cases with score differences no greater than ± 2. Individuals classified as having a lower aspiration level after the conference than before therefore showed a *drop* of at least 3 points on the 12-point score between their pre- and postconference responses. (Reciprocally, change in the direction of higher aspiration levels in February is defined as a score *increase* of at least 3 points on the 12-point score in February as compared to October.)

The distribution of individual change in aspirations is shown in Table 8.2. It is readily seen that the change profile on the individual level mirrors that shown on the aggregate level. Roughly two-thirds of the delegates showed no significant shift in aspirations for either type of office-seeking. Political aspirations are quite stable in this politically experienced sample, a tendency similar to that shown in the preceding chapter for subjective ratings of political competence.

Among the third of the delegates who did show aspiration change, the pattern also repeats that shown in the net effect table: More delegates lowered than raised their aspirations between the two surveys, though more strongly so for movement than for mainstream political aspirations (a difference of 10.5% between the percentage who lowered and the percentage who raised their movement aspirations, to only 4.5% in the case of mainstream aspirations).

Table 8.3 permits a closer inspection of how the two change measures relate to each other. In the top one-half of Table 8.3, the two measures are cross-tabulated, with all cell cases percentaged against the total case base.

Table 8.2
Mainstream and Movement Political Aspiration Change (in percent)[a]

Direction of Change	MOVEMENT Aspirations	MAINSTREAM Aspirations
LOWER after the conference	22.5	20.6
NO or slight change	65.5	63.3
HIGHER after the conference	12.0	16.1
100% =	(875)	(875)

[a]Score difference between pre- and post conference measures of political aspirations. Lower scores are differences from −3 to −12; no or slight changes ±2; higher scores are differences from +3 to +12.

Table 8.3

Stability and Change in Mainstream and Movement Political Aspirations between Pre- and Post-Conference Surveys (in percent)

A. CROSS-TABULATION OF CHANGE INDICES (Total Percentage Distribution)

MAINSTREAM Aspiration Change	MOVEMENT Aspiration Change[a]		
	LOWER after Conference	STABLE	HIGHER after Conference
LOWER after Conference	7.5	11.5	1.6
STABLE, No Change	11.7	45.4	6.3
HIGHER after Conference . . .	3.3	8.6	4.1
			100%=875

B. CHANGE/STABILITY PATTERN

NO Change in either Movement or Mainstream Aspirations 45.4

Change in either Movement OR Mainstream Aspirations 38.1

       Movement 18.0

       Mainstream 20.1

Change in BOTH Movement and Mainstream Aspirations 16.5

    SAME direction of change (both up or both down) 11.6

    SEE-SAW change (one up, one down) 4.9

                            100% = (875)

[a] Stable aspirations between surveys are defined as the same score ±2; decreases (lower scores) as differences between −3 and −12; increases (higher scores) as differences between +3 and +12 between surveys.

The percentage of the sample that showed no change of any significant sort on *either* mainstream or movement aspirations is 45%, a considerable drop from the 65% shown when the two change scores were examined separately. It is clear that many delegates changed their aspiration levels only in one political sphere rather than in both. This is shown in the more detailed pattern in the bottom one-half of Table 8.3: Thirty-eight percent of the delegates show aspiration change in one sphere of politics, whereas 16% changed in both spheres.

The subclassification in Table 8.3 also indicates two additional pieces of information. For one, there is roughly the same proportion of cases of change only in mainstream (20%) or only in movement (18%) aspirations. Of particular interest is the pattern shown where change occurred in both spheres of political aspirations: Here, more than twice as many delegates changed in the same direction on both mainstream and movement politics (12%) as showed the seesaw pattern of raising aspirations in one sphere while lowering aspirations in the other (5%).

Thus far it has been seen that more women aspire for movement prominence than for mainstream prominence; the net effect of the conference was more a lowering than a raising of political aspirations; close to one-half the delegates showed no or minor change over the 5-month period; where change did occur, it was more apt to involve one sphere than both political spheres; and when both spheres were involved, changes were more synchronous than crossovers from one to the other political sphere.

Aspiration Typology

Another approach to the aspiration data is to sketch the major characteristics of delegates who fall into one of four basic types: Those who have low aspirations in both spheres, high aspirations in both, and the two alternate types of aspiring only for mainstream or only for movement elective office. (I used the last reading on aspirations from the postconference survey in this typology, with a simple dichotomy of each of the two measures into high and low aspiration levels). Aspiration levels are of a piece in the two spheres for two-thirds of the delegates: Forty-two percent report high aspirations in both mainstream and movement politics, 26% low aspirations in both spheres. Another 23% show high movement but low mainstream aspirations, and a mere 9% aspire for significant mainstream but not movement elective office. Table 8.4 shows in detail, and Table 8.5 in summary form, some of the main political and demographic characteristics associated with the four aspiration types.

All four measures of past political activity level show a predictable relationship to political aspirations: Women who are ambitious to seek elective office in both mainstream and movement politics are young, have held public office, have been active in both sex- and gender-issue politics and in mainstream politics in the past, and are of a liberal, rather than conservative or radical, political orientation.

Those with low aspirations in both spheres of politics show a reciprocal

Table 8.4

Political Aspiration Typology by Selected Background Characteristics, Post-Conference Survey (in percent)

Background Characteristic	BOTH HIGH	HIGH on Movement only	HIGH on Mainstream only	BOTH LOW	100%=	Chi-Square
POLITICAL ASPIRATION TYPOLOGY						
PAST POLITICAL ACTIVITY						
OFFICE HOLDING:						
Neither	38.3	25.8	7.7	28.2	(574)	38.2***
Appointive Only	46.0	22.4	9.2	22.4	(174)	
Elective Only	57.9	13.2	18.4	10.5	(38)	
Both	52.7	9.9	18.7	18.7	(91)	
MAINSTREAM POLITICS						
Very Low	31.6	23.3	5.7	39.4	(193)	51.7***
Low	40.0	21.9	9.0	29.0	(155)	
High	44.4	28.1	8.3	19.1	(324)	
Very High	50.0	15.9	16.5	17.7	(164)	
GENDER POLITICS						
Very Low	29.0	19.7	12.6	38.7	(269)	59.4***
Low	44.2	24.8	10.2	20.8	(226)	
High	46.6	24.1	10.9	18.3	(174)	
Very High	53.0	23.5	3.7	19.8	(217)	
SEX POLITICS						
Very Low	31.4	20.9	11.9	35.9	(354)	65.4***
Low	40.9	26.0	10.6	22.6	(208)	
High	51.3	22.2	7.6	19.0	(158)	
Very High	60.1	24.8	3.3	11.8	(153)	
PERSONAL CHARACTERISTICS						
AGE						
Under 30	54.2	21.1	8.5	16.2	(142)	31.8***
31–50	44.0	22.4	10.5	23.2	(514)	
51 or Older	31.3	24.2	7.9	36.5	(252)	
RACE/ETHNICITY						
White	41.5	23.0	10.3	25.2	(709)	n.s.
Black	45.9	18.8	7.1	28.2	(85)	
Ethnic	41.6	24.8	5.3	28.3	(113)	
POLITICAL ORIENTATION						
Radical	36.6	22.5	8.5	32.4	(71)	58.5***
Very Liberal	49.4	25.1	7.1	18.2	(350)	
Liberal	41.9	25.7	8.9	23.4	(303)	
Moderate	36.9	13.9	13.1	36.1	(122)	
Conservative	17.5	14.0	17.5	50.9	(57)	
TOTAL:	42.1	22.9	9.3	25.6	(903)	

*** p ≤ .001

profile: They are older, report no previous office-holding, have low activity levels in all three measures of past political involvement, and are from the tails of the political spectrum—moderate and Conservative at one end, radical on the other. This profile suggests a tendency among at least some delegates at

Table 8.5
Most Significant Political and Demographic Characteristics of Four Aspiration Types

P O L I T I C A L   A S P I R A T I O N   T Y P O L O G Y

HIGH Aspirations in BOTH Mainstream and Movement Politics	HIGH Aspirations in MOVEMENT Politics only	HIGH Aspirations in MAINSTREAM Politics only	LOW Aspirations in BOTH Mainstream and Movement Politics
Very High Past Activity in: Sex Politics Gender Politics Mainstream Politics	NO Past Public Office or ONLY Appointive Office	HELD Elective Office or BOTH Elective and Appointive Office	NO Past Public Office
Under 30 Years of Age	Not Very High Mainstream Political Activity	Very High Activity in Mainstream Politics	Very Low Activity in: Sex Politics Gender Politics Mainstream Politics
Very Liberal Political Orientation	Liberal to Radical Political Orientation	Moderate or Conservative Political Orientation	Over 50 Years of Age
			Moderate/Conservative or Radical Political Orientation

the extremes of the political continuum to be active politically not out of personal ambition, and not through focusing on a broad span of issues but, as suggested in the introduction, through concentration on one or two specific political or moral causes. Three prominent examples come to mind: The recent involvement of women from traditional women's organizations to work on ERA ratification; the older conservative women whose energies are concentrated on opposition to the ERA or abortion; and the younger, radical lesbians whose political energies are highly concentrated on lesbian rights. All three groups show low scores on the general measures of feminist and mainstream political activity because they are single-issue activists.

The third aspiration type—women who show high aspirations only in mainstream politics—tend to be moderate or conservative in outlook, are very experienced already in mainstream politics, and have held elective or appointive office. They probably include many highly political women who have been latecomers to the feminist cause, as feminism became a political asset, rather than a liability, in party politics.

Last, the women whose ambitions are restricted to feminist politics are more liberal, have held only appointive office if any at all, and show considerable variety in the degree to which they have been active in mainstream politics. It is curious that these women are just as prevalent among those who have not been active in feminist politics as among those with high levels of past feminist activity, suggesting that some women seek visibility in movement politics as an entry phase to politics generally. Among such women who had limited involvement in the movement until very recently, are Black women and, especially, Latinas. Though overall, race/ethnicity is the only variable in Table 8.4 that is not significantly related to the political aspiration typology, many Latinas have had less involvement in mainstream politics than white and Black delegates, and five times as many aspire only to movement office as to only mainstream office (compared to a ratio of two to one among white delegates). Some of them may be thinking of feminist Latina organizations that have formed only in very recent years, so there is clearly a pioneer phase of Latina feminism that may be reflected here. Many Latinas today are at the stage of feminist awakening and organization that Black women were at a decade ago. Many Black women in the 1960s shifted from civil rights activism to neighborhood and community work on women's issues, which in turn brought them into the larger feminist movement by the early 1970s, but with a focus on welfare, training, and job access issues. Only in very recent years has any significant proportion of Black feminists become active and visible in mainstream politics. Latinas may show a comparable pattern in the 1980s, organizing Latina feminist groups and organizations, working within the larger feminist movement on a narrower set of issues than white feminists are involved in and, perhaps by the late 1980s, becoming a visible presence in mainstream politics as well.

The typological approach to the analysis of political aspirations is crude at best. For one, it is based on a simple dichotomy of the two 12-point aspiration scales. For another, many of the political and personal characteristics that are significantly related to the typology are themselves highly interrelated. To find, for example, that activity level in sex-issue politics is significantly related to both mainstream and movement aspirations may be a spurious reflection of the role of age on all three variables.

Indeed, age plays a different part in the analysis of political aspirations than it played in previous analyses that looked backward to the political biographies of the delegates. Older delegates have had more political and organizational experience than younger delegates as a simple function of having lived longer. By the same token, older delegates have shorter futures than younger delegates and, perhaps, a more realistic vision of the time remaining for them to develop political careers. Since the delegates have a mean age of 42, this may help to explain why the net effect of the conference appears to have lowered political aspirations. The opportunity to observe other women at close range and on a persistent and intense basis during the Houston experience may have encouraged younger women to raise, and older women to lower, their own aspirations in politics. Since there are more older than younger women in the sample, this differential impact of the conference may account for the negative net effect profile.

Determinants of Political Aspirations

Table 8.6 shows the first step in the regression analysis of political aspirations. The 11 predictor variables in the equations were chosen on the basis of the analysis in the preceding chapter on the political development of the women. It is assumed that aspirations for office-seeking are rooted in past levels of political activity. Very few women in this sample are likely to express high aspirations (e.g., for a seat in the U.S. Senate) unless they have already tested themselves in the political arena of their communities and states. Hence, a major set of variables in the equations on aspirations consists of previous levels of political activity (in mainstream, gender- and sex-issue politics), previous experience as elected or appointed officials, and service as a delegate to a political party convention. Since significant political careers are associated with organizational embeddedness, three measures of organizational membership are included in the equations (political, feminist, and traditional women's organizations). My expectation was that specific spheres of political activity or type of organizational membership would differentiate aspirations for prominence in mainstream as compared to movement politics. General political orientation is included in the equations on the expectation that it is very liberal delegates who will aspire for prominence in movement politics, while a broader range of political perspectives may be congenial to mainstream aspirations. Politically active husbands are included as a dummy variable, to test whether such domestic proximity to politics elevates aspirations as it has clearly done for past political activity. Finally, age is a necessary control variable in the equations, since past experience is strongly affected by length of life and we wish to see the influence of past experience net of its age correlate.

Mainstream versus Movement Aspirations
before the Conference

First let us compare the determinants of mainstream with those of movement aspirations as reported before the Houston conference (the first and third columns in Table 8.6). Four variables are highly predictive of both types of political aspiration: Past involvement in mainstream politics, membership in traditional women's organizations, being young, and not having a spouse active in politics are significantly related to both mainstream and movement aspirations. By contrast, three variables predict movement, but not mainstream, political aspirations: past feminist political activity level, membership in feminist organizations, and a more liberal-to-radical political orientation. The only variable that is significant for mainstream, but not movement, aspirations is political competence level, an interesting finding that suggests many women may *acquire* political competence from participation in the feminist movement before attempting any significant entry into mainstream politics.

These results underline the continuity between experience and aspirations, for the women who hold high mainstream political aspirations are very like those profiled in Chapter 7 as the most active in mainstream politics in the past: They share high political competence, direct experience in party politics, and involvement in traditional women's organizations. The aspirants for future public office are different from those active in the past only in being younger and not having a political spouse. The political wife has had a great deal of political experience, including holding elective party office, but she tends not to aspire for a political career of her own.

High aspirations in movement politics are significantly associated with extensive membership in both traditional and feminist organizations, and activity in gender- but not sex-issue politics. The latter finding suggests it is age that is the stronger variable in the tendency shown for sex politics activists to be ambitious in both mainstream and movement politics (see Table 8.4). That high activity levels in sex-issue politics is not predictive of high aspirations in the feminist movement may be partly an artifact of our measure of movement aspirations: The scale refers to "women's rights organizations," which exist at

Table 8.6

Regressions on Political Aspirations: Mainstream versus Movement, Pre- and Post-Conference (Beta Coefficients)[a]

Predictor Variables	MAINSTREAM Political Aspirations		MOVEMENT Political Aspirations	
	PRE-Conference	POST-Conference	PRE-Conference	POST-Conference
PAST POLITICAL ACTIVITY				
Mainstream Politics	.151 ***	.085 *	.099 **	.068 +
Gender-Linked Movement Politics	.065 +	.075 +	.109 **	.153 ***
Held Elective/Appointive Public Office	.054	.133 ***	-.012	-.012
Sex-Linked Movement Politics	.049	-.013	.075 +	.075 +
Served as Party Convention Delegate	.035	.041	-.046	-.038
ORGANIZATIONAL MEMBERSHIP				
# Traditional Women's Organizations	.151 ***	.147 ***	.121 ***	.163 ***
# Feminist Organizations . . .	-.027	.039	.111 **	.162 ***
# Political Organizations . . .	.026	.035	-.016	-.059
PERSONAL CHARACTERISTICS				
Age	-.298 ***	-.356 ***	-.208 ***	-.191 ***
Political Competence	.135 ***	.157 ***	.032	.024
Politically Active Husband . .	-.059 *	-.008	-.079 *	-.014
Political Orientation (Conservative=High)	-.008	-.015	-.129 ***	-.114 ***
R^2 =	.180 ***	.208 ***	.171 ***	.181 ***
(N=786) F =	14.1	17.0	13.3	14.3

[a] The direction of change between equations is the same for both metric and beta coefficients for the 12 variables in the comparisons on both Mainstream and Movement aspirations. There is a slight decrease in variance on mainstream aspirations between surveys (S.D.=4.72 versus 4.61) and a slight increase in variance on movement aspirations between surveys (S.D.=4.71 versus 4.95), but these are minor changes for 12-point scores.

+ $p \leqslant .10$
* $p \leqslant .05$
** $p \leqslant .01$
*** $p \leqslant .001$

the national level on gender issues rather than sex issues. Should there be more extensive organizational developments at a national level to serve as coalitions for the numerous local activities on sex-linked issues that currently characterize political activity in this area, the profile shown in Table 8.6 may well change, with the younger sex-issue activists then aspiring for movement prominence beyond the local level.[1]

One further finding in Table 8.6 worth noting is the part played by political orientation as a predictor of political aspirations: Only movement aspirations are significantly affected by political orientation, with a tendency for very liberal delegates to aspire for movement visibility; by contrast, ambitious mainstream aspirations are found at a more varied range of positions on the political spectrum.

Pre- and Post-Conference Aspirations

What happened to the influence of the predictor variables after the Houston conference can be seen by comparing the first with the second column in Table 8.6 (mainstream aspirations) and the third with the fourth column (movement aspirations). Looking first at mainstream aspirations, two variables increased in importance by the second survey: age and political competence. This is consistent with findings reported in previous chapters, that is, that a larger proportion of younger women and a smaller proportion of older women played significant active roles during the Houston conference, with some spill-over effect on their own expectations for the future, particularly if they had the kinds of skills tapped by the political competence scale.

A particularly interesting shift is shown on the significance of previous office-holding. Having held public office did not predict aspirations before the conference ($\beta = .054$), but did so strongly 5 months later ($\beta = .133$). This is the opposite of the pattern shown in an earlier analysis of expected versus actual leadership roles at the conference, where it was found that office-holders had expected to be more important conference leaders than they actually were to

---

[1]On the other hand, many observers of sex-issue politics might disagree with this prediction. Sex-issue activists are strongly motivated to effect change in consciousness among local women, not only on political issues but at a deeply personal level. Those who work in shelters for battered wives, for example, pour enormous energy into the difficult task of encouraging their shelter guests to redefine themselves from women responsible for their own victimization to autonomous, confident women able to take charge of their own lives. The key concept in shelter counseling programs is the *empowerment* of women. This is an enormously difficult task, and the rewards are hidden from public view. The qualities of those attracted to such work are not apt to be the same as those seeking careers in the organizational and party life of a community or at a state level. Even assuming that such shelter programs survive the budget-cutting 1980s, it is difficult to predict what proportion of such sex-issue activists in the feminist movement will acquire the conviction that their goals can be furthered by moving to state and national levels of political action.

experience. In light of the fact that the overall net impact of the conference was to dampen, rather than to raise, political aspirations, previous office-holding may be one of the characteristics that helped to restrain the general drift toward lower aspirations. Although office-holders may have been frustrated by their roles in Houston, they were more apt to retain a good assessment of their skills and, in some cases, to expand their horizons for future office-holding. A delegate who flew back to New England on my flight touched on this point in the course of our conversation. She had served on a state commission (by appointment) and the city council in her hometown (by election). Asked about her reaction to the conference, she linked her assessment to her own political plans:

> Well, I didn't make quite the splash I thought I would in Houston. I don't have the connections with national feminist leaders that would have taken. But watching those women in action made me feel good about myself. I've been thinking about running for the state legislature in a vague sort of way. Now I think I'll give it a serious try. A state senator's job is a lot closer to my experience on the city council than being a hotshot or star in Houston.

It is also of special interest to note the declining significance of spouse's political activity between the pre- and postconference surveys. For many women whose husbands had been politically active, the Houston conference was a first experience of playing a political role in their own right in an almost exclusively female political arena. Like the office-holder, they have had sufficient political experience to find the Houston conference format similar to party conventions they had attended. Many may have found to their surprise that such knowledge was of help to less experienced women in their delegations. It would be unrealistic to expect the political wife to shift from showing no aspirations to high ones merely as a consequence of the Houston experience, but that there was some impact is suggested by the finding that having a politically active husband changed from a significant negative predictor before the conference to a nonsignificant coefficient by the February survey, for both mainstream and movement aspirations. The Houston experience, then, may have provided them with their first intense opportunity to think of themselves as autonomous political actors rather than political helpmates to their husbands.

One new contact I made in Houston illustrates what may be happening among other delegates as well. This was a woman in her late forties whose husband had been very prominent in the political life of their midwestern state. She had been active in his campaigns for more than a decade, and had filled a party office herself 5 years before. In the course of our conversations in Houston, we talked about the ebb and flow during our lives of interest in various political issues and of personal hobbies. In exchange for my point that I had given up a passion for growing iris when my political involvement increased in the late 1960s, she sketched her own shelving of an old passion for creative needlework as the pressures of her husband's political activity increased. We have exchanged several letters since the Houston conference, and in one she referred to that conversation about changes in activity profiles over the years, but with a new twist:

> I have often thought about our conversation in Houston—the ebb and flow bit— and wondered whether it could also apply to a kind of balance between marriage partners. A kind of "one up, one down" thing. My husband has been saying this year that he is losing interest in a lot of the things he does in politics. But curiously, my own interest has increased. In fact, I have even begun to think that it would be a neat change if I got into politics on my own, though I am not at all sure he would campaign for me the way I have for him.

I do not know if this woman's role in Houston contributed to her possible entry into mainstream politics in her state, but it would be consistent with the analysis results on politically active spouses for the Houston experience to make that contribution.

Change in Predictors of Mainstream versus Movement Aspirations

An examination of changes in the significance and magnitude of the beta coefficients between the pre- and postconference surveys suggests a winnowing-out effect of the intervening experience in Houston. On mainstream aspirations, three variables increased in significance following the conference: previous experience in holding office, being young, and political competence. Two factors declined in significance: activity level in mainstream politics and having a politically active spouse. Overall, such a profile of changing influence suggests that more specific and focused factors (office-holding, competence rating) became more predictive, whereas more diffuse factors like political activity level became less predictive. That age became a more powerful predictor for mainstream aspirations may reflect differential impact of the conference on younger compared to older women, the younger delegates taking heart from their more active and successful participation in Houston and their exposure to effective younger political models like Carol Bellamy or Anne Saunier, and the older delegates taking heart from the certainty that more vigorous and younger women could replace them in the decade ahead. Either or both of these changes would help to explain the increased significance of age as a predictor of mainstream aspirations in the postconference survey.

Changes in the predictors of movement aspirations also show a winnowing-out effect. A diffuse variable like political orientation declined as a significant predictor, whereas very specific variables like membership in traditional and feminist organizations and gender-issue political activity level show increases in the magnitude of the beta coefficients after the conference. Since the women with the greatest experience in gender-issue politics worked through organizations like NOW and were closely involved with the Pro-Plan caucus in Houston, their effectiveness in the important caucuses may have stimulated the increase of these variables as predictors of movement aspirations by the second survey.

Political Aspirations within Age Groups

Age is an important factor in analyzing expectations or aspirations in any sphere of inquiry. In a study of feminists, it takes on an added dimension of importance precisely because the feminist movement has a short history and has shown great changes in the expansion and diversity of issues on its agenda. Older women who became active in the mid-1960s brought very different backgrounds to their initial involvement as feminists than younger women in the late 1970s. To the extent this is true, we should find different predictors of political aspirations among younger women than among older women delegates. Using postconference political aspirations as dependent variables, Table 8.7 shows the regression coefficients that predict mainstream and movement aspirations within three age-groups of women: those under 35, those in the middle years of 36−50, and the older women 51−81 years of age.

It is readily seen that there are several sharp differences in the determinants of high political aspirations among younger women as compared to older women. Among older women, past activity in party politics and membership in traditional women's organizations are the strongest predictors of *mainstream* political aspirations, whereas for younger women, a high level of political competence, past experience in holding public office, involvement in feminist organizations, and not having a politically active husband are the top predictors of mainstream aspirations.

There are equally sharp age differences in what predicts aspirations for prominence in *movement* politics. Among older women, membership in traditional women's organizations and feminist organizations are strong predictors, followed by a high activity level in gender-issue politics and a very liberal political orientation. For the younger women, it is direct political action rather than organizational membership that is the strongest predictor. For the first time in the analysis, both gender- and sex-issue politics activity levels are strong and significant predictors of movement aspirations.

One of the difficulties in interpreting these different profiles of political aspirations between younger and older women is the question of whether such differences reflect maturational or cohort-historical factors. The finding that older aspiring women seem far more embedded in organizational life and

Table 8.7

Regressions on Mainstream and Movement Political Aspirations by Age
(Post-Conference Survey)[a]

Predictor Variables	Age 35 or Younger		Age 36 – 50		Age 51 or Older	
M A I N S T R E A M A S P I R A T I O N S						
PAST POLITICAL ACTIVITY						
Mainstream Politics	.037		.058		.220	***
Gender Politics	.002		.128	*	.058	
Sex Politics	.062		-.005		-.055	
Held Elective/Appointive						
Public Office	.141	*	.191	***	.014	
ORGANIZATIONAL MEMBERSHIP						
# Traditional Women's						
Organizations	.056		.132	*	.244	***
# Feminist Organizations . .	.151	*	.007		.066	
PERSONAL CHARACTERISTICS						
Political Competence	.221	***	.158	**	.129	*
Politically Active						
Husband	-.126	*	-.064		-.041	
Political Orientation						
(High=Conservative)	.096		-.042		-.042	
R^2 =	.145	***	.197	***	.182	***
M O V E M E N T A S P I R A T I O N S						
PAST POLITICAL ACTIVITY						
Mainstream Politics	.001		.058		.099	+
Gender Politics	.179	**	.058		.177	*
Sex Politics	.158	*	.109	*	-.016	
Held Elective/Appointive						
Public Office	.041		-.033		-.077	
ORGANIZATIONAL MEMBERSHIP						
# Traditional Women's						
Organizations	.107	+	.080		.249	***
# Feminist Organizations . .	.083		.107	*	.185	**
PERSONAL CHARACTERISTICS						
Political Competence	-.027		.057		.023	
Politically Active						
Husband[b].	-.167	**	-.137	*	-.074	
Political Orientation						
(High=Conservative)	-.084		.073		-.177	**
R^2 =	.164	***	.146	***	.241	***
N =	(276)		(324)		(232)	

[a] When the coefficients are ranked by size for the three age groups, there are
no differences between the metric and beta coefficients for any of the 9 predictor variables for movement aspirations, and only one minor difference out of
9 predictor variables for mainstream aspirations. The variance on the dependent
variable is greater for the oldest delegates than the youngest on both mainstream
(S.D.=4.64 versus 4.13) and movement (S.D.=5.14 versus 4.64) aspirations,
but these are minor differences on a 12-point score.

[b] Dummy variables.

   + p ≤ .10
   * p ≤ .05
  ** p ≤ .01
 *** p ≤ .001

that younger aspiring women seem to base their aspirations on direct political activity rather than organizational affiliations, could be interpreted in either of two ways: Either younger women have yet to acquire a network of ties with organizations, which they may do over the next decade before they try to implement their political aspirations (a maturational interpretation), or younger women have joined at a different phase of the feminist movement, when there is an emphasis not on traditional organizations but on loose coalitions and issue-focused interest groups whose members tend to stay away from the formality of dues-paying, large organizations that have at-tracted women in the past (a cohort-historical interpretation). The cohort interpretation of the age difference is consistent with sociological observations that young people in the 1960s and 1970s have been more likely to base their social activities on informal peer groups than on teenage or adolescent formal organizations like the Boy or Girl Scouts or church groups. On the other hand, the younger delegates are less apt to be embedded in marital and family ties as well. A large proportion are unattached adult women whose personal intimate circles consist of friends, work colleagues, and political allies.

There may be a mix of both maturational and cohort factors in the age differences shown in the political aspiration data. The older women may gravitate to traditional party politics and highly structured programs of action sponsored by traditional women's organizations. Undoubtedly, some of the younger women will acquire formal connections as they move into their middle years, but a residue may remain of a new-style politics of loose coali-tions, no regular party affiliations, and shifting alliances in the political arena as feminist goals shift with the press of the time and the nature of the political forces at the national level. So long as there are occasions and issues on which older and younger politically ambitious women connect and work together, the two political styles suggested above need not clash, but may extend the reach of feminism to more varied groups within the society.

Impact of the Conference on Political Aspirations

I turn now to an examination of the direct effects of conference participa-tion on the postconference reports of political aspirations, controling for the aspirations reported in the preconference survey. In light of the fact that the net effect of the conference was a decrease in high political aspirations, I expect the exposure variables to function not only as boosters in the direction of raising aspirations but as restraints against the general tendency to lower aspirations.

Most of the exposure variables are familiar from their use in the preceding two chapters: the extent to which the delegates played an active role in the plenary sessions, the number of groups they worked with in Houston, their actual leadership role, and the number of new contacts they made during the conference. In addition, three new variables are entered into the equations, so a word on the expected contribution of these variables to the change analysis is appropriate.

The first of the new variables is a rating of the effectiveness of the contacts made in Houston. These are subjective ratings of the extent to which the delegates thought their new contacts would be helpful in three areas: in local and state political activities they expect to engage in, in their job opportunities and effectiveness on their jobs, and in their work in voluntary associations. The number of contacts and the rated effectiveness of the contacts are only modestly correlated ($r=.23$), so there is room for both variables to show independent effects on aspiration levels. That the correlation is low may reflect different motivations behind the delegates' acquisition of new contacts. For some women, the new contacts may fulfill nonpolitical motivations, flowing from their generally gregarious and affiliative nature. For others, the new contacts may be more purposefully linked to political network expansion.

The second new variable in the equations is an index of attitudes toward conference management, a 4-item index that taps the delegates' judgments that the conference was controlled by "big-city eastern Democrats," or that resolutions were "railroaded through." (The remaining items are identified in a footnote to Table 8.8.) It is expected that those who assessed the conference as highly controlled and managed reacted with disappointment and anger that perhaps spilled over, lowering their own aspirations for office-holding.

The third variable is a summary measure on the extent to which the delegates said they expected to work toward the implementation of the resolutions. Each of the 26 resolutions was rated on this dimension, and the index is a simple measure of how many resolutions the delegates expected to work on themselves. Since the implementation of the resolutions requires political activity (as lobbyists and campaigners on a wide array of issues) through formal organizations dedicated to feminist goals as well as through changes in law and government regulations, I expected this measure to either contribute positively to an expansion of political aspirations or to restrain the downward tendency in the conference aftermath.

Table 8.8 shows the results of this second step in the regression analysis of political aspirations, which are the direct effects of the seven exposure variables on postconference aspirations, controlling for preconference aspirations in the two spheres of politics. As expected, there are significant contributions of at least some of the predictor exposure variables in the two equations.

The *contact effectiveness* index shows a highly significant positive coefficient in both equations. Those who came away from Houston with a conviction that they had significantly enlarged their effective network of people to call on for help in their jobs, politics, or organizations, showed a significant

Table 8.8

Regression on Post-Conference Mainstream and Movement Political Aspirations, Controlling for Pre-Conference Aspirations (Beta Coefficients)

Predictor Variables	POST-Conference Political Aspirations	
	MAINSTREAM Politics	MOVEMENT Politics
Pre-Conference Political Aspirations[a] . . .	.661 ***	.514 ***
Effectiveness of Contacts Made in Houston[b]	.091 ***	.148 ***
Active Plenary Session Role	.089 **	.057 +
Commitment to Implementation of Resolutions	.063 *	.108 ***
# Groups Worked With in Houston	.029	.050
Actual Leadership Role in Houston	-.016	.047
# New Contacts Made in Houston	.012	-.061 *
Conference Highly Controlled[c]	-.004	-.061 *
R^2 =	.538 ***	.444 ***
F =	112.5	77.67
$R^2 - r^2$ =	.032	.067

(N = 786)

[a]Mainstream political pre-conference aspirations in the equation on mainstream post-conference aspirations, and a comparable matching for pre- and post-conference movement aspirations.

[b]Four items rating how helpful contacts made in Houston will be to activity in local and state politics, in their job opportunities and effectiveness, and as a volunteer in organizations.

[c]Four attitude items on management of the conference: High scores indicate agreement that the conference was managed by "big city eastern Democrats," resolutions were "railroaded through," floor management was not democratic, and access to microphones needed the approval of Pro-Plan floor managers.

+ $p \leqslant .10$
* $p \leqslant .05$
** $p \leqslant .01$
*** $p \leqslant .001$

increment to their political aspirations, over and above the level reported before the conference. Network-building of an effective variety is therefore a significant benefit of large-scale conferences of this sort. The effectiveness measure is clearly the important aspect of network expansion, for the sheer number of contacts contributed no independent effect on mainstream aspirations and, in fact, shows a modest negative effect on movement aspirations. For many delegates, a long list of contacts may simply have satisfied their social needs rather than political purposes.

Commitment to the implementation of the resolutions passed in Houston contributes significantly to both types of aspirations, though more strongly so for movement than mainstream politics. This is an understandable difference, since mainstream politics deals with many more issues than just those affecting women. On the other hand, that resolution commitment is modestly significant in raising aspirations in mainstream politics is an important finding, since this suggests that some proportion of highly committed feminists will work *within* the traditional political hierarchy as well as in the parallel political movement that has absorbed so much female political energy in the past.

The experience of playing an active role in the plenary sessions gave a significant increment to mainstream political aspirations, but only a modest one to movement aspirations. The skills used in such active plenary roles are more adaptable to regular party politics than to movement politics. By contrast, neither the number of groups worked with in Houston nor the rated leadership role the women played there reach any statistical significance.

Last, a judgment that the conference was a tightly controlled and managed affair served to dampen political aspirations, though significantly so only for movement politics. Since many of the people conspicuous in the management of the conference were women active in leadership roles in women's rights organizations like NOW, or political coalitions like the NWPC, delegates who objected to the way the conference was handled rejected the political models represented by the conference organizers. This does not mean that the political energies of such women are lost to the feminist cause; many of them may simply divert their energies to work in the less-structured coalitions dealing with local and state issues with a decision-making mode more akin to their democratic preferences.

With the exception of the new contacts and conference control variables, the exposure variables all worked by expanding aspirations beyond those reported before the conference. To be a visible activist in a pressure-cooker event like the Houston conference provides some small increment to political aspirations. The experience of playing an active and important role in Houston shows a much greater contribution to movement aspirations than mainstream aspirations, since it involves experiences and contacts of direct relevance to movement politics, but not necessarily to mainstream political careers. Consistent with this, the overall effect of the exposure variables (as measured by the $R^2 - r^2$ at the bottom of Table 8.8) was a minimum of 7% for movement aspirations, double that shown for mainstream aspirations (3%).

Commitment to Implementation of Conference Resolutions

Although no formal records were kept in Houston of the actual vote cast on each of the 26 resolutions on the agenda, it was widely observed that 80% or more of the delegates voted favorably on all but one resolution before the body.[2] In Chapter 3, details were given on the level of activity the delegates had engaged in on 16 specific issues and their plans for activity on all 26 resolutions. Table 3.19 showed great variation in the extent of commitment to future political activity on these issues: Over 70% expected to be active on ERA ratification, battered women, employment, minority women, education, and elective or appointive office; between 50% and 70% expected to be active on child abuse, reproductive freedom, child care, rape, homemakers' rights, welfare and poverty, older women, health, credit, and disabled women; and from 30% to 50% expected to be active to some degree on the resolutions concerning media, offenders, business, rural women, insurance, international affairs, sexual preference, arts and humanities, and statistics (see Appendix C for the full wording of the resolutions on each of these issues). No resolution fell below 30% in the proportion of delegates with some level of commitment to its implementation.

Intentions concerning political action have much softer edges than reports of past activity, so that despite the considerable variation in level of commitment by the kind of resolution involved, intercorrelations among the resolutions were quite high. Hence the subscores that cluster resolutions into a manageable set for more detailed analysis were constructed on a criterion of $r = .50$ or better for all coefficients among pairs in the correlation matrix. Three subscores were constructed in this effort at data-compression, and since they will be used in the regression analysis reported later, a brief summary sketch is a necessary reminder (details are given in Chapter 3):

Victims of violence ($r = .62 - .71$): Rape, battered wives, and child abuse.
Victims of society ($r = .52 - .67$): Minority women, welfare and poverty, offenders, disabled women, older women, health, and rural/farm women.
Money management ($r = .57 - .69$): Business, credit, insurance, and statistics.

In addition to the 14 resolutions classified into these three scores, separate

---

[2]The delegates rejected a resolution to establish a separate Cabinet post to oversee all government activities affecting women.

analyses are presented on the two most controversial resolutions on reproductive freedom and sexual preference.

One last set of findings reported in the earlier chapter merits repetition here; it deals with the relation between past spheres of feminist activity and plans for political activity. Overall, there was a high correlation between past and future levels of activity ($r=.461$), hardly a surprising finding since one expects continuity of effort in women involved enough to be elected delegates to the national conference. Of greater interest was the finding that past activity in gender-issue politics was more strongly correlated with plans for activity on all the subscores than past activity in sex-issue politics (see Table 3.20). The impression was strong from these results that older women who became involved in feminist politics a decade or more ago, on issues affecting education and job opportunities for women, have taken on new issues as the movement agenda expanded, whereas younger women who have become involved in the movement in more recent years show a narrower range of issue-commitments, perhaps because political efforts were already relatively well organized on the earlier issues, as well as the younger women's greater personal and political involvement in the newer issues like rape, battered wives, child abuse, and sexual preference. The resolutions included in the victims of violence index are close to the issues in the sex politics index, whereas the resolutions in the victims of society index match most closely the issues in the gender politics index. But the correlation between past gender politics and victims of violence is higher ($r=.405$) than the correlation between past sex politics and the victims of society score ($r=.224$) (Table 3.20). This suggests that sex-issue politics may be added to gender-issue politics more readily than the reverse.

The major question underlying the analysis of what determined the level of commitment to implementing the resolutions was whether such planned political action drew on different combinations of experience and personal characteristics. To the extent that they do, it is assumed that this demonstrates a combination of personal salience and political salience that strengthens the effectiveness of the larger political movement: It means that there is issue-differentiation along the lines that are most likely to stoke high levels of motivation and persistence in the political energy needed to implement the resolutions. So long as there are broad commitments to a generalized sense of what needs doing to improve the position of women in American society, such differentiation of effort contributes to the strength of a political movement. It also means that those who are privately ambivalent or even opposed to the feminist position on one issue have no need to betray their own beliefs but can simply concentrate their efforts on other issues of salience to them. The sum total of all such specialized political efforts is a contribution to the collective goals of the social movement.

To test the extent of this issue-differentiation in the delegates' plans for working toward the implementation of the resolutions, I have drawn on three major categories of variables—the most obvious are the two measures of past feminist activity—to test whether they contribute differently and independently to future action on issue-commitments. The second set contains two measures of organizational involvement (traditonal and feminist organizations), on the assumption that organizational loyalty rooted in membership in such organizations may press for action-commitments on those grounds alone, independent of other predictors of future action. The third set are those personal characteristics that were strongly associated with specialization in the analyses of past political activity and beliefs of the delegates: age, religiosity, employment, marital status, minority-group membership, and general political orientation are the variables included in the equations.

Table 8.10 shows the results of the regression analysis of the five dependent variables tapping commitment to implementation of the resolutions. The equations are ordered in a way that most differentiates the contribution of the predictor variables to the dependent variables; hence the sharpest contrast is provided by the first and last columns (money management and sexual preference). Delegates committed to implementing resolutions dealing with money management tended to be conservative, to be full-time employees of all ages and degrees of religiosity, to belong to traditional women's organizations, and to show a past pattern of high activity levels in gender-issue politics. By contrast, those committed to implementation of the sexual preference resolution were young, unmarried women, very liberal or radical in political persuasion, and decidedly low in religiosity; they were members of feminist organizations, and their past feminist activities were in sex-issue politics—they were rarely involved in traditional women's organizations.

The profile of significant predictors of the victim of society index is familiar from the liberal, reformist agenda of NOW in its earliest years: Delegates who planned to work on these issues were older, employed full-time, liberal in political orientation, and had high levels of activity in gender-issue politics. It is the only resolution index on which minority-group membership is a highly significant positive predictor of future political efforts, understandably so in light of its inclusion of issues dealing with welfare, poverty, and minority women.

Only two variables are significant predictors of future action on the victims of violence index: a high level of past activity in both gender- and sex-issue politics. Apparently, such past concentration of effort absorbs whatever personal characteristics would otherwise relate to feminist political activity. Involvement in traditional and feminist organizations adds nothing independent of direct political activity, though both beta coefficients are positive.

Future action on the abortion issue is associated with many of the same

Table 8.9
Regressions on Commitment to Implementation of Conference Resolutions (Beta Coefficients)

Predictor Variables	Resolution Focus[a]				
	Money Management	Victims of Society	Victims of Violence	Reproductive Freedom	Sexual Preference
PAST FEMINIST ACTIVITY LEVEL					
Gender Politics	.403 ***	.382 ***	.294 ***	-.024	-.020
Sex Politics	-.054	.033	.166 ***	.371 ***	.366 ***
ORGANIZATIONAL MEMBERSHIP					
# Traditional Women's Organizations	.066 *	.058 +	.050	-.002	-.056 +
# Feminist Organizations . .	.056	.031	.030	.097 **	.085 **
PERSONAL CHARACTERISTICS					
Full Time Employed[b]	.093 **	.072 *	.039	.022	.059 +
Political Orientation (High= Conservative)	.071 *	-.064 *	.006	-.087 **	-.126 ***
Minority Group Member[b] . . .	.049	.137 ***	.038	-.018	-.017
Age	.042	.103 **	.030	.001	-.080 *
Unattached Marital Status[b] .	.035	.054	.021	-.016	.099 **
Religiosity	-.011	.048	.021	-.209 ***	-.098 **
R^2 =	.189 ***	.257 ***	.186 ***	.294 ***	.307 ***
F =	20.31	30.11	19.90	36.18	38.63

(N=881)

[a] The Money Management index is based on degree of commitment to work on resolutions concerning business, statistics, credit and insurance; the Victims of Society index is based on resolutions concerning Minority Women, health, disabled, older women, rural women, welfare and poverty; the Victims of Violence index is based on resolutions concerning battered women, child abuse and rape. The remaining two variables are single items on reproductive freedom and sexual preference.

[b] Dummy variables.

+ $p \leqslant .10$
* $p \leqslant .05$
** $p \leqslant .01$
*** $p \leqslant .001$

characteristics as sexual preference: liberal to radical political orientation, low levels of religiosity, high levels of membership in feminist organizations, and past involvement in sex-linked issues. Beyond these shared determinants, high commitment to the abortion issue cuts across all marital statuses (unlike sexual preference, which is far more associated with an unattached status) and age groups (again, unlike sexual preference, which attracts more younger than older women).

Conclusion

The general impression given by these results is the embeddedness of planned political action in the existential concerns of the women delegates. Older, employed, more conservative women worry about economic security in their future years; if they have expertise on financial or fiduciary issues, they may be the activists who work to improve the retirement benefits for their own cohort of women, as well as for younger women when they reach their retirement years. Young radical women who entered the feminist movement to further the civil rights of lesbian women, clearly plan to persist in their efforts toward implementing the sexual preference resolution. Those who are members of disadvantaged minority groups, or are employed and carrying difficult family responsibilities, gravitate to political action on the bread-and-butter issues of child-care, welfare and poverty assistance, health and disability.

The most differential profiles are those on the two most controversial issues of abortion and sexual preference. It is also of interest that none of the personal characteristics contribute any independent effect on issues concerning victims of violence: Child abuse, battered wives, and rape involve issues that affect or concern women of all ages, ethnicity, political orientation, and earning ability. The fact that sexual preference did not correlate highly enough to be included with these sex-linked issues as it did in the index on past sex-issue political activity suggests a continuing axis of differentiation among feminists on this issue. I suspect that age and its associated link to marital and family involvement plays an important role here. Older feminists have been open and willing to add many, but not all, of the new issues on the feminist agenda to their own concerns: Displaced homemakers, rape, and women's health issues have blended with the older concerns for school access, job promotion, equal pay, and greater representation in politics in a way that sexual preference has not. Minority women have their own special reasons for withholding open support for sexual preference issues: Their concern for family and community cohesion on racial and ethnic grounds makes any issue that implies sexual segregation or anti-male hostility a sensitive, if not impossible, issue to lend support to.

There is another side to this issue as well. It did not go unnoticed, particularly by minority women, that once the sexual preference resolution was passed in Houston, there was a considerable drop in the lesbian presence in the Coliseum, despite the fact that the resolution considered next dealt with welfare and poverty. It is important for lesbian feminists to be more conspicuous in their support for and political action on nonlesbian issues. Unless that occurs, there is little chance that sexual preference will become a widely supported component of a feminist agenda among more moderate women. And it may not happen, despite such activity, if lesbian feminists do not extend the same tolerance for the life styles of heterosexual women that they expect for themselves.

There were both disturbing and encouraging political developments in the years immediately following the conference. On the encouraging side is the fact that the 1980 election was a first-ever historical event in the voting patterns of men and women: Far more men than women voted for Reagan. Also encouraging has been a new kind of coalition of organizations in opposition to the economic policies of the Republican administration. It would not be surprising to find a coalition of such organizations as NOW, NARAL, and the NWPC. What is new and something of a political surprise is the fact that such feminist organizations have been joined by many quite traditional women's organizations in a coalition led by the NWPC. Among the 40 organizations signing the NWPC statement in opposition to the Reagan economic policies were the AAUW, the League of Women Voters, the Y.W.C.A., and the National Federation of Business and Professional Women's Clubs (*Women's Political Times,* April 2, 1981). It is tempting to believe that the cooperation of feminist and traditional women's organizations behind the NWPC leadership is partially the consequence of the Houston conference.

The concern shared by the diverse organizations behind the NWPC effort was the conviction that the Reagan policies would have a particularly harsh impact on women and children: Cutbacks on food stamps, welfare payments, health and legal services for the poor, reduced federal staff size, and an erosion of affirmative action—all these elements of the Reagan policies have harsher impact on women than men. It is predominantly women who are below the poverty line, in need of welfare support and legal and social services; it is predominantly women who work in public rather than private employment; and it is women, the last hired, who would be affected most by the general economic downturn expected to accompany the sharp rise in national expenditures on the military. The expanded military budget was contrary to the persistent and growing anti-war and antinuclear views of women, and its economic impact would be to expand fields like engineering,

electronics, and heavy metal industries in which women are poorly represented.

The analysis of determinants of commitment to implementing the diverse
resolutions passed in Houston suggested a great deal of differentiated action
among feminists in the political arena. Many women will be contributing their
political efforts through their work; others through organizations; still others
through coalitions associated with sex-issue politics; and yet others through
seeking office in mainstream politics. It is encouraging to note that when core
issues of major concern to women are challenged by the opponents of sexual
equality and the rights of women, many women's groups and organizations
quickly formed coalitions despite their diversity of interests and commitments.

We may be in sore need of such coalitions as the decade unfolds. It will
be a long time before even one-third of our national legislators are women;
longer still before women hold any significant proportion of the positions in
key decision-making posts in the Cabinet or the White House. But there is a
vast mushrooming of local, state, and national activist groups and organizations honeycombing the nation in the long tradition of women's political roles
through voluntary associations outside the structure of political parties. This
augurs well for quick response by women if and when political developments
threaten their private and public rights.

9

Summary of Findings and Their Political Implications

Introduction

The preceding eight chapters have presented a great deal of detailed quantitative analysis. In this concluding chapter, I shall stand back from such detail to discuss the unique characteristics of the study design, summarize the major findings of the study and assess the significance of the findings for the current and future position of women in American politics.

Unique Features of the Study

Five characteristics of the study are unique in the sense that they rarely have been investigated in any systematic way and have never been brought together in the same research design. Two of these characteristics are intrinsic to the study: (a) that this was a study of an event, the Houston national women's conference and (b) that the central focus was on the impact of that event, through the use of a longitudinal, or panel, design. Joined to this short-term change analysis was the focus on three substantive issues: (a) the consistency of belief and affect structures that differentiate members of voluntary associations or caucuses, as in the comparisons of NOW with LWV members and Pro-Plan with Anti-Plan caucus activists; (b) the political biographies of the delegates, which we traced from their families of origin through schooling, employment, organizational involvement, and political activities; and (c) the determinants of political aspirations in mainstream and feminist politics. The impact of the conference was an analysis dimension on each of these three substantive issues.

Event Analysis

Neither contemporary sociology nor history pay much attention to the study of events, though for different reasons. Sociology has neglected the study of events, prefering to study ongoing and presumed universal features of social structures and the underlying causes of social change. The reason for such preferences has been the desire of sociologists to establish their field as a scientific, rather than a historical, discipline. An exception to this general tendency has been a long tradition of conducting voting studies in political sociology, but elections are repetitive events, and sociological interest was on changes in the underlying dispositions of voters toward one or another party or in voter responsiveness to a particular electoral campaign or personality. Studies of unique events are rare in sociology. Indeed, it was to break this long-standing tradition that Kai Erikson adopted as a theme for the annual meeting while he was president of the Eastern Sociological Society in 1980–1981 the neglect of systematic studies of significant events. To counter such neglect, Erikson organized plenary sessions around such topics as the Attica prison riot, the Jonestown massacre, and landmark events in recent feminist history, of which Houston was surely one.

The neglect of event analysis in the field of history has a different context. Historical analysis had once been heavily involved with event analysis: A description and analysis of military, political, and diplomatic events used to be standard fare in any history of a particular period or nation. In recent years, the study of events has declined, as historians adopted more abstract guiding concepts for their work (e.g., the study of *structure* or *conjuncture* over long stretches of time, or the search for changes in a national *mentalité* rather than the detailed time–place–event focus of earlier historical work). My concern that future historians have access to more sophisticated data on contemporary events in feminist history provided one motivation for this study of the 1977 women's conference, yet such event analysis is out of fashion in historical circles today.

I do not agree with the judgment that event analysis is unimportant. That historians have drawn such a conclusion may reflect the inadequacy of the methods and theories they brought to bear on event analysis, not that the events themselves do not impact powerfully on contemporaries and hence on societal change. If one had to rely simply on the descriptions provided by journalists and participant observers of the Houston conference, it could well be that future historians would find the data wanting; they would even be misleading, as I shall illustrate. It may also be the case that event analysis is more appropriate to historical studies of social and political movements rather than to stable national or governmental structures. Those who participate in social movements are likely to have sensitive appreciation of landmark events in their own history. Indeed, one empirical indicator of the vitality of a social movement may be the level of awareness and agreement among members concerning highpoint dates and events in its own history. Robert Darnton made this point in his assessment of the 1981 political developments in Poland: He said that members of the Solidarity movement took very seriously the search for the "real" events in their own history. Darnton suggested that a series of dates projected to contemporary Poles the whole meaning of the Solidarity movement—1956, 1968, 1970, 1980 (Darnton, 1981).

Whether the same sensitivity to landmark dates is characteristic of contemporary American feminists, we do not know. At the founding meeting of NOW in Washington, D.C., 1966, several women raised the question of whether anything special had taken place that affected women 100 years before, in 1866, and one woman commented ruefully that it was too bad we were not meeting in 1948, since then we could clearly link our efforts to the first convention to call for suffrage for women, which took place in Seneca Falls, New York, in 1848. The women's studies movement today is giving back to women their own history, so that as the larger movement progresses, American women, like Poles, may find that a series of dates will project the meaning of the feminist movement to them—1848, 1920, 1966, 1973, and perhaps 1977. Major events like Seneca Falls, the ratification of suffrage, the founding of NOW, the Supreme Court decision on abortion, and perhaps the Houston national conference, help to shape and affirm a consciousness of one's own significance in history.

Impact Analysis

An event can be studied in a variety of ways using a variety of methods. One can study the event while it is taking place, as journalists or participant observers do. One can study the event retrospectively, by interviewing people after the fact and combining their comments with documentation on the event itself. Or, as in this study, one can conduct a short-term longitudinal study through the use of a before−after design with repeat measures in both surveys and with indicators of the level and extent of participation in the event (e.g., the exposure variables used in previous chapters to explain change in such things as political competence or political aspirations). For an event to be significant must surely mean it has had an impact of some kind on participants and possibly on a larger public that learns of the event and is affected by that knowledge.

There are good reasons to believe that a before–after design is preferable to a situational analysis of an event and its impact on participants. For one thing, significant events are *greedy* in the sense that people become totally caught up in them, temporarily shelve other roles and obligations, and often behave out of character, sometimes to their own surprise in retrospective musing on their role in the event.[1] By these standards, Houston was a greedy event par excellence: It was marked by long hours, sleep and food deprivation, disruption of ordinary daily habits, intensity of social interaction, underlying anxiety concerning political disruption, sheer people density, excessive sensory stimulation, ear and eye strain for those trying to follow events on the Coliseum podium over the buzz of delegates in front of them, etc. Such a combination opens mind and body to profound vulnerability. It is little wonder that crying, singing, and dancing in the aisles were frequently observed and reported by the delegates themselves. Not only would it have been nearly impossible to secure data from participants *during* such an event on any systematic sampling basis, but there is considerable question how stable and meaningful their responses to the questions would have been. The duration of an event is a time for action and interaction, not for the expression of considered opinions and plans in a research interview. But if the event really has political and psychological consequences, then a panel design should be able to pinpoint the level and direction of such impact. Compared to the frenzy so often shown during the event, the impact is apt to be a modest one, and possibly a disappointment to a political advocate or social researcher.

Events that are anticipated and planned for carry a special risk in research designed to study their impact. Perhaps to the extent that an event is unique, there is an anticipatory rise in expectations concerning the importance of the event and of one's role in it. We know too little at this juncture of what this process entails but, throughout the analysis of the data, I have been concerned that the October survey might have been too close to the event to obtain a stable first reading on the panel variables. The drop in actual leadership role compared to the expected role reported in October may reflect some anticipatory halo effect. So, too, it may have been the same anticipatory euphoria that artificially raised the political aspirations reported in October: They may have been higher than we would have obtained had the survey

---

[1] I am indebted to Rose and Lewis Coser for this observation, which draws on the analogous concept of *greedy institutions* (Coser & Coser, 1981, personal communication). Rose Coser also provided many insightful comments on an earlier draft of this summary, as a discussant of a paper presented at the March 1981 convention of the Eastern Sociological Society, for which I am very grateful.

been fielded several months before the conference rather than 5 or 6 weeks before it. On the other hand, the exposure variables that measured what people actually did during the Houston conference yielded meaningful explanations of the changes found in the panel variables. Only further experience with studies of events and their impact will provide a basis in empirical data with which to settle some of the methodological questions raised by this first study.

The Houston conference was a unique event for the researcher as well as for the delegates: With the benefit of hindsight, I now wish that the study had included variables to tap personal capacity to sustain the demands on psyche and physique of such a greedy event: Measures such as how many hours people usually sleep each night; how regular or routinized their sleeping and eating habits are; whether they are in good physical health or suffer some chronic disability; what their usual reactions are to situations of high stress, etc. Some hints of the potential relevance of such variables were suggested in the analysis, since age was found to be negatively related to high scores on the major exposure variables in the study, suggesting that lower levels of physical stamina may have reduced political activity levels among many of the older delegates. Under normal circumstances in a home community, an active political role may be filled as well by older women as by younger women, but the program-packed days and nights of the national conference may have taken a differential toll on the older participants. Hence, in this study, age not only has cohort significance in the usual sense, but the physical maturation dimension of age had a direct political significance since the decisions reached were heavily influenced by young people with the stamina to press their views vigorously in the caucuses, delegation meetings, and inordinately long plenary sessions. Direct measures of physical stamina might have helped to explain the meaning of the strong age correlates found in the analysis of the Houston experience and its impact.

Belief and Affect Consistency

Event analysis is necessarily behavior-oriented, since an event involves people coming together to engage in some action and reach some decisions through a process of interpersonal persuasion, organizational pressure, collective deliberation. Thus, the exposure variables focused on who did what with what frequency: working with caucuses, attending delegation meetings, passing messages, speaking from microphones on the floor, influencing others or being influenced by others in voting for or against a resolution. Such behavior is an acting-out of the less visible values and beliefs of the participants; this was therefore an unprecedented opportunity to explore the underlying affect and beliefs of the delegates.

To someone observing the Coliseum floor when resolutions were voted on, the most visible cleavage seemed to be that between Pro-Plan and Anti-Plan delegates. The Anti-Plan delegates were a tiny, but highly visible, minority in what appeared to be an otherwise highly cohesive body. But voting for a resolution masks reservations and ambivalence, if not decided opposition, even among ardent advocates of feminism. Houston was not the occasion for participants to express such ambivalence, but the study provided an opportunity for the impact researcher to explore the extent to which beliefs and affect show varying levels of consistency between members of specific voluntary associations and caucuses. The 25 resolutions endorsed by the overwhelming majority of the delegates were not equally important to, or approved by, all the delegates, just as the delegates' past and planned political activity did not show uniform levels of involvement and commitment to the many issues covered by the resolutions.

The belief and affect analysis, then, helped to probe beneath the behavior demonstrated during the event itself. In light of the intense pace, frequent demonstrations of anger and euphoria, and the public nature of the conference, it would have been easy to make erroneous inferences about belief consistency among the delegates. The analysis demonstrated that affect and belief are structured along organizational, racial, ethnic, and age lines to a much greater extent than met the public eye. That there was considerable anxiety about whether certain resolutions would receive majority support when they came to an actual vote (as there was on sexual preference and reproductive freedom), reflects not only an underestimation of the power of a greedy event to create at least momentary cohesion but an awareness of the ambivalence or qualified support many women have expressed under quieter circumstances in their usual habitats.

Political Development

It would have been quite consistent with numerous studies of women in politics to have designed this one with a time frame of merely 1 year or so before and after the national conference. One could have tapped political aspirations as they existed in the summer or fall of 1977 and simply explained the impact of the conference on political aspirations in the narrow framework of how event participation affected those aspirations several months later, as I did in one part of the analysis in Chapter 8. In a similar way, many studies of women and men who serve on school boards or in state legislatures have confined their analyses of gender differences to the time devoted to official duties or to intentions to run for a higher office, with few variables on background experiences. Budget restraints often impose restrictions on the scope of a study design, or the researcher fears the response rate might be too low if a longer survey were used.

Since I was very optimistic that this particular sample would be highly motivated to respond, I ran the risk of using a longer instrument in order to enlarge the analysis framework to cover the life experiences that characterize various routes to political activity. Hence the study was able to provide insight into the political development of women. What makes this emphasis of the study relatively unique is that I have linked this more static, but important, focus on political development to the differential impact of the Houston experience on women with different kinds of past political, family, and organizational experiences.

Mainstream versus Movement Political Activity and Aspirations

A number of studies have been published on women in politics, using specialized samples of party convention delegates (Kirkpatrick, 1976); members of state legislatures (Diamond, 1977; Dubeck, 1976; Githens, 1977; King, 1977; Kirkpatrick, 1974; Werner, 1968); women political elite in the United States compared to European countries (Epstein & Coser, 1981); and women who have served in the U.S. Congress (Gehlen, 1977; Johnson & Carroll, 1978; Johnson & Stanwyck, 1976). Almost without exception, the emphasis in such research on political women has been restricted to women who ran for or held *elective public office*.[2] Appointive office has not been a focus of much research, nor have there been any studies that compare those active in feminist politics with those active in mainstream electoral politics. Hence the study makes a unique contribution to the analysis of what differentiates electoral from appointive office-holding and to analysis differentiating mainstream from movement political activity and aspirations.

It is more than 100 years since Margaret Fuller drew the distinction between feminist pioneers who were "passionate rebels" serving as harbingers of future change and those who were "severe lawgivers to themselves" seeking reforms in the legal system of their society (Fuller, 1855). In the late 1960s, one could draw the same distinction between those active in the "liberation" wing of the feminist movement (who were more likely to be passionate rebels) and those active in the "women's rights" wing (who tended to be reformists). This distinction had blurred by the late 1970s, partly because the dramatic public displays of protest that marked the 1960s and early 1970s had given way to more highly organized tactics that require persistence, financial re-

[2]Two excellent collections of essays on women in politics are edited by Githens and Prestage (1977) and Epstein and Coser (1981). Githens and Prestage provide a good selection of work on women in American politics, with a special focus on Black women, whereas Epstein and Coser included essays on political women in West Germany, Finland, Norway, Poland, Yugoslavia, and Austria as well as the United States. Epstein's review essay is an excellent overview of the literature on women in American politics (Epstein, 1981a:124–146).

sources, and the political clout of large memberships. Hence it is probably the case that the Houston delegate body included few passionate rebels in Fuller's sense and more "severe lawgivers to themselves." Whatever their personal history, by 1977 almost all the energies of the women in the IWY Commission sample were channeled into organized efforts toward regulatory and legal changes in mainstream American life, a reformist rather than revolutionary, agenda.

Despite the reformist bent of almost all the Houston delegates, the study has shown that there is an analytic utility to the distinction between gender and sex-issue politics (roughly, the difference between issues affecting the status of women in formal institutions and issues rooted in the unique reproductive and sexual functioning of women). Many feminists who were pioneers in the 1960s have added sex-linked issues to their original gender-linked issues agenda for social change. But a significant number from that pioneer cohort have not done so, either because they consider sex-linked issues so volatile and controversial as to limit the potential for successful attainment of gender-issue political goals or because, on the grounds of religion, race, or ethnicity, their own beliefs preclude acceptance of feminist views on sex-linked political issues. Younger feminists who became active in the 1970s frequently left gender-issue politics to those already involved with such issues in organizations like NOW or the NWPC, and have concentrated their own political commitments on such sex-linked issues as women's health, rape, sexual preference, and battered wives.

Consequently, political activity within the feminist movement is to some extent age-stratified, with older women working on gender-linked issues, younger women on sex-linked issues. The interesting exception to this is that many younger women from racial and ethnic minority groups limit their own feminist efforts to gender-linked issues. Indeed, for many Black women and Latinas, religious, community, and family values do not permit acceptance of feminist views in the area of sex and family (Rodriquez, 1981). Consistent with the age-stratified nature of activism among majority women, we have found that aspirations for prominence in movement politics are determined mostly by membership in a large-scale organization among older women, whereas younger delegates with similarly high aspirations are more apt to report high levels of direct political action rather than activity channeled through formal organizations.

As a unique characteristic of the study, then, I have given attention throughout the analysis not only to the comparison of mainstream with movement politics but to the three-way comparison of mainstream, gender- and sex-issue politics.

Although the study has as a central focus the historically unique event of the Houston national women's conference, the research design linked the event analysis to broader ongoing variables of sociological and political importance. We were not merely interested in the 3 days people spent in Houston and what they did there. That was merely the tip of our substantive interest. Of equal importance were the antecedents and consequences of event participation: relating event participation to *antecedents* such as political experience and commitments, involvement in state committees, organizational membership and membership in a state delegation prior to Houston; to event *consequences* such as the new organizations or committees that replaced some of the state delegations, the expansion of individual political networks through contacts made in Houston with like-minded women from one's own or other states, and changes in delegates' personal aspirations to enter mainstream or movement politics.

Historians may have rejected event analysis because the data they had access to was limited to reports in the media, official records, and participants' personal accounts of a qualitative variety; in other words, data were restricted largely to who did what during a narrowly defined event. Only systematic sociological research can tap the more basic questions regarding the influences of the past on the activity level during the event and the ripple-out effects of such activity on the participants' plans and aspirations. It was my hope that the design and results of the study reported in this volume would contribute to a more vital connection between history and sociology.

Major Findings

Much material had accumulated on the Houston conference before the publication of this study: There had been countless newspaper articles across the country, television programs, personal talks in home communities by those who had been in Houston as delegates, and the final report of the IWY Commission itself, *The Spirit of Houston* (1978). In attempting an overview of study findings, I opted for a particular device that relates the study to these more qualitative media and official reports. Hence the underlying question in this summary is simply this: What does one learn from a systematic, quantitative study of an event that one cannot learn from either media accounts or personal observations of participants themselves? A second question is, What are the implications of the results of this study for the role of women in politics in the years ahead?

Conference Impact on Political Aspirations

The first major finding provides a good example of the gap that can exist between *in situ* impressions captured by observation and media reports, on the one hand, and the impact results from a panel analysis of a sample of participants, on the other. A reporter or participant observer in Houston could not help but catch the euphoric atmosphere of much of the conference. I suggested earlier that this is in the nature of a greedy event such as the conference, where tension is high, one's usual roles and predispositions are temporarily shelved, and there are frequent moments of intense emotional unity or tension in the body politic. One was impressed in Houston by the many skillful, politically astute women in leadership roles and was tempted to believe that there were surely future senators and governors among the women in attendance. Press interviews with Anne Saunier, Carol Bellamy, Ellie Smeal, and others like them furthered this impression, and it would have been easy to believe that participation in a national conference of this sort would have a wide impact on the rest of the delegates, who would go home with their own sights on political posts of greater stature and visibility than they had ever considered for themselves in the past.

In fact, the net effect of the conference, as shown in the panel results, seems to have been quite the opposite. For one thing, as a group, the delegates are politically experienced women, among whom personal political aspirations are quite stable. Whatever their momentary flights of fantasy or self-deflation during the Houston event itself, pre- and postconference surveys showed that the majority of the delegates did not change their political aspirations for holding office in either mainstream or movement politics. But among those who did show a significant change in aspirations, twice as many lowered their aspirations as raised them. Thus, 15% raised their aspirations for prominent movement political office, but 31% lowered their aspirations. The ratio was slightly less extreme in mainstream politics; still, 15% raised, and 24% lowered, their aspirations for holding public office.

I must admit that these results, when they first showed up on computer printouts, were disappointingly at odds with my own predictions. Those predictions were rooted, I now realize, more in political wishful thinking than in sober sociological thought. I wanted to believe that the conference had influenced more women to seek national prominence in the feminist movement, thus infusing new vigor by replacing those women long associated with the national movement. Still others, I naively hoped, would raise their sights from a local school board election to the state legislature, and eventually to the U.S. Congress.

There is, however, an underside to a powerful event: To come from a small town, where one enjoys some local political visibility and influence, to a national conference necessarily means that one is exposed to some national political stars, women with far more political astuteness, more political connections that can be used, for example, to successfully amend a resolution on the floor, than the majority of the delegates could conceivably possess. The sum total of top leaders from the hundreds of communities across the country is far in excess of the leadership slots available at one large-scale national conference.

At this conference, not all the delegates were well known even in their own cities and states, because the IWY Commission at the national level, and the coordinating committees on the state level, were dedicated to serious outreach, actively seeking women from less well-represented groups to assure age, class, and ethnic diversity in the conference delegate body. The unintended net effect of that outreach may have been to depress rather than to raise the personal political aspirations of the delegates as a group.

Many feminist psychologists and sociologists have argued that women are deprived of adequate role models of competent, successful women as teachers, mentors, or employers. This has provided one rationale for urging the hiring and promotion of more women to significant posts in public bureaucracies and private businesses. In the course of our ordinary lives as a student or employee, however, it may be the case that we do not find a single individual who serves as our role model or mentor. Rather, our tendency may be to draw up a composite role model, one trait or ability drawn from one teacher or mentor, another from a second person, and still a third from a very different model, just as we select among the qualities shown by our parents. I do not know if this is the way the process works in an empirical sense; hence I am drawing more on personal observation than published evidence. In my own experience, the kind of sociologist I had hoped to become drew on such a composite: I wanted to be a person with the political views and aesthetic taste of Professor X, the theoretical knowledge and conceptual flair of Professor Y, and the research and method skills of Professor Z. But I also remember the depressing impact of my first attendance at a national sociology meeting: In that intense, highly packed experience, running from one session to another to listen to the prominent sociologists whose work I had admired in the quiet of a library stall, I lost self-confidence and came away convinced I could never really be an outstanding sociologist at all.

Analogously, the greedy event of Houston may have led many delegates to fuse the array of qualities shown by the superstars they met, observed, and admired into a composite image of what it might take to "go do likewise." If such a composite model fused the parliamentary skills of Anne Saunier, the conceptual and linguistic flair of Jill Ruckelshaus, the political savvy of Bella Abzug, and the charisma of Barbara Jordan, it is little wonder that many delegates might have felt relatively deprived, concluding that they personally fell short of what it takes to be a competent political leader. What we tend to forget is that such leaders are themselves swept up into performances of an outstanding quality in situations like the Houston conference: They, too, have shelved the ordinariness of daily functioning as political animals. As we say, they "rose to the occasion." The underside of admiration under such circumstances can be self-devaluation.

Although the study included no variable on general self-confidence or self-esteem, a specific manifestation of such confidence is the variable of political competence. Since this was a repeat-panel measure, I analyzed the impact of conference participation on subjective competence in the political realm. Independent of the women's rating of their own political competence before the conference, their level of *activity* in conference politics increased their political competence self-rating in the postconference survey. Reciprocally, the more passive the women were during the conference, the lower their competence rating became in the second survey. Furthermore, increasing the size of their networks with new contacts made in Houston had a positive effect on postconference competence ratings, and the more the delegates judged these new network contacts as helpful to their jobs and political roles, the greater the rise in their own political aspirations.

Two points are important to stress on the pragmatic political implications of these findings. First, there are probably structural limitations to the proportion of people at any large meeting, conference, or convention that can play significant, active roles in the deliberations. If passive roles depress and active roles enlarge individual self-confidence and competence, then the results argue for reducing the size of delegate bodies, perhaps by holding smaller, regional conferences rather than national conferences. (Interestingly, this is precisely what the Continuing Committee recommended in its early plans concerning a second women's conference in the IWY Commission mode).

Second, the results give some corrective to what many of us have taken to be only good news, that is, that national political party conventions since 1972 have contained larger proportions of women among the delegates. This trend is itself of interest: It may reflect not merely the successful pressure of women's groups to enlarge their representation in the party conventions, but an increased willingness of the national parties to do so as such conventions more and more became "media events" rather than critical decision-making occasions. This is consistent with Epstein's judgment, in a review of the role of women in American politics, that *women tend to make progress when social institutions lose power* (Epstein, 1981a). The admission of women to elite schools, private clubs, and many occupations has tended to occur when such institutions were losing their power to competing institutions. Epstein comments, "There is no doubt that women benefit in such cases, but the institutions to which they are thus admitted are no longer the same, and it is often questionable whether the prize has the value originally attributed to it" [Epstein, 1981a:13].

In the case of party conventions, the delegate role may no longer facilitate access to power the way it once did, but the role provides opportunities to expand networks that may be politically useful, to acquire and practice political skills, and to extend practical political knowledge. My findings suggest that this only occurs if delegates have opportunities to be genuinely active. If the enlarged representation of women in party conventions merely provides female faces to television viewers and a spectator audience to male leaders on the convention floor, the net effect of such enlarged female representation could be to depress the women's sense of political competence and to lower their personal aspirations for office-seeking.

Another set of findings on political aspirations is of interest in a historical and cross-cultural framework. Epstein (1981a) has noted that one unique aspect of American women in elite political positions, compared to their European counterparts, is a background route to political power through voluntary associations. The findings on political aspirations of older women delegates are consistent with this historical tendency: Those with the highest aspirations for mainstream political prominence tended to be women with high levels of past political party activity and extensive membership in traditional women's organizations. The profile of younger women delegates differed from that of the older women: For the younger women, the most powerful predictors of high mainstream political aspirations were having already held some public office, a history of direct political action on issues, high political competence levels, membership in feminist organizations, and *not* being married to a politically active man. This age differentiation among the background predictors of political aspirations may represent a harbinger of change in the recruitment paths of political careers among the upcoming generation of younger American women, who are experienced in coalition-building rather than formal organizations and possess greater autonomy and independence, as suggested by their being either unattached or married to a man with no political career of his own.

A counterpart age differentiation was also found for movement aspirations. Older women who aspire for prominence in feminist politics tend to be liberal and to have extensive memberships in traditional, political, and women's rights organizations. Examples of such women in the top ranks of the Democratic party, the NWPC, and the coordinators of ERA ratification coalitions in the unratified states come readily to mind. Younger women with aspirations for prominence in feminist politics, like their counterpart aspirants for mainstream prominence, show profiles of high direct political action rather than extensive organizational membership, and past involvement with both gender- and sex-linked issues. It is difficult to tell if this is a maturational tendency or a cohort difference, though other trends support the idea that they are cohort differences. Young people, since the mid-1960s at least, have shown a lesser tendency to be "joiners" of formal clubs and organizations and a preference for informal peer groups: For example, enrollments in formal youth organizations like the Girl and Boy Scouts have shown a steady decline. Political party attachments are similarly less central nowadays than they once were, with a larger proportion of voting adults defining themselves as

Independents and with more crossover voting patterns at the polls. Trends like these suggest that the predictors of aspirations among the younger delegates are cohort, rather than maturational, characteristics. It will be interesting to explore the biographies of those women now in their twenties and thirties who move into prominence in either mainstream or movement politics to see whether or not they continue to show greater past involvement in informal political coalitions on specific issues rather than formal party and organizational memberships. Carol Bellamy and Patricia Schroeder exemplify this trend, both having moved into mainstream public office from liberal—leftist opposition to the Vietnam war.

Lines of Cleavage in Affect and Belief

Most of the media coverage of the Houston conference projected the view that the basic cleavage in the delegate body was between Pro-Plan and Anti-Plan activists, particularly on the issues of ERA, reproductive freedom, and sexual preference. Media reports also suggested that the one great highpoint that even the Anti-Plan delegates shared was the passage of the composite Minorities resolution. Clearly, an observer would readily note that both white and Black Pro-Plan delegates hugged and danced with many Anti-Plan women who voted for the Minorities resolution. It was transparent to all how intense the feelings were on the Reproductive Freedom resolution: This was the only resolution whose passage triggered equally intense pro- and anti-demonstrations. For one half-hour, there was pandemonium on the floor, as pro-abortion delegates screamed at the anti-abortion demonstrators, some attempting to rip down the photographs of fetuses that were being carried through the aisles. Although the demonstrations and cheering lasted equally as long when the Sexual Preference resolution was passed, this was a far more one-sided celebration, with a large proportion of the delegates standing quietly by their seats observing the euphoria felt by others.

A crowd and a demonstration can be very misleading. When the noise and excitement have taken over a hall, one does not notice those who stand or sit quietly and do not participate. One's attention as a participant or media observer is riveted on the fast-moving activities of the most conspicuous demonstrators. But beneath the noise, there is a great deal of variance in the feelings people have and the beliefs behind those feelings, and it is this variance that can be measured with quantitative data to correct often misleading impressions during the event itself.

As reported in Chapter 6, the empirical analysis was consistent with other observations that the greatest polarization of affect was on the abortion issue. A comparison of the delegates active in the Anti-Plan caucus with those active in the Pro-Plan caucus showed the sharpest contrast in feelings toward pro-abortion groups: On a 7-point scale, the mean score of Anti-Plan activists was close to the pole of hostility ($M=1.2$), whereas Pro-Plan activists scored close to the positive end of the barometer ($M=6.2$).

On the other hand, despite the observers' sense that Anti-Plan delegates shared the views of Pro-Plan delegates on the Minorities resolution, the Anti-Plan delegates showed less positive feelings toward racial and ethnic groups (a neutral $M=4.4$ toward Blacks and Latinas) than the Pro-Plan activists, who were clearly on the positive side, with $M=5.9$. The issue on which the Pro-Plan activists showed a comparable neutrality of feeling was sexual prefer-ence: Here the Pro-Plan activists showed a mean affect score toward lesbian groups of $M=4.7$ and the Anti-Plan activists were decidedly hostile, with $M=1.4$.

A similar profile was found in a comparison of NOW members with League of Women Voters members. With the scores converted to a $0-100$ range (where 100 represents the most feminist response), NOW members show mean scores over 90 on belief indices on marital equity, economic rights, and abortion, but their mean drops to 62 on the belief measure that includes two items on the sexual preference issue (the bottom-line feminism index). On affect scales, NOW members show a mean over 90 in feelings toward pro-abortion groups and pro-ERA groups, but one of only 73 toward lesbian groups. Of course, League of Women Voters members show a similar ten-dency to differentiate among issues and groups, though consistently with lower, less "feminist" responses than NOW members in every index in the analysis.

Furthermore, an analysis of the degree of variance in affect and belief also tends to correct the misleading impression of great and uniform emotional unity among Pro-Plan or NOW activists in Houston: Although there is very little variance on ERA, marital equity, and child-care, there was a moderate level of variance on abortion and a very high variance on lesbian issues.

Last, an enthusiasm scale that measured the feelings of enthusiasm or depression the delegates felt when resolutions were voted on showed that there had been a markedly higher positive response to the passage of the ERA and Minorities resolutions than to the Reproductive Freedom and Sex-ual Preference resolutions.

The change analysis on the affect scores also helps correct a misleading impression formed from both the coverage by the media and from the qualita-tive comments so many delegates made to the open-ended question at the end of the second survey. Many of these comments, like those made during interviews and reported by the press in Houston, spoke of contacts made and of informal conversations engaged in by Pro-Plan delegates with their Anti-Plan opponents. Many noted their surprise at finding so much common ground in their life experiences—hardships related to family illnesses, coping with adolescent children, difficulty finding jobs, etc.—with the result that they claimed to feel more sympathy and respect for the conservative Anti-Plan delegates by the end of the conference. That said, many Pro-Plan delegates went on to describe how they watched the Anti-Plan women with whom they had talked when votes were taken, and were pleased to see them vote in support of several resolutions. They took this to be evidence of their own personal powers of persuasion.

In actuality, there is evidence that feelings were not softened, but were polarized even further by the Houston conference. Many Anti-Plan delegates came to Houston with intentions to vote for certain of the resolutions. Several described how they had examined the resolutions and decided in advance which they would favor and which they would oppose. Furthermore, the areas in which the delegates reported their surprise at similar life experiences were not political areas, but personal and family matters—illness, child-rearing, job experiences. On measures tapping affect toward groups of political relevance, the views and feelings of the Pro- and Anti-Plan delegates were even further apart *after* the conference than before. Two kinds of evidence demonstrate this point. When individual scales were compared, the Anti-Plan delegates showed more negative affect toward all the liberal, feminist groups by the second survey and more positive affect toward Conservative groups; the Pro-Plan activists showed the reciprocal profile: more positive affect toward liberal feminist groups and more negative feelings toward Conservative groups. Second, the average within-individual variability across 10 affect scales was lower after the conference than before, and more strongly so for the embattled minority of Anti-Plan delegates than the victorious Pro-Plan activists, suggesting that the Anti-Plan group emerged from the conference even more united than the majority Pro-Plan delegates. Contrary to the impression held by many Pro-Plan delegates that they had influenced their opponents, the Anti-Plan women were not influenced to even moderate, much less change, their views. Major dramatic events may stimulate fleeting emotional unity but sharpen and polarize political beliefs.

Commitment to Future Political Action

Like affect and belief, there is considerable variation among the delegates in the extent to which they are personally committed to work toward the implementation of the resolutions passed in Houston. Predictably, ERA ratification heads that list, with 74% of the delegates claiming they would definitely be active in working on campaigns to secure final ratification, and only 13% with no plan to be active. Beyond this single issue, there was considerable variation in the overall level of commitment and in the kinds of personal characteristics or experiences that predict future commitment on the various issues covered by the resolutions.

Issues that bear on the general position of women in major institutions of society—for example, education, employment, and political life—continue to head the list of feminist concerns, with over 70% of the delegates claiming they will be active in implementing resolutions on these basic issues. In addition to these female-status issues, two issues that affect particular categories of women—minority women and battered wives—are high on the list of future commitments to action by the delegate body. The minority issue has been central to NOW's concerns since its founding, whereas battered wives, and efforts to secure community and federal support to establish shelters for such women, are issues of more recent concern to feminists.

Between 50% and 70% of the delegates expect to be active politically to implement the resolutions on child abuse, child care, rape, homemakers' rights, reproductive freedom, welfare and poverty, older women, health, credit, and disabled women. From 30% to 50% of the delegates expect to be active on such issues as international affairs, sexual preference, or insurance. On none of the resolutions did fewer than 30% of the respondents plan to be active. Only those delegates identified with the Anti-Plan caucus expressed any intention of working against the implementation of any of the resolutions.

The findings suggest that feminists tend to show a high level of mutual tolerance: They may not all agree on all the issues, but where there is ambivalence or even personal objection there is silence or nonactivity rather than opposition. There is no reason to attribute this to feminists *qua* feminists, since Gehlen's (1977) analysis of the voting record of the 69 women who served in the House of Representatives from 1915 to 1976 showed a comparable reluctance of the women members to oppose programs they did not support: "More so than the men, they tend to opt out rather than go on record as opposed" [Gehlen, 1977: 314].

The analysis of what predicts high commitment to future political action on the various resolutions suggested a considerable degree of issue-differentiation on personal grounds. Women select issues to work on that are meaningful to them, drawing on deeper personal motivations as well as a political agenda that dictates the importance of a particular issue for women at large. The sharpest contrast of this sort was the profile of predictors of future action on a cluster labeled *money management* and the Sexual Preference resolution. Those who expect to be very active on such matters as credit and insurance policies are somewhat more conservative than the average delegate, employed full-time, members of traditional women's organizations, and have already been active on a broad range of gender-linked issues. By contrast, the sexual preference activist of the future tends to be young, unmarried, very liberal or radical in political persuasion, decidedly low in religious observance, has been active in feminist organizations on other sex-linked issues, and is rarely a member of a traditional women's organization. Abortion activists of the future are similar to the sexual preference activists on all the above characteristics except age and marital status: Abortion activists are found among both married and unmarried, younger and older women, whereas sexual preference activists are younger unmarried or divorced women, for the most part.

The findings of rather sharp contrasts in predictors of future political action in terms of personal characteristics raises two interesting questions. For one, does such an issue differentiation mean possible fragmentation within the feminist movement? We tend to think not, since there is a high level of agreement on a set of central issues affecting the general position of women: These are equal and expanded opportunities for women in schooling, employment, and politics. Beyond this, differentiation of political effort can contribute to the strength of the movement since those who are privately ambivalent or even opposed to a particular issue need not betray their own beliefs but simply concentrate their efforts on issues of greater salience to them. The data show, for example, that abortion and sexual preference are issues that majority white women, but not minority-group women will be active on in the future. But this does not mean that Black women and Latinas will oppose white feminists on these issues. They will merely concentrate their political efforts on resolutions of greater concern to them, whether child care, welfare, women's rights, job training, or shelters for displaced homemakers. When personal salience is joined to overall political salience, the sum total of specialized political efforts is a contribution to the collective goals of the social movement.

The second question is, Does such self-motivation suggest that feminists are more often motivated by self-serving goals than women have been reported to be? Other studies of political activists that have compared women and men have reported that women are less likely than men to be motivated by self-serving goals. Throughout American history, women have been attracted to issues that are defined as altruistic, moral, or public-serving rather than self-serving. More recently, Costantini and Craik's (1972) study of party and public office-holders in California concluded that politics for men centers on personal enhancement and career advancement, whereas for women it centers on party loyalty, a labor of love, and service to others. But one must look closely at such imputations of motives. The female moral crusaders of the 1830s seem, at one level, to be morally motivated by a desire to lift prostitutes from "lives of sin"; yet from another point of view, they may have been just as concerned for their own protection from venereal disease. Epstein (1981a) urges a similar second look at the motivation of women who worked for Prohibition. On one level, this seems to be a moral crusade, but many such women were motivated by self-interest: They wanted to be protected from drunken husbands who deprived them and their children of needed food and clothing and often abused them physically and sexually (Epstein, 1981a:134). Opposition to liberal divorce laws does not stem simply from religious and moral objection to marriage termination, but from awareness that easy divorce is a threat to many women's economic interests. Personal and collective realism is also at work in contemporary feminist efforts to rid the workplace of sexual harassment: This is no moral purity campaign, but an effort rooted in the hard realization that, in general, women stand to lose in any physical encounter with men, coupled with the equally pragmatic realization that so long as power and high status positions are unequally distributed between the sexes, women will be the targets of unwanted sexual approaches unless there are firm guidelines and firm sanctions against men who harass women at work.

We are only slowly shifting away from stereotypic thinking about women in many areas of life, nowhere more so than in politics. Even at the level of women as voters rather than as candidates or office-holders, it has been assumed by many political scientists that women are motivated by the personality of the candidates rather than by policy issues. Much of *Women and Politics*, by Baxter and Lansing (1980), is devoted to a careful reexamination of voting studies over the last several decades. They point out that, in election after election, it was critical policy issues and not personality that tipped women's votes away from those of men: Women voters registered their greater opposition to corruption, war, political extremism, military expansion, and inflation. Women did not support Ronald Reagan to the extent that men did in the 1980 elections, and in doing so they were responding to issues, not personalities. Women sensed that Republican party economic policies would penalize women workers while benefiting male bosses; that expanded military expenditure would benefit men rather than women because it would improve the job situation in technical occupations in which men predominate; and that a hard-line foreign policy could only increase the risk of war, this in addition to the fact that Reagan was opposed to the inclusion of ERA support in the party platform and had taken stands against the pro-choice position on abortion.

Neither political party has yet reckoned with the political implications of the major shift in women's relation to the labor force: As stable rather than intermittent employees, women are going to show increasing sensitivity to their own economic positions and needs when they enter the voting booth. When they defined their own position largely in terms of their husbands' social status, support by women for the Republican party was more assured. But now women are defining themselves in terms of their own employment:

As workers in lower-status, lower-paid positions, their economic interests no longer make for any easy or natural affiliation with the Republican party. It would be politically expedient for a Republican administration to improve the economic status of women. Urging higher pay and higher positions for women could yield the political advantage of increased support by women of the Republican party.

Social movements often affect the consciousness of their members by stripping away illusions. It is a feminist perception to observe that if women appear to be more altruistic and pure than men in politics, this reflects the fact that women have been kept out of the centers of power in the political system. As feminist sociologist Cynthia Epstein put it, if women have played cleaner politics than men, this may relate "less to their superior morality than to the structure of their political position" [Epstein, 1981a: 137]. I would merely add, and to the structure of their economic position.

Marriage to a Politically Active Husband

Perhaps the most surprising set of findings in the study involved the variable of marriage to a politically active husband. Had the sample been drawn from the general population or from a special sample of those active in mainstream politics, the results would not have been so surprising. I found that marriage to a politically active husband is strongly related to having grown up in a family with politically active parents, having been active in mainstream politics, and having held elective office in a political party some time in the past. This whole profile might be expected to have a further extension into higher-than-average plans for political activity and, in particular, to higher aspirations for office-holding. But this is decidedly not the case. In fact, women married to politically active men show lower self-ratings of political competence and lower aspirations for office than women without such domestic proximity to politics.

Why should this be so? Why does a political spouse take away from, rather than increase, political competence? I suggested this is rooted in the fact that such wives are not playing autonomous roles of their own in politics, but adjunct roles in support of their husbands' political careers. This could explain why such women do not report high political aspirations of their own, but why do they also show lower ratings of political competence? They are after all, very knowledgeable and experienced in political affairs. Stoper (1977) has suggested that there is an intrinsic contradiction between a wife role and a political role. Political roles are public, power-oriented, and egoistic (one has to "sell" oneself in politics), whereas the wife role focuses on service and love, not power. Hence the two roles are neither *congruent* (that is, they do not harmonize) nor *convergent* (i.e., they require different skills or qualities). Rose

Coser (1981, personal communication) makes the further important point that self-confidence is not just due to past experience but is a property of social structure: Competence or self-confidence is nourished in relationships in which one obtains *recognition,* feedback for being skillful. From this perspective, the political wife has experience but is deprived of the feedback of recognition as a political person. Her rewards are for her behavior as a wife of a politician, not as a political person in her own right. To be approached by the media or to be asked to speak before local groups as the wife of a candidate is not an invitation to defend one's own ideas, but to be a conduit for a husband's ideas or to supplement those ideas with some personal tidbits concerning the husband's passion for jelly beans or fast cars.

Of course, there are many more wives of politicians in the country than there are married women politicians, but the same points made concerning the political wife also apply to those women who try to combine marriage with political careers of their own: Their two roles are neither congruent nor convergent, but in conflict with each other, as Stoper shows in her study (1977). Nor do such women get the backing and help from their husbands that men get from their wives, as Kirkpatrick (1974) found in a study of state legislators.

The only evidence in the study of any conference impact on the wives of politically active husbands is a very slight effect. Whereas such marriages showed a significantly negative Beta coefficient for political aspirations of the women in the *preconference* survey, the coefficient was no longer significant (though still negative), in relation to *postconference* ratings of political aspirations. I suggested that, for many such women, the conference itself may have been a first experience in an all-women political event on a scale that made political experience highly relevant. Recognition and positive feedback may have been the intervening experience for many such women, whose knowledge of procedures and effective caucusing may have been helpful to other, less experienced women delegates. In time, and through additional reinforcement of this kind through future women's political activities, even political wives may become a source of feminist candidates for public office, not as widows, as in the past, but through independent political careers paralleling those of their husbands. In light of the fact that a larger proportion of young women are remaining unmarried and more married women are remaining childless, the combined effect of these trends can be an enlarged pool of women available to enter the political arena.

Economic Roles and Political Competence

One last finding has great interest and relevance for the future role of women in American politics: The level of a woman's own earnings is a significant and independent determinant of her self-rating on political competence.

The higher her paycheck, the higher the woman rated her political competence. Own earnings was second only to the amount of experience the woman had in mainstream politics in explaining political competence level. It is important to note that the earnings level is *independent* of total household income, suggesting it is not simply high socioeconomic status that stimulates the general confidence in self that ripples out to the political arena but the educational attainment, job experience, economic independence, and self-sufficiency of the high-earning woman. Such women in the IWY Commission sample held demanding professional and public service jobs that have often nourished skills that are transferrable to politics, such as learning the skill of persuasian from debating an issue, defending a preferred decision against opposition, or chairing or participating effectively in work sessions and conferences. The fact that a large proportion of the sample reported that they were employed in the public sector means that they had high-level jobs in civil service where they had access to political figures and an opportunity to learn how to work with the political process outside of electoral politics.[3]

That skills developed through high-paying jobs can be transferred to the political sphere has interesting implications for what will facilitate the movement of more women into significant political careers: not simply more experience in party politics or service as delegates to party conventions; not entry to political clubs or to the inner sanctum of politics per se; not even larger numbers of women with legal training. Indeed, political parties have declined in significance and local electoral politics and law degrees are no longer as necessary as they once were for an ascent into the centers of political power. Prewitt and McAllister (1976) have shown that the executive elite in administrations from Hoover through Nixon were more likely to have backgrounds of appointive office than elected office. Epstein (1981a:14) reminds us that the same point was made by C. Wright Mills in 1956, who showed that 62% of higher politicians in the federal executive in the United States were *appointed* to all or most of their political jobs before reaching top positions between 1933 and 1953. With increasingly complex issues confronting legislators and political administrations, sophisticated professional skills are called for to staff commissions, agencies, and the executive offices at all levels of government. The appointive route so neglected in the literature on women in politics may become an increasingly important one. Hence continued pressure to remove the barriers to high-paying jobs and to recruit and promote more women to them will not only yield an *economic* advancement of women, but provide a route to the *political* advancement of women as well.

---

[3]On the other hand, it should be borne in mind that public employees cannot draw salaries from other jobs, which means that legislators have had to either give up their civil service jobs or to come from private sector employment (Githens, 1977: 197).

The Houston National Women's Conference Study

October Survey (1977)

SECTION I. EXPECTATIONS FOR THE HOUSTON CONFERENCE

1. What is your relationship to the National IWY Commission?
    (Circle one)
    1. Elected state/territory *delegate* to Houston
    2. Elected state/territory *alternate* to Houston
    3. Appointed *delegate-at-large* to Houston
    4. Current National Commissioner
    5. Former National Commissioner
    6. Secretariat, professional staff
    7. Secretariat, support staff
    8. Other

2. Are you planning to attend the National Women's Conference in Houston in November?
    (Circle one)
    1. Yes
    2. Uncertain
    3. No

3. People attending the Houston Conference will probably vary in their degree of participation. Which of the following best describes YOUR probable role? (Even if you do not plan to attend, answer AS IF you expect to be present)
    (Circle one)
    1. a KEY PERSON, someone whose views will be sought and taken into account.
    2. an IMPORTANT PERSON, someone whose views will be paid attention to.
    3. an INTERESTED PARTICIPANT, someone who will try to make their views known.
    4. an INTERESTED BYSTANDER, someone concerned with the issues but who will not influence decisions.
    5. NOT MUCH OF A PARTICIPANT
    0. Don't know

4. How often have you travelled more than 500 miles from your home in the past two years?
    (Circle one)
    1. Never
    2. Once or twice
    3. Three to six times
    4. Seven to twelve times
    5. More than twelve times

5. Rate how you feel about the Houston Conference on the Low-to-High Scale below. (Even if you do not plan to attend, answer AS IF you expect to be present.)
    (Circle one in each row)

	Very Low	Low	Un-certain	High	Very High	Does Not Apply
a. Enthusiasm about attending	1	2	3	4	5	
b. Anxiety about travel	1	2	3	4	5	
c. Optimism about outcome	1	2	3	4	5	
d. Concern about political disruption	1	2	3	4	5	
e. Anxiety about family while away	1	2	3	4	5	8

345

6. How optimistic are you that the Congress and the President will act favorably on at least some of the recommendations made by the IWY Commission in its final report? (Circle one)

1. Very optimistic
2. Somewhat optimistic
3. Uncertain, Don't know
4. Somewhat pessimistic
5. Very pessimistic

7. How committed are you personally to work toward the implementation of at least some of the resolutions to be voted on in Houston (A) in your own community and/or state, and (B) at a national level? (Circle one in Column A and one in Column B)

	A Community/State	B National
Top priority commitment	1	1
Major commitment	2	2
Minor commitment	3	3
No commitment	4	4
Don't know	0	0

8. For each of the following groups, indicate your feeling toward it on what can be called a "feeling thermometer" or "feeling scale," where "1" means NEGATIVE or COLD, a "4" means NEUTRAL (neither cold nor warm), and "7" means POSITIVE or WARM. (Circle one in each row)

	NEGATIVE (Cold)			NEU- TRAL		POSITIVE (Warm)		Don't Know
a. Anti-abortion groups	1	2	3	4	5	6	7	0
b. Anti-ERA groups	1	2	3	4	5	6	7	0
c. Black/Afro-American groups	1	2	3	4	5	6	7	0
d. Business/professional groups	1	2	3	4	5	6	7	0
e. Chicano/Hispanic/Latino groups	1	2	3	4	5	6	7	0
f. Conservative groups	1	2	3	4	5	6	7	0
g. Farm/rural groups	1	2	3	4	5	6	7	0
h. Labor unions	1	2	3	4	5	6	7	0
i. Lesbian groups	1	2	3	4	5	6	7	0
j. Liberal groups	1	2	3	4	5	6	7	0
k. National IWY Commissioners	1	2	3	4	5	6	7	0
l. National Organization for Women (NOW)	1	2	3	4	5	6	7	0
m. National Women's Political Caucus (NWPC)	1	2	3	4	5	6	7	0
n. Pro-Abortion groups	1	2	3	4	5	6	7	0
o. Pro-ERA groups	1	2	3	4	5	6	7	0
p. Radical groups	1	2	3	4	5	6		0

QUESTIONS 9 through 19 SHOULD BE ANSWERED BY ELECTED DELEGATES AND ALTERNATES ONLY. ALL OTHERS PLEASE SKIP TO SECTION II, Question 20, on Page 5.

9. In the delegate election at your State Meeting, were you in the top third, middle third, or the bottom third in the number of votes you received?
(Circle one)

1. Top third
2. Middle third
3. Bottom third
4. Don't know

10. Rate the extent to which each of the following factors played a role in your desire to be a delegate to the Houston conference.
(Circle one in each row)

	None	A Little	Some	Great Deal
a. To represent a particular organization	1	2	3	4
b. To strengthen my position in local or state party politics	1	2	3	4
c. To participate in an historic event	1	2	3	4
d. To have influence on a particular issue	1	2	3	4
e. To help my political career	1	2	3	4

11. As a nominee for election as a delegate, did you have the support of any organization, caucus or coalition of the following types?
(Circle one in each row)

	Yes	No	Don't Know
a. State Coordinating Committee nominee	1	2	0
b. Women's rights organization, caucus or coalition	1	2	0
c. Racial/ethnic organization, caucus or coalition	1	2	0
d. Pro-ERA organization, caucus or coalition	1	2	0
e. Professional or union caucus, organization or coalition	1	2	0
f. Anti-abortion or Pro-Life organization, caucus or coalition	1	2	0
g. Anti-ERA organization, caucus or coalition	1	2	0
h. Lesbian organization, caucus or coalition	1	2	0
i. Other formal or informal groups	1	2	0

12. A. Did you campaign or lobby in behalf of your own nomination?
B. Did you campaign or lobby for any other nominee(s) in the election?
(Circle one in each column)

	A For Yourself	B For someone else
Yes	1	1
No	2	2

13. Are you personally acquainted with any elected delegates from states or territories OTHER THAN YOUR OWN?
(Circle one)

1. Yes, at least a dozen
2. Yes, fewer than a dozen
3. Not sure yet
4. No

14. What proportion of your state delegation were you personally acquainted with (A) BEFORE your State Meeting? (B) SINCE your election as a delegate or alternate?
(Circle one in each column)

	A BEFORE State Meeting	B SINCE State Meeting
80% or more...	1	1
50 to 79%	2	2
25 to 49%	3	3
Less than 25% .	4	4
None	5	5

15. Rate how SATISFIED you were with your State Meeting on each of the dimensions listed below.
(Circle one in each row)

	Very Dis- satisfied	Dissa- tisfied	Mixed	Satisfied	Very Satisfied
a. Registration procedures	1	2	3	4	5
b. Nomination procedures	1	2	3	4	5
c. Voting procedures	1	2	3	4	5
d. Time allotted for voting	1	2	3	4	5
e. Delegation elected............	1	2	3	4	5
f. Resolutions Adopted	1	2	3	4	5
g. Your overall reaction	1	2	3	4	5

16. Has your state delegation held any meeting(s) in preparation for the National Women's Conference in Houston?
(Circle one)

1. Yes, and I attended at least one meeting
2. Yes, but I did not attend
3. No, but meeting is scheduled
4. No, and no meeting is scheduled
0. Don't know

17. Which of the following best describes your state delegation?
(Circle one)

1. Largely Feminist
2. Mixed
3. Largely Anti-Feminist
0. Don't know

18. How closely do you expect to work with each of the following groups during the Houston conference?
(Circle one in each row)

	Not at all	Not Much	Some	Great Deal	Don't Know
a. An issue-oriented caucus..................	1	2	3	4	0
b. Your state delegation.....................	1	2	3	4	0
c. Delegates who belong to the same organization(s) you do.....................	1	2	3	4	0
d. Delegates who belong to the same political party you do.....................	1	2	3	4	0

19. Which of the following BEST describes how you think of yourself at the Houston conference?
(Circle one)

1. As an individual delegate
2. As a member of a state delegation
3. As a member of an issue-oriented caucus
4. As a representative of a particular organization
0. Don't know

SECTION II. GENERAL POLITICAL EXPERIENCE AND OPINIONS

20. How would you describe your general political views?
(Circle one)

1. Radical
2. Very liberal
3. Somewhat liberal
4. Moderate
5. Somewhat conservative
6. Very conservative
7. Extremely conservative

21. Have you ever attended a Democratic or Republican national convention as a delegate or alternate?
(Circle one)

1. No, I never did
2. Yes, once
3. Yes, twice
4. Yes, three or more times

22. How would you feel about serving as a delegate to a national political party convention in the future?
(Circle one)

1. Very positive
2. Mostly positive
3. Mixed or Don't Know
4. Mostly negative
5. Very negative

23. Which of the following best describes your political party preference?
(Circle one)

      1. Strongly Republican
      2. Republican
      3. Independent, but closer to Republican
      4. Independent
      5. Independent, but closer to Democratic
      6. Democratic
      7. Strongly Democratic
      8. Other party

24. Have you been a member of your IWY State Coordinating Committee?

      1. Yes
      2. No

25. How active have you been politically in recent years on each of the following levels?
(Political activity of ANY kind, not just party politics)
(Circle one in each row)

	Not at All	Somewhat	Very	Extremely
a. Precinct or neighborhood	1	2	3	4
b. Town or city	1	2	3	4
c. State	1	2	3	4
d. National	1	2	3	4

26. How much INTEREST do you have personally in holding an ELECTED PUBLIC OFFICE at each of the following levels?
(Circle one in each row)

	None	A Little	Moderate	High	Don't Know
a. National level	1	2	3	4	0
b. State level	1	2	3	4	0
c. Local level	1	2	3	4	0

27. How much INTEREST do you have personally in holding an ELECTED POLITICAL PARTY POSITION at each of the following levels?
(Circle one in each row)

	None	A Little	Moderate	High	Don't Know
a. National level	1	2	3	4	0
b. State level	1	2	3	4	0
c. Local level	1	2	3	4	0

28. How much INTEREST do you have personally in holding an ELECTED OFFICE in a WOMEN'S RIGHTS ORGANIZATION at each of the following levels?
(Circle one in each row)

	None	A Little	Moderate	High	Don't Know
a. National level	1	2	3	4	0
b. State level	1	2	3	4	0
c. Local level	1	2	3	4	0

29. Do you think you WILL hold an ELECTED OFFICE of the following sorts sometime in the future?
(Circle one in each row)

	Yes	No	Don't Know
a. National Public Office	1	2	0
b. State Public Office	1	2	0
c. Local Public Office	1	2	0
d. National Political party position	1	2	0
e. State Political party position	1	2	0
f. Local Political party position	1	2	0

30. A. Have you ever held public office? (Circle one in column A)
    B. Have you ever held a political party position (Circle one in column B)

	A Public Office	B Political Party
Yes, both elected & appointed	1	1
Yes, elected only	2	2
Yes, appointed only	3	3
No	4	4

31. If you could achieve national prominence as a leader in ONLY ONE of the following ways, which one would you MOST PREFER?
(Circle one)
   1. Elected public official
   2. Appointed public official
   3. Elected political party officer
   4. Appointed political party officer
   5. Women's rights organization officer
   6. Job-related organization officer
   7. None of these
   0. Don't know

32. Has any member of the family you grew up in ever held any of the following political offices?
(Circle one in each row)

	Yes	No
a. Local office (eg. mayor, city council)	1	2
b. State office (e.g. governor, state legislator, judge)	1	2
c. National office (eg. Senator, federal judge, Congressman) ..	1	2

33. Have (or are) any of the following people in your life been active politically? (eg. ran for or held public office, active in political party or political organization)
(Circle one in each row)

	Yes	No	Does not apply
a. Your mother	1	2	
b. Your father	1	2	
c. Your brother	1	2	8
d. Your sister..........	1	2	8
e. Your spouse	1	2	8

34. Since you came of voting age, how often have you voted in (A) NATIONAL elections? (B) LOCAL elections?
(Circle one in each column)

	A National	B Local
Every election................	1	1
Most elections	2	2
Some elections	3	3
None or hardly any elections ..	4	4
Not yet of voting age	5	5

35. Which of the following best describes your participation in the 1976 Presidential election?
(Circle one)
1. Campaigned and voted for Carter
2. Voted for Carter, but did not campaign for him
3. Voted for Ford, but did not campaign for him
4. Campaigned and voted for Ford
5. Voted for someone other than Ford or Carter
6. Did not vote in 1976 election
7. Not yet of voting age in 1976

36. When you vote in a general election, do you vote a straight party ticket?
(Circle one)
1. All the time
2. Most of the time
3. Some of the time
4. Almost never
5. Never
6. Do not vote
7. Not yet of voting age

37. Enter in the boxes below, the NUMBER of groups or organizations you belong to of each type listed. Do NOT count any organization in which you are employed, but DO count informal local groups as well as formal national organizations. (If you do not belong to any group of a given type, enter "00" in the box.)

a. [ ]   CIVIC organizations (eg. environmental, better government, youth, energy)

b. [ ]   CIVIL RIGHTS organizations (eg. ACLU, racial/ethnic rights, local civil rights coalitions)

c. [ ]   EDUCATIONAL organizations (eg. PTA, Alumnae associations, AAUW, local school-improvement or alternative education groups)

d. [ ]   FEMINIST organizations (eg. NOW, WEAL, women's consciousness raising or support groups)

e. [ ]   JOB-RELATED organizations (eg. unions, professional associations, FEW)

f. [ ]   POLITICAL organizations (eg. political party, League of Women Voters, DSOC, Women's Political Caucus, issue-oriented groups or coalitions, eg. abortion, ERA)

g. [ ]   RELIGIOUS organizations (eg. church, synagogue, missionary society, Hadassah)

h. [ ]   SERVICE organizations (eg. Rotary, veterans, Altrusa, Zonta, crisis groups, health service groups)

i. [ ]   SOCIAL OR CULTURAL organizations (eg. country club, symphony, gallery, craft clubs, sports or garden organizations)

j. [ ]   OTHER organizations, not classifiable above

38. Thinking over the full range of groups or organizations you belong to:

A. What is their general political perspective?
(Circle one)

1. All or mostly radical
2. All or mostly liberal
3. All or mostly conservative
4. Mixed radical and liberal
5. Mixed liberal and conservative
6. Too varied to classify
0. Don't know

B. What is the predominant size and scale of the groups and organizations you belong to?
(Circle one)

    1. Mostly small, local
    2. Mostly large, national
    3. Too varied to classify
    0. Don't know

C. What is the general sex composition of the groups and organizations you belong to?
(Circle one)

    1. Mostly women-only
    2. Mostly women-predominant
    3. Mostly mixed men-women
    4. Mostly men-predominant
    5. Mostly men-only
    6. Too varied to classify
    0. Don't know

D. Apart from your participation in IWY activities, are you MORE or LESS active now than a few years ago in organizations that deal exclusively or primarily with women's issues?
(Circle one)

    1. MORE active in such groups now
    2. LESS active in such groups now
    3. NO change over the past few years
    4. Have never been active in organizations primarily dealing with women's issues
    0. Don't know

39. How would you rate yourself on each of the following things?
(Circle one in each row)

	Very Low	Low	Moder- ate	High	Very High	Don't Know
a. Speaking well before a large audience	1	2	3	4	5	0
b. Knowledge of parliamentary procedures	1	2	3	4	5	0
c. Remaining alert for long hours at a time	1	2	3	4	5	0
d. Getting acquainted with a large number of people ...	1	2	3	4	5	0
e. Debating an issue well	1	2	3	4	5	0
f. Accepting compromises well	1	2	3	4	5	0

40. How would you describe the general political position concerning SEX EQUALITY taken by EACH of the following persons?
   A. You yourself (Circle one in Column A)
   B. Your spouse (Please answer even if now separated or divorced; if never married, circle "8" in Column B)
   C. Your best friend (Circle one in Column C)
   D. Your oldest son (If you have no son OVER 12 YEARS OF AGE, circle "8" in Column D)
   E. Your oldest daughter (1f you have no daughter OVER 12, circle "8" in Column E)

	A You	B Spouse	C Friend	D Son	E Daughter
Strongly Feminist	1	1	1	1	1
Moderately Feminist	2	2	2	2	2
Mixed	3	3	3	3	3
Moderately Anti-Feminist	4	4	4	4	4
Strongly Anti-Feminist	5	5	5	5	5
Don't Know	0	0	0	0	0
Does not apply		8	8	8	8

41. Have you given time and/or money to actively SUPPORT or OPPOSE the following social movements?
   (Circle one in each row)

	Yes, Actively SUPPORT	Yes, Actively OPPOSE	No, Not Active
a. Anti-abortion	1	2	3
b. Anti-ERA	1	2	3
c. Anti-nuclear energy	1	2	3
d. Anti-war	1	2	3
e. Civil rights	1	2	3
f. Cooperation with Third World people or countries ...	1	2	3
g. Pro-abortion	1	2	3
h. Pro-ERA	1	2	3
i. Pro-environmental protection	1	2	3
j. Zero Population Growth	1	2	3

42. Rate the following tactics on how well you think they contribute to the achievement of greater equality for women.
   (Circle one in each row)

	Very Poor Tactic	Poor Tactic	Not Sure	Good Tactic	Very Good Tactic
a. Lobbying legislatures on women's issues	1	2	3	4	5
b. Sit-ins to dramatize a bad situation affecting women	1	2	3	4	5
c. Forming coalitions to elect more women to public office	1	2	3	4	5
d. Civil disobedience when other tactics fail	1	2	3	4	5
e. Pressure on state and national leaders to appoint more women	1	2	3	4	5
f. Public demonstrations/marches on women's issues	1	2	3	4	5
g. Boycotts of firms discriminating against women	1	2	3	4	5

43. Indicate whether or not you think it should be possible for a pregnant woman to obtain a legal abortion under each of the following circumstances.
(Circle one in each row)

	Yes	No	Don't Know
a. If there is a strong chance of serious defect in the baby	1	2	0
b. If she is married and does not want any more children	1	2	0
c. If a woman's own health is seriously endangered by the pregnancy	1	2	0
d. If the family has a very low income and cannot afford any more children .	1	2	0
e. If she is not married and does not want to marry the man	1	2	0

44. Do you favor or oppose the use of public funds to pay for abortions?
(Circle one)

1. Strongly favor
2. Favor
3. Mixed, or Don't Know
4. Oppose
5. Strongly oppose

45. How much SUPPORT do you think there is among each of the groups listed below for political and economic change that would increase the equality of the sexes?
(Circle one in each row)

	Strong Support	More Support than Opposition	Mixed or Neutral	More Opposition than Support	Strong Opposition	Don't Know
a. The General Public	1	2	3	4	5	0
b. The Congress	1	2	3	4	5	0
c. The Courts	1	2	3	4	5	0
d. Labor Union Leaders	1	2	3	4	5	0
e. Labor Union Members	1	2	3	4	5	0
f. Employers	1	2	3	4	5	0
g. Mass Media	1	2	3	4	5	0
h. The MEN in your community	1	2	3	4	5	0
i. The WOMEN in your community . .	1	2	3	4	5	0
j. Your MEN friends	1	2	3	4	5	0
k. Your WOMEN friends	1	2	3	4	5	0

46. Which of the following best describes your idea of the kind of society in which sex equality would be possible.
(Circle ONE)

1. Sex equality would require a radical change in our political and economic system.
2. Sex equality can be achieved within our present political and economic system.
3. Sex equality is not desirable.
4. Sex equality can not be achieved in any society.
5. Sex equality already exists in the United States.
0. Don't know

47. Indicate whether you AGREE or DISAGREE with each of the following statements about sex roles in American society.

(Circle one in each row)

	Strongly Agree	Agree	Not Sure	Disagree	Strongly Disagree
a. It is more important for a wife to help her husband than to have a career herself	1	2	3	4	5
b. Preschool children are likely to suffer if their mothers work	1	2	3	4	5
c. Men and women should be paid the same money if they do the same work	1	2	3	4	5
d. It is much better for everyone involved if the man is the achiever outside the home and the woman takes care of the home and family	1	2	3	4	5
e. A working mother can establish just as warm and secure a relationship with her children as a mother who does not work	1	2	3	4	5
f. A woman should have exactly the same job opportunities as a man	1	2	3	4	5
g. Men should share the work around the house with women such as doing dishes, cleaning and so forth ...	1	2	3	4	5
h. A woman's job should be kept for her when she is having a baby	1	2	3	4	5
i. Women should be considered as seriously as men for jobs as executives or politicians or even President	1	2	3	4	5

48. Indicate whether you AGREE or DISAGREE with each of the following views towards the IWY Commission.

(Circle one in each row)

	Strongly Agree	Agree	Not Sure	Disagree	Strongly Disagree
a. The IWY Commission is an appropriate use of public funds	1	2	3	4	5
b. The IWY Commission is NOT an effective way to try to improve the status of women	1	2	3	4	5
c. By and large the IWY Commission has done a poor job	1	2	3	4	5
d. Congress should pass a new law to continue the IWY Commission beyond March 1978	1	2	3	4	5

49. Indicate whether you are POLITICALLY ACTIVE or NOT on each of the following issues AS THEY AFFECT WOMEN (Do not count job-related activity.)
(Circle one in each row)

	Not Active	Somewhat Active	Very Active
a. Abortion	1	2	3
b. Child care	1	2	3
c. Education	1	2	3
d. Employment	1	2	3
e. ERA ratification	1	2	3
f. Family planning	1	2	3
g. Farming/rural life	1	2	3
h. Health care	1	2	3
i. Homemaker legal rights ...	1	2	3
j. Housing	1	2	3
k. International relations	1	2	3
l. Mass media	1	2	3
m. Rape	1	2	3
n. Retirement benefits	1	2	3
o. Sexual Preference	1	2	3
p. Sexuality	1	2	3

50. To what extent do you work for women's rights in your present job?
(Circle one)
1. A great deal
2. Somewhat
3. Not much
4. Not at all
5. Not employed

51. Here are some statements about which people disagree nowadays. For each statement, circle whether you AGREE or DISAGREE.
(Circle one in each row)

	Strongly Agree	Agree	Not Sure	Disagree	Strongly Disagree
a. It's more important for women to get along with other women than with men	1	2	3	4	5
b. People can not be considered Feminists if they oppose the ERA	1	2	3	4	5
c. I would not place a pre-school child of mine in a child-care center no matter how good it was	1	2	3	4	5
d. I get along better with men than with women	1	2	3	4	5
e. People can not be considered Feminists if they oppose abortion	1	2	3	4	5
f. A "women-only" club or restaurant is discriminatory	1	2	3	4	5
g. A pre-school child would benefit from attending a child care center	1	2	3	4	5
h. The lesbian-rights issue is doing more harm than good to the women's movement	1	2	3	4	5
i. I would rather have a relative take care of my child than a child-care center	1	2	3	4	5
j. People can not be considered Feminists if they do not work for lesbian rights	1	2	3	4	5
k. Women in top leadership positions seldom do anything for other women	1	2	3	4	5
l. A "men-only" club or restaurant is discriminatory	1	2	3	4	5

52. How much INEQUALITY among men and women do you think presently exists in each of the following areas?
(Circle one in each row)

	None	Not Much	Some	Great Deal	Don't Know
a. Employment	1	2	3	4	0
b. Home maintenance	1	2	3	4	0
c. Marriage	1	2	3	4	0
d. Parenthood	1	2	3	4	0
e. Politics	1	2	3	4	0

53. Rate the extent to which you believe it is IMPORTANT for men and women to PAR-
TICIPATE EQUALLY in each of the following areas.
(Circle one in each row)

	Not at All	Not Very	Very	Extremely	Don't Know
a. Employment	1	2	3	4	0
b. Home maintenance	1	2	3	4	0
c. Marriage	1	2	3	4	0
d. Parenthood	1	2	3	4	0
e. Politics	1	2	3	4	0

SECTION III. PERSONAL AND BACKGROUND INFORMATION

54. What is your sex?
1. Female
2. Male

55. What is your current marital status?
(Circle one)
1. Single
2. Married
3. Separated or divorced
4. Widowed

56. What is your age? (Write directly in the box below)

57. How many children do you have?
(Circle one)
0   1   2   3   4   5   6   7   8 +

58. What is the age of your YOUNGEST child, to his/her nearest birthday?
(Write directly in the box below, using "00" if you have NO children.)

59. What is your share of the responsibility for the care of your child(ren)? (If you have no children,
circle "0". If you have no children under 12 years of age, circle "1".)
0. Have no children
1. Have no children under 12 years of age
2. All or almost all my responsibility
3. Mostly my responsibility
4. About half my responsibility
5. Less than half my responsibility
6. Little or no responsibility

60. How many years have you lived in your present community? (Write directly in the box below, using "01" for anything less than ONE year.)

```
┌──────────┐
│          │
│          │
└──────────┘
```

61. Which of the following best describes who lives with you?
(Circle one)

01. Live alone
11. Spouse only
12. Spouse and child(ren)
13. Spouse and relative(s)
14. Spouse and non-related adult(s) (eg. friend, tenant)
15. Spouse, child(ren) and non-related adult
16. Spouse, child(ren) and relative(s)
21. Child(ren) only
22. Child(ren) and relative(s)
23. Child(ren) and non-related adult (eg. friend, lover)
30. Relative(s) only
40. Non-related Adult only (eg. friend, lover, tenant)
50. Other

62. To what racial or ethnic group do you belong?
(Circle one)

1. White
2. Black
3. Hispanic origin
4. Asian origin
5. American Indian or Alaskan native
6. Pacific Islander
7. Other

63. In which social class would you place yourself?
(Circle one)

1. Lower class
2. Working class
3. Middle class
4. Upper middle class
5. Upper class
0. Don't Know

64. What social class best describes the family you grew up in?
(Circle one)

1. Lower class
2. Working class
3. Middle class
4. Upper middle class
5. Upper class
0. Don't Know

65. A. Where did you grow up? (Circle one in column A)
    B. Where do you live now? (Circle one in column B)

	A Grew Up	B Live Now
On a farm	1	1
In a rural area, not on farm	2	2
Small town or city (500-24,999)	3	3
Medium sized central city (25,000-300,000)	4	4
Suburb of medium sized city	5	5
Large size central city (over 300,000)	6	6
Suburb of large city	7	7

66. A. In what state or U.S. territory do you NOW LIVE? (Locate the name of your state of residence on the list below and enter the code number that appears in brackets, in the box below.)

B. In what state or U.S. territory were you BORN? (Use the code number that appears in brackets following the name of the state of your birth. If you were born in a foreign country, enter the code number "00" in the box.)

Alabama (41)	Illinois (21)	Nebraska (28)	Samoa (94)
Alaska (81)	Indiana (22)	Nevada (74)	South Carolina (48)
Arizona (61)	Iowa (23)	New Hampshire (04)	South Dakota (31)
Arkansas (42)	Kansas (24)	New Jersey (12)	Tennessee (54)
California (82)	Kentucky (52)	New Mexico (62)	Texas (64)
Colorado (71)	Louisiana (45)	New York (13)	Trust territory (95)
Connecticut (01)	Maine (02)	North Carolina (47)	Utah (75)
Delaware (11)	Maryland (53)	North Dakota (29)	Vermont (06)
Dist. of Col. (51)	Massachusetts (03)	Ohio (30)	Virgin Islands (96)
Florida (43)	Michigan (25)	Oklahoma (63)	Virginia (49)
Georgia (44)	Minnesota (26)	Oregon (84)	Washington (85)
Guam (91)	Mississippi (46)	Pennsylvania (14)	West Virginia (55)
Hawaii (92)	Missouri (27)	Puerto Rico (93)	Wisconsin (32)
Idaho (72)	Montana (73)	Rhode Island (05)	Wyoming (76)

67. Are you currently attending any school, college or university?
(Circle one)

    1. Yes, full time
    2. Yes, part time
    3. No

68. What is your current employment status?
(Circle one)

    1. Full time job plus part time job(s)
    2. Full time job only
    3. Part time job(s) only
    4. Unemployed and looking for a job
    8. Not employed

69. Who is your employer? (If you hold more than one job, code for the job with the longest number of hours. If you are not currently employed, code in terms of your LAST job).
(Circle one)

      1. Federal government
      2. State or local government
      3. Private business/corporation
      4. Non-profit service organization
      5. Self-employed, free lance
      8. Never employed

70. Which of the following best describes how you feel about your job compared to other parts of your life.
(Circle one)

      1. My job is the most important part of my life.
      2. My job is more important than my private life.
      3. My job is just as important as my private life.
      4. My job is less important than my private life.
      8. No regular paid employment
      0. Don't know

71. What was the approximate annual income YOU YOURSELF EARNED last year, before taxes?
(Circle one)

0.	None, not employed	5.	$20,000-$24,999
1.	Under $4,999	6.	$25,000-$29,999
2.	$5,000-$9,999	7.	$30,000-$49,999
3.	$10,000-$14,999	8.	$50,000 and over
4.	$15,000-$19,999		

72. What was the approximate TOTAL ANNUAL INCOME of your PRESENT FAMILY last year, before taxes, from all sources?
(Circle one)

1.	Under $4,999	5.	$20,000-$24,999
2.	$5,000-$9,999	6.	$25,000-$29,999
3.	$10,000-$14,999	7.	$30,000-$49,999
4.	$15,000-$19,999	8.	$50,000 and over

73. Has the amount of money you live on per year undergone any major increase or decrease over the last few years?
(Circle one)

      1. Annual income VERY MUCH LOWER now
      2. Annual income SOMEWHAT LOWER now
      3. No significant change in annual income
      4. Annual income SOMEWHAT HIGHER now
      5. Annual income VERY MUCH HIGHER now
      0. Don't know

74. Which of the following best describes the current source of your household income?
(Circle one)

      1. Only spouse's earnings
      2. Largely spouse's earnings
      3. About equally from spouse and my earnings
      4. Largely my earnings
      5. Only my earnings
      6. Mostly from welfare
      7. Mostly from pension/social security/savings
      8. Other

75. What is your occupation? (Code in terms of your main line of work, whether or not you are currently employed. If you work in more than one occupation, code in terms of MAIN job.)
(Circle ONLY One).

- 1. Professional /technical (eg. teacher, lawyer, social worker, nurse)
- 2. Manager/administrator (eg. store owner/manager, union official, government administrator)
- 3. Sales/clerical/office machine worker (eg. salesperson, secretary, computer technician, typist)
- 4. Craft worker (eg. plumber, potter, lab technician)
- 5. Operative (eg. factory assembler, bus driver, presser)
- 6. Farmer, farm worker
- 7. Service worker (eg. building maintenance or food service worker, hairdresser, school guard, child care worker)
- 8. Other

*Which of the following professional or technical occupations are you in? (If you work at more than one occupation, code in terms of your MAIN job.)
(Circle one)

01. Accountant	12. Pharmacist, dietitian
02. Architect	13. Physician, dentist
03. Artist, sculptor	14. Research scientist, natural or social
04. Author, poet	15. Social/welfare worker
05. Clergy, religious worker	16. Teacher, college/university
06. Editor, reporter	17. Teacher, elementary/high school
07. Engineer, Physical or Computer Scientist	18. Teacher, pre-school
08. Lawyer, judge	19. Teacher, other
09. Librarian	20. Therapist/counselor
10. Nurse, dental hygienist	21. Other
11. Performing artist (drama, dance, music)	

76. What is your best estimate of the proportion of women in your occupation? (Code in terms of your main line of work, whether or not you are currently employed).
(Circle one)

- 1. Largely women (80% or more women)
- 2. More women than men (55 to 79% women)
- 3. Roughly equal proportions of men and women (45% to 54% women)
- 4. More men than women (20% to 44% women)
- 5. Largely men (Less than 20% women)
- 8. Never employed
- 0. Don't know

77. A. How many years of education have YOU completed? (Circle one in column A)
B. How many years of education has YOUR SPOUSE completed? (Circle one in column B. Please answer even if you are now separated, divorced or widowed.)

A	B	
You	Your Spouse	
	0	Never married
1	1	Some High School or less (11 years or less)
2	2	High school graduate (12 years)
3	3	Community college graduate or Some College (13-15 years)
4	4	College graduate (16 years)
5	5	Some graduate work
6	6	Master's degree (M.A., M.S., M.S.W.)
7	7	Ph.D., M.D., Ed.D.
8	8	LL.B., LL.D.

78. What is your religious preference?
(Circle one)

01	Agnostic	11	Jewish
02	Atheist	12	Latter Day Saints, Mormon
03	Baptist	13	Lutheran
04	Catholic	14	Methodist
05	Christian Scientist	15	Pentecostal or Assembly of God
06	Church of Christ	16	Presbyterian
07	Church of God	17	Unitarian
08	Congregational	18	United Church of Christ
09	Eastern Orthodox	19	Other
10	Episcopalian		

79. How often do you attend religious services?
(Circle one)

1. Never
2. Almost never
3. Once or twice a year
4. Several times a year
5. Once or twice a month
6. Almost every week
7. At least once a week

That is the end of the questionnaire. Thank you for your help.
Please return your questionnaire in the envelope provided, at your earliest convenience.

February Survey (1978)

SECTION I. THE HOUSTON EXPERIENCE

1. Which of the following describes your relationship to the National Women's Conference?
(Circle one)
   1. Elected *delegate*
   2. Elected *alternate* who became a delegate for part or all of the conference
   3. Elected *alternate* who remained an alternate
   4. Appointed *delegate-at-large*
   5. Current National Commissioner
   6. Former National Commissioner
   7. Secretariat, professional staff
   8. Secretariat, support staff

2. Did you attend the National Women's Conference in Houston?
(Circle one)
   1. Yes (GO to Q. 3)
   *2. No

→ *IF NO:

> a. Which of the following is the MAIN reason you did not attend the conference?
> (Circle one)
>   1. *Illness*: self or family member
>   2. *Financial*: expenses not reimbursed by IWY
>   3. *Job*: responsibilities and/or problems
>   4. *Family*: responsibilities and/or problems
>   5. *Political*: disapproval of IWY and/or conference plans
>   6. Other
>
> **IF YOU DID NOT ATTEND, PLEASE SKIP TO Q. 35, Page 9**

3. When did you ARRIVE in Houston?
(Circle one)
   1. Thursday, Nov. 17 or earlier
   2. Friday, Nov. 18
   3. Saturday, Nov. 19
   4. Sunday, Nov. 20 or later

4. When did you LEAVE Houston?
(Circle one)
   1. Sunday, Nov. 20 or earlier
   2. Monday, Nov. 21
   3. Tuesday, Nov. 22 or later

5. Which of the following best describes your role at the Houston meeting?
(Circle one)
   1. a KEY PERSON, someone whose views were sought and taken into account
   2. an IMPORTANT PERSON, someone whose views were paid attention to
   3. an INTERESTED PARTICIPANT, someone who tried to make their views known
   4. an INTERESTED BYSTANDER, someone concerned with the issues but who did not influence decisions
   5. NOT MUCH OF A PARTICIPANT
   0. Don't know

6. Which of the following BEST describes how you thought of yourself at the Houston conference?
(Circle *one*)
   1. As an individual delegate
   2. As a member of a state delegation
   3. As a member of an issue-oriented caucus
   4. As a representative of a particular organization
   5. As an IWY Commission or staff member
   6. Other
   0. Don't know

367

7. Did you attend any meetings of the following CAUCUSES during the Houston conference?
(Circle one in each row)

	NO, None	YES, One	YES, more than one
a. Asian	1	2	3
b. Black	1	2	3
c. Disabled	1	2	3
d. Hispanic	1	2	3
e. Labor	1	2	3
f. Lesbian	1	2	3
g. "Majority" (anti-plan)	1	2	3
h. Native American	1	2	3
i. "Pro-Plan"	1	2	3
j. Welfare	1	2	3
k. Youth	1	2	3

8. While you were in Houston, did you attend any of the following events?
(Circle one in each row)

	Yes	No
a. Torch Rally, Friday afternoon	1	2
b. ERA Ratification Assembly, Friday	1	2
c. ERA Reception, Friday evening	1	2
d. NOW reception, Friday evening	1	2
e. Exhibits in Albert Thomas Convention Center	1	2
f. Seneca Falls South activities	1	2
g. Peace & Disarmament Hearing, Sunday	1	2
h. International Visitors reception	1	2
i. Workshops/lectures	1	2
j. Music Hall gala, Sunday evening	1	2

9. How much did you work with each of the following groups during the Houston conference?
(Circle one in each row)

	Not at all	Not Much	Some	Great Deal
a. An issue-oriented caucus	1	2	3	4
b. Your state delegation	1	2	3	4
c. Delegates who belong to the same organization(s) you do	1	2	3	4
d. Delegates who belong to the same political party you do	1	2	3	4
e. Individual IWY Commissioners	1	2	3	4
f. IWY Secretariat staff	1	2	3	4
g. Non-delegate observers	1	2	3	4
h. Pro-Plan caucus	1	2	3	4
i. "Majority" (anti-plan) Caucus	1	2	3	4

10. Were you personally involved in any effort to AMEND or SUBSTITUTE a resolution in the Plan of Action?
(Circle one)

    1. No (Go to Q. 11)

    2. Yes

    → *IF YES:

    a. Did your effort begin before you arrived in Houston or during your stay in Houston?
       (Circle one)

         1. Before I arrived
         2. During my stay

    b. Did your effort involve any of the following groups?
       (Circle one in each row)

	Yes	No
(1) Your state delegation	1	2
(2) A caucus	1	2
(3) An organization you belong to	1	2

    c. Were you involved in the efforts that SUCCEEDED in changing any of the following resolutions in the Plan of Action?
       (Circle one in each row)

	Yes	No
(1) Disabled Women	1	2
(2) Education	1	2
(3) Minority Women	1	2
(4) Older Women	1	2
(5) Rape	1	2
(6) Rural Women	1	2
(7) Women, Welfare & Poverty	1	2

11. When did you first hear about the "Pro-Plan Caucus"?
(Circle one)

    1. Before leaving home for Houston
    2. On the way to Houston
    3. After arriving in Houston
    4. I don't remember when

12. Which of the following best describes your feeling about the Pro-Plan Caucus . . .
A. While you were in Houston (Circle one in column A)
B. Now (Circle one in column B)

	A In Houston	B Now
Enthusiastic support	1	1
Moderate support	2	2
Too mixed to say	3	3
Moderate opposition	4	4
Extreme opposition	5	5
Don't Know	0	0

13. What proportion of the total delegate body to the Houston conference would you estimate are members or supporters of the Democratic Party?
(Circle one)

    1. 90% or more
    2. 80% to 89%
    3. 70% to 79%
    4. 60% to 69%
    5. 50% to 59%
    6. 40% to 49%
    7. Less than 40%
    0. Don't know

QUESTIONS 14 through 17 SHOULD BE ANSWERED BY **ELECTED DELEGATES AND ALTERNATES** ONLY. ALL OTHERS PLEASE SKIP TO Q. 18

(ELECTED DELEGATES AND ALTERNATES ONLY)

14. How many times did your state delegation meet (a) BEFORE the Houston conference? (b) DURING the conference? and (c) SINCE the conference?
(Circle one in each row)

	None	Once	2 or 3 times	4 or more times	Don't Know
a. Before the conference	1	2	3	4	0
b. During the conference	1	2	3	4	0
c. Since the conference	1	2	3	4	0

15. How much consensus was there in your state delegation on the Plan of Action?
(Circle one)
1. Very High, Pro-Plan consensus
2. High Pro-Plan consensus: most delegates supported all but a few resolutions
3. Delegation split on most resolutions
4. High Anti-Plan consensus: most delegates opposed all but a few resolutions
5. Very high, Anti-Plan consensus
0. Don't Know

16. Did you carry any of the following responsibilities in your state delegation?
(Circle one)
1. No special responsibilities
2. Yes, chair or co-chair
3. Yes, vice-chair
4. Yes, committee chair or task force leader
5. Yes, committee member or task force member
6. Yes, other

17. A. What proportion of the delegates from your state are you NOW personally acquainted with?
(Circle one in column A)

B. What proportion of the delegates from your state do you think share YOUR political views on women's issues? (Circle one in column B)

	A Proportion Known Personally Now	B Proportion Share My Political Views
80% or more	1	1
50% to 79%	2	2
25% to 49%	3	3
Less than 25%	4	4
None	5	5
Don't Know	0	0

18. From Saturday morning through Monday noon, the Houston conference was in plenary session for approximately 23 hours. What is your best estimate of the number of hours you attended the plenary sessions?
(Circle one)
1. 22 to 23 hours
2. 20 to 21 hours
3. 15 to 19 hours
4. 10 to 14 hours
5. 5 to 9 hours
6. Less than 5 hours
0. Don't know

19. During the plenary sessions, how often did you do each of the following?
(Circle one in each row)

		Not at all	Once	A few Times	Many Times
a.	Stood on microphone lines	1	2	3	4
b.	Attended a caucus meeting	1	2	3	4
c.	Asked someone to explain a procedure	1	2	3	4
d.	Left the floor to just "get away from it all"	1	2	3	4
e.	Voted for something you personally opposed	1	2	3	4
f.	Dozed off or lost track of what was going on	1	2	3	4
g.	Voted against something you personally supported	1	2	3	4
h.	Explained a procedure to someone else	1	2	3	4
i.	Looked to others for how you should vote	1	2	3	4
j.	Tried to persuade someone how to vote	1	2	3	4
k.	Passed along messages as part of floor operations	1	2	3	4

20. If time had permitted, would you have preferred to further amend any of the resolutions adopted in Houston?
(Circle one)

1. No
2. Yes, one or two
3. Yes, three or four
4. Yes, five or more
0. Don't know

21. Many people at the Houston conference felt great time pressure because of the length of the agenda and the shortness of the conference. If you had to decide to reduce the number of resolutions OR add a day to the duration of the conference, which would you do?
(Circle one)

1. Reduce the number of resolutions
2. Add a day to the conference
3. Neither: it was fine as it was
4. Both: more time and fewer resolutions would have made for a better conference
0. Don't know

22. **A.** As best you remember, how did you vote on each of the resolutions in the Plan of Action? (If you were not on the floor for the vote, indicate how you *would have* voted were you present. If you were an *Alternate,* indicate how you *would have* voted if you were on the floor.)
(Circle one in each row in Column A)

B. If time, technology or the rules had permitted a secret ballot rather than a standing vote, how would you have voted for each of the resolutions?
(Circle one in each row in Column B)

| | A | | | B | | |
| | **Actual Vote** | | | **Would have Voted on a Secret Ballot** | | |
	FOR	Abstain or Don't Know	AGAINST	FOR	Abstain or Don't Know	AGAINST
a. Arts and Humanities	1	2	3	1	2	3
b. Battered Women	1	2	3	1	2	3
c. Business	1	2	3	1	2	3
d. Child Abuse	1	2	3	1	2	3
e. Child Care	1	2	3	1	2	3
f. Credit	1	2	3	1	2	3
g. Disabled Women (Substitute)	1	2	3	1	2	3
h. Education (amended)	1	2	3	1	2	3
i. Elective & Appointive Office	1	2	3	1	2	3
j. Employment	1	2	3	1	2	3
k. Equal Rights Amendment	1	2	3	1	2	3
l. Health	1	2	3	1	2	3
m. Homemakers	1	2	3	1	2	3
n. Insurance	1	2	3	1	2	3
o. International Affairs	1	2	3	1	2	3
p. Media	1	2	3	1	2	3
q. Minority Women (substitute)	1	2	3	1	2	3
r. Offenders	1	2	3	1	2	3
s. Older Women (amended)	1	2	3	1	2	3
t. Rape (amended)	1	2	3	1	2	3
u. Reproductive Freedom	1	2	3	1	2	3
v. Rural Women (amended)	1	2	3	1	2	3
w. Sexual Preference	1	2	3	1	2	3
x. Statistics	1	2	3	1	2	3
y. Women, Welfare & Poverty (substitute)	1	2	3	1	2	3
z. Women's Department	1	2	3	1	2	3
aa. Committee of the Conference (new)	1	2	3	1	2	3

23. Do you think the political differences between "Pro-Plan" and "Majority" anti-plan delegates were REDUCED or INCREASED as a result of the conference?
(Circle one)

1. Differences were *reduced*
2. No change
3. Differences were *increased*
0. Don't know

24. How would you compare the Pro-Plan and Anti-Plan delegates in the extent to which they voted as a bloc?
(Circle one)

1. Pro-Plan delegates did more bloc voting
2. Anti-Plan delegates did more bloc voting
3. No difference: both groups did a lot of bloc voting
4. No difference: neither group did much bloc voting
0. Don't know

25. How would you compare the Pro-Plan and Anti-Plan delegates in the extent to which they voted against their individual beliefs?
(Circle one)

    1. Pro-Plan delegates did more voting against their individual beliefs
    2. Anti-Plan delegates did more voting against their individual beliefs
    3. No difference: both groups did a lot of voting against their beliefs
    4. No difference: neither group did much voting against their beliefs
    0. Don't know

26. Political controversy and emotional intensity in the delegate body were greater on some resolutions than on others. For each of the four resolutions listed in columns A, B, C and D below, rate the extent to which you were ENTHUSED or DEPRESSED when it passed.
(Circle one in each column)

	A Equal Rights Amendment	B Minority Women (subst.)	C Reproduc- tive Freedom	D Sexual Prefer- ence
Extremely enthusiastic	1	1	1	1
Very enthusiastic	2	2	2	2
Enthusiastic	3	3	3	3
Neutral	4	4	4	4
Depressed	5	5	5	5
Very Depressed	6	6	6	6
Extremely Depressed	7	7	7	7
Don't Know	0	0	0	0

27. If you had it to do over again, would you attend the Houston conference?
(Circle one)

    1. Definitely yes
    2. Probably yes
    3. Not sure
    4. Probably not
    5. Definitely not

28. Here are some opinions about the Houston Conference. Please indicate how much you agree or disagree with each of them.
(Circle one in each row)

	Strongly Agree	Agree	Neu- tral	Dis- Agree	Strongly Disagree	Don't Know
a. Supporting lesbian rights was absolutely critical to the conference	1	2	3	4	5	0
b. Most delegates showed respect for dissenting views	1	2	3	4	5	0
c. The conference was controlled by big city Eastern Democrats	1	2	3	4	5	0
d. The resolutions passed in Houston were "railroaded" through	1	2	3	4	5	0
e. The chair was generally fair in its interpretation of the rules	1	2	3	4	5	0
f. Supporting lesbian rights endangers Congressional implementation of other resolutions in the Plan of Action	1	2	3	4	5	0
g. The resolutions adopted show too much dependence on the federal government	1	2	3	4	5	0
h. No one could get to a mike without the approval of a Pro-Plan floor manager	1	2	3	4	5	0
i. The floor management was inconsistent with a democratic process	1	2	3	4	5	0
j. The conference was one of the peak experiences of my life	1	2	3	4	5	0
k. Mike monitors were fair and helpful to anyone wishing to speak	1	2	3	4	5	0
l. Tight floor management was necessary to get through the long agenda	1	2	3	4	5	0

SECTION II.   CONFERENCE AFTERMATH

29. Rate the extent to which you felt each of the following when you FIRST ARRIVED HOME from the Houston conference.
(Circle one in each row)

	Not at all	A Little	Very	Extremely
a. Happy	1	2	3	4
b. Pessimistic	1	2	3	4
c. Inspired	1	2	3	4
d. Defeated	1	2	3	4
e. Exhilarated	1	2	3	4
f. Disillusioned	1	2	3	4
g. Victorious	1	2	3	4
h. Depressed	1	2	3	4
i. Optimistic	1	2	3	4
j. Angry	1	2	3	4

30. When you returned from Houston, did you do any of the following things?
(Circle one in each row)

	Yes	No
a. Appear on local radio or TV	1	2
b. Give an interview to a local paper	1	2
c. Give a talk about the conference to local group(s) ...	1	2

31. What was your overall reaction to the Houston Conference at each of the following points in time?
(Circle one in each row)

	Very Satis- fied	Somewhat Satis- fied	Mixed	Somewhat Dissatis- fied	Very Dissatis- fied
a. When you were leaving Houston	1	2	3	4	5
b. A week after you got home from Houston ...	1	2	3	4	5
c. Now	1	2	3	4	5

32. What is your best estimate of the number of people you MET FOR THE FIRST TIME in Houston, WITH WHOM YOU PLAN TO KEEP IN TOUCH? (eg, "20", or "00" if you have no plans to keep in touch with people you met.)
(Enter the number in the boxes to the right)

    a.   People from your local community or city ....

    b.   People from outside your city but within your state ......

    c.   People from another state ....

33. To what extent do you think the relationships you formed or reinforced through the Houston conference will contribute to each of the following?
(Circle one in each row)

	Not at all	A Little	Some	Great Deal	Don't Know	Does Not Apply
a. Your personal social life	1	2	3	4	0	8
b. Your political effectiveness in your local community	1	2	3	4	0	8
c. Your political effectiveness at the state and/or na- tional level	1	2	3	4	0	8
d. Your *job* opportunities or effectiveness	1	2	3	4	0	8
e. Your effectiveness as a *volunteer* in organizations ..	1	2	3	4	0	8

34. A. Do you think most delegates came away from the Houston conference feeling more solidary and united as women, or more divided than they were when they arrived? (Circle one in column A)
B. How did the conference affect your own feeling of solidarity with other women? (Circle one in column B)

	A Most Delegates	B You Yourself
Very much more solidary	1	1
Somewhat more solidary	2	2
No change, feel solidary anyway . . .	3	3
No change, feel divided anyway	4	4
Somewhat more divided	5	5
Very much more divided	6	6
Don't know	0	0

35. Which of the following is closest to your view of how pre-school child care services should be funded?
(Circle one)

    1. Completely public funds
    2. Largely public funds
    3. Mixed public and private funds
    4. Largely private funds
    5. Completely private funds
    6. Pre-school child care should be left in the family
    0. Don't know

36. Which of the following is closest to your view of the proper role of the FEDERAL GOVERNMENT in relation to pre-school child care?
(Circle one)

    1. Provide funds, establish standards, and manage the programs
    2. Provide funds and establish standards, but leave program management to the local level
    3. Establish standards, but leave funding and management to the local level
    4. Stay out of the pre-school child-care area altogether
    0. Don't know

37. How do you feel about the establishment of a national health security (or insurance) program by Federal legislation?
(Circle one)

    1. Strongly support
    2. Moderately support
    3. Mixed or Don't Know
    4. Moderately oppose
    5. Strongly oppose

38. How would you feel about serving as a delegate to a NATIONAL POLITICAL PARTY CONVENTION sometime in the future?
(Circle one)

    1. Very positive
    2. Mostly positive
    3. Mixed or Don't Know
    4. Mostly negative
    5. Very negative

39. How would you rate yourself on each of the following things?
(Circle one in each row)

	Very Low	Low	Moder- ate	High	Very High	Don't Know
a. Speaking well before a large audience	1	2	3	4	5	0
b. Knowledge of parliamentary procedures	1	2	3	4	5	0
c. Remaining alert for long hours at a time	1	2	3	4	5	0
d. Getting acquainted with a large number of people . .	1	2	3	4	5	0
e. Debating an issue well	1	2	3	4	5	0
f. Accepting compromises well	1	2	3	4	5	0

40. Looking ahead to the coming year or so, how committed are you to work FOR or AGAINST the implementation of each of the resolutions adopted in Houston?
(Circle one in each row)

	Definitely Work FOR	Probably Work FOR	No Commitment to be Active	Probably Work AGAINST	Definitely Work AGAINST
a. Arts & Humanities ...	1	2	3	4	5
b. Battered Women	1	2	3	4	5
c. Business	1	2	3	4	5
d. Child Abuse	1	2	3	4	5
e. Child Care	1	2	3	4	5
f. Credit	1	2	3	4	5
g. Disabled Women	1	2	3	4	5
h. Education	1	2	3	4	5
i. Elective & Appointive Office	1	2	3	4	5
j. Employment	1	2	3	4	5
k. Equal Rights Amendment	1	2	3	4	5
l. Health	1	2	3	4	5
m. Homemakers	1	2	3	4	5
n. Insurance	1	2	3	4	5
o. International Affairs	1	2	3	4	5
p. Media	1	2	3	4	5
q. Minority Women	1	2	3	4	5
r. Offenders	1	2	3	4	5
s. Older Women	1	2	3	4	5
t. Rape	1	2	3	4	5
u. Reproductive Freedom	1	2	3	4	5
v. Rural Women	1	2	3	4	5
w. Sexual Preference	1	2	3	4	5
x. Statistics	1	2	3	4	5
y. Women, Welfare & Poverty	1	2	3	4	5
z. Committee of the Conference	1	2	3	4	5

41. How much interest do you have personally in holding an ELECTED PUBLIC OFFICE at each of the following levels?
(Circle one in each row)

	None	A Little	Moderate	High	Don't Know
a. National level	1	2	3	4	0
b. State level	1	2	3	4	0
c. Local level	1	2	3	4	0

42. How much interest do you have personally in holding an ELECTED OFFICE in a WOMEN'S RIGHTS ORGANIZATION at each of the following levels?
(Circle one in each row)

	None	A Little	Moderate	High	Don't Know
a. National level	1	2	3	4	0
b. State level	1	2	3	4	0
c. Local level	1	2	3	4	0

43. Do you think you WILL hold an ELECTED OFFICE of the following sorts sometime in the future?
(Circle one in each row)

	Yes	No	Don't Know
a. National Public Office	1	2	0
b. State Public Office	1	2	0
c. Local Public Office	1	2	0

44. If you could achieve national prominence as a leader in ONLY ONE of the following ways, which one would you most prefer?
(Circle one)

1. Elected public official
2. Appointed public official
3. Elected political party officer
4. Appointed political party officer
5. Women's rights organization officer
6. Job-related organization officer
7. Volunteer head of an organization
8. None of these
0. Don't know

45. For each of the following groups, indicate your feeling toward it on what can be called a "feeling thermometer" or "feeling scale," where 1 means NEGATIVE or COLD, a "4" means NEUTRAL (neither cold nor warm), and "7" means POSITIVE or WARM.
(Circle one in each row)

	NEGATIVE (Cold)			NEU-TRAL			POSITIVE (Warm)	Don't Know
a. Anti-abortion groups	1	2	3	4	5	6	7	0
b. Anti-ERA groups	1	2	3	4	5	6	7	0
c. Black/Afro-American groups	1	2	3	4	5	6	7	0
d. Business/professional groups	1	2	3	4	5	6	7	0
e. Chicano/Hispanic/Latino groups	1	2	3	4	5	6	7	0
f. Conservative groups	1	2	3	4	5	6	7	0
g. Farm/rural groups	1	2	3	4	5	6	7	0
h. Labor unions	1	2	3	4	5	6	7	0
i. Lesbian groups	1	2	3	4	5	6	7	0
j. Liberal groups	1	2	3	4	5	6	7	0
k. National IWY Commissioners	1	2	3	4	5	6	7	0
l. National Organization for Women (NOW)	1	2	3	4	5	6	7	0
m. National Women's Political Caucus (NWPC)	1	2	3	4	5	6	7	0
n. Pro-choice abortion groups	1	2	3	4	5	6	7	0
o. Pro-ERA groups	1	2	3	4	5	6	7	0
p. Radical groups	1	2	3	4	5	6	7	0

46. Are you a member of any of the following national organizations?
(Circle one in each row)

	Yes	No
a. Coalition of Labor Union Women (CLUW)	1	2
b. Eagle Forum	1	2
c. Federally Employed Women (FEW)	1	2
d. National Congress of Neighborhood Women	1	2
e. National Gay Task Force	1	2
f. National Abortion Rights Action League	1	2
g. National Organization for Women (NOW)	1	2
h. American Association of University Women	1	2
i. Business & Professional Women's Club	1	2
j. League of Women Voters	1	2

47. If a Second National Women's Conference were called a few years from now, would you want to attend it?
(Circle one)

1. Definitely Yes
2. Probably Yes
3. Not sure
4. Probably Not
5. Definitely Not

48. Which of the following two options do you think is the wiser course to follow in 1978?
(Circle one)

    1. Seek Congressional appropriations to continue the IWY Commission beyond March 31, 1978
    2. Seek private funds and establish a National Assembly of Women independent of government
    3. Do both of the above
    4. Do neither of the above
    0. Don't know

49. If you are willing to share it, could you describe your most memorable experience in connection with the Houston conference?

_____

_____

_____

_____

_____

_____

50. Did you return the first questionnaire in this study in October or November?
(Circle one)

    1. Yes ⟶ YOU MAY END HERE, WITH OUR HEARTY THANKS FOR YOUR COOPERATION.
    2. No ⟶ PLEASE FILL OUT SECTION III, which contains background and other information useful to the study.

SECTION III. PERSONAL AND BACKGROUND INFORMATION. (To be filled out by those who did NOT return an October questionnaire).

51. What is your sex?
    1. Female
    2. Male

52. What is your current marital status?
(Circle one)
    1. Single
    2. Married
    3. Separated or divorced
    4. Widowed

53. What is your age? (Write directly in the box below)

54. How many children do you have?
(Circle one)
    0   1   2   3   4   5   6   7   8+

55. What is the age of your YOUNGEST child, to his/her nearest birthday?
(Write directly in the box below, using "00" if you have NO children)

56. To what racial or ethnic group do you belong?
(Circle one)
    1. White
    2. Black
    3. Hispanic origin
    4. Asian origin
    5. American Indian or Alaskan native
    6. Pacific Islander
    7. Other

57. In which social class would you place yourself?
(Circle one)

1. Lower class
2. Working class
3. Middle class
4. Upper middle class
5. Upper class
0. Don't Know

58. What social class best describes the family you grew up in?
(Circle one)

1. Lower class
2. Working class
3. Middle class
4. Upper middle class
5. Upper class
0. Don't Know

59. In what state or U.S. territory do you NOW LIVE? (Locate the name of your state of residence on the list below and enter the code number that appears in brackets, in the box below.)

Alabama (41)	Illinois (21)	Nebraska (28)	Samoa (94)
Alaska (81)	Indiana (22)	Nevada (74)	South Carolina (48)
Arizona (61)	Iowa (23)	New Hampshire (04)	South Dakota (31)
Arkansas (42)	Kansas (24)	New Jersey (12)	Tennessee (54)
California (82)	Kentucky (52)	New Mexico (62)	Texas (64)
Colorado (71)	Louisiana (45)	New York (13)	Trust territory (95)
Connecticut (01)	Maine (02)	North Carolina (47)	Utah (75)
Delaware (11)	Maryland (53)	North Dakota (29)	Vermont (06)
Dist. of Col. (51)	Massachusetts (03)	Ohio (30)	Virgin Islands (96)
Florida (43)	Michigan (25)	Oklahoma (63)	Virginia (49)
Georgia (44)	Minnesota (26)	Oregon (84)	Washington (85)
Guam (91)	Mississippi (46)	Pennsylvania (14)	West Virginia (55)
Hawaii (92)	Missouri (27)	Puerto Rico (93)	Wisconsin (32)
Idaho (72)	Montana (73)	Rhode Island (05)	Wyoming (76)

60. Are you currently attending any school, college or university?
(Circle one)

1. Yes, full time
2. Yes, part time
3. No

61. What is your current employment status?
(Circle one)

1. Full time job plus part time job(s)
2. Full time job only
3. Part time job(s) only
4. Unemployed and looking for a job
8. Not employed

62. A. How many years of education have YOU completed? (Circle one in column A)
B. How many years of education has YOUR SPOUSE completed? (Circle one in column B. Please answer even if you are now separated, divorced or widowed.)

A You	B Your Spouse	
	0	Never married
1	1	Some High School or less (11 years or less)
2	2	High school graduate (12 years)
3	3	Community college graduate or Some College (13-15 years)
4	4	College graduate (16 years)
5	5	Some graduate work
6	6	Master's degree (M.A., M.S., M.S.W.)
7	7	Ph.D., M.D., Ed.D.
8	8	LL.B., LL.D.

63. What was the approximate annual income YOU YOURSELF EARNED last year, before taxes?
(Circle one)

0.	None, not employed	5.	$20,000-24,999
1.	Under $4,999	6.	$25,000-$29,999
2.	$5,000-$9,999	7.	$30,000-$49,999
3.	$10,000-$14,999	8.	$50,000 and over
4.	$15,000-$19,999		

64. What was the approximate TOTAL ANNUAL INCOME of your PRESENT FAMILY last year, before taxes, from all sources?
(Circle one)

1.	Under $4,999	5.	$20,000-$24,999
2.	$5,000-$9,999	6.	$25,000-$29,999
3.	$10,000-$14,999	7.	$30,000-$49,999
4.	$15,000-$19,999	8.	$50,000 and over

65. How would you describe your general political views?
(Circle one)

1. Radical
2. Very liberal
3. Somewhat liberal
4. Moderate
5. Somewhat conservative
6. Very conservative
7. Extremely conservative

66. Which of the following best describes your political party preference?
(Circle one)

1. Strongly Republican
2. Republican
3. Independent, but closer to Republican
4. Independent
5. Independent, but closer to Democratic
6. Democratic
7. Strongly Democratic
8. Other party

67. A. Have you ever held public office? (Circle one in column A)
B. Have you ever held a political party position? (Circle one in column B)

	A Public Office	B Political Party
Yes, both elected & appointed	1	1
Yes, elected only	2	2
Yes, appointed only	3	3
No	4	4

68. How would you describe the general political position concerning SEX EQUALITY taken by EACH of the following persons?
A. You yourself (Circle one in Column A)
B. Your spouse (Please answer even if now separated or divorced; if never married, circle "8" in Column B)
C. Your best friend (Circle one in Column C)
D. Your oldest son (If you have no son OVER 12 YEARS OF AGE, circle "8" in Column D)
E. Your oldest daughter (If you have no daughter OVER 12, circle "8" in Column E)

	A You	B Spouse	C Friend	D Son	E Daughter
Strongly Feminist	1	1	1	1	1
Moderately Feminist	2	2	2	2	2
Mixed	3	3	3	3	3
Moderately Anti-Feminist	4	4	4	4	4
Strongly Anti-Feminist	5	5	5	5	5
Don't Know	0	0	0	0	0
Does not apply		8	8	8	8

69. What is your religious preference?
(Circle one)

01	Agnostic	11	Jewish
02	Atheist	12	Latter Day Saints, Mormon
03	Baptist	13	Lutheran
04	Catholic	14	Methodist
05	Christian Scientist	15	Pentecostal or Assembly of God
06	Church of Christ	16	Presbyterian
07	Church of God	17	Unitarian
08	Congregational	18	United Church of Christ
09	Eastern Orthodox	19	Other
10	Episcopalian		

70. How often do you attend religious services?
(Circle one)

1. Never
2. Almost never
3. Once or twice a year
4. Several times a year
5. Once or twice a month
6. Almost every week
7. At least once a week

That is the end of the questionnaire. Thank you for your help. Please return your questionnaire in the envelope provided, at your earliest convenience.

Alphabetical List of Indices, Operational Definitions, and Location in Surveys

Index name	Operational definition	Raw score range	Survey/Question number
Abortion	Approval of legal abortion access on 5 counts: fetal defect, maternal health, low income, not married, married but no desire for more children.	0–5	Pre-43a–e
Active plenary role	Frequency of active roles during plenary sessions on 5 items: stood on mike lines, attended caucus meeting, explained procedure to someone, tried to persuade someone how to vote, passed messages on floor.	5–20	Post-19a,b,h,j,k
Bottom line feminism	Agree–Disagree on 4 items on definition of feminist in relation to stand on ERA, abortion, and lesbian rights.	4–20	Pre-51b,e,h,j
Caucus meetings	Number of meetings attended in Houston at 11 caucuses.	11–33	Post-7a–k
Child care	Agree–Disagree on 5 items on child care away from mother.	5–25	Pre-47b,e; 51c,g,i
Conference control	Agree–Disagree on 4 items on conference management.	4–20	Post-28c,d,h,i
Contact effectiveness	Extent to which new contacts made in Houston will contribute to effectiveness in politics, job, organizations.	4–20	Post-33b–e

(continued)

Index name	Operational definition	Raw score range	Survey/Question number
Contacts made	Number of new contacts made in Houston with people from own city, own state, other states.	Open	Post-32a−c
Delegation meetings	Number of delegation meetings before, during, and after conference.	3−12	Post-14a−c
Economic rights	Agree−Disagree on 3 items on women's economic rights.	3−15	Pre-47f,h,i
Family political activity	Political office holding and/or activity of parents and/or siblings; more weight for state/national than local, mothers than fathers.	0−19	Pre-32a−c,33a−d
Feminist organizations	Membership in NOW, NARAL and/or National Gay Task Force.	0−3	Post-46e,f,g
Gender-linked feminist activity	Ratings of political activity level on issues affecting public roles of women: child care, education, employment, health care, housing, retirement.	6−18	Pre-49b,c,d,h,j,n
Groups supported nomination	(Delegates only) Whether nomination at state meeting supported by 5 types of groups.	0−5	Pre-11a−e
Groups worked with	Extent of political work with 9 groups in Houston.	9−36	Post-9a−i
Liberal causes	Gave time/money to 6 liberal causes in past.	0−6	Pre-41c−f,i,j
Mainstream political activity	Ratings of political activity level in neighborhood, city, state and national politics; more weight given to state/national activity than local.	0−11	Pre-25a−d
Mainstream political aspirations	Ratings of interest level in holding elective public office on local, state, national levels, for both pre- and post-conference surveys.	0−12	Pre-26a−c Post-41a−c
Marital equity	Agree−Disagree on 3 items on spouse roles.	3−15	Pre-47a,d,g
Money management	Level of commitment to future political action on resolutions dealing with credit, insurance, business, statistics.	4−12	Post-40c,f,n,x
Movement political activity	Ratings of political activity level on 16 issues affecting women.	16−48	Pre-49a−p
Movement political aspirations	Ratings of interest level in holding elective office in women's rights organizations on local, state, national levels, for both pre- and post-conference surveys.	0−12	Pre-28a−c Post-42a−c
Nonpolitical organizational membership	Total number membership in educational, job-related, religious, service, social, and cultural organizations.	Open	Pre-37c,e,g,h,i
Passive plenary role	Frequency of passive responses during plenary sessions on 3 items: asked for procedural explanations, lost track or dozed off, looked to others for how to vote.	3−12	Post-19c,f,i

(continued)

Index name	Operational definition	Raw score range	Survey/Question number
Political competence	Ratings of political skills on 6 items: public speaking, parliamentary savvy, staying power, sociability, debating issues well and accepting compromises well; pre- and post-conference surveys.	6−30	Pre-39a−f Post-39a−f
Political organizations	Total number membership in civic, civil rights, feminist and political organizations.	Open	Pre-37a,b,d,f
Post-conference public relations	Level of activity post-conference in home community: TV, radio, and organizational.	0−3	Post-30a−c
Sex-linked feminist activity	Ratings of political activity level on issues affecting private lives of women: abortion, family planning, rape, sex preference, sexuality.	5−15	Pre-49a,f,m,o,p
Special events	Attendance at 10 specific kinds of events in Houston apart from plenary sessions.	0−10	Post-8a−j
Total organization membership	Sum of organizational membership across 10 types of organizations.	Open	Pre-37a−j
Traditional women's organizations	Membership in LWV, AAUW, BPW.	0−3	Post-46h−j
Victims of violence	Level of commitment to future political action on resolutions dealing with: rape, child abuse, battered women.	3−9	Post-40b,d,t
Victims of society	Level of commitment to future political action on resolutions dealing with: minorities, poverty, offenders, disabled, older women, health, rural.	7−21	Post-40g,l,q,r,s,v,y

APPENDIX C

Resolutions Endorsed by National Women's Conference

1. Arts and Humanities

The President should take steps to require that women:

... Are assured equal opportunities for appointment to managerial and upper level posts in Federally-funded cultural institutions, such as libraries, museums, universities and public radio and TV.

... Are more equitably represented on grant-awarding boards, commissions and panels.

... Benefit more fairly from government grants, whether as individual grant applicants or as members of cultural institutions receiving Federal or State funding.

Judging agencies and review boards should use blind judging for musicians, including singers, in appraising them for employment, awards, and fellowships as well as for all articles and papers being considered for publication or delivery and for all exhibits and grant applications, wherever possible.

2. Battered Women

The President and Congress should declare the elimination of violence in the home to be a national goal. To help achieve this, Congress should establish a national clearinghouse for information and technical and financial assistance to locally controlled public and private nonprofit organizations providing emergency shelter and other support services for battered women and their children. The clearinghouse should also conduct a continuing mass media campaign to educate the public about the problem of violence and the available remedies and resources.

Local and State government, law enforcement agencies and social welfare agencies should provide training programs on the problem of wife battering, crisis intervention techniques, and the need for prompt and effective enforcement of laws that protect the rights of battered women.

State legislatures should enact laws to expand legal protection and funds for shelters for battered women and their children; remove interspousal tort immunity in order to permit assaulted spouses to sue their assailants for civil damages; and provide full legal services for victims of abuse.

Programs for battered women should be sensitive to the bilingual and multicultural needs of ethnic and minority women.

3. Business

The President should issue an Executive Order establishing as national policy:

> . . . The full integration of women entrepreneurs in government-wide business-related and procurement activities, including a directive to all government agencies to assess the impact of these activities on women business owners.
> . . . The development of outreach and action programs to bring about the full integration of women entrepreneurs into business-related government activities and procurement.
> . . . The development of evaluation and monitoring programs to assess progress periodically and to develop new programs.

The President should amend Executive Order 11625 of October 13, 1971 to add women to its coverage and to programs administered by the Office of Minority Business Enterprise.

The President should direct the Small Business Administration (SBA) to add women to the definition of socially or economically disadvantaged groups as published in the *Code of Federal Regulations* and take all steps necessary to include women in all the services and activities of the SBA. These steps should include community education projects to encourage women to participate in SBA programs, particularly minority women, including Blacks, Hispanic Americans, Asian Americans and Native Americans.

The President should direct all contracting agencies to increase the percentage of the annual dollar amount of procurement contracts awarded to women-owned businesses and to maintain records by sex and race or ethnicity for monitoring and evaluation.

The President should direct the General Services Administration to amend, so as to include women, the Federal Procurement Regulations requiring that all firms holding government contracts exceeding $5,000 insure that "minority business enterprises have the maximum practicable opportunity to participate in the performance of Government contracts."

The President should direct the Department of Labor, Office of Federal Contract Compliance Programs to assure that compliance officers monitor the awards of subcontracts in order to assure that women-owned businesses are equitably treated.

4. Child Abuse

The President and Congress should provide continued funding and support for the prevention and treatment of abused children and their parents under the Child Abuse Prevention and Treatment Act of 1974.

States should set up child abuse prevention, reporting, counseling and intervention programs or strengthen such programs as they already have. Child abuse is defined, for this purpose, as pornographic exploitation of children, sexual abuse, battering, and neglect.

Programs should:

. . . Provide protective services on a 24-hour basis.
. . . Counsel both victim and abuser.
. . . Create public awareness in schools and in communities by teaching how to identify and prevent the problems.
. . . Encourage complete reporting and accurate data collection.
. . . Provide for prompt, sensitive attention by police, courts, and social services.

5. Child Care

The Federal government should assume a major role in directing and providing comprehensive, voluntary, flexible hour, bias-free, non-sexist, quality child care and developmental programs, including child care facilities for Federal employees, and should request and support adequate legislation and funding for these programs.

Federally funded child care and developmental programs should have low-cost, ability-to-pay fee schedules that make these services accessible to all who need them, regardless of income, and should provide for parent partici-pation in their operation.

Legislation should make special provision for child care facilities for rural and migrant worker families.

Labor and management should be encouraged to negotiate child care programs in their collective bargaining agreements.

Education for parenthood programs should be improved and expanded by local and State school boards, with technical assistance and experimental programs provided by the Federal government.

City, county and/or State networks should be established to provide par-ents with hotline consumer information on child care, referrals, and follow-up evaluations of all listed care givers.

6. Credit

The Federal Equal Credit Opportunity Act of 1974 should be vigorously, efficiently and expeditiously enforced by all the Federal agencies with en-forcement responsibility.

The Federal Reserve Board should conduct a nationwide educational cam-paign to inform women of their rights under the law.

7. Disabled Women

The President, Congress, and State and local governments should rigor-ously enforce all current legislation that affects the lives of disabled women.

The President, Congress, and Administration should expeditiously imple-ment the recommendations of the White House Conference on Handicapped Individuals and develop comprehensive programs for that purpose.

Disabled women should have access to education, training and employ-ment based on their needs and interests rather than on the preconceived notions of others.

The Federal government should enact legislation which will provide higher income levels so that disabled women can afford to live independently and at a decent standard of living. The disabled woman must have the right to determine for herself whether she will live in or out of an institutional setting. Funds and services should be available to make independent living a reality.

Congress should appropriate sufficient funds to ensure the development of service programs controlled by disabled people.

Disabled women should have the right to have and keep their children and have equal rights to adoption and foster care.

Congress should mandate health training and research programs focused on the health needs of the disabled.

Information developed by disabled women should be disseminated to medical professionals and women so that all women can make decisions about children based on knowledge rather than fear.

National health care legislation must provide for the unique requirements of disabled women without reference to income.

Congress should enact legislation to remove all work disincentives for all disabled individuals who wish paid employment.

The President and Congress should work closely with disabled individuals in the development of the welfare reform act and all other legislation concerning disabled persons.

Medicaid and Medicare should cover all the medical services and supplies that are needed by disabled women.

The President and Congress should encourage all States to utilize Title XX funds for the provision of attendant care and other such services for disabled women.

The President and Congress should enact legislation to include disabled women under the 1964 Civil Rights Act and afford them judicial remedy.

The President and Congress and International Women's Year must recognize the additional discrimination disabled women face when they are members of racial, ethnic and sexual minority groups and appropriate steps must be taken to protect their rights.

In the passage of the National Plan of Action, the word "woman" should be defined as including all women with disabilities. The term "bilingual" should be defined as including sign language and interpreter for the deaf. The term "barriers" against women and "access" should be defined as including architectural barriers and communication barriers.

Congress and the President should support U.S. participation in and funding for the International Year of the Handicapped as proclaimed by the United Nations for 1981.

8. Education

The President should direct the vigorous and expeditious enforcement of all laws prohibiting discrimination at all levels of education and oppose any amendments or revisions that would weaken these laws and regulations.

Enforcement should apply to elementary, primary, secondary, post-secondary, graduate, vocational and technical schools, including sports and other programs and granting of scholarships and fellowships.

Federal surveys of elementary and secondary schools should gather data needed to indicate compliance with Federal anti-discrimination laws, and these data should be collected by sex as well as race or ethnicity. The Civil Rights Commission should conduct a study to evaluate the enforcement of laws prohibiting sex discrimination in physical education and athletics, and to consider the usefulness and feasibility of per capita expenditure in physical education and athletics as a measure of equal opportunity.

Leadership programs for working women in post-secondary schools should be upgraded and expanded, and private foundations are urged to give special attention to research on women in unions.

Bilingual vocational training, educational and cultural programs should be extended and significantly expanded, with particular attention to the needs of Hispanic Americans, Native Americans, Asian Americans and other minority women.

State school systems should move against sex and race stereotyping through appropriate action, including:

. . . Review of books and curriculum.

. . . The integration into the curriculum of programs of study that restore to women their history and their achievements and give them the knowledge and methods to reinterpret their life experiences.

. . . Pre-service and in-service training of teachers and administrators.

. . . Non-sexist and non-racist counseling at every level of education, with encouragement of women to increase their range of options and choices to include both non-traditional and traditional occupations and to increase understanding of women's rights and status in various occupations.

9. Elective and Appointive Office

The President, Governors, political parties, women's organizations and foundations should join in an effort to increase the number of women in office, including judgeships and policy-making positions, and women should seek elective and appointive office in larger numbers than at present on the Federal, State and local level.

The President and, where applicable, Governors should significantly increase the numbers of women appointed as judges, particularly to appellate courts and supreme courts.

Governors should set as a goal for 1980 a significant increase and, by 1985, equal membership of men and women serving on all State boards and commissions. Concerted efforts should be directed toward appointing women to the majority of State boards and commissions which have no women members.

Political parties should encourage and recruit women to run for office and adopt written plans to assure equal representation of women in all party activities, from the precinct to the national level, with special emphasis on equal representation on the delegations to all party conventions.

The national parties should create affirmative action offices for women. Women's caucuses and other women's organizations within the party should participate in the selection of its personnel and in the design of its program, which should include greatly improved financial assistance for female delegates and candidates.

10. Employment

The President and Congress should support a policy of full employment so that all women who are able and willing to work may do so.

The President should direct the vigorous and expeditious enforcement of all laws, executive orders and regulations prohibiting discrimination in employment, including discrimination in apprenticeship and construction.

The Equal Employment Opportunity Commission should receive the necessary funding and staff to process complaints and to carry out its duties speedily and effectively.

All enforcement agencies should follow the guidelines of the EEOC, which should be expanded to cover discrimination in job evaluation systems. These systems should be examined with the aim of eliminating biases that attach a low wage rate to "traditional" women's jobs. Federal legislation to provide equal pay for work of equal value should be enacted.

Congress should repeal the last sentence of Sec. 703(h) of Title VII, Civil Rights Act (1964) which limits enforcement of that law by incorporating the more restrictive standards of the Equal Pay Act.

As the largest single employer of women in the nation, the President should require all Federal agencies to establish goals and timetables which require equitable representation of women at all management levels, and appropriate sanctions should be levied against heads of agencies that fail to demonstrate a "good faith" effort in achieving these goals and timetables.

The Civil Service Commission should require all Federal agencies to establish developmental and other programs in consonance with upward mobility and merit promotion principles to facilitate the movement of women from clerical to technical and professional series, and make all Federal women employees in Grades (GS) 11 through 15 eligible for managerial positions.

Agencies and organizations responsible for apprenticeship programs should be required to establish affirmative action goals and timetables for women of all racial and ethnic origins to enter into "non-traditional" training programs.

Federal laws prohibiting discrimination in employment should be extended to include the legislative branch of the Federal government.

In addition to the Federal government, State and local governments, public and private institutions, business, industry and unions should be encouraged to develop training programs for the employment and promotion of women in policy-level positions and professional, managerial and technical jobs.

Special attention should be given to the employment needs of minority women, especially Blacks, Hispanics, Asian Americans and Native Americans, including their placement in managerial, professional, technical and white collar jobs. English-language training and employment programs should be developed to meet the needs of working women whose primary language is not English.

The Congress should amend the Veteran Preference Act of 1944 (58 Stat. 387, Chapter 287, Title V, US Code) so that veterans preference is used on a one-time-only basis for initial employment and within a three-year period after discharge from military service, except for disabled veterans. It should modify the "rule of three" so that equally or better qualified non-veterans should not be unduly discriminated against in hiring.

Title VII of the 1964 Civil Rights Act should be amended to prohibit discrimination on the basis of pregnancy, childbirth or related medical conditions.

The President should take into account in appointments to the National Labor Relations Board and in seeking amendments to the National Labor Relations Act of 1936 the obstacles confronting women who seek to organize in traditionally nonunionized employment sections.

Unions and management should review the impact on women of all their practices and correct injustices to women.

Enforcement of the Fair Labor Standards Act and the Social Security Act as they apply to household workers and enforcement of the minimum wage should be improved.

Federal and State governments should promote Flexitime jobs, and pro-rated benefits should be provided for part-time workers.

All statistics collected by the Federal government should be gathered and analyzed so that information concerning the impact of Federal programs on women and the participation of women in the administration of Federal programs can be assessed.

11. Equal Rights Amendment

The Equal Rights Amendment should be ratified.

12. Health

Federal legislation should establish a national health security program. Present Federal employees' health insurance policies and any future national health security program should cover women as individuals.

Health insurance benefits should include:

. . . Preventive health service.
. . . Comprehensive family planning services.
. . . Reproductive health care.
. . . General medical care.
. . . Home and health support services.
. . . Comprehensive mental health services.

States should license and recognize qualified mid-wives and nurse practitioners as independent health specialists and State and Federal laws should require health insurance providers to directly reimburse these health specialists.

States should enact a patient's bill of rights which includes enforceable provisions for informed consent and access to and patient ownership of medical records.

Federal legislation should be enacted to expand the authority of the Food and Drug Administration to:

. . . Require testing of all drugs, devices and cosmetics by independent sources other than the manufacturers.
. . . Extend test periods beyond the present grossly inadequate one year or 18 months.
. . . Have immediate recall of hazardous, unsafe or ineffective drugs, devices and cosmetics.
. . . Require a patient information package insert with every drug and device marketed. This insert should include warnings about possible risks.
. . . Require by law the reporting of significant adverse reactions noted by physicians or by the manufacturers of drugs, devices and cosmetics.

Congress should appropriate funds for increased research on safe, alternative forms of contraception, particularly male contraception. Research to identify the risks of present forms of contraception and estrogen-based drugs should be given higher priority. Outreach programs should be established by the Department of Health, Education, and Welfare to identify and provide services for victims of hazardous drug therapy.

The Department of Health, Education, and Welfare should provide additional funds for alcohol and drug abuse research and treatment centers designed to meet the special needs of women.

Federal and State governments should encourage fair representation of women on all Federal, State and private health policy and planning bodies.

Congress should appropriate funds to establish and support a network of community-based health facilities to offer low cost-reproductive health services.

The President should appoint a special commission to conduct a national investigation of conditions in nursing homes and mental institutions and propose standards of care.

Congress should appropriate funds to encourage more women to enter the health professions and Congress should allocate funds only to those health professions schools whose curricula are clearly non-sexist.

The Secretary of Health, Education, and Welfare should undertake a special investigation of the increase in surgical procedures such as hysterectomy, Caesarean section, mastectomy and forced sterilization.

13. Homemakers

The Federal Government and State legislatures should base their laws relating to marital property, inheritance, and domestic relations on the principle that marriage is a partnership in which the contribution of each spouse is of equal importance and value.

The President and Congress should support a practical plan of covering homemakers in their own right under social security and facilitate its enactment.

Alimony, child support, and property arrangements at divorce should be such that minor children's needs are first to be met and spouses share the economic dislocation of divorce. As a minimum every State should enact the economic provisions of the Uniform Marriage and Divorce Act proposed by the Commissioners on Uniform State Laws and endorsed by the American Bar Association. Loss of pension rights because of divorce should be considered in property divisions. More effective methods for collection of support should be adopted.

The Census Bureau should collect data on the economic arrangements at divorce and their enforcement, with a large enough sample to analyze the data by State.

The Federal and State Governments should help homemakers displaced by widowhood, divorce, or desertion to become self-sufficient members of society through programs providing counseling, training and placement and counseling on business opportunities; advice on financial management; and legal advice.

14. Insurance

State legislatures and State insurance commissioners should adopt the Model Regulation to Eliminate Unfair Sex Discrimination of the National Association of Insurance Commissioners. The Regulation should be amended and adopted to include prohibition of the following practices:

... Denial of coverage for pregnancy and pregnancy-related expenses for all comprehensive medical/hospital care.
... Denial of group disability coverage for normal pregnancy and complications of pregnancy.
... Denial of health insurance coverage to newborns from birth.
... Requiring dependents who convert from spouses' contracts to their own to pay increased premiums for the same coverage or be forced to insure for lower coverage.
... Denial of coverage to women with children born out of wedlock and denying eligibility of benefits to such children.
... Using sex-based actuarial mortality tables in rate and benefit computation.

15. International Affairs

Women and Foreign Policy

The President and the Executive Agencies of the government dealing with foreign affairs (Departments of State and Defense, USIA, AID and others) should see to it that many more women, of all racial and ethnic backgrounds, participate in the formulation and execution of all aspects of United States foreign policy. Efforts should be intensified to appoint more women as Ambassadors and to all U.S. Delegations to international conferences and missions to the United Nations. Women in citizen voluntary organizations concerned with international affairs should be consulted more in the formulation of policy and procedures.

The foreign affairs agencies should increase with all possible speed the number of women at all grade levels within the agencies, and a special assistant to the Secretary of State should be appointed to coordinate a program to increase women's participation in foreign policy and to assume responsibility for U.S. participation in and the funding of the UN Decade for Women. All concerned agencies of the Executive Branch should strive to appoint women on an equal basis with men to represent the U.S. on all executive boards and governing bodies of international organizations and on the UN functional commissions. A permanent committee composed of government officials and private members, the majority of them women, should be appointed to advise the State Department of the selection of women candidates for positions on U.S. delegations, on governing bodies of international agencies, and in the UN system.

UN Commission on the Status of Women

The U.S. Government should work actively for the retention and adequate funding of the UN Commission on the Status of Women, and it should recommend that the Commission meet annually rather than biennially.

Women in Development

The U.S. Agency for International Development and similar assistance agencies should give high priority to the implementation of existing U.S. legislation and policies designed to promote the integration of women into the development plans for their respective countries. They should also continue to study the impact on women in the developing world of U.S. government aid and commercial development programs over which government has any regulatory powers. These agencies should actively promote the involvement of these women in determining their own needs and priorities in programs intended for their benefit.

Human Rights Treaties and International Conventions on Women

In pressing for respect for human rights, the President and the Congress should note the special situation of women victims of oppression, political imprisonment and torture. They should also intensify efforts for ratification and compliance with international human rights treaties and conventions to which the United States is signatory, specifically including those on women's rights.

Peace and Disarmament

The President and the Congress should intensify efforts to:

- ... Build, in cooperation with other nations, an international framework within which serious disarmament negotiations can occur.
- ... Reduce military spending and foreign military sales, convert excessive weapons manufacturing capacity to production for meeting human needs.

. . . Support peace education in schools and advanced study in the fields of conflict resolution and peace keeping.

To this end the United States should take the lead in urging all nuclear powers to start phasing out their nuclear arsenals rather than escalating weapons development and deployment, and should develop initiatives to advance the cause of world peace.

International Education and Communication

Government agencies, media, schools, and citizen organizations should be encouraged to promote programs of international education and communication emphasizing women's present and potential contribution, particularly in developing countries, to economic and social well-being. Improved methods should be devised for collection and dissemination of this needed information in order to make adequate data available to policy makers and the public.

International Women's Decade

The U.S. should give vigorous support to the goals of the UN Decade of Women, Equality, Development and Peace, in the General Assembly and other international meetings; should give financial support to Decade activities and should participate fully in the 1980 mid-Decade World Conference to review progress toward targets set in the World Plan of Action adopted unanimously by the World Conference of International Women's Year, 1975.

16. Media

The media should employ women in all job categories and especially in policy-making positions. They should adopt and distribute the IWY media guidelines throughout their respective industries. They should make affirmative efforts to expand the portrayal of women to include a variety of roles and to represent accurately the numbers and lifestyles of women in society. Training opportunities should be expanded so that more women can move into all jobs in the communications industries, particularly into technical jobs.

Appropriate Federal and State agencies, including the Federal Communications Commission, U.S. Commission on Civil Rights, Department of Health, Education, and Welfare, Department of Justice, and State civil rights commissions should vigorously enforce laws which prohibit employment discrimination against women working in the mass media. These agencies should continue studying the impact of the mass media on sex discrimination and sex-role stereotyping in American society.

Special consideration should be given to media which are publicly funded or established through acts of Congress. Particularly, public broadcasting should assume a special responsibility to integrate women in employment and programming.

Women's groups and advocacy groups should continue to develop programs to monitor the mass media and take appropriate action to improve the image and employment of women in the communications industries. They should join the campaign to de-emphasize the exploitation of female bodies and the use of violence against women in the mass media.

17. Minority Women

Minority women share with all women the experience of sexism as a barrier to their full rights of citizenship. Every recommendation of this National Plan of Action shall be understood as applying equally and fully to minority women.

But institutionalized bias based on race, language, culture and/or ethnic origin or governance of territories or localities has led to the additional oppression and exclusion of minority women and to the conditions of poverty from which they disproportionately suffer.

Therefore, every level of government action should recognize and remedy this double-discrimination and ensure the right of each individual to self-determination.

Legislation, the enforcement of existing laws and all levels of government action should be directed especially toward such problem areas as involuntary sterilization; monolingual education and services; high infant and maternal mortality rates; bias toward minority women's children, confinement to low level jobs; confinement to poor, ghettoized housing, culturally biased educational, psychological and employment testing (for instance, civil service); failure to enforce affirmative action and special admission programs; combined sex and race bias in insurance; and failure to gather statistical data based on both sex and race so that the needs and conditions of minority women may be accurately understood.

Minority women also suffer from government failure to recognize and remedy problems of our racial and cultural groups. For instance:

American Indian and Alaskan Native Women

American Indian/Alaskan Native women have a relationship to Earth Mother and the Great Spirit as well as a heritage based on the sovereignty of Indian peoples. The Federal government should guarantee tribal rights, tribal sovereignty, honor existing treaties and Congressional acts, protect hunting, fishing, and whaling rights, protect trust status, and permanently remove the threat of termination.

Congress should extend the Indian Education Act of 1972, maintain base funding of education instead of replacing it with supplemental funding, provide adequate care through the Indian Health Service, forbid the systematic removal of children from their families and communities and assure full participation in all Federally-funded programs.

Asian/Pacific American Women

Asian/Pacific American Women are wrongly thought to be part of a "model minority" with few problems. This obscures our vulnerability due to language and culture barriers, sweatshop work conditions with high health hazards, the particular problems of wives of U.S. servicemen, lack of access to accreditation and licensing because of immigrant status, and to many Federally-funded services.

Hispanic Women

Deportation of mothers of American-born children must be stopped and legislation enacted for parents to remain with their children; citizenship provisions should be facilitated.

Legislation should be enacted to provide migrant farm working women with the Federal minimum wage rate, collective bargaining rights, adequate housing, and bilingual-bicultural social services delivery.

Classification of existing Hispanic American media as "Foreign Press" must be stopped to ensure equal access to major national events.

Additionally, the Federal Communications Commission must provide equal opportunity to Hispanic people for acquisition of media facilities (radio and television), for training and hiring in order to provide Spanish-language programming to this major group.

Puerto Rican Women

Puerto Rican women emphasize that they are citizens of the United States and wish to be recognized and treated as equals.

Black Women

The President and Congress should provide for full quality education, including special admission programs, and for the full implementation and enforcement at all levels of education.

The President and Congress should immediately address the crisis of unemployment which impacts the Black community and results in Black teenage women having the highest rate of unemployment.

The Congress should establish a national program for the placement of "children in need of parents," preferably in a family environment, where the status of said children is affected by reason of racial or ethnic origin.

The President and Congress should assure Federally assisted housing to meet the critical need of Black women, especially of low and moderate income, should direct the vigorous enforcement of all fair housing laws, and provide the allocation of resources necessary to accomplish this housing goal.

The President, Congress and all Federal agencies should utilize fully in all deliberations and planning processes, the Black Women's Plan of Action which clearly reflects and delineates other major concerns of Black women.

18. Offenders

States should review and reform their sentencing laws and their practices to eliminate discrimination that affects the treatment of women in penal facilities. Particular attention should be paid to the needs of poor and minority women.

States should reform their practices, where needed, to provide legal counseling and referral services; improved health services emphasizing dignity in treatment for women in institutions; and protection of women prisoners from sexual abuse by male and female inmates and by correctional personnel.

Corrections Boards must provide improved educational and vocational training in a non-stereotyped range of skills that pay enough for an ex-offender to support her family.

Law enforcement agencies, courts, and correctional programs must give special attention to the needs of children with mothers under arrest, on trial, or in prison.

States must increase efforts to divert women offenders to community-based treatment facilities such as residential and non-residential halfway houses, work releases, or group homes as close to the offender's family as possible.

Disparities in the treatment of male and female juvenile offenders must be eliminated; status offenses must be removed from jurisdiction of juvenile courts; and States are urged to establish more youth bureaus, crisis centers and diversion agencies to receive female juveniles detained for promiscuous conduct, for running away, or because of family or school problems.

19. Older Women

The Federal and State governments, public and private women's organizations and social welfare groups should support efforts to provide social and health services that will enable the older woman to live with dignity and security. These services should include but not be limited to:

> . . . Innovative housing which creates as nearly as possible an environment that affords security and comfort.
> . . . Home health and social services, including visiting nurse services, homemaker services, meals-on-wheels and other protective services that will offer older women alternatives to institutional care, keeping them in familiar surroundings as long as possible.
> . . . Preventive as well as remedial health care services.
> . . . Public transportation in both urban and rural areas for otherwise housebound women.
> . . . Continuing education in order to insure that the older woman will be an informed and intelligent user of the power which will be hers by virtue of the increase of her numbers.
> . . . Immediate inclusion of geriatric education in the curriculum and training of all medical personnel in order that the elderly will receive optimum medical attention. This applies particularly to nursing home staff.
> . . . Bilingual and bicultural programs, including health services, recreation and other programs to support elderly women of limited English-speaking ability.
> . . . Elimination of present inequities in social security benefits.
> . . . Recognition of the economic value of homemaking in social security benefits.
> . . . Passage of the Displaced Homemakers bill.
> . . . Expansion of coverage for medical and health care costs.
> . . . Older women should be included as active participants in all kinds of policy-making positions at every level of government.
> . . . The image of the older woman is changing and there should be wide publicity focused on this. The effective use of the media is essential to furnishing information to the older woman so as to insure her informed participation in the decision-making process which continuously affects the quality of her life and the life of her community.
> . . . Mandatory retirement shall be phased out.

20. Rape

Federal, State and local governments should revise their criminal codes and case law dealing with rape and related offenses to:

> . . . Provide for graduated degrees of the crime with graduated penalties

depending on the amount of force or coercion occurring with the activity.

. . . Apply to assault by or upon both sexes, including spouses as victims.

. . . Include all types of sexual assault against adults, including oral and anal contact and use of objects.

. . . Enlarge beyond traditional common law concepts the circumstances under which the act will be considered to have occurred without the victim's consent.

. . . Specify that the past sexual conduct of the victim cannot be introduced into evidence.

. . . Require no more corroborative evidence than is required in the prosecution of any other type of violent assault.

. . . Prohibit the Hale instruction* where it has been required by law or is customary.

Local task forces to review and reform rape law and practices of police, prosecutors, and medical personnel should be established where they do not now exist. Such task forces should also mobilize public support for change. Rape crisis centers should be established (with Federal and State funding) for the support of victims and the confidentiality of their records should be assured. Bilingual and bicultural information resources should be made available where necessary.

Federal and State funds should be appropriated for educational programs in the public school system and the community, including rape prevention and self-defense programs.

The National Center for the Prevention and Control of Rape within the National Institute of Mental Health should be given permanent funding for operational costs, for staff positions, research and demonstration programs and for a clearinghouse on sexual assault information and educational material with regard to prevention, treatment of victims and rehabilitation of offenders. In addition, rape centers should be consulted by NIMH in the setting of priorities and allocation of funds. The National Center should be continued in order to insure community involvement and the composition of the committee should be reviewed to assure minority representation and a majority of women.

State legislatures should expand existing victim compensation for the cost of medical, surgicial, and hospital expenses; evidentiary examinations; counseling; emergency funds for housing, etc., and compensation for pregnancy and pain and suffering.

*Some states require judges to instruct the jury as prescribed by a 17th Century jurist, Lord Chief Justice Matthew Hale: "Rape is an accusation easily to be made and hard to be proved, and harder to be defended by the party accused, tho never so innocent."

21. Reproductive Freedom

We support the U.S. Supreme Court decisions which guarantee reproductive freedom to women.

We urge all branches of Federal, State and local governments to give the highest priority to complying with these Supreme Court decisions and to making available all methods of family planning to women unable to take advantage of private facilities.

We oppose the exclusion of abortion or childbirth and pregnancy-related care from Federal, State or local funding of medical services or from privately financed medical services.

We urge organizations concerned with improving the status of women to monitor how government complies with these principles.

We oppose involuntary sterilization and urge strict compliance by all doctors, medical and family planning facilities with the Dept. of Health, Education & Welfare's minimum April 1974 regulations requiring that consent to sterilization be truly voluntary, informed and competent. Spousal consent should not be a requirement upon which sterilization procedures are contingent. If the patient does not speak English, appropriate staff must be found to explain the procedures and HEW regulations in the primary language of the patient.

Particular attention should be paid at all levels of government to providing confidential family-planning services for teen-agers, education in responsible sexuality, and reform of laws discriminating against unwed parents and their children.

Programs in sex education should be provided in all schools, including elementary schools.

Federal, State and local governing bodies should take whatever steps are necessary to remove existing barriers to family planning services to all teenagers who request them.

Each school system should assist teen-age parents with programs including child care arrangements that will encourage them to remain in school, provide educational and vocational training leading to economic independence, and teach prenatal health and parenting skills.

22. Rural Women

The President and Congress should establish a Federal rural education policy designed to meet the special problems of isolation, poverty and underemployment that characterize much of rural America. Such a policy must be consciously planned to overcome the inequality of opportunities available to rural women and girls.

The Office of Management and Budget should set and enforce a policy that data collected on beneficiaries of all Federal programs shall be reported by sex, by minority status, and by urban/rural or metropolitan/non-metropolitan areas, based on a standard definition.

Data on employment of women and public programs on behalf of working women should include in their definitions farm wives and widows who perform the many tasks essential to the farm operation.

A farm wife should have the same ownership rights as her spouse under State inheritance and Federal estate laws. Tax law should recognize that the labor of a farm wife gives her an equitable interest in the property.

The President should appoint a joint committee from the Department of Labor, Agriculture, and Justice to investigate the Louisiana sugar plantations system's violations of human rights, especially of women. This commission should also investigate conditions of other seasonal and migratory workers in all States and Territories of the United States.

All programs developed on behalf of rural women should be certain to include migrant, Black, Native American, Alaskan, Asian, and Hispanic women and all isolated minorities, and affirmative action programs should be extended to include all disenfranchised groups.

23. Sexual Preference

Congress, State, and local legislatures should enact legislation to eliminate discrimination on the basis of sexual and affectional preference in areas including, but not limited to, employment, housing, public accommodations, credit, public facilities, government funding, and the military.

State legislatures should reform their penal codes or repeal State laws that restrict private sexual behavior between consenting adults.

State legislatures should enact legislation that would prohibit consideration of sexual or affectional orientation as a factor in any judicial determination of child custody or visitation rights. Rather, child custody cases should be evaluated solely on the merits of which party is the better parent, without regard to that person's sexual and affectional orientation.

24. Statistics

The Office of Management and Budget should require all departments and agencies to collect, tabulate, and analyze data relating to persons on the basis of sex in order to assess the impact of their programs on women.

The U.S. Census Bureau should aggressively pursue its efforts to reduce the undercounts of minority Americans, including Blacks, Hispanic Americans, Asian Americans, and American Indians. The Department of Health, Education, and Welfare should continue its efforts to implement the usage of special group identifiers in all vital statistics record-keeping. These statistics should be recorded and reported by sex and subgroup.

25. Women, Welfare, and Poverty

The Federal and State governments should assume a role in focusing on welfare and poverty as major women's issues. All welfare reform proposals should be examined specifically for their impact on women. Inequality of opportunity for women must be recognized as a primary factor contributing to the growth of welfare rolls.

Women in poverty, whether young or old, want to be part of the mainstream of American life.

Poverty is a major barrier to equality for women. Millions of women who depend on income transfer programs or low paying jobs for their basic life support may be subject to the multiple oppression of sexism, racism, poverty and they are often old or disabled.

Many other women, because of discriminatory employment practices, social security laws, differential education of men and women, and lack of adequate child care are just one step away from poverty. Consequently, the elimination of poverty must be a priority of all those working for equal rights for women.

Along with major improvements in the welfare system, elimination of poverty for women must include improvements in social security and retirement systems, universal minimum wage, non-traditional job opportunities, quality child care, comprehensive health insurance, and comprehensive legal services. A concerted effort must be made to educate the public about the realities of welfare, the plight of the blind, the aged, the disabled, single-parent families and other low income women.

We support increased Federal funding for income transfer programs (e.g. Social Security, SSI, AFDC). Congress should approve a Federal floor under payments to provide an adequate standard of living based on each State's cost of living for all those in need. And, just as with other workers, homemakers receiving income transfer payments should be afforded the dignity of having that payment called a wage, not welfare.

We oppose the Carter Administration proposal for welfare reform (HR 9030), which among other things eliminates food stamps, threatens to eliminate CETA training and CETA jobs paying more than minimum wage, and does not guarantee adequate day care, and we oppose proposals for "workfare" where welfare mothers would be forced to "work off" their grants which is work without wage, without fringe benefits or bargaining rights, and without dignity. HR 9030 further requires those individuals and families without income to wait weeks or even months before even the inadequate grant is available.

We strongly support a welfare reform program developed from ongoing consultation with persons who will be impacted.

This program should 1) be consistent with the National Academy of Science recommendation that no individual or family living standard should be lower than half the median family income level for substantial periods (after taxes) and this income should not fall below the government defined poverty level of family income even for shorter periods; 2) help sustain the family unit; and 3) insure that women on welfare and other low income women who choose to work not be forced into jobs paying less than the prevailing wage.

In order to improve the status of women, the following actions should be taken:

  a. To insure that welfare and other poor are not discriminated against as an economic class, affirmative action guidelines should be drawn up to provide that all employers who are recipients of Federal and/or State contract monies be required to show that they are hiring recipients.
  b. There should be targeting of funds by local CETA advisory boards for the placement and training of women in nontraditional higher paying jobs, consistent with the original mandate.
  c. The Department of Labor should make a study of jobs and wages based on a standard of comparable worth, and speedily move the implementation of that study in all government positions.
  d. Unions should devote additional energy to the organization of women to upgrade pay and working conditions for women in traditional employment.

Quality child care should be a mandated Title XX service, available to all families on an ability to pay basis throughout training, education, job search and employment.

Congress should encourage education of women by insuring that Federal and other education grants do not reduce an individual's or family's eligibility for public assistance in AFDC or any other program.

Comprehensive support services and social services must be provided and adequately funded.

References

Almond, G. A., & Powell, G. B. (1966) *Comparative politics: A developmental approach.* Boston, Massachusetts: Little, Brown.

Baxter, S., & Lansing, M. (1980) *Women and politics: The invisible majority.* Ann Arbor: Univ. of Michigan Press.

Brewster-Smith, M., Block, J., & Haan, N. (1968) Activism and apathy in contemporary adolescents. In J. F. Adams (Ed.), *Understanding adolescence.* Boston, Massachusetts: Allyn & Bacon.

Brim, O. G., Jr., & Kagan, J. (1980) *Constancy and change in human development.* Cambridge, Massachusetts: Harvard Univ. Press.

Carden, M. L. (1974) *The new feminist movement.* New York: Russell Sage Foundation.

Chafe, W. (1972) *The American woman: Her changing social, economic, and political roles, 1920–1970.* London and New York: Oxford Univ. Press.

Costantini, E., & Craik, K. (1972) Women as politicians: The social background, personality and political careers of female party leaders. *Journal of Social Issues, 28*(2), pp. 217–236.

Darnton, R. (July 16, 1981) Poland rewrites history. *New York Review of Books 28*(12), pp. 6–9.

Davies, J. C. (1962) Toward a theory of revolution. *American Sociological Review, 27,* pp. 5–19.

Diamond, I. (1977) *Sex roles in the state house.* New Haven, Connecticut: Yale Univ. Press.

Dubeck, P. J. (1976) Women and access to political office: A comparison of female and male state legislators. *Sociological Quarterly, 17,* pp. 42–52.

Epstein, C. F. (1981a) Women and power: The roles of women in politics in the United States. In C. F. Epstein & R. L. Coser (Eds.), *Access to power: Cross-national studies of women and elites.* London: Allen & Unwin.

Epstein, C. F. (1981b) *Women in law.* New York: Basic Books.

409

Epstein, C. F., & R. L. Coser, (Eds.). (1981) *Access to power: Cross-national studies of women and elites.* London: George Allen & Unwin.

Ferree, M. M., & Miller, F. (1978) *Winning hearts and minds: Some social psychological contributions to the resource mobilization perspective on social movements.* Unpublished manuscript.

Feuer, L. S. (1969) *The conflict of generations.* New York: Basic Books.

Firestone, S. (1970) *The dialectic of sex: The case for feminist revolution.* New York: William Morrow.

Flacks, R. (1967) The liberated generation: An exploration of the roots of student protest. *Journal of Social Issues, 23*(3), pp. 52–75.

Freeman, J. (1972–1973) The tyranny of structurelessness. *Berkeley Journal of Sociology: A Critical Review, 17,* pp. 151–64.

Freeman, J. (1975) *The politics of women's liberation.* New York: David McKay.

Friedan, B. (1963) *The feminine mystique.* New York: Norton.

Fuller, A. B. (1855) *Woman in the nineteenth century and kindred papers by Margaret Fuller Ossoli.* Boston, Massachusetts: John P. Jewitt.

Gehlen, F. L. (1977) Women members of Congress: A distinctive role. In M. Githens & J. L. Prestage (Eds.), *A portrait of marginality: The political behavior of the American woman.* New York: Longman.

Githens, M. (1977) Spectators, agitators and lawmakers: Women in state legislatures. In M. Githens & J. L. Prestage (Eds.), *A portrait of marginality: The political behavior of the American woman.* New York: Longman.

Githens, M., & Prestage, J. L. (Eds.). (1977) *A portrait of marginality: The political behavior of the American woman.* New York: Longman.

Gurr, T. R. (1970) *Why men rebel.* Princeton, New Jersey: Princeton Univ. Press.

Haan, N., Brewster-Smith, M., & Block, J. (1968) Moral reasoning in young adults: Political–social behavior, family background and personality correlates. *Journal of Personality and Social Psychology, 10*(3), pp. 183–201.

Hansen, M. L. (1952) The third generation in America. *Commentary,* 14(5), pp. 492–500.

Hole, J., & Levine, E. (1971) *Rebirth of feminism.* New York: Quadrangle.

Johnson, M., & Carroll, S. (1978) *Profile of women holding office,* (Vol. 2). New Brunswick, New Jersey: Center for the American Woman and Politics, Eagleton Institute of Politics, Rutgers—The State University.

Johnson, M., & Stanwick, K. (1976) *Profile of women holding office,* (Vol. 1). New Brunswick, New Jersey: Center for the American Woman and Politics, Eagleton Institute of Politics, Rutgers—The State University.

Keniston, K. (1967) The source of student dissent. *Journal of Social Issues, 23*(3), pp. 108—137.

Keniston, K. (1968) *Young radicals: Notes on committed youth.* New York: Harcourt Brace.

King, E. G. (1977) Women in Iowa legislative politics. In M. Githens & J. L. Prestage (Eds.), *A portrait of marginality: The political behavior of the American woman.* New York: Longman.

Kirkpatrick, J. (1974) *Political woman.* New York: Basic Books.

Kirkpatrick, J. (1976) *The new presidential elite: Men and women in national politics.* New York: Russel Sage Foundation.

Klotzburger, K. (1973) Political action by academic women. In A. S. Rossi & A. Calderwood (Eds.), *Academic women on the move.* New York: Russell Sage Foundation.

Lindsey, K. (1980) Organizing: Women's commissions-in-exile—the perils of working inside the system. *Ms. Magazine, 8*(8), pp. 23–25.

Lipman-Blumen, J. (1973) Role de-differentiations as a system response to crisis: Occupational and political roles of women. *Sociological inquiry, 43*(2), pp. 105–129.

McCloskey, H. (1958) Conservatism and personality. *American Political Science Review, 52,* pp. 27–45.

McCloskey, H. (1960) Issue conflict and consensus between party leaders and followers. *American Political Science Review, 54,* pp. 406–427.

McCloskey, H. (1964) Consensus and ideology in American politics. *American Political Science Review, 58,* pp. 361–382.

Millett, K. (1970) *Sexual politics.* Garden City, New York: Doubleday.

Mills, C. W. (1956) *The power elite.* London and New York: Oxford Univ. Press.

Mueller, C. M., & Judd, C. M. (August, 1979) *Belief constraint and belief consensus: Towards an analysis of social movement ideologies.* Paper presented at the 74th Annual Meeting of the American Sociological Association, Boston, Massachusetts.

National Commission on the Observance of International Women's Year. (1978) *The spirit of Houston: The First National Women's Conference.* Washington, D.C.: US Govt. Printing Office.

O'Neill, W. (1969) *Everyone was brave: The rise and fall of feminism in America.* New York: Quadrangle.

Prewitt, K., & McAllister, W. (1976) Changes in the American executive elite, 1930–1970. In H. Eulau & M. M. Czudnowski (Eds.), *Elite recruitment in democratic politics: Comparative studies across nations.* New York: Sage & Wiley.

Rodriquez, A. (1981) *Racial and ethnic variation among feminists: The women at the 1977 First National Women's Conference.* Unpublished master's thesis, department of sociology, University of Massachusetts, Amherst.

Rossi, A. S. (1973) *The feminist papers: From Adams to deBeauvoir.* New York: Columbia Univ. Press.

Rossi, A. S., & Calderwood, A. (Eds.). (1973) *Academic women on the move.* New York: Russell Sage Foundation.

Stoper, E. (1977) Wife and politician: Role strain among women in public office. In M. Githens & J. L. Prestage (Eds.), *A portrait of marginality: The political behavior of the American woman.* New York: Longman.

Thornton, A., & Freedman, D. (1979) Changes in the sex role attitudes of women, 1962–1977: Evidence from a panel study. *American Sociological Review, 44*(5), pp. 831–842.

Werner, E. E. (1966) Women in Congress, 1917–1964. *Western Political Quarterly, 19*(1), pp. 16–30.

Werner, E. E. (1968) Women in the state legislatures. *Western Political Quarterly, 21*(1), pp. 40–50.

Women's Political Times, 6(2), April 2, 1981.